Remembering Chinook Country

Told and Untold Stories of Our Past

The Chinook Country Historical Society

DETSELIG
ENTERPRISES LTD

Remembering Chinook Country: Told and Untold Stories of Our Past

© 2005 The Chinook Country Historical Society

Library and Archives Canada Cataloguing in Publication

Remembering chinook country: told and untold stories of our past/the Chinook Country Historical Society.

Includes bibliographical references.

ISBN 1-55059-287-4

1. Calgary Region (Alta.)--History. 2. Calgary Region (Alta.)--Biography. I. Chinook Country Historical Society.

FC3695.S65R45 2005   971.23'4   C2005-901104-1

Detselig Enterprises Ltd.
210, 1220 Kensington Road NW
Calgary, Alberta T2N 3P5

Phone: (403) 283-0900
Fax: (403) 283-6947
Email: temeron@telusplanet.net
www.temerondetselig.com

We acknowledge the support of the Government of Canada through the Book Publishing Industry Development Program (BPIDP) for our publishing program.

We also acknowledge the support of the Alberta Foundation for the Arts for our publishing program.

COMMITTED TO THE DEVELOPMENT OF CULTURE AND THE ARTS

SAN 113-0234
ISBN 1-55059-287-4
Printed in Canada

Cover Design by Alvin Choong

Henry Klassen
(1931-2005)

As a member of the Department of History at the University of Calgary from 1968 to 1998, and then as a professor emeritus, Henry Klassen made an enormous contribution to the study of Western Canadian history. Born and raised in Manitoba, he studied at the University of Manitoba (B.A., B.Ed., and M.A.) and completed his Ph.D. at the University of Toronto. A meticulous researcher and devoted scholar, he published numerous academic articles and two major books on Western Canada, *A Business History of Alberta* (1999), and *Eye on the Future: Business People in Calgary and the Bow Valley, 1870-1900* (2002). He also published in Canadian Business History, his major publication being *Luther Holton* (2001), a biography of the important mid-nineteenth century Montreal entrepreneur.

Henry was a role model for the rest of us in the profession. Self-effacing, he was invariably more interested in the person to whom he was speaking than in discussing his own successes. He was blessed with a wonderful sense of humor, conveyed in a soft-spoken voice and could always be relied upon to give a balanced opinion on a contentious issue. A gifted teacher, he encouraged students to express their opinions and to pursue their interests, always providing welcome scholarly advice. He cared about and took deep interest in the research of others in Canadian history, both at the university and in the community.

For years, Henry assisted the Chinook Country Chapter of the Historical Society of Alberta. He served as president, and in numerous executive positions. How appropriate, therefore, that this anthology is dedicated to this outstanding individual, who, several years ago, proposed such a volume in honor of the province's 100th birthday. He also wrote one of the essays included here as well as the book's introduction. *Remembering Chinook Country* is a great tribute to this warm and generous scholar who gave so much to his students, his colleagues, and his community. We are greatly indebted to him.

Donald Smith
Department of History
University of Calgary
February 28, 2005

Table of Contents

Acknowledgements

The Chinook Country Historical Society would like to acknowledge those individuals who were instrumental in the publication of *Remembering Chinook Country: Told and Untold Stories of Our Past.*

First and foremost, we are indebted to Kate Reeves and Harry Sanders for the countless hours they have spent contacting and making arrangements with writers to participate in the Anthology. Special thanks go to all the authors who agreed to write a chapter for this provincial Centennial project. Our thanks also go to Carrol Jaques for her kind support.

Our thanks to Roberta Hersey and the past presidents of the CCHS who initiated the publication of the Anthology for Alberta Centennial 2005.

Thank you to Diana Horsman for lending her legal expertise in acquiring funding for the Anthology.

To Ted Giles of Detselig Publishers, thank you for taking on our project; and to Kim-Marie Ward and Linda Berry, our thanks for editing this anthology.

Finally, we owe a debt of gratitude to the Calgary Foundation without whose financial support, the publication of Anthology 2005 would never have been realized.

Diana Ringstrom
President, Anthology Coordinator
Chinook Country Historical Society

Introduction

by Henry C. Klassen

Remembering Chinook Country presents a lively and informed account of how one small town and its surrounding area grew from a tiny urban and rural community into a major Alberta zone. Written to commemorate the 100th Anniversary of the province of Alberta, with emphasis on Calgary and its region, the book is more than an urban publication. It is a history of aspects of this constantly changing area.

From the days when Calgary's streets were lined with ox-drawn wagon trains from all over the prairie West, the northwestern Great Plains, and British Columbia, and both Canadian and American monies were financing frontier expansion, Calgary and its region have been leading forces for economic, social, and political development – in spite of setbacks along the way. In the late nineteenth century, the area contributed to Alberta's trade and manufacturing industries as well as to the expansion of the railway and telegraph network. By the early twentieth century, Calgary was helping to develop the automobile trade, social institutions, electrical utilities, and the telephone system. Today, the city and the outlying areas provide support for Alberta's high-tech industries. The story of Chinook Country, then, is one of constant change.

The twentieth century was a risky time for people in the Calgary area as it was a time of dramatic ups and downs in the economic cycle. Again and again, hopes for expansion were temporarily shattered due to the nationwide depressions in 1907, 1913, the post-World War I years, the Great Depression of the 1930s, and recessions in the mid-1950s, 1961, 1981, and the early 1990s. There were winners and there were losers in the Calgary region in the playing out of Canada's fluctuating economy.

Many of the area's current traditions – both conservative and liberal policies, dedication to the well-being of the city, region, and province, and even some of the principal social interests – can be traced to our beginnings in the early twentieth century. Nonetheless, no one individual determined its shape; no one decade dictated its evolution. Over the years, as Canadian civilization has changed and the notion of community has broadened to embrace not only the immediate vicinity but also the nation and finally, the world, these interests and traditions have been modified, enlarged, or augmented. Chinook Country's story is that of many responsible people working over several generations to ensure ongoing growth and development of a vibrant and forward-looking region, as well as a dedication to the preservation of our shared history.

Assembled here is a group of contributors who are experts in their respective fields of social, economic and legal history. Together, we have created a book that is a story of our heritage. An important, fresh look at Chinook Country and Canadian history, *Remembering Chinook Country* will interest anyone who wants to understand how a region has stepped so confidently into the modern age.

All Things Remembered
The History of the Chinook Country Historical Society
by Harry M. Sanders*

In February 1896, the *Alberta Tribune* – forerunner of the *Albertan*, which eventually became the *Calgary Sun* – advocated the formation of "a Historical Society for Alberta."[1] "The means of obtaining authentic information as to the early history of the Far West are rapidly decreasing, owing to the passing away of the pioneers and the disappearance of old landmarks," the *Tribune* observed.

> There are certainly sufficient people of culture in Alberta to successfully sustain such a Society here. It only remains for them to get together and organize. They will not only find much pleasure in the systematic prosecution of their researches, but they will be laying posterity under a deep obligation of gratitude to them for their labours.[2]

Evidently the writer was unaware that several lofty attempts had already been made. In 1884, a Literary, Scientific & Historical Society had been organized in Fort Macleod. The following year in Calgary, pioneer Roman Catholic missionary Father Albert Lacombe became president of the newly-formed Historical & Scientific Society of Alberta,[3] and in 1886, the Calgary Institute of Literature, Science & History was formed. Each of these efforts was short-lived, and it took until 1907 – 11 years after the *Tribune*'s editorial, and 18 months after the formation of the province – for the Historical Society of Alberta (HSA) to be formed. Premier Alexander Rutherford served as president for the first 32 years, and all 25 members of the Legislative Assembly were charter members. But the organization remained virtually dormant until 1919, and it remained largely an Edmonton organization for decades. The society again became inactive during the Second World War (1939-1945). It took until 1959, more than three years after Alberta's golden jubilee, for the establishment of a Calgary Branch of the society to be initiated. A corresponding Edmonton Branch was also formed, leaving the HSA as an umbrella provincial body. A third branch in Lethbridge was organized in 1961. The branches were colorfully renamed in 1970 to reflect the broad district each one covered outside its main urban area. They became Amisk-Waskahegan Chapter (Edmonton), Chinook Country Chapter (Calgary), and Whoop-Up Country Chapter (Lethbridge). Chinook's region stretched from Red Deer in the north to Nanton in the south, and from the Saskatchewan to British Columbia borders. After the formation of a Red Deer-based chapter in 1995, Chinook's northern border shifted south to Olds.

Long before the Calgary Branch was organized, there were other serious efforts to create an historical society in what is now the Chinook Country region. On December 4, 1901, the newly-formed Calgary Old-Timers' Association held its first annual dinner at the Criterion Restaurant on Stephen Avenue. Membership was limited to those who had arrived in the district prior to 1884 – in the *Calgary Herald's* words, "those who metaphorically came over on the Mayflower."[4] But guests of the association, who reached Alberta after the cut-off date, were also allowed to attend the dinner. Among them were Reverend James Chalmers Herdman (1855-1910), who had come to Calgary as the new Presbyterian minister in 1885, and William Pearce (1848-1930), the Dominion Superintendent of Mines, Minerals, and Resources, who had moved from Winnipeg in 1887. Rev. Herdman spoke on behalf of the clergy. He pointed out the need to record the stories of the district's early figures who were even then passing away. When it was his turn to speak, Pearce returned to Rev. Herdman's point "with regard to the desirability of collecting statistics, and the formation of an historical society," as the *Herald* summarized Pearce's remarks.[5]

William Pearce in his Canadian Pacific Railway office in 1914. Pearce was president of the local historical society in 1902-1903 and 1926-1927. Glenbow Archives, NA-325-1

The organization that first met at that December 1901 dinner was the forerunner of the present Southern Alberta Pioneers and Their Descendants. Herdman's suggestion, however, quickly resulted in the establishment of an entirely separate organization. On January 14, 1902, Herdman and Pearce met with 18 other men at the Dominion Lands Office, where they established an historical society. The distinction between the two new organizations comprised both philosophy and membership eligibility. The pioneers' group focus was to preserve memories of an era and the personalities who shaped it; membership was open to those who arrived before a certain date, and eventually, to their descendants. The historical society's focus embraced broader academic questions; membership would be open to all, regardless of arrival date. Not insignificantly, neither Herdman nor Pearce qualified for membership in the Calgary Old Timers' Association.

Both men were named to a committee that met two weeks later to outline the scope of the new organization. Pearce chaired both the inaugural meeting and the committee, which proposed a broad program of study that included cartography, ethnology, and toponymy, in addition to history. The committee also recommended that women be included as society members, and encouraged the collection of a wide range of records and photographs and the establishment of an archives. The committee offered three possible names, depending on the geographic scope chosen for the organization – the Canada Intra Western Historical Society, the Western Canada Historical Society, or the Rocky Mountain Historical Society. It eventually became the Western Canada Historical Society, with Pearce as founding president.

The new organization received excellent press coverage in Calgary. The 18 men who attended the organizational meeting included William McCartney Davidson (1872-1942), owner and editor of the *Albertan* (and a future biographer of Louis Riel), and Thomas B. Braden (1851-1904), founder and business manager of the *Herald*, who acted as the meeting's secretary. Both journals approved of the organization in their editorials, and the *Albertan* even published a front-page story about the group, titled "Vision of What Might Be."[6] All the more surprising, then, that the society was so short-lived: it evidently disbanded within a year.[7]

Five years later, on March 15, 1907, the HSA was created by provincial statute – the Historical Society of Alberta Act. Its mandate comprised the whole of the new province, which had come into being on September 1, 1905. The new society's goals were defined in the statute:

> The object of the society shall be to encourage the study of the history of Alberta and Canada, to rescue from oblivion the memory of the original inhabitants, the early missionaries, fur traders, explorers, and settlers of the north and west of Canada, to obtain and preserve narratives in print, manuscript or otherwise of their travels, adventures, labours and observations, to secure and preserve minerals, archaeological curiosities and objects generally illustrative of the civil, religious, literary and natural history of the country and to establish a museum and library.[8]

The Edmonton-based society limited its activities to the capital city, and became dormant during the First World War. On its post-war revival in 1919, HSA member Edward Higinbotham recommended "that associate societies or groups should be formed throughout Alberta."[9] It took another quarter century for the society to reach out as Higinbotham suggested, and nearly 40 years for the first branch to be formed. In the meantime, the 1920s saw a second great effort to establish an historical society in southern Alberta. It involved some of the same personalities who had been involved in 1902.

The same year that the provincial government established the HSA in Edmonton, the Historic Landmarks Association of Canada was founded in Ottawa. In 1922 it was reorganized as the Canadian Historical Association (CHA), and began publishing the *Canadian Historical Review*. The following year, CHA president Lawrence Burpee sought local support in Calgary for the national organization. On the recommendation of Alexander Calhoun, chief librarian of the Calgary Public Library, Burpee wrote to businessman George Coutts (1886-1974) requesting the names of Calgarians who might be interested in joining the CHA. The correspondence led Coutts, who owned and managed a legal publishing firm, to join with a group of like-minded men to form their own local organization. The Historical Society of Calgary (HSC) held its founding meeting at the Calgary Public Library (now the Memorial Park Branch) on October 18, 1923. Just like its predecessor two decades earlier, the historical society's establishment followed the lead of the local pioneers' organization. In 1921, the group that began as the Calgary Old Timers' Association was formalized as the Southern Alberta Pioneers' & Old Timers' Association. The cut-off date for membership was adjusted from 1884 to 1891. As with the Western Canada Historical Society in 1902, most founding members of the HSC were ineligible for membership in the pioneer club. James Nevin Wallace

(1870-1941), an amateur historian and one of the pillars of the new society, outlined the philosophical distinction between the Pioneer organization and the Historical Society as he saw it:

> The weak point of allowing confusion between a Historical Society and an Old-Timers Society is that very few indeed of the Old-Timers are sufficiently acquainted with the written records to appreciate the relation between their reminiscences and the history of the west. . . . Calgary is peculiarly liable to a substitution of roving reminiscences for plain historical accuracy, and it has resulted in a want of proper proportion when dealing with various events of past years, too much attention being given to matters which were really more or less of little consequence, and too little to the unseen forces behind the scenes which were bearing on these writers much more than they seem to realize. It was not the individual old-time rancher who made the West, but he was himself carried along on a tide whose existence even was unknown to him.[10]

That the new Calgary group began as an independent society, and not as an affiliate or junior partner of the Edmonton-based HSA, may reflect the persistent rivalry between the two cities.

Through its constitution, the HSC adopted four principal tasks: to provide a forum for people in Calgary and its region who were interested in history; to prepare papers on historical subjects, to be read at society meetings and published if possible; to collect historical books and documents; and to promote historical research and public interest in history, "particularly in the history of Western Canada."[11] The founding president was John Edward Annand Macleod (1878-1966), a Nova Scotia-born lawyer and amateur historian who settled in Calgary in 1909. Macleod became a self-taught expert on the fur trade, and is credited with establishing the location of the Old Bow Fort. His paper on the subject was later published in the *Canadian Historical Review*.[12] William Pearce, who had presided over the 1902 historical society, served as vice-president and succeeded Macleod in 1926. George Coutts served as secretary, and Mr. Justice Duncan Stuart was the honorary president. Members included Charles O. Smith, editorial writer for the *Herald*, and William Davidson, still the owner and editor of the *Albertan*, with the happy result that in Calgary, historical society meetings were always news. Typed transcripts of papers presented to the society are preserved in the Calgary Public Library's Local History Collection.

Curiously, given Pearce's emphasis on the preservation of records and the documentation of history, extant records of the HSC end with his assumption of its leadership in 1926. While its exact date and cause of dissolution is forgotten, the society did not last beyond 1927.[13] Limited membership (which peaked at 60), combined with the death or departure from the city of key members, evidently contributed to its demise. Through the Great Depression and the Second World War, there was no historical society activity in Calgary. This was also true in wartime Edmonton, where the HSA entered its second period of dormancy in 1939. When it was revived in 1947, the Edmonton-based group reached beyond the capital by appointing more than a dozen district conveners in points across the province; the Calgary representative was J. E. A. Macleod, one of the pillars of the old HSC.[14] In 1953 the HSA launched *Alberta Historical Review*, a quarterly journal edited by Rev. W. Everard Edmonds, who had been instrumental in reviving the society in 1947. The *Review* brought historical articles and society news to members across the province. The magazine's title, styled after the *Canadian Historical Review*, was changed to *Alberta History* in 1975.

In the spring of 1956, Hugh A. Dempsey, vice-president of the HSA and associate editor of *Alberta Historical Review*, moved to Calgary. The former *Edmonton Bulletin* reporter and provincial civil servant had been hired to create an archives for the Glenbow Foundation, an historical institute that had recently been founded by Calgary oilman Eric L. Harvie (1892-1975).[15] Dempsey immediately made plans to expand the society's activities in Calgary and involve the city's 138 members. In a "Notice to Calgarians" published in the Summer 1956 *Review*, Dempsey proposed a series of winter lectures, but the idea met with little interest. Dempsey remained the city's only representative on the HSA's executive, and in 1958 was elected president. He resigned a few months later to take over the editorship of the *Review*.

Meanwhile, Dempsey had recruited two Glenbow colleagues, director Jack D. Herbert and historical researcher Sheilagh S. Jameson (1914-1997), to help drum up local interest in the society. Dempsey also took an important step in establishing a relationship with the Calgary Allied Arts Centre and its longtime director, Archibald F. Key (1894-1986). The Allied Arts Centre was a cultural facility established in 1946 and housed in the Coste House, a city-owned mansion in the posh Mount Royal district that had been acquired years earlier through non-payment of taxes. In the summer of 1958, Key conducted a series of historical tours in Drumheller (where he had once edited a newspaper),

Blackfoot Crossing, the Old Bow Fort, and the Old Women's Buffalo Jump. He opened the tours to members of the Historical Society, and the tours proved a great success. Dempsey outlined the following course of events in the *Review*:

> Because of the success of these tours, it was felt that an attempt should be made to form a branch of the Society in the city. As the only Calgarian on our Executive, it fell to my lot to make these arrangements. Accordingly, the Society took out an affiliate membership in the Calgary Allied Arts Council which gave us a meeting place in the Coste House and other privileges of the Council.
>
> As we did not know what kind of support we would receive, it was decided to hold the first few meetings without an elected Executive. This would give us a chance to determine the interest in our group and also to look over the members for good executive material.[16]

On October 3, 1958, the city's first historical society meeting in more than 30 years – and the first ever under the aegis of the HSA – took place in Room 104 of the Coste House. Una MacLean, an historical researcher at the Glenbow, spoke on the life of Irene Parlby, one of five Alberta women (the Famous Five) instrumental in the 1929 Persons Case, a landmark step in the progress toward equality for women in Canada.[17] The November speaker was Norman T. Macleod, the son of Commissioner James F. Macleod of the North-West Mounted Police. At a third meeting in February, members watched the Pierre Berton-narrated film *City of Gold*, a documentary about Dawson City, Yukon. The turnout of 50 to 60 people on cold winter evenings convinced the organizers to formally establish a Calgary Branch and elect an executive. This took place at the Coste House on March 6, 1959, when Jack Herbert was elected president. In a nod to local history, J. E. A. Macleod was chosen as honorary

J. E. A. Macleod, circa 1910s. Macleod was president of the Calgary Historical Society from 1923-1926. He later became Honorary President of the HSA's Calgary Branch. Glenbow Archives, NA-4150-2

president, establishing a tangible link between the old Historical Society of Calgary and the new Calgary Branch of the Historical Society of Alberta. (George Coutts, Macleod's old colleague on the HSC executive, later joined the Calgary Branch's executive.) Norman T. Macleod became the honorary vice-president, and later in 1959, Benton Mackid – a descendant of Dr. H. G. Mackid, a pioneer Calgary physician – became the branch's second president.

The Calgary Branch continued its program of tours in the summer and lectures, panel discussions, and film nights at the Coste House in the fall and winter. In 1962 its meetings moved to the new campus of the University of Alberta, Calgary (now the University of Calgary), whose principal, Dr. Malcolm G. Taylor, became the branch's second honorary vice-president. Meetings moved to the new Glenbow Museum when it opened in 1965 in Calgary's historic 1914 sandstone courthouse. The Chinook Country Chapter (as it was renamed in 1970) later met regularly in a variety of facilities, including the Memorial Park Branch of the Calgary Public Library, likely in the very room where the Calgary Historical Society had gathered in the 1920s. By the 1970s the chapter adopted a tradition of hosting an annual Christmas dinner for members and guests, in venues ranging from the Palliser Hotel's Crystal Ballroom to Gunn's Dairy Barn at Heritage Park Historical Village, and from the reconstructed Wainwright Hotel at Heritage Park to the Officer's Mess at historic Mewata Armouries. Besides its bus tours and regular meetings, the chapter and its members advocated for heritage awareness and education, participated in the unveiling of cairns at historic sites, and urged the preservation of the Fort Calgary site, which had become an industrial site and was threatened in the 1960s by proposed freeway construction. The site was reclaimed in the 1970s as Fort Calgary Historic Park as part of Calgary's centennial celebration of the arrival of the North-West Mounted Police in 1875.

The centennial of Confederation was the first significant anniversary after the branch's formation. Members celebrated the nation's birthday through participation in the Western Canada History Conference, a Centennial project jointly sponsored by the HSA and the University of Alberta, and held in Banff in May 1967. Two years later, the branch published *Calgary in Sandstone*, a 29-page illustrated booklet written by member Richard Cunniffe, documenting the many extant and demolished buildings that once gave Calgary the moniker "Sandstone City." The next significant anniversary, the centennial of Fort Calgary in 1975, provided an occasion for a successful two-part collaboration with the

History Department at the University of Calgary. In May 1975, the chapter and the department jointly organized and sponsored a successful conference on Calgary's history. It was followed by *Frontier Calgary: Town, City, and Region 1875-1914* (University of Calgary/McClelland and Stewart West, 1975), a scholarly anthology of the conference's papers edited by the university's Anthony Rasporich and Henry C. Klassen (Klassen later served as chapter president.).

This successful publication venture was followed by *Citymakers: Calgarians After the Frontier* (1987), a collection of 27 biographical essays edited by Sheilagh Jameson and Max Foran. Conceived in 1984, the centennial of Calgary's incorporation as a town, the book's essays explored the city's post-frontier experience between the first and second world wars. The present volume, occasioned by Alberta's centennial of provincehood, is the third in what has become a series. Other publication projects have included Bruce W. Gowans' *Wings Over Calgary: 1906-1940* (1990) and participation with Detselig Enterprises in publishing Doug Nelson's *From Hotcakes to High Stakes: The Chuckwagon Story* (1993), edited by former chapter president Trudy Cowan.

In 1992 the chapter began participating in Historic Calgary Week, a city-wide program of exhibits, lectures, and guided tours that had been inaugurated the previous year. When the festival's organizing committee dissolved in 1995, the Chinook Country Historical Society (as the chapter became known after its incorporation in 1993) took over management of the annual event, which has become its key outreach program and membership drive. The chapter was represented on the City of Calgary Heritage Advisory Board (HAB), created in 1978 as an advisory body to city council on heritage matters. Three of Chinook's presidents – Trudy Cowan, Elise Corbet, and Neil Watson – also chaired the HAB. (In 2002, the HAB was superceded by the Calgary Heritage Authority, on which the chapter is not directly represented.) Chinook also funds the Elise Corbet Scholarship, named for former chapter president Elise A. Corbet (1926-1996) and awarded annually to an undergraduate history student at the University of Calgary.

In 1988, the HSA debated where to house its first permanent office since the society's formation in 1907. The Chinook Country president suggested to the provincial council that the then-vacant historic Lougheed House be considered. A committee was established, ostensibly a provincial group, but comprised solely of Chinook Country members. Out of that committee grew the Lougheed House Conservation Society, formed in 1995. The HSA, through Chinook, maintained a seat on that group's board until 2004. The HSA opened its first office in Calgary's historic Lancaster Building in 1991 and moved it to the historic Barron Building in 2002. Chinook opened its first office in the Old Y, Calgary's historic Young Women's Christian Association building, in 2002.

The incorporation of HSA chapters in the 1990s (Amisk-Waskahegan became the Edmonton and District Historical Society, Whoop-up Country became the Lethbridge Historical Society, and the new Red Deer-based chapter was organized as the Central Alberta Historical Society) did not sever their link to the provincial body, which remains an important source of funding, coordination, and fellowship across the province, maintained through a governing council, annual conferences, *Alberta History*, and the newsletter *History Now*. Each chapter hosts the annual conference in rotation, and Chinook's contributions have included the military-themed "Guns and Wild Roses" conference (Carriage House Inn, 1991), "From Cross to Crisis: A Century of Health Care in Alberta" (Palliser Hotel, 1998), and "Friends and Neighbourhoods" (former Highlander Hotel, 2002). Chapter members also took part in the November 1987 conference on winter sports in western Canada, jointly sponsored by the HSA and the University of Calgary History Department, and held at the university in advance of the XV Olympic Winter Games in Calgary in February 1988. The HSA later published *Winter Sports in the West* (1990), an anthology of the conference's papers, edited by Prof. Rasporich and Elise Corbet.

In January 1902, the *Albertan* predicted the important role that the newly-formed (though short-lived) Historical Society would play:

> As time goes on the district will more and more conform to the ways of the rest of the country and will lose its indi-viduality and some of its peculiar beauty. The chronicler, who can place before the world scenes as they were will be performing a duty for which future generations in Alberta and the student of men and nature will rise up and call him blessed.[18]

Though it took far longer for the Historical Society to be founded on a permanent basis, its members have taken seriously the weighty role of "chronicler." Through its efforts and those of its nearly 500 members (representing almost half the membership of the entire provincial organization), the Chinook Country Historical Society has made a long-standing, substantial contribution to heritage education, awareness, and advocacy. Its programs and publications offer a balance between scholarship and popular history. In a fast-growing city and region, whose petroleum-based wealth constantly draws newcomers, CCHS ensures that local history is not lost on the public imagination.[19]

In an article written during Alberta's 75th anniversary year, Sheilagh Jameson cast the society's goals in a profound context that remains true a quarter-century later.

> It is said that a knowledge of the past is essential for an understanding of the present and as a foundation upon which to build the future. . . . At a time when so much in the world is cause for pessimism, I feel that the place of history in Alberta today warrants optimism. General public awareness, a strong interest in preserving and using historical materials, governmental concern, a new emphasis on history in education – surely these bode well for Alberta's future.[20]

Notes

1. At that time, Alberta was a district in the North-West Territories. It comprised an area considerably smaller than the province created under that name in 1905.

2. "A Historical Society," *Alberta Tribune* 22 February 1896, 4.

3. Hugh A. Dempsey, "Four Early Alberta Historians," *Alberta History* 45:2 (Spring 1997) 2-3.

4. "The Old Timers Hold Their First Great Banquet in Calgary," *Daily Herald*, 5 December 1901, 1.

5. *Ibid.*

6. "Vision of What Might Be," *Albertan and the Alberta Tribune* 31 January 1902, 1, 4.

7. On 2 January 1903, the *Weekly Albertan* reported that "The Historical Association will de [sic] revived early in the year." ("Local News," *Weekly Albertan* 2 January 1903: 2). This suggests the organization had become inactive during 1902. At a meeting held on 28 January 1903, members announced their intention to apply for a charter for the Western Canada Historical Association. There is no known evidence that they did so.

8. Statutes of Alberta 1907 c. 23.

9. Glenbow Archives, Historical Society of Alberta fonds, HSA minutes, 10 Jan. 1919.

10. Calgary Public Library, Local History Collection, Minutes of Historical Society of Calgary 1923-26, Constitution, 18 October 1923. The inclusion of Wallace's critique here should not be taken as a modern criticism of the Southern Alberta Pioneers and Their Descendants, which has long maintained an active historical research committee.

11. Ibid.

12. J. E. A. Macleod, "Old Bow Fort," *Canadian Historical Review* xii, 407, December 1931.

13. Pearce's legendary crusty personality might have contributed to the demise of both historical societies that he chaired. Pearce's life was the subject of Chinook's September 1983 program, "William Pearce: His Calgary Connexions," delivered by then-HSA president Dr. Alyn Mitchener.

14. "Alberta Historical Society Reorganizes," *Edmonton Journal* 9 February 1948.

15. Harvie established the Glenbow Foundation in 1954, on the eve of Alberta's golden jubilee. The anniversary inspired the formation of historical societies in smaller centres across the province, whose project ranged from establishing small museums to publishing local histories. Similarly, the centennial of Confederation in 1967 and the province's 75th anniversary in 1980 stimulated the activities of local historical societies. Such groups remained independent of the HSA, however, and their stories lie beyond the scope of this chapter.

16. Hugh A. Dempsey, "Calgary Report," *Alberta Historical Review* 7:2 (Spring 1959), 31.

17. Irene Parlby (1868-1965) was still living at the time, and Una MacLean sent a copy of her article ("Honourable Irene Parlby," *Alberta Historical Review* 7:2 [Spring 1959]: 1-6) to Parlby at her ranch near Alix, Alberta. Parlby wrote a letter to the *Review's* editor, published in the Winter 1960 issue, correcting a few minor points.

18. "The Historical Association," *Albertan and the Alberta Tribune* 21 January 1902, 6.

19. Many other historical, commemorative, and preservation societies have emerged in Calgary in recent decades. They remain independent of the HSA and beyond the scope of this chapter.

20. Sheilagh Jameson, "Historical knowledge a blueprint," undated newspaper clipping, circa 1980.

* This chapter is based, in part, on research the author conducted with Jennifer Cook Bobrovitz for her article, "Historical Society of Calgary: A Lasting Legacy," *Alberta History* 45:3 (Summer 1997) 2-11.

Reasoned Speculation:
The Challenge of Knowing Isabella Clarke Hardisty Lougheed

by Jennifer Cook Bobrovitz and Trudy Cowan

Using only fragments of the past: infrequent photographs, occasional letters, overzealous newspaper reports, and fading memories, to create a whole person is no easy task. Yet, to tell the tale of this amazing woman, one must collect the fragments together and bring Isabella Clarke Hardisty Lougheed to life. But how? A Métis woman born at a remote fur trade post in 1860, she later entertained royalty at "the most beautiful home in the North-West," and died almost penniless during the Depression – but these are events. Who *was* she?

We know people laugh, therefore Isabella must have laughed. But did she revel in the joys of a humorous story? Did she tell a good one? We know that mothers experience unquenchable sorrow when a child dies. Frail for some time, Marjorie, the youngest child, died at age 12. We are left to imagine Isabella's grief. We know she was involved with many community service organizations. Was she committed to the groups that boasted her name on their letterheads, or was it simply her social duty as the Senator's wife? We know that her home was filled with books, and that gifts of books were given even as wedding presents. Did Isabella like to read, and if so, what books did she select for her own enjoyment?

Who was Belle Lougheed?

Isabella Clarke Hardisty Lougheed (1859-1936). Calgary, Alberta. Glenbow Archives NA-3232-5

Isabella Clarke Hardisty was born at Fort Resolution, Northwest Territories on April 18, 1861, to William Lucas Hardisty and Mary Anne Allen.[1] She was one of nine children. For 36 years, her father was an officer of the Hudson's Bay Company (HBC), rising to the position of Chief Factor for the Mackenzie District. Born circa 1822, probably at Waswanipi House in the Prince Rupert District (now part of Quebec),[2] he was the second child of the Hudson's Bay Company Chief Trader, Richard Hardisty, who was a native of London, England. His mother Margaret Sutherland was of First Nations and Scottish parentage. He had five siblings including Richard Charles Hardisty, who became Chief Factor for the Upper Saskatchewan District. In 1888, our heroine's uncle, Richard Charles, was appointed to the Canadian Senate representing the District of Alberta. Her aunt Isabella Sophia (for whom she was presumably named) married Donald Smith (First Baron Strathcona and Mount Royal), who began his career as an employee of HBC. Lord Strathcona eventually rose to the position of governor and principal shareholder of the company. He helped finance the Canadian Pacific Railway and was also president of the Bank of Montreal. Later, his wife's family connections would be helpful to James Lougheed's career.

According to genealogical research on the Hardisty family, our Isabella's mother, Mary Anne Allen (daughter of Robert Allen and Charlotte Scarborough), was born at Fort Dunvegan on August 10, 1840. Isabella's parents had an unusual relationship in that her father expected his wife to take a more prominent role in HBC society than was the norm. In November 1857 William Lucas Hardisty wrote to Sir George Simpson.

> I was up at Fort Simpson in August and got married there in a very offhand way to a Miss Allen – she is an orphan, her parents having died when she was an infant – her education has been very much neglected, and it is my intention to send her to school for a year or two. It is a very unusual thing to send a Wife to school and no doubt will cause a laugh at my expense, but I don't care a fig and won't mind the expense, so long as she is enable thereby to act her part with credit in the society among which she is placed – as for the rest, the woman who I consider good enough to live with, is good enough for my friends to look at.[3]

Schooling for their children was also unusually important. Isabella was well educated. When still not more than a child of six or seven years of age, she was sent to the Red River to begin her formal education at Miss Davis' School.[4] Within a year or two, she left because of poor health. In a 1922 interview with Elizabeth Bailey Price, Lady Lougheed said that she went to stay with her grandmother in Lachine, Quebec (Hudson's Bay Company headquarters) until she was well enough to return to school.[5] She was later sent to the Wesleyan Ladies College in Hamilton, Ontario where she was registered as a student for six years.[6] By her own account she left Hamilton at age 18 and returned to Fort Simpson where she lived with her family for three years.[7] But the archival records and reminiscences do not always concur.

Isabella apparently left the Wesleyan Ladies College in the spring of 1875 although she was still listed as a student. According to a letter written to Richard Hardisty, Isabella spent the winter of 1876 at Fort Chipewyan, although the correspondent mentioned that she would benefit from more education.[8] A letter written to Isabella in September 1877 refers to her return to school, although it does not mention which one.[9]

In 1878, William Lucas Hardisty retired from the HBC. He and his family (including Isabella) arrived in Winnipeg in October, having left Fort Simpson in June. The family spent the winter of 1878-1879 in Winnipeg at the residence of Isabella's uncle, Donald Smith.[10] The next spring, they moved to Lachine, Quebec, where William died less than two years later. Isabella's mother, Mary Anne Allen Hardisty, returned to Winnipeg where she married Edwin Stewart Thomas.

Whether Isabella stayed at Lachine after her father's death, or moved back to Winnipeg with her mother, is not known. However, in August 1883 she made another move, this time to Calgary, along with brothers Frank and Thomas, to live with her Uncle Richard Charles Hardisty and her Aunt Eliza (nee McDougall).[11] She soon met a young man, a newly arrived lawyer by the name of James Lougheed. They may have met at the Methodist Church (which in those days was a tent) or it might have been at the Hardisty home. Wherever they initially met, church gatherings provided the young couple with an opportunity to develop their friendship. In the spring of 1884 the *Calgary Herald* reported that "Miss Hardisty and Lougheed" were among the performers at a church concert that packed the pews on Good Friday.[12]

Six months later, on September 16, 1884, the young couple were married in a ceremony performed by Reverend J. McDougall.[13] The *Calgary Herald* published an account of the event.

> Last evening the youth and beauty of our town, might be seen wending their way towards the Methodist Church, where a scene of no common interest was being enacted – a marriage

ceremony. The principals were James A. Lougheed, Esq. Barrister, and Miss Hardisty. The bride was waited upon by Miss Clara Hardisty, Calgary, and Miss McDougall of Morley. Messrs. Parlow and Andrews performed similar services for the groom. Before the hour the building was packed, a number having to satisfy themselves with a peek through the windows. After the ceremony had been performed and the usual congratulations indulged in, a large company repaired to the residence of Chief Factor Hardisty, where a sumptuous feast awaited the guests. We extend our congratulations to the happy couple and wish them a happy sail o'er the sea of life.[14]

Of the early years of the Lougheed marriage, we know very little, although in a 1922 interview, Lady Lougheed recalled the early days and the couple's association with the Methodist Church. "I played the organ – my husband who was a young lawyer then, was superintendent of the Sunday school."[15]

From the family Bible we know that their first child, Clarence Hardisty Lougheed, was born July 29, 1885, and on December 6, christened in Calgary by Reverend J. McDougall of Morley.[16]

James Lougheed's November 1885 letter to Belle's uncle, Senator Richard Hardisty, provides a rare insight into the couple's personal lives. His affection for Belle and pride in his four-month old son Clarence shines through in an unusual display of prosaic wit and humor.

We have nothing blood thrillingly new down here. Everything moves along in the even tenor of its way. A new baby comes along by weekly clock-work. When you were here we had a fresh arrival daily, but the strain was so great and the wear and tear so heavy that it has been reduced to a weekly arrival, instead of a daily one. The last week being the term of the Presbyterian Minister, the bairn came duly to hand. The preceding week was the Doctor's week, and the arrival was satisfactory, father, mother and child doing well, especially the father. If Belle were within hearing distance I might find out the report for this week, but my enquiring mind has not been equal to the information.

Our son and heir is growing like a weed in the potato field. The women state emphatically that he is a wonder and as against all the other babies of the place, he takes the proverbial bun. This little eulogy is not made in a moment of impulse and parental pride, but made after solemn and serious consideration.

I miss greatly the sociabilities which you carried off in your retinue when you left. Belle and I threaten at times to fall into a state of rust and dumbness by having so few to brush elbows and tongues against.[17]

To date the only surviving letter written by Belle was penned on Beaulieu stationery to her Auntie Eliza (McDougall) Hardisty on November 24, 1903. It is necessary to read between the lines, as some topics were not openly discussed, even in correspondence with Auntie. At the time this letter was written, the weary Belle was seven months pregnant with her sixth child and second daughter, Marjorie Yolande. Four children still lived at home; the youngest, Douglas, had just turned two in September. Eighteen-year-old Clarence, no longer a child growing like a weed in the potato field, was living in Edmonton with his Aunt Eliza and Uncle Richard. The strain of maintaining the household while "Mr. Lougheed," as Belle referred to her husband, was in Ottawa and otherwise engaged in business affairs, was wearing on the normally stalwart Belle.

I must ask you to forgive me for not writing you long before this, but since I returned from my trip east, I have been kept so busy all day long that I always felt too tired to do anything but rest. I have had to do all the housework for nearly two months, so that my health nearly gave way. The doctor ordered me off to bed one day and there I had to stay for a week or so, which accounts for the report that I was very ill. However I am glad to say that there was nothing to it and I am getting quite strong again. You know there is a great deal to do in a house of this size.[18]

As well as being mother and household manager, she was involved with, and supported, several women's organizations. She was a member of the executive or patron of the Imperial Order Daughters of the Empire (IODE), Victorian Order of Nurses (VON), both the Local and National Councils of Women, Methodist Ladies Aid and Women's Association, Calgary Children's Aid Society, Calgary Society for the Protection of Cats, the Women's Pioneer Association of Southern Alberta, and the General Hospital Women's Auxiliary – all worthy organizations working for health, education, social, and even animal welfare. Like many political wives of the time, Isabella seemed to deliberately avoid controversy.

Although there is little evidence to suggest that she was involved in any overtly political activities, Isabella occasionally made her views known.

In the fall of 1909, she joined with other Calgary women to protest "an omission in the draft city bill" which deprived married women of the municipal vote that they had exercised since 1894. The move rankled Mrs. Lougheed to the point that she spoke to an *Albertan* reporter who quoted her along with a number of other dissatisfied women. She said, "I have always voted and I should dislike very much to give up the privilege. It would not be fair. Married women have more right to vote than single women."[19] On the following day the newspaper reported that the Honorable W. H. Cushing, Minister of Public Works, had phoned his wife in Calgary with assurances that the government would not insist on withdrawing the franchise.

We know little of Belle's private life or her relationship with her children. Film footage from the 1930s reveals a short, small-boned, lively woman.[20] It is possible to visualize Belle as a woman of iron will, strength, and fortitude. In later years her son-in-law, J. A. Hutchison, hints at Belle's stubborn streak in a 1935 letter to R. B. Bennett:

> "[Dorothy] is a fine cook though Lady Belle claims she is too fussy. It was amusing the last time mother [Belle] was up [to Edmonton] from Calgary to see both in the kitchen. Lady Belle had her opinion as to how things should be done and likewise Dorothy. Sometimes one or the other would appeal to the only male present for his opinion – train your diplomats under similar circumstances."[21]

In spite of a rigorous schedule, Isabella found time to golf and drive her automobile. She seemed to do everything with zest. Along with her husband, she was a founding member of the Calgary Golf and Country Club, established in 1910. Her enthusiasm for motoring caught the attention of the local media and the entire community. At a time when the Traffic Act discriminated against women, Mrs. Lougheed prevailed.[22] In 1913 the *Albertan* reported that many women "own cars built especially for their private use, and not a few of these handle a car with the skill of an expert." One was Mrs. James A. Lougheed (who as owner of Calgary's first large automobile was hardly typical): "Mrs. Lougheed is very fond of motoring and one of her pet luxuries is her garage and her motor driven equipages. Her cars are probably the finest in the province."[23]

Lady Lougheed and daughter, Marjorie, Calgary, Alberta. Glenbow Archives, NA-3232-6

One of Belle's most passionate interests was history. At a time when there were few historical societies and no organizations like the Heritage Canada Foundation, promoting the preservation of Canada's buildings or the study of history in schools, newspaper articles suggest that Lady Lougheed supported both. Privately, she kept meticulous records of births, deaths, and marriages in the family Bible and throughout her life stayed actively involved with the Southern Alberta Pioneers and Old Timers.

She spoke with regret about the fact that she and the Senator "did not move their first house on Stephen Avenue to their new 13th Avenue property and remodel it for some useful purpose as it was the scene of many important historical events and of happiness peculiar to those early days." The *Calgary Daily Herald's* 1932 series "Alberta Women We Should Know," captured her sentiments.

> In seeing the old order pass, Lady Lougheed regretfully notes the demolition of landmarks and buildings that recall the beginnings of this city. Like many others she believes that a society for the preservation of these historical spots would be of great value in the west, although too late to save Calgary's first structures. The old fort, the old barracks, the house where the women and children were huddled together for two days during the Indian rebellion scare, the first store, the first community hall and school, the early mission houses and hostelries could not all be preserved and handed down to posterity as of artistic or historical value.

> Nevertheless, their destruction, necessary though it undoubtedly was brought a pang of regret to many of the oldtimers who, like Lady Lougheed, have taken such a consistent and active interest in this community for nearly half a century.[24]

Throughout Belle's life she balanced many roles. But the role that was most widely reported in the press, and therefore about which we know the most, was that of hostess both at Beaulieu and in Ottawa. Mrs. Lougheed's calendar was public information and the newspapers reported on most aspects of her life. Whether it was the endless rounds of tea and afternoon socials, the first "at home" held at Beaulieu after renovations in 1908,[25] hosting the inaugural meeting of the Victorian Order of Nurses in the drawing room in 1909, providing accommodation for the Duke and Duchess of Connaught during their 1912 visit, or entertaining the Prince of Wales at a garden party in 1919, both the events and the clothes she wore were described in minute detail.

Belle unfailingly supported her husband's political career, hosting and attending events in the senator's absence, often accompanied by her eldest son Clarence. She frequently joined her husband on official engagements both in Ottawa and Europe. She and Clarence accompanied the senator as a representative of the Canadian Senate at the coronation of King George V in the summer of 1911. Five years later, Belle became Lady Lougheed when King George knighted her husband for his contribution to the war effort.

Clearly her reputation as a hostess was not confined to Calgary or Alberta. On April 4, 1912, the Calgary *Albertan* reported an article in a Montreal newspaper about Mrs. Lougheed's position in Ottawa society, "An Alberta Woman who Leads In the Official Set at Ottawa."

> In the *Montreal Star* over the signature of Chesterfield, appears the following which is an appreciation of one of the leading women of Calgary and the province, and an outline of the patriotic services of a woman whose family for two generations has contributed to the development of the Canadian west.
>
> 'Quite a loss has been temporarily sustained by the official social set at the Capital by the return to Calgary of Mrs. James A. Lougheed, wife of the government leader in the Senate, who has been one of the most active and most popular official hostesses since the Borden Government came into power.

> In Calgary, where Mrs. Lougheed has [lived] since she first went there in 1884, been considered a leader in society, and either at her beautiful city residence or in her summer bungalow at Banff has entertained many of the distinguished visitors to the west. She is an ideal hostess, full of honest fun and unassuming; but putting her face unobtrusively but firmly against the nasty innovations such as cigarette smoking, playing cards for money etc.'

Her ability to connect with people from all walks of life earned her the reputation as an "ideal hostess," a role she retained even after Senator Lougheed's death in 1925.

Although life as a widow was less hectic, she maintained the friendships and connections of her once very public life, hosting or attending functions for the Earl of Minto, Lord and Lady Byng, Prince Erik of Denmark, and Lord and Lady Willingdon. During the summer of 1932, Belle entertained visitors to the Canadian Law Society Convention at a five o'clock reception in the gardens of the Lougheed House. The *Calgary Herald* observed, "it is only suitable that this summer the Lougheed residence be the rallying ground for one of the most important gatherings of the year."[26]

The Prince of Wales continued to send her Christmas cards and even invited her to dinner at his E. P. Ranch south of Longview, along with other dignitaries, during one of his infrequent visits in 1928. Friends, family, and many of the senator's former colleagues looked forward to Belle's New Year's Day open house held annually at Beaulieu.

In spite of a brave public face, Lady Lougheed found herself in dire financial straits in the years following her husband's death. The Alberta drought of the 1920s exacerbated by a nation-wide slide into the Depression of the 30s, all but decimated the senator's estate, most of which was invested in real estate. Like many Canadians, the Lougheeds suffered a drastic change in lifestyle. In 1934, the City of Calgary assumed title to Beaulieu for non-payment of taxes. Out of respect and in recognition of the Lougheed family's enormous contribution, city officials allowed Lady Lougheed to continue living in the house where she and the senator had raised their family, the house they had graciously opened to the world.

In October 1935, Belle's daughter, Dorothy, shared her perspective about her mother's circumstances in a letter to an old family friend, her father's former law partner, Prime Minister R. B. Bennett. "My poor mother is nearly heart broken. I want her to come and live with us. It is such a tragedy to me that her last years should be filled with worry and unhappiness."[27] Dorothy, who was living in Edmonton with her husband J. A. Hutchison, was also feeling the pinch of poverty, claiming that she had not received "a cent" from the estate. Despite the fact that Lougheed and Bennett's business break-up had not been amicable, Bennett's response was quick and heart-warming. "I can only say that I have been worried more than I can tell you about your affairs. . . . I want you to assure your mother that whatever happens I will see that she is looked after. I never forget her and her kindness to me in days that are past, and she must not be permitted to suffer because of what has transpired."[28]

In spite of an invitation from Dorothy to come live with her family, Lady Lougheed continued to stay on at her beloved Beaulieu until her death on the 13th of March 1936. Son Norman and his family, and the butler, Grierson, stayed there with her until the end.

The Albertan headline read, "First Lady of Early Days Succumbs after Colorful Life in West" and went on to inform Calgarians that, "Latterly as health failed, Lady Lougheed participated less and less in the social activities of the city. Since New Year's Day, when she kept open house as usual during the afternoon, she has been confined to her home and two weeks ago suffered the illness that resulted in her death today."[29]

From noon Sunday until Monday at 3:30 p.m., her remains rested at Beaulieu, as was the practice at the time. The Venerable Archdeacon Cecil Swanson then conducted a private service at the family residence. Jacques Funeral Home made arrangements for Belle to be buried at Union Cemetery in the family plot following the very crowded public service at 4:00 p.m. at the Cathedral Church of the Redeemer. The service was led by Anglican church officials, Rt. Rev. L. Ralph Sherman, Bishop of Calgary, Archdeacon Swanson, Venerable Archdeacon J. W. Tims, with the Very Reverend Dean H. R. Ragg assisting.

Despite her highly public position and her large family, surprisingly few photographs or personal documents have thus far come to light. Lady Isabella Clarke Hardisty Lougheed was a wife, mother, grandmother, daughter, sister, aunt, and niece. She was a friend, colleague, employer, and patron. She was a leader, and at times found her life daunting. Despite all of these roles, despite her position in society, she was "a private person" and for as much as we are able to learn of her life, knowing Belle Lougheed remains a challenge.

Notes

1. The family bible held by Donald Lougheed provides two different years for Belle's birth, 1860 and 1861. In the 1901 census Mrs. Lougheed's birth date is recorded as 18 April 1861. Canada. *Census of Canada, 1901*. Province of Alberta, District of Central Alberta, 13

2. Biographical information on William Lucas Hardisty is from the *Dictionary of Canadian Biography, 1881-1890*, Vol. XI (Toronto: University of Toronto Press, 1982), 384-385.

3. Winnipeg. Provincial Archives of Manitoba, Hudson's Bay Archives, Letter from Chief Trader William Lucas Hardisty to Sir George Simpson-Fort Yukon, 10 November 1857. D5/45,fo264d, 10 November 1856 to George Simpson. Cited from J. G. MacGregor, *Senator Hardisty's Prairies 1840-1889*. (Saskatoon: Western Producer Prairie Books, 1978), 46-47.

4. Manitoba Archives, Miss Davis Collection. See also Elizabeth B. Price "Alberta's Women Pioneers will form Organization," *Calgary Herald*, 21 March 1922.

5. "Alberta's Women Pioneers Will Form Organization," The *Calgary Daily Herald*, 20 March 1922, 13. In an interview with Elizabeth Bailey Price, Lady Lougheed says that during the trip out of the north to attend Miss Davis's school she contracted scarlet fever and "lay ill in bed for a year and a half afterward."

6. Hamilton Public Library, Special Collections Department, records of the Wesleyan Ladies College. Isabella Hardisty is listed in the college catalogue from school year 1868 to 1874/75. The 1868-1869 calendar lists Elizabeth and Nellie McDougall of Saskatchewan H. B. T. as Isabella's classmates. The records of the Wesleyan Ladies College consists of early histories, letters, speeches, reminiscences, commencement exercises, school essays, and annual reports. The school closed in 1898.

7. Isabella's account may be inaccurate as she is listed in the Wesleyan Female College Calendars from 1868 until 1875. Since she was born in 1861, she would have been 14 when she left the college.

8. Calgary. Glenbow Archives, Richard C. Hardisty fonds, Box 5, Item 808. Letter from Fort Chipewyan to Richard Hardisty, 22 December 1876. The letter refers to the fact that "Miss Bella Hardisty is passing the winter at this place - it is to be regretted that she was removed so soon from the Canadian Institution where she was being educated- 2 or 3 years longer would have turned out a highly accomplished and charming young lady."

9. Calgary. Glenbow Archives, Richard C. Hardisty fonds, Box 5, Item 8983. Letter from John Bunn, Fort Calgary, to Bella Hardisty, 5 September 1877. The letter refers to her "safe arrival" and "I am sure that you are both happy together at school . . ."

10. "William Lucas Hardisty," *Dictionary of Canadian Biography 1881-1890*. Vol. XI. (Toronto: University of Toronto Press, 1982), 385. This information concurs with Lady Lougheed's own account of her childhood which appeared in Elizabeth B. Price, "Alberta Women Pioneers will form Organization," *Calgary Herald*, 21 March 1922.

11. J. G. MacGregor, *Senator Hardisty's Prairies: 1840-1889*, 193.

12. "Concert," in the *Calgary Herald*, 16 April 1884.

13. Methodist Church Mission, Morleyville, North West Territories, Marriage Register, Glenbow Archives, Calgary, McDougall Family Papers, M732, file 12.

14. "Wedding Bells," *Calgary Herald*, 17 September 1884.

15. "Alberta's Women Pioneers Will form Organization," The *Calgary Daily Herald*, 20 March 1922, 13

16. Family Bible held by Donald Lougheed.

17. Calgary. Glenbow Archives, Hardisty Fonds, Series 23-5. M5908/1688. Letter from James A. Lougheed to Richard Hardisty, 25 November 1885.

18. Calgary. Glenbow Archives, Hardisty Fonds, Series 23-7, M5908/1779. Letter from Belle Lougheed to Eliza (McDougall) Hardisty, 24 November 1903. Eliza was married to Belle's uncle Richard Hardisty. The Lougheed's eldest son Clarence, who was 18 years old, was living with the Hardistys in Edmonton at the time this letter was written.

19. "Calgary Women Will Likely Make Protest," *The Morning Albertan*, 28 October 1909.

20. Calgary. Glenbow Archives, Dr. Burwell J. Charles Fonds, F 168, [1930s].

21. Public Archives of Canada, R. B. Bennett Fonds, MG 26, K, Vol. 956: 0605391 – 0605394. Letter from (Lady Lougheed's son-in-law – Dorothy's husband) James A. Hutchison to R. B. Bennett dated 20 December 1935.

22. *The Boom and Bust.* 51-52. Edmonton: United Western Communications, 1994. "One interesting side-effect of early motoring was its wary recognition of women as people, after a bad start. The 1911 Traffic Act was flat-out discriminatory, allowing males to drive at the age of 16 but females only at 18. Bruce Watson, solicitor for the Calgary Auto Club, felt it was justified because the city had, "too many show-off girls who simply haven't strength enough to stop a car quickly."

23. *The Boom and Bust.* 51-52. Edmonton: United Western Communications, 1994. The specific date for the 1913 *Albertan* was not cited.

24. "Alberta Women We Should Know," The *Calgary Daily Herald*, 17 December 1932.

25. "Social and Personal," The *Calgary Daily Herald*, 12 September 1908.

26. "Prominent Canadian Hostess Opens Home for Law Reception," *Calgary Herald*, 27 August 1932.

27. Public Archives of Canada, R. B. Bennett Fonds, MG 26, K, Vol. 956: 060536 – 060537. Letter from Dorothy Lougheed Hutchison to R. B. Bennett dated 15 October 1935.

28. Public Archives of Canada, R. B. Bennett Fonds, MG 26, K, Vol. 956: 0605390. Letter from R. B. Bennett to Dorothy Lougheed Hutchison dated 6 November 1935.

29. "First Lady of Early Days Succumbs after Colorful Life in West," *Albertan.* 14 March 1936.

A Francophone Community Leader
Édouard-Hector Rouleau
by Jim Bowman

At one time, a substantial proportion of the population in the Prairie Provinces was Francophone – the region could easily have become bilingual. But the defeat and resulting dispersion of the largely Francophone and Catholic Métis communities in 1870 and 1885 determined that the region would be dominated by Anglophone and Protestant interests. In spite of the difficulties, some Francophone colonies persevered. One such stalwart community was the Village of Rouleauville, named in honor of its two most prominent citizens: Chief Justice Charles-Borromée Rouleau and his brother, Dr. Édouard-Hector Rouleau.

The area around the junction of the Bow and Elbow rivers was a traditional location for Blackfoot wintering camps, and in the 1870s it developed into a scattered settlement of Métis subsistence farms. In 1873, the largely French-speaking missionary order, the Oblates of Mary Immaculate, established a mission named Notre Dame de la Paix about 35 kilometres upstream on the Elbow. In 1875, still consisting of little more than a log cabin, it was relocated at the approximate site of present-day 1st Street and 24th Avenue in southwest Calgary.

In 1884 the Oblate Fathers acquired the land title to the area known as The Mission, and they subdivided it into residential lots. The subdivision was located at the outskirts of the town of Calgary, and only a few families settled there. Whether or not it had been intended as a Catholic Francophone enclave is not known, as it soon had a higher population of Anglophones than Francophones.[1] Even so, it was one of the few places in southern Alberta where Francophones could feel at home, and from 1899 to 1907 the Mission had its own municipal government, the Village of Rouleauville.

The Rouleau brothers were born in l'Isle-Verte, a picturesque village on the Saint Lawrence estuary, about 200 kilometres northeast of Quebec City. They were great-grandsons of Jean Rouleau, who immigrated to Canada from Normandy shortly after 1745. The boys' father, Joseph Rouleau, was a successful merchant who encouraged his

Doctor Édouard Hector Rouleau, Calgary Alberta. Glenbow Archives, NA-2953-1

sons to seek professional careers.[2] Heeding their father's wishes, one became a doctor; the other, a magistrate.

Édouard-Hector was born in 1843, and over the next 27 years gained a varied education and vast life experience. While still a mere teen by today's standards, he studied at Laval Normal School and in 1861 qualified for teaching, a profession that was then something of a gateway to other professional careers for young men from rural communities. Possibly interested in joining the priesthood, he then undertook classical studies at the Séminaire de Nicolet. During the American Civil War the defence of Canada was a national concern. Rouleau set aside his studies to become a captain in the militia and while in service, attended the School of Military Instruction of Quebec in 1864. Finally, he studied medicine at l'Université Laval in Quebec City, graduating in 1870.

Dr. Rouleau practiced medicine at Bic (a small community on the lower Saint Lawrence), Ottawa, and Bryson (in the Ottawa Valley). In 1883, at the age of 40, the career-minded bachelor at last took time from his work to invite love into his life. He married Catherine O'Meara of Bryson, daughter of a prominent Irish merchant. Two years later as the North West Rebellion broke out, Édouard again came to the aid of his country and joined the Medical Corps of the Canadian Army. He was stationed at the Mounted Police post at Battleford, where his brother Charles had been serving as a magistrate until he was forced to flee with his family to Calgary. As the rebellion came to a close, Édouard treated the wounded on the battlefield at Batoche. He returned to his medical practice at Bryson, but in 1887 came west to join his brother in the town of Calgary. Édouard was the third physician to settle in the young frontier town. He became the surgeon at the Mounted Police post at Fort Calgary, and was the medical chief of staff at Holy Cross Hospital when it was founded in 1891.

As a frontier physician, Rouleau was a general practitioner, but he also specialized in obstetrics. He was said to have an uncommon ability to ease his patients' stress and discomfort during the birthing process. Édouard was also known for his humanitarianism, for his generosity, and for his contributions to community life. He often provided free medical services to the poor, and never charged a fee to patients treated on the Sabbath.

Édouard was the founder of the Societé Saint-Jean-Baptiste in 1888. He was appointed Honorary Consul of Belgium that same year, and in 1901 was made a Chevalier de l'Ordre de Leopold II in recognition of his services to Belgian immigrants. He was also chancellor of the Catholic Mutual Benefit Association, an active member of the Knights of Columbus, and served on the Catholic School Board for 23 years. In the short-lived and unstable Village of Rouleauville, he never held political office, but on several occasions Édouard was often called upon to step into the breach, acting as Returning Officer and organizing municipal elections. Politically, he was an outspoken Liberal, even though his brother had been a Conservative candidate for Parliament and received his judicial appointment from Sir John A. Macdonald.

Édouard-Hector and Catherine had five children, born between 1889 and 1897. Four survived infancy. Daughter Albertine spent her adult life with the teaching order, the Sisters, Faithful Companions of Jesus; Albert became Calgary's first native-born priest; Bernadette died in her early 20s; and Henri was killed in action in France during the First World War.[3]

Soon after their arrival in Calgary in 1887, Dr. Rouleau and his wife took up residence in a house in the Mission at the corner of St. Joseph Street and Scarth Street (present-day 18th Avenue and 1st Street SW), located directly across the street from the mission church of Notre Dame de la Paix (which later became St. Mary's Cathedral). The house was a simple, box-like one and three-quarter story structure, but with a bay window in the front facade and some decorative gingerbread at the peak of the front gable. The tall, segmental-arched windows suggested an influence of the Italianate architectural style, popular in Central Canada in the mid-19th century, and possibly served as a reflection of the Rouleau family's architectural tastes at the time. Recent research discoveries indicate that the house was probably built in 1885, for Edwin B. Rogers, a hardware merchant who also worked with Édouard's brother, as the Clerk of Judge Rouleau's court. The design may have come from a commercial architectural plan book. It bears a remarkable resemblance to the Commanding Officer's residence at Fort Battleford, which coincidentally would have been familiar to Rouleau while he was stationed there.[4]

In 1902 or 1903 the house was moved two lots to the east, and Dr. Rouleau built a larger house for himself on the original site. The first house was then operated as a boarding house by his neighbors, the McHugh family. It has been used as a boarding house, rooming house, or single-family rental property ever since. Because the Rouleaus had no grandchildren, the family connection with the house was forgotten. It wasn't until the early 1990s that the architectural significance of the house was observed. A photograph of the Rouleau family standing in front of the house was discovered in the Glenbow Archives, and further research established its historical significance.[5]

In 1996 the Rouleau House was inventoried as a Class A heritage building (recommended for preservation because of high historical or architectural significance). But in July 2003 its owner, the owner of the office building immediately to the north, announced its intention to demolish the house in order to expand its parking lot. An informal coalition of Francophone community organizations, historical

Dr. Édouard Rouleau and family outside of their family home. Calgary, Alberta.
Glenbow Archives, NA-5222-2

organizations, the Cliff Bungalow-Mission Community Association, and individuals formed the Friends of the Rouleau House/Les amis de la maison Rouleau. With the active support of Alderman Madeleine King, Calgary City Council allocated funds to move the house to nearby City-owned land, thereby ensuring the survival of the house.

Notes

1. Census of Canada, 1891, District No. 197, Sub-District No. 24 (Calgary C.); Census of Canada, 1901, District No. 202 (Central Alberta), Polling Sub-Division No. 52 (South Calgary).

2. Corinne Dumouchel, *Genealogy of the Rouleau Family* (Ottawa, privately printed, 1960). Photocopy in Glenbow Archives, M 7864.

3. Archibald Oswald MacRae, "Edward Hector Rouleau, M.D." in *History of the Province of Alberta* (n.p., Western Canada History Co., 1912), vol. 1, 507-508; George D. Stanley, "Medical Pioneering in Alberta: Edward Hector Rouleau," *Historical Bulletin of the Calgary Associate Clinic,* vol. 5, no. 4 (May 1940), 4-10; Max Foran, "Rouleau, Édouard-Hector," *Dictionary of Canadian Biography,* vol. 13, 899-900.

4. "Local Intelligence," *Calgary Tribune,* 4 November 1885, 3; 25 March 1887, 3. The Fort Battleford house is depicted in Glenbow Archives image no. NA-1353-8 which can be viewed at [www.glenbow.org/lasearch/photo.htm] (viewed September 2004). The author wishes to thank Harry Sanders, who kindly shared his discovery of these items.

5. Harry M. Sanders, "The Rouleau House," unpublished report, 1996, copy held by Glenbow Library; "Paper Trail," *The Beaver,* vol. 84:3 (June/July 2004), 8. The photograph of the Rouleau family standing in front of their house is Glenbow Archives image no. NA-5222-2 which can be viewed at [www.glenbow.org/lasearch/photo.htm] (viewed September 2004). It was also published *The Beaver* (loc. cit.) and in *Picturesque Calgary* (Calgary: *Calgary Herald,* [1900]). An annotation on the copy of the latter pamphlet in Calgary Public Library, Local History Room, indicates it was published in 1900. The author wishes to thank Trudy Cowan, Deb AuCoin, Greg Lang, Harry Sanders, and David Mittelstadt, who contributed to the research on the Rouleau House.

Everybody's Favorite
Eva Reid
by Jennifer Hamblin

Regaling friends with amusing anecdotes from her long career in journalism, Eva Reid once suggested that a suitable title for her autobiography would be "Dope Fiends and Debutantes."[1] In her 40-year career with the *Albertan*, she interviewed and wrote about interesting characters from the top to the bottom of the Calgary social scene, and in all that time, she never lost her abiding interest in people and their stories. Today, Eva is remembered mainly for her social columns,

Eva Reid, circa 1937. Glenmore Archives, PB-760-1

particularly the ever-popular "Eavesdrop with Eva," but there were a few significant "firsts" along the way, and Eva's survival and success in the traditionally male-dominated newspaper world served as an inspiration and role model for several generations of young female journalists.

Intrigued by the stories of transient hired hands, Eva's greatest wish while growing up in southern Alberta during the teens and twenties was to see life beyond the family farm. She and her older siblings, Lavina and Dalton (Don), were born in Orangeville, Ontario, but in 1908, when Eva was just two years old, Willie-John and Annie Reid relocated their young family to the Hazelmere district of Alberta, south of (Fort) Macleod. Although the family prospered at first, variable agricultural conditions during the 1920s convinced John Reid that his children would do better in life off the farm. With his blessing, but with very little in the way of financial support, one by one they headed to Calgary.

Don found work in agricultural sales, but the girls studied business in high school at Mount Royal College, working part time in exchange for room and board. After graduation, Lavina worked as a stenographer for a number of years, but restless Eva quickly tired of the work, and in 1924 she left Calgary for Detroit. Encouraged by Dr. Hobart Reed, along with his nurse-wife, Anna – friends who had moved to Detroit from Calgary a year earlier – Eva planned to train as a nurse while boarding with the Reeds. An untimely accident delayed the start of her training and she began working for Dr. Reed instead. Four years later, she was still in Detroit, working as a stenographer, nursing ambitions forgotten, and there she might have stayed if not for her sister's unexpected death in January 1928.

Lavina had been battling a mysterious and debilitating intestinal illness for over a year when she died, but her death shook Eva badly, and she did not return to Detroit after the funeral. Instead, she stayed on in Calgary to comfort her parents, who had temporarily moved into the city from the farm. She soon found work as a stenographer. Seeking understanding of the tragedy that had befallen his family, John Reid discovered the Calgary Prophetic Bible Institute and its charismatic preacher, William Aberhart. Eva attended meetings reluctantly at first, but soon she too found solace in Aberhart's impassioned sermons and his wife's generous friendship. In 1929, she accepted the Aberharts' offer to become a boarder in their spacious Mission area home.

Eva boarded with the Aberharts for 14 memorable months during which time she grew very fond of the family, in particular the younger daughter, Ola, who was Eva's age, and Jessie Aberhart, who became something of a second mother to the lonely young woman. When she found herself with time to spare after losing her job during the height of the Depression, Eva started attending free classes at the Calgary Prophetic Bible Institute, eventually completing the first two years of a three-year program in biblical scholarship. Impressed with the religious fervor of the Institute students, especially Aberhart's star student, Ernest Manning, Eva also started attending the newly formed Bible Institute Baptist Church, where she became friendly with teen-aged organist, Muriel Preston.

Eva found the atmosphere in these various organizations stimulating, but her intimate association with the Aberharts eventually proved too restrictive for the fun-loving young woman. Although she admired Mr. Aberhart's intellect and never questioned his religious sincerity and devotion to family, she remained wary of the big man with the loud voice and quick temper, and chafed under his household dominion. Some time after confessing to him her indulgence in forbidden pleasures such as dancing, drinking, and card playing, she moved into another boarding house a few blocks away, thereby making room for the Aberhart's next boarder, Ernest Manning.

Although Eva's tenure in the Aberhart home was relatively brief, her involvement with the family and with the Bible Institute continued throughout the late twenties and early thirties, determining the major themes of her life for all the years to come: her strong Baptist faith, her lifelong support of the Social Credit party, and her career as a journalist.

William Aberhart only adopted social credit theories after Eva had ceased to be his boarder, but she may well have witnessed the early development of his ideas regarding social and economic policy during lively evening discussions with followers and friends at the Aberhart home. Certainly, she was well aware of his feelings of helpless frustration when confronted with students and parishioners caught by the Depression. Originally voiced simply as an extension of the religious message in his regular Sunday broadcasts, Aberhart's social credit ideas soon fired the imagination of ordinary Albertans hungry for economic relief and social change. Social Credit study groups only began forming in Calgary in 1933 and around the province by 1934, but the movement soon gained such political momentum that Aberhart and his Social Credit Party swept to power in the provincial election of 1936.

Eva was an eager participant in all these developments, serving as Secretary of the Central Council of the Alberta Social Credit League and president of the Original Young People's Social Credit Group. During the election campaign of 1936, she assisted local candidates, once even substituting for an absent Edith Gostick during a radio debate. Her faith in Aberhart and Social Credit was such that when the party came to power, she signed the Alberta Citizen's Registration Covenant, indicating that she would support the government in whatever economic measures they chose to implement. For a time, she even received half her pay in Social Credit Prosperity Certificates, Aberhart's so-called "funny money."[2]

That Eva even had a job after a long period of unemployment in the early 1930s was due entirely to her involvement with Social Credit. The mainstream press had watched the quick evolution of the movement from social-religious to political with concern and, in some cases, overt antagonism. Therefore, it was a relief to Aberhart in the summer of 1934 when veteran publisher, Charles K. Underwood, proposed the creation of the *Social Credit Chronicle*, a newspaper devoted exclusively to the ideals, policies, and personalities of Social Credit.[3] Underwood, who knew the Reid family from his Macleod days, was happy to offer Eva a position on his small staff as circulation manager. But the *Chronicle* grew so quickly that Eva soon found herself writing up reports, interviewing candidates, and producing human interest articles as well as a weekly social column called "Here and There with Eva." During this whirlwind period of Eva's life, she may well have had a brief love affair with Underwood, but more importantly, she discovered her love of journalism.

In 1936, a syndicate of Social Creditors acquired the Calgary *Albertan* for a brief period, but Eva's main focus remained the *Chronicle*, which was produced as a weekly supplement to *The Albertan* for several years. When financial arrangements with the party fell through in 1938, Max Bell (who had inherited *The Albertan* when his father died in 1936) reasserted the newspaper's independence from the Social Credit government and dropped the *Chronicle*. Eva, who had impressed the editors with her journalistic ability, was offered the opportunity to train as a junior reporter with *The Albertan*. She accepted gladly, conforming to the newspaper's expectations by withdrawing from active political involvement with the party. However, she remained a lifelong Social Credit supporter and continued her close personal relationship with the Aberhart family.

With no formal background in journalism, Eva's training as a reporter was very much on the job. Under the watchful eye of managing editor Bill Hall, she spent six weeks on the proof desk and tackling rewrites. Occasionally, she was allowed to do some writing, but since she could not leave the office, even she judged her attempts "feeble." Phase two of her training proved much more interesting: she was allowed to accompany senior reporters on their various beats. However, her first foray as a junior reporter nearly changed her mind about her chosen career when she witnessed the distressing carnage at the scene of a local car crash.[4]

She soon toughened up, and when war was declared and the news-room emptied of men, Eva was ready to take on the challenging job of provincial editor. Well aware that it was unusual for a woman to hold such a position (at the time, most female editors were relegated to the social pages), Eva was determined to excel in her new job. She organized and trained a string of local correspondents "from Barrhead to the border,"[5] paying them 15 cents a copy-inch and leaving them in no doubt about her high expectations and tough standards. Although the job lasted little more than a year (during wartime, international events often pushed provincial news to the back pages, thereby eliminating the need for an editor), Eva had proven her ability as an editor and earned the respect of her male co-workers as well as her female peers. At their triennial convention in 1949, the Canadian Women's Press Club recognized Eva's unique achievement as one of the first female provincial editors in Canada.[6]

In 1940, Eva took on another unusual job for a woman when she became *The Albertan's* police court reporter. At the time, crime reporting was considered too sordid for a female reporter's delicate sensibilities, but once again, Eva gained a unique opportunity because of the scarcity of male reporters during wartime. However, she quickly proved her compe-tence and affinity for the job, and once the war ended there was no thought of replacing her with a man. Showing a great empathy for people and their stories, and employing a chatty, confidential writing style, for the first time the police court reports were interesting to the average reader. Eva's column was popular and she continued to produce it for 14 years until changes in the court system eliminated the need for a special reporter.

Although she was sympathetic to minor misdeeds, and could be selective and "charitable" in her coverage, especially when dealing with the social elite, Eva was considered a very fair reporter and earned the respect of both "the bench and the bar."[7] Since she was in the police court whenever it sat, hers was a very familiar face for some of the more notorious habitues of the court system, leading to many amusing incidents of mistaken identity. One of her favorite stories occurred late one night when a male colleague walked her home from work. Spotting Eva, a police court "regular" turned to a friend and confided, "see that woman over there, she's the worst little prostitute in the city!"[8]

In 1941, Eva took on a second job at *The Albertan* when she became women's editor. With this position, she was responsible for producing the women's pages on a daily basis with the help of just one assistant. Her days became a curious patchwork: police court in the morning with afternoons back in the office writing up that column, and gathering information for the women's page or rewriting stories received over the wire services that were mainly of interest to women. Afternoons and most evenings were spent attending club meetings and social functions, and it was not unusual for Eva to arrive back in the office late at night still attired in evening wear to produce her social reports for the next day's paper.

Even though her days were hectic, Eva thrived on the pace, never considering the time involved or poor rate of pay, anxious only to do whatever was required to get both jobs done, and done well. This attitude was common enough during wartime, but Eva's continuing devotion to her job, and loyalty to the often financially struggling *Albertan*, earned her the admiration and respect of editors and co-workers alike, even the crusty and demanding Art Raymond, Bill Hall's successor as managing editor. Observers admired the ease with which she was accepted into what was then very much a man's world while at the same time maintaining both her professionalism and essential femininity.[9]

Eva was friendly and popular, often organizing and hosting social events for friends and colleagues who substituted for family with her parents gone and her brother living in Edmonton. Her Baptist religious affiliation never interfered with her love of parties; she was known to drink and even smoked for a time. But in spite of her sociable personality, Eva was a very private person and never divulged the details of her unhappy love affairs (there were several). Usually cheerful and projecting confidence, Eva was admired as a successful single career woman, and even her good friends never realized the extent of her feelings of loss and regret regarding marriage and family.

Women's editor of *The Albertan* for nearly 20 years, Eva became something of an authority on local social, arts, and cultural organizations and events which, at the time, were run mostly by women and consequently reported on the women's pages. An important, if invisible, cog in the local social structure, Eva was invited to important local events, consulted on matters of etiquette, and granted interviews with celebrities passing through the city. Readers loved her informal interviews with big name visitors such as the Duchess of Windsor, Eleanor Roosevelt, Marjorie Lawrence, Cary Grant, and Walter Pidgeon. Courted by the social elite, and dependent on them for "news" of note, sometimes the distinction between Eva's two jobs blurred, especially when a court case involved misdemeanors by social leaders or their families. However, Eva usually managed the gracious wearing of two such different hats, earning a reputation for her charitable handling of some of the more socially challenging cases with which she was confronted.

Eva discovered fellowship with other female journalists when she joined the Canadian Women's Press Club in the late 1930s. The Calgary Branch of the club had gone dormant some years before, but local press women provided support on an informal basis and through their continuing involvement in the national club. In 1950, Eva was instrumental in reorganizing the Calgary club, serving as president for several years and playing an active leadership role until the club again disbanded in 1974. At the local level, her favorite activities included the annual media competition (she won four writing awards in the 1950s) and the Calgary Branch's annual Stampede luncheon. Local involvement stimulated her interest in the national organization, and she served as Alberta Regional Director (1954-1956), national Vice President (1956-1959), chair of the Memorial Awards Committee (1956-1959), and chair of the Beneficiary Fund (1962-1971). In 1959, local press colleagues recognized her dedication to the field by inviting her to serve on the board of the newly formed Calgary Press Club – the only female director at the time.

Another indication of Eva's growing local reputation came in the form of a very flattering job offer in 1957. Although she never seriously considered leaving *The Albertan* to become women's editor of the *Calgary Herald*, nevertheless Eva cleverly negotiated a raise by threatening to accept their generous offer of nearly double her salary. More importantly, the *Herald's* job offer helped to raise her value in the eyes of her old employer. After years of doing double duty, once the police court column ended in 1954, Eva had gone back to a single job, women's editor. But years of social visibility had made her a popular local figure and potentially a great asset to *The Albertan*, although it was several years before she was given the opportunity to prove her worth to the paper by becoming a regular columnist.

Cleaning house at *The Albertan* in 1960, new managing editor Ed Romaine proposed that Eva move from women's editor to social columnist on the women's page. After some delicate negotiations in which Eva won the freedom and flexibility to make her column much broader and richer than first envisioned, "Eavesdrop with Eva" began appearing in September that year. It was an instant success with its pleasing mixture of current local social and cultural events and personal profiles. Written in Eva's inimitable breezy style, the "Eavesdrop" column proved enormously popular and continued for 20 years until Eva finally retired in 1980. Anyone who was "anyone" wanted to get into Eva's column, and she was more than happy to profile interesting people, using their stories to promote local causes. As she grew more comfortable with her column, she occasionally used it to express her own opinions on a variety of social issues (everything from feminism to drugs and crime) or to broaden her readers' horizons by reporting on her travels abroad. She enjoyed the freedom and latitude of writing a column and appreciated the easier pace of a more settled working day. Always humble and self-deprecating, she ignored the snobbery of fellow writers producing harder-edged columns for more "important" pages of the newspaper, and focused instead on feedback from her readers, which was uniformly positive. Not surprisingly, when she retired she termed the "Eavesdrop" years as the happiest of her long journalistic career.

Capitalizing on her popularity, Eva was given a second column to write in 1964. Called "Socially Speaking," occasionally it included personality profiles, but was really just an extension of the newspaper's traditional "Social Notes" feature, with its news of the parties and travels of the social elite. Although it was very popular with those whose names were featured and with readers interested in news of Calgary's social leaders, by 1972 the column was considered outdated and was dropped. In 1968, Eva was given another weekly column, "Eva Reid's Television," but this venture proved short-lived, lasting less than a year. More successful was "About the Churches," which debuted in 1970. Eva had been writing articles on religion for *The Albertan* ever since she was appointed editor of the church page in 1967. Inclusive of all faiths, her "Churches" column proved very popular and ran until the paper adopted a tabloid format in 1978. Over the years, Eva also continued to research and write other articles, mainly for *The Albertan*, including a seven part series on LSD in 1963 and an article on Calgary's business leaders in 1979 entitled "The Ten Most Vaunted List."

As Eva aged, eventually allowing her dark hair to whiten so that she looked like "everyone's favourite grandmother,"[10] she became something of an icon at *The Albertan*, welcoming all comers to afternoon tea in her office. She had a real fondness for "young cubs," and over the years served as a role model for many young women who drew inspiration from her confidence and early success in a male-dominated field.[11] Generous with advice and support, Eva was well liked among her press colleagues and a 1971 celebration of her career saw a record turnout by journalists from all over the city anxious to honor their old friend. Hosted jointly by the Calgary Press Club and the Calgary Branch of the Canadian Women's Press Club, "Eva Reid Night" was a touching testimony to Eva's popularity and professionalism. Other honors followed: honorary lifetime memberships in the Southern Alberta Old Timers' Association (1971) and the Women's Canadian Club of Calgary (1976), the Distinguished Community Service Award from the Altrusa Club of Calgary (1976), and one of the first Women of the Year Awards presented by the Calgary YWCA (1979).

When the *Sun* newspaper chain took over *The Albertan* in 1980, Eva decided, at age 74, that it was time to retire. Facing a meager retirement (privately promised a pension years before by former owner Max Bell, she had never joined the company plan[12]) she hired a lawyer who negotiated a comfortable settlement. With time on her hands, Eva planned to do a bit of writing, but without pressing deadlines she found she was unable to persevere. Instead, she found more time for Baptist church activities and bible study. Her health declined steadily, making travel difficult, and in 1988 friends helped her to move from her long-time apartment in the Hull Estates to the Beverley Nursing Home. Unfortunately, she never settled into her new surroundings and during an ill-advised trip at Christmastime to visit her brother in Edmonton, she suffered a stroke. She was returned to the Holy Cross Hospital in Calgary, where she died of another stroke on March 8, 1989 at the age of 82.

Eva's funeral service was attended by an eclectic mixture of friends and colleagues, attesting to her wide popularity and her many years of mixing with all levels of Calgary society. Termed by one observer "the last great gathering of the Social Credit party,"[13] many of her old friends from the Aberhart years also came to say goodbye. Her press colleagues wrote many kind words about her warmth and hospitality, one even remembering her sentimentally as "the most respected woman journalist ever to toil in Alberta."[14] But perhaps the most fitting tribute came from her dearest friends some six months after her death when they established a journalism scholarship in her name at Mount Royal College. Called the "Eva Reid Memorial Scholarship," and created mainly by the innumerable small donations of sincere admirers touched by Eva during her lifetime,[15] it continues to be awarded annually to an enthusiastic student in the field of journalism – precisely the kind of "young cub" whose encouragement would have given Eva so much personal delight and professional satisfaction.

Notes

Unless otherwise noted, information in this article was drawn from the business and personal papers comprising the Eva Reid fonds at the Glenbow Archives (M 7957).

1. Detlifsen, Karen. Interview with Eva Reid, June 8, 1982 (M 7957/RCT-945-9).

2. "The Albertan: 1902-1980," *The Albertan*, 27 July 1980.

3. Groves, Keith Franklin. "The Alberta Social Credit Chronicle." Unpublished essay. Department of Political Science, University of Calgary, 1972, 172 (M 7957/176).

4. Detlifsen. Op cit.

5. Braun, Sandy. "Eva Reid: Profile," *The Albertan*, ca. 1980 (M 7957/169).

6. Drysdale, Ruth. "Eva Reid," *My Golden West*, Vol. V, Spring 1970, 28-29.

7. Ramondt, Joanne. "Newswoman shuns her own story," *Calgary Herald*, 6 November 1983.

8. *Ibid.*

9. Ford, Catherine. "Chance meeting began a career," *Calgary Herald*, March 9, 1989; Evans, Art. Untitled column, *Edmonton Journal*, 2 August 1980.

10. Tennant, Jack. "Eva Reid wrote the book on style," *The Calgary Sun*, 10 March 1989.

11. Olsen, Tom. "Cancer takes local writer," *The Calgary Sun*, March 9, 1989; "News 'dean' dies at 82," *Calgary Herald*, 9 March 1989.

12. "After 44 years, time to retire," *Alberta Report*, 15 August 1980.

13. Scott, Susan and Marilyn Wood. Interview with author, 18 August 2003.

14. Tivy, Patrick. "You, too, can set up a fund with aid of foundation," *Calgary Herald*, 22 November 1989.

15. Bredin, Ed and Nan. Interview with author, 2 September 2003.

Machinist, Foreman, Superintendent
Thomas Harrison
by Henry C. Klassen

For the Canadian Pacific Railway's Ogden Locomotive and Car Shops in Calgary, the beginning of history – that is, a written record of their evolution and culture – is a fairly recent phenomenon. With some exceptions, most notably newspaper articles, which were published in the early twentieth century, the Ogden community became truly conscious of itself only after World War II. It was in 1975 that Walter H. S. Boote wrote *Ogden Whistle*, the story of the Ogden district and the first study of this community. Covering a great deal of important ground, the book became must-reading for anyone interested in the history of the Ogden Shops.

The role of Thomas Harrison in the development of the Ogden Shops is briefly acknowledged in *Ogden Whistle*, but his work and his standing need to be examined more fully.[1] Harrison's chosen trade did not give him the power we associate with the bold vision of a great entrepreneur. He was a machinist, then a foreman, and finally super-intendent as he toiled in the yards of the Canadian Pacific Railway. Instead of being celebrated for commanding a huge corporation, he was respected for playing an important part in the affairs of the Ogden Shops since their establishment in 1913. During his tenure at the Ogden Shops, the Canadian Pacific Railway (CPR) enjoyed a long period of growth. Investors watched happily as the railway grew despite periodically facing economic miseries in most corners of Canada during the first half of the twentieth century. This positive growth was not Harrison's accomplishment alone, of course, but he deserves more credit for it than might be evident at first glance.

Thomas Harrison's roots were firmly in the nineteenth century. He was born in Manchester, England, in 1882.[2] His father, Thomas Senior, was a boilermaker at the North London Railway shops in Manchester, and among the "aristocrats of labor." The elder Thomas Harrison's work was a real craft that required dexterity and imagination. To be recognized as a gifted boilermaker, as the father was, meant attending to one's own task and overseeing several apprentices, as well as making a superior product. His work at the railway fascinated his son, who in one way or another expected to follow in his father's footsteps.

The Harrison family left Manchester in 1886 so that the father could accept an appointment at the North London Railway (NLR) shops in London, where he became head of the department responsible for the production of boilers.[3] Even before the family's move to London, the father, wanting his bright son to have a good education, had enrolled him in an elementary school in Manchester at the age of three. He did not merely attend this school out of duty – he loved it. Young Thomas lived life in the academic fast lane, and he continued to do very well throughout elementary and in a London high school, from which he graduated in 1896, at the age of 14. He excelled in geometry, algebra, and chemistry, as well as everything else.[4] With his high school record, Thomas could have attended any university in England.

Thomas Sr. always encouraged his son, but Thomas Jr. did not proceed to get a university degree. Instead, he focused on a habit he'd developed in his youth, of tinkering with mechanical devices. "I had mechanics in my blood and I wanted to learn a trade," Thomas Harrison recalled many years later.[5] In 1896, his working life and fortunes became closely linked with railway shops. During that year, he was apprenticed to learn the craft of machinist in the NLR shops in London where his father also worked. Thomas was phenomenally talented at his job. By the time he completed his apprenticeship in 1901 at the age of 19, he possessed a clear understanding of the most advanced work in the use of machine tools. Adept at dealing with the complicated parts of steam engines, he came to know how to make and rebuild railway locomotives. Inspired by the example of his father as a superb boilermaker, Thomas became an expert machinist. The successful father conferred on his son the priceless endowment of a rock-solid sense of self-worth.

But young Thomas Harrison felt that his job at the NLR shops had little potential. As apprentices, "we were exploited in those days. You'll hardly believe this. I'd get up at ten to five in the morning and start work at six o'clock and get home at six in the evening for 6 shillings (about a dollar and a half) a week in London. I got an increase of 2 shillings (about 50 cents) every year," Thomas remembered.[6] Disillusionment with the NLR shops came quickly. By the spring of 1902, Harrison, like many other junior machinists, was looking elsewhere for work.

Harrison was young and vigorous, and the future in Canada looked promising. Erect and square-shouldered, he was a solidly set man, with a handsome, strong-featured face, bright, flashing eyes, and a rich voice. His personality was as strong as his appearance, and when he made a plan, he followed through on it. "I went into London," Thomas recalled, "and there was an exhibition of Canada and I'll never forget it. They had a map of Canada, and on that they had antelope and prairie chickens and some bears. Then they had one of British Columbia, beautiful, showing all the orchards and everything else. They had a big picture of a fellow who went to Manitoba, and they showed him knocking up a shack; they showed him 10 years later and he had a house. Of course, I went back to my father and I said, 'Dad, I'm going to go to Canada.'"[7] Thomas did not have the funds to move to Canada, but his father came to his aid. Besides giving his son 10 pounds, on April 17, 1902, Thomas Sr. paid the fare to Quebec City. London's port was filled with hundreds of Britons ready to emigrate to Canada. The ship was swarming with people looking for a better life.

Two weeks later, Thomas Harrison Jr. found himself in Montreal. Building railway locomotives was his trade, and he immediately went to the Canadian Pacific Railway's large Angus Shops hoping to find a job.[8] When he suffered rejection trying to sell himself there, he left Montreal and went directly to the railway's shops in Toronto. Harrison had confidence in himself. If he could get a foot in the door, he felt he could take the remaining steps to reach his goal. He got his opportunity, then had to prove himself in the face of a doubting foreman in Toronto's Canadian Pacific shops. Fortunately for Harrison, a demanding practical test on a steam engine was no trouble for him and he passed with flying colors. He began working in the shops on May 1, 1902. The pay was 20 cents an hour. Despite his success in securing a job, he was soon unhappy. He said, "after that I got all the lousy work."[9]

But Harrison persisted, at least until September 1903, when people he knew in Toronto were saying to him, "Go West, young man." What to do? He responded to this challenge by obtaining a transfer to the Canadian Pacific's Weston Shops in Winnipeg, where he worked as a machinist and draftsman for 32 cents an hour.[10] From the beginning, Harrison showed great energy, personal magnetism, and a strong desire to be productive. He knew how to make technology serve the Canadian Pacific. Walter Boyd, general foreman in the Weston Shops, was pleased with his work. "Boyd kind of took a fancy to me for some reason," Harrison recalled.[11] But the weather in Winnipeg that winter was not all that appealing as the temperature dropped down to 45 below zero Fahrenheit (-43°C). This was enough to make Harrison want to leave the city for a warmer climate.

His chance came the following year. By this time, Samuel James Hungerford had replaced Boyd, who had moved on to become general foreman in the Canadian Pacific's shops in Calgary. One day Hungerford, a self-educated native of Quebec who later became president of the Canadian National Railways, called Harrison into his office and said, "I've got a letter here from Mr. Boyd in Calgary and he wants to know if you would like to work for him." Harrison jumped at the opportunity. "That was right up my alley, so I got to Calgary in December of 1904," he remembered.[12] So did many other newcomers, a number of whom came with the encouragement of Irish-born William Toole, the Canadian Pacific's land agent in Calgary who energetically promoted immigration to Alberta.[13]

Thomas immediately began working as a machinist at the Canadian Pacific's Calgary shops on 10th Avenue and 6th Street East, where about 75 men were employed.[14] Built of local sandstone back in 1898, the $50 000 structure consisted of an engine house, a machine shop, and a boiler and blacksmith shop.[15] Harrison was 22 years old. His pay was now 40 cents an hour, up 8 cents from the 32 cents he had made at the railway's Weston Shops in Winnipeg.[16]

Even more important than the money was his position. Harrison stood at the centre of transportation and communication for one of the fastest-growing cities in the Canadian West.[17] He had, by diligence and talent, become the protégé of a man – Walter Boyd – whose origins were nearly as humble as his own, and whose rise had been as steady as his own would be. Above all, he had faith in himself. He was a young man of remarkable ability.

Boyd's confidence in Thomas was repaid in striking fashion soon after he was employed at the Canadian Pacific's shops in Calgary.[18] In the operational conditions of the growing railway and of an expansive national economy, the exceptional mechanical skills of Thomas Harrison flourished. The interplay between personal talents of a high order and favorable external circumstances shaped the course of his career. In Calgary, the Canadian Pacific's shops concentrated on rebuilding steam engines. Harrison immediately became a noted figure in the workforce through his attention to precision and quality. Never bored with the routine of his shop tasks, he took pride in dismantling the engines, repairing the various parts, and then putting them all together again.[19]

Those close to Harrison at this time knew that he also was an ardent union man. Like many other machinists at the Canadian Pacific's shops on 10th Avenue and 6th Street East, he was a member of the International Association of Machinists. Before long, he became familiar with the names of the union leaders and immersed himself in salient union issues such as the demand for improved working conditions and higher wages. He regularly attended union meetings. After some time, he became a member of the machinists' three-man shop committee. "I was a strong union man, no kidding," recalled Harrison.[20]

An important event in Thomas Harrison's life came in 1907, when he was promoted to a gang foreman at the age of 25 and assigned the general supervision of all unskilled workers. The promotion meant he had to relinquish his interest in the International Association of Machinists. He had begun to climb a ladder of success, and his salary was now $90 a month.[21] By this time, the Canadian Pacific employed about 407 workers in its 10th Avenue shops. Nearby were large railway yards for hundreds of freight and passenger cars that congregated daily. Every day, 30 trains arrived in and departed from Calgary, whose population had reached about 14 000.[22] The Canadian Pacific was not simply a passive enterprise: it interacted directly with other businesses, providing crucial inputs in businesses as diverse as retailing, farming, ranching, and coal mining. Like many other remarkable Calgarians, Harrison learned as much from the world around him as from the newspapers and books he read at his leisure. While the *Calgary Herald* – of which he had been an avid reader since his arrival in the city – helped keep him in touch with local developments outside his personal experience as well as national and international events, his interest in Calgary's growth was stimulated by strolls through the city, and walks in the scenic countryside with his friends.

Since his arrival in Calgary, Harrison had become well known among the workers and within the top tier at the Canadian Pacific shops. He met not only the ordinary employees, but also the movers and shakers themselves. Harrison befriended English-born Arthur G. Graves, a boilermaker who had started working in the shops in 1900 for $2 a day and who was to become City of Calgary public utilities commissioner, as well as another native of England, Thomas B. Riley, a machinist.[23] Harrison also had the opportunity to meet senior officers. As one who loved to play the violin and the piano, a passion he had brought with him from England where he had played in a London orchestra, he was popular among Canadian Pacific employees when they gathered in their Calgary homes for musical evenings.[24] These evenings did a great deal to create a close-knit family atmosphere. Bonds of friendship were forged, and the festivities established Harrison as one of the group. Although he never nursed an ambition to make music his career, he was a proficient musician and the piano and the violin remained important to him. "I lived for music. I could eat music. Music was my life," Harrison recalled.[25]

Against this happiness was a downside. During the summer of 1908, the Canadian Pacific shops in Calgary, as in Winnipeg, Toronto, and Montreal, experienced labor unrest. The economic depression in 1907 had dealt harshly with Canada. Slumping industries cut back orders for raw materials, spelling doom for many workers. As the depression became national, the economic downturn hurt hundreds of businesses. Many business firms failed, and a number were on the brink of bankruptcy. The Canadian Pacific faced unprecedented problems. Some of the railway's branch lines were not operating profitably. Unemployed men drifted into Calgary and other Canadian cities.[26] In the labor-intensive railway industry, wage-rates were a principal consideration and industrial conflict a constant threat to the steady course of the work in the shops. During the early days of August in 1908, many machinists, boilermakers, blacksmiths, and other workers at Canadian Pacific across the nation went on strike demanding better wages.[27] The strike crippled the railway in Calgary during the late summer. As a foreman, however, Thomas Harrison helped to keep the shops in the city open with non-union labor.[28] The strike dragged on into early fall, its course being marked by the usual features – rallies, negotiations, and picketing.[29] But its organizational and financial structure was fragile, and in the end the corporation prevailed. The strikers, including Tom Reddick, a machinist in the Canadian Pacific shops in Calgary, made no gains and lost their pension rights.[30] They also lost wages. By October 6, the strike had come to an end.[31]

For the Canadian Pacific, already struggling in a competitive industry, the costs of lost revenues and profits were high. After the strike, and with the return of prosperity in 1909, the railway's executives tried to prevent conflict in the future. To solve their labor problems and to keep workers loyal to their company, they built on earlier corporate welfare programs for employees. In Calgary, they showed their commitment to welfare capitalism, which meant that business firms should look after the best interests of workers, by continuing to sponsor athletic activities such as hockey.[32] Canadian Pacific officers also renewed their emphasis on retirement pension benefits for employees who had not walked out in the 1908 strike.[33] Back in 1902, the company had established a pension program for its employees, bearing the whole cost of the pensions and making no assessments on workers' wages.[34] The executives viewed foremen as members of management, and like the other foremen, Harrison remained satisfied with his relationship to senior management. At the same time, he sought to avoid labor-management antagonism by building good personal relations with the workers in his department.[35] Largely successful in their efforts to achieve a sense of harmony with their workforce, Canadian Pacific executives kept their shops in Calgary free of labor strife for a number of years.

Of course, this road was not without some bumps. Certainly, it was a difficult task to keep all the workers content all the time. But Harrison believed that a sense of community and shared purpose was essential for developing a pioneering venture such as the Canadian Pacific shops in Calgary. Always a stickler for high-quality production, he tried to build consensus by helping the men do their work well and making them feel central to the organization. Throughout this period of growing pains, he remained unflappable, establishing and maintaining a supportive work environment for Canadian Pacific employees and instilling a feeling of company excellence.

Thomas Harrison was doing much else besides demonstrating his human relations skills at the Canadian Pacific shops during these years. In 1911, he married Jenny Crawford, whose father left Ottawa, together with his family, to work as a land agent for the Grand Trunk Pacific Railway in Wainwright, Alberta. Jenny was a graduate of Dunham Ladies' College in the Eastern Townships, where she was the roommate of Grace Elliott, who in the future was to become the mother of Pierre Elliott Trudeau.[36] Evidently Jenny was a very good student. A warm admirer of higher education for women, Harrison was proud of his wife's accomplishments at Dunham Ladies' College.

Fortified with a salary of $120 a month at the Canadian Pacific shops in Calgary, Harrison was now able to support a family. A meticulous planner, he had obviously given considerable thought to where he and Jenny might make their home. In 1911, he purchased three lots in East Calgary near the shops, building a modest four-room cottage on each, one for himself and his wife, and the other two for tenants. From each of the tenants, Harrison collected a monthly rent of $18, providing him with funds to pay for his properties.[37] One of the things Jenny brought to their new home was her fine piano. If Jenny heightened Thomas's appreciation of music, he reciprocated by doing everything he could to give her a warm, comfortable home.

Harrison would remember the next year of work at the Canadian Pacific shops in the city as the most hectic of the entire period before World War I. As he saw the situation, the company's executives became more aggressive in pushing ahead with the locomotive and car repairs at their old shops on 10th Avenue that serviced the rapidly expanding railway in the Canadian West, while at the same time building new and much larger shops in the future Ogden community just east and south of Calgary in order to carry out their repair work to better advantage.[38] On January 27, 1912, there appeared in the *Calgary Herald*, a picture showing the proposed shops soon to be known as the Ogden Shops in honor of veteran railway-man I. G. Ogden, Canadian Pacific's vice-president of finance and accounting. The proposed name was thanks to a request made by company president, Thomas G. Shaughnessy.[39]

In mid-March 1912, Shaughnessy wrote to vice-president and general manager George J. Bury:

> I prefer that the shops near Calgary should be given some other name than that suggested in your letter of the 8th instant, although, of course, I appreciate the implied compliment. The length of my name does not lend itself to purposes of this kind; indeed, I have always thought that 'Shaughnessy Heights' at Vancouver was a mistake. . . . How would 'Ogden' shops do? We have no 'Ogden' station on the lines of the Road, and Mr. Ogden is really our oldest officer now, that is, he has been connected with the Company in an official capacity longer than anybody else."[40]

While the Canadian Pacific's locomotive and car repair work was to be dominated by its new Ogden Shops, its old shops on 10th Avenue continued to repair some of the locomotives and cars for a number of years.

When the Canadian Pacific opened its Ogden Shops, covering an area of 213 acres with shop floor space of 10 acres, in mid-March 1913, Thomas Harrison was transferred there and started his new job as foreman of the wheel shop. The promotion authorized him to assume direct supervision of this shop's daily operations.[41] Under his trained and watchful eye in the wheel shop that was equipped with steel tire wheel lathes, axle machinery, and other tools, a workforce of about 20 machinists resurfaced the wheels that needed to be repaired. Every aspect of the Ogden Shops was of public interest, and the wheel shop was no less so. Repair work at the Ogden Shops progressed through several stages as an electric travelling overhead crane carried the steam engines to the various shops.[42] The first step was to take the engines to the locomotive shop, where they were dismantled. Depending on what repairs were required, the remaining steps varied. But usually work had to be done in the wheel shop and the tender shop (the tender was a car attached to the steam locomotive for carrying a supply of coal and water), as well as in the boiler shop and the blacksmith shop. Last came the erection shop, where the engines were put together.

Harrison's commitment and enthusiasm – his willingness to endure at the Ogden Shops through thick and thin – made him an asset to the Canadian Pacific. A severe depression in 1913 hurt the railway, so much so that restructuring at its Ogden Shops led to many job losses as the original workforce of about 1 200 shrank rapidly.[43] "On 1 July 1913, they laid off five hundred men just like that," recalled Tom Reddick.[44] But with its persistent entrepreneurship, the company survived the economic downturn and mounted vigorous marketing attacks against the growing competition in railway services. It is powerful testimony to the spirit of early twentieth-century boosterism sweeping through Canadian towns and cities, especially in the West, that many businessmen had a positive attitude toward the Canadian Pacific. Like Harrison, Calgary's business leaders were optimistic about the future of their city and the Ogden Shops. The impact of the Ogden Shops went far beyond their essential role in railway operations. Resting on electrical power and possessing a large industrial workforce that helped the Calgary economy become increasingly diversified, the Ogden Shops played a critical part in the city's development.

Harrison dreamt the immigrant generation's dream of getting ahead. He never wondered if the promise of Canadian life was an impossible dream. In 1914 Thomas, together with Jenny and their one-year-old daughter Dorothy, moved into their new $2 500 home at 1340-12th Avenue S. W., which he had built with the help of a mortgage loan.[45] "If you worked for the C.P.R., your credit was good," remembered one of Harrison's friends.[46] In this two-story home, with four bedrooms and a fireplace, their son Thomas Crawford (known as Crawford) was to be born two years later. Back in 1912, Thomas Harrison had purchased a new automobile, a Model T. Ford, for $750. The Model T was the car that put Canada on wheels, and Harrison often used his automobile to drive visiting Canadian Pacific executives to the Ogden Shops and back to the railway's Palliser Hotel.[47]

In 1914, on the outbreak of World War I in Europe, when the weapons which the Germans and British had been selling globally were turned against each other, there was an increased demand in Canada for railway services by the military. World War I brought relatively low military involvement and only a few changes to work at the plant; rather, existing trends in the plant's operations were reinforced, particularly its emphasis on repairing Canadian Pacific locomotives and cars. With Canada's entry into World War I in August 1914, however, the railway's Montreal executives and the management at the Ogden Shops began to plan for possible small-scale production of materials for war purposes, and by World War II, the Ogden Shops revolutionized their military operations.

In their most noteworthy departure from past operations, from May 1915 onward the Ogden Shops, along with the Canadian Pacific's Angus Shops in Montreal, manufactured shells for the Canadian and British armies.[48] At the same time, the Angus Shops pursued the shell contracts much more aggressively. Thomas Harrison was quite visible at the Ogden Shops during the war and appreciated for his involvement, especially in repairing steam engines and, perhaps indirectly, in making shells.

In 1915, Harrison was promoted to foreman of the erection shop, where he supervized a number of men as they put together the parts of engines and delivered one engine every day.[49] Given the staff shortages at the Ogden Shops during the war, he also oversaw the work of three gang foremen with their gangs of unskilled laborers. "As roustabouts, they did the cleaning up and general work. In a big plant like that, there was a lot of cleaning up to do, for instance when you were turning out an

Canadian Pacific Railway machinists carry out the precise work of turning a high-quality steel naval gun barrel on a large lathe at the Ogden Locomotive and Car Shops during World War II, expanding on a service begun during World War I. Courtesy of the Naval Museum of Alberta.

engine a day there were tons and tons of scrap that went out. They'd pick all that up, they'd collect all that scrap, clean up the shops, clean the windows, all that kind of work," recalled Harrison.[50] Over the next few years, he brought a strong desire for excellent performance to his jobs, a vision that served the Canadian Pacific well.

An economic depression hurt the Canadian Pacific, as well as many other Canadian businesses, after World War I. Trends in the postwar national economy also produced labor unrest. During the war, the federal government attempted to control inflationary pressures, but these measures broke down in peacetime, and the Canadian cost of living started to rise. As workers at the Canadian Pacific and other companies asked for commensurate wage increases, they encountered resistance from executives. In the summer of 1919, a strike hit the Canadian Pacific's Ogden Shops. The railway's executives still viewed foremen as members of management. As a foreman, Harrison continued to maintain good relations with senior management, as well as the men in the labor unions at the Ogden Shops. "The big strike in 1919 started in Winnipeg and it spread out here. I was a foreman and we, the staff, tried to keep the railway going. The sad part about the situation was that the strikers, after losing the strike, lost their pensions," remembered Harrison.[51]

Prosperity, although tempered by growing competition in the railway industry, returned to the Canadian Pacific in the mid-1920s.[52] Thomas Harrison participated in the prosperity at the Ogden Shops. In 1927, he became general locomotive foreman, a position that increased his salary and saw him meeting the administrative challenge of supervising the foremen who oversaw the machine shop, boiler shop, tender shop, wheel shop, blacksmith shop, foundry, pattern shop, and erection shop.[53]

Harrison's success in the Ogden Shops was paralleled by his happiness at home with his wife Jenny and their children Dorothy and Crawford.[54] Thomas Harrison may have gotten his start in England, but Canada was where he truly put down roots and helped Canada grow.

Notes

1. Walter H. S. Boote, *Ogden Whistle A History of Millican, Ogden Flats, Maryland, Valleyfield, Bonnybrook, South Hill, Cepeear, Lynnwood, Lynnwood Ridge, River Glen, Crestwood, C.P.R Ogden Shops* (Calgary: Ogden Area History Committee, 1975), 13.

2. Interview by the author with Thomas Harrison, 9 May 1974.

3. For a brief history of the North London Railway, see H. P. White, *A Regional History of the Railways of Great Britain* Volume III Greater London (London: Phoenix House, 1963), 73-81.

4. Thomas Harrison interview, 9 May 1974.

5. Ibid.

6. Ibid.

7. Ibid.

8. The Angus Shops were named after R. B. Angus, an original member of the Canadian Pacific board of directors. See *Canadian Pacific Facts and Figures,* Compiled and Edited by the General Publicity Department (Montreal: Canadian Pacific Foundation Library, 1937), 135.

9. Thomas Harrison interview, 9 May 1974.

10. Thomas Harrison interview, 9 May 1974; John A. Eagle, *The Canadian Pacific Railway and the Development of Western Canada* (Montreal: McGill-Queen's University Press, 1989), 222.

11. Thomas Harrison interview, 9 May 1974.

12. Thomas Harrison interview, 9 May 1974; *Financial Post of Canada*, 24 February 1934; G. R. Stevens, *History of the Canadian National Railways* (New York: The Macmillan Company, 1973), 363.

13. Interview by the author with Barbara Connelly, 21 May 1974; Tyler Trafford, *Toole Peet 1897-1997: An Enduring Partnership* (Calgary: Toole, Peet & Co. Limited, 1997), 6-8.

14. Interview by the author with Arthur G. Graves, 24 October 1973.

15. *Calgary Herald*, 17 November 1898.

16. Thomas Harrison interview, 9 May 1974.

17. Max Foran, *Calgary: An Illustrated History* (Toronto: James Lorimer & Company, 1978), 67-70; Hugh A. Dempsey, *Calgary, Spirit of the West: A History* (Calgary: Glenbow and Fifth House Publishers, 1994), 75-86.

18. *Henderson's Manitoba and Northwest Gazetteer and Directory for 1905*, 243.

19. Thomas Harrison interview, 9 May 1974.

20. Ibid.

21. Ibid.

22. *Calgary Herald*, 7 September 1907.

23. Arthur G. Graves interview, 24 October 1973; Thomas Harrison interview, 9 May 1974.

24. Thomas Harrison interview, 9 May 1974.

25. Ibid.

26. *Albertan*, 21 January 1908.

27. Thomas Harrison interview, 9 May 1974; *Albertan*, 7, 8 August 1908; Elizabeth Ann Taraska, "The Calgary Craft Union Movement, 1900-1920," (M. A. thesis, University of Calgary, 1975), 18-19.

28. Thomas Harrison interview, 9 May 1974.

29. Glenbow-Alberta Institute Archives, M3973, George Gooderham interviews, file 7, Thomas Booth Riley.

30. Interview by the author with Tom Reddick, 11 February 1976.

31. *Albertan*, 6 October 1908.

32. *Calgary Herald*, 1 February 1902; 11 February 1903; 6 July 1903; 11 December 1907; 24 February 1909.

33. *Calgary Herald*, 9 February 1909.

34. *Canadian Pacific Facts and Figures*, 197.

35. Thomas Harrison interview, 9 May 1974.

36. Thomas Harrison interview, 9 May 1974; Stephen Clarkson & Christina McCall, *Trudeau and Our Times Volume 1: The Magnificent Obsession* (Toronto: McClelland & Stewart, 1990), 26.

37. Thomas Harrison interview, 9 May 1974.

38. Canadian Pacific Archives, Shaughnessy Correspondence, Montreal, 7 June 1911, Thomas G. Shaughnessy to William Whyte; Winnipeg, 23 October 1911, George J. Bury to Thomas G. Shaughnessy.

39. *Calgary Herald*, 27 January 1912.

40. Shaughnessy Correspondence, Montreal, 12 March 1912, Thomas G. Shaughnessy to George J. Bury.

41. Thomas Harrison interview, 9 May 1974; *Canadian Facts and Figures*, 135.

42. Interviews by the author with James Holmes, 25 January, 2002; 1 February 2002; 22 April 2002; *Engineering Record*, vol. 67, no. 24, n. d., 658.

43. Thomas Harrison interview, 9 May 1974; J. Lorne McDougall, *Canadian Pacific: A Brief History* (Montreal: McGill University Press, 1968), 93; *Albertan*, 27 April 1914; David Bright, *The Limits of Labour: Class Formation and the Labour Movement in Calgary, 1883-1929* (Vancouver: UBC Press, 1998), 100.

44. Tom Reddick interview, 11 February 1976.

45. Thomas Harrison interview, 9 May 1974; *Calgary Herald*, 3 November 1977.

46. Tom Reddick interview, 11 February 1976.

47. Thomas Harrison interview, 9 May 1974.

48. *Calgary Herald*, 1, 3 May 1915; 1, 4 June 1915; 13 August 1915.

49. Thomas Harrison interview, 9 May 1974.

50. Ibid.

51. Ibid.

52. McDougall, *Canadian Pacific*, 104.

53. Thomas Harrison interview, 9 May 1974.

54. Ibid.

Apostle of the Arts
Stanford Perrott
by Maxwell Foran

Stanford Perrott was undoubtedly one of the most pivotal figures in the development of the visual arts in Alberta in the second half of the twentieth century. A superb watercolorist, he ranks with the best in Western Canada in using color, composition, and conformation to depict a unique sense of place. More significantly however, Perrott was also a brilliant teacher. For 27 years at the Provincial Institute of Technology and Art (later the Alberta College of Art), he employed varied and innovative techniques to help students see art and creativity in different ways. In so doing, he was instrumental in breaking the colonial shackles to British traditions that had bound formal art in the province. Stan Perrott's overall contribution to Alberta and Western Canadian art was enormous. Through his own art and his exceptional teaching skills, he empowered hundreds of students to seek new visions and ways of portraying Alberta and Western Canada to Canadians and to the world.

Stanford Perrott was born in Claresholm, Alberta, on March 11, 1917, and grew up on his English-born parents' farm near Stavely. The second of five children, Stan Perrott faced early life with mixed blessings. He was highly intelligent and displayed an early artistic promise. At two years of age he recognized his aunt's kitchen linoleum pattern in an Eaton's catalogue. He was also small for his age, sickly, and burdened with a harelip. The result was a sheltered, self-absorbed, creative child, very much at home in the world of make-believe. It is likely that a low self-image contributed to the sensitivity he had towards the shortcomings of others.

In 1935 Perrott entered art school at the Provincial Institute of Technology and Art in Calgary. It was hardly an ambitious move. Not knowing what to do following high school and disdainful of a career in farming, he drifted into art education almost by default. In fact, one of the most enduring themes in Perrott's later reflections was a conviction that good things happened to him accidentally. Over the ensuing 4 years he earned superior grades as well as half a dozen art scholarships and awards, one of which enabled further study at the Banff School of

Fine Arts. While he was not impressed with A. C. Leighton, he enjoyed the teachings of Leo Pearson, Henry George Glyde, and Arthur Adam.[1] Most of all, he was in awe of Marion Nicoll, who became his lifelong friend and the closest he ever had to a mentor. He enjoyed the more robust social activities associated with student life, and counted among his close friends the noted ceramist, Luke Lindoe. Perrott's progress towards maturity was enhanced through operations that remedied his harelip. A more confident Stan Perrott graduated from art school in 1939. With it came impishness, a ready wit, and a love of company. Artistically, he had developed considerably. He had a small but steady demand for his lino prints and Christmas cards. Later, on a trip east with his parents, he was exposed to the work of the Masters in Chicago art galleries. The result was the sort of catharsis often associated with creative breakthroughs. He now saw art in a different light and possibly as something he might want to pursue seriously.

Four years at art school had given Perrott a diploma but not a job. In 1941, he chose Normal School – not so much because he wanted to be a teacher but because there was no better alternative. A year later he graduated with the highest grades in the student body and with two practice teaching assessments that had marked him as a teacher of great promise. The fall of 1942 saw him teaching Elementary and a year later, Junior High students in Turner Valley, an oilfield town southwest of Calgary. Perrott liked teaching. More importantly, he discovered that he was good at it. For example he took particular satisfaction from his ability to motivate grade nine boys more interested in working on the rigs than in staying in school, or from employing the new but challenging enterprise method of integrating inquiry-based learning around a single theme. After two years, he left public school teaching for good and took a drafting position with Royalite Limited, a major operator in the Valley's oilfields. However, by this time he had decided his future lay in the world of art. He was considering an application to the University of Toronto to study art when a chance meeting on a Calgary street with James Fowler, Principal of the Alberta Institute of Technology and Art, changed his mind. Fowler persuaded him to apply for a vacant teaching position with the Art Department. In the fall of 1946, Perrott began the 27 year career that would place his name in the forefront of Western Canadian art education

Perrott soon earned a reputation as a brilliant teacher, one reinforced by a keen mind, a powerful work ethic, a wonderful presence, and strongly held beliefs about the learning process. By his own admission, his success in teaching figure drawing to classes formerly taught by the renowned Henry George Glyde boosted his initial confidence immeasurably. Students recall his teaching as entertaining and valuable but never watered-down. One student noted that "he could substitute the fist with gentle wit and cool, clear intelligence."[2] Perrott always maintained that he was a designer first and foremost. To him, design was the key to opening the doors to creativity and that, regardless of medium, design should precede drawing in order for students to realize that "originality and individuality are the basis of ultimate success." He realized that artistic fulfillment required creative confidence as well as skill mastery. In short, Stanford Perrott empowered students to reach their potential. As one student put it, "he could criticize your work and make you feel good about it."[3] Perrott's students provide the best testimony not only to his effectiveness but also to his wider role as art educator. Several went on to success as artists, art administrators, and teachers nationally and internationally. They include Katie Ohe, Bernadette Law, Karen Moller, Les and Jackie Graff, Wayne and Gitta Whillier, John Hall, Doug Haynes, Ted Diakow, Herb Sellin, and Ed Drahanchuk to name just a few. Perrott's role as a teacher did not end with the classroom. He supported his students through his ready ear and counsel, and on several occasions, financially. His rustic home in Bragg Creek was crammed with works purchased from his students and not all solely for their artistic merits. Les Graff, former Director of Visual Arts for the Province of Alberta, summed up Perrott's contribution to art education when he said that "his students, friends and graduating disciples are impacting on the visual arts of this nation."[4]

Stan Perrott grew as a person through his association with Illingworth Kerr, his immediate superior in the Art Department, which would later become the College of Art. A superb painter in his own right, Kerr earned international acclaim as one of the leading Canadian artists of his generation. As an administrator he was relentless in his efforts to advance the status of the Art Department both within the Institute of Technology and beyond. However, he was not so effective in the realm of staff and student relations. Perrott, on the other hand, was a consummate communicator. In Kerr's words, Perrott became his "right hand man" and together they forged an almost symbiotic relationship. The interaction between Perrott and Kerr provides an illuminative window into a fuller understanding of both men. Perrott admired Kerr for all the things Perrott felt he himself was not. For instance, he envied Kerr for his proactiveness in securing time away from his administrative and teaching duties to paint, and Perrott blamed himself for not being so assertive. For his part, Kerr respected Perrott for his ability to keep harmony among students and staff. Combining their abilities, they moved the Art Department into a higher profile within the Institute and were together in 1960 when the study of art in Calgary was formally removed from technological training and the former art department was renamed The Alberta College of Art. According to the student newsletter, *Tech-Art*, the change represented "the end of an era." When Kerr died in 1989, it fell to his lifelong colleague and *alter ego* to deliver an inspirational eulogy that poignantly touched the essence of their relationship.

In 1967, by the time Kerr was ready to quit the College of Art, Perrott was there to take his place. There was simply no one else. Perrott stayed as Head for seven years, during which time he spearheaded the drive to secure a separate building for the college. Responding to prevailing opinion in government circles that the college was a haven for "ne'er-do-wells, old ladies and drug addicts,"[5] Perrott painstakingly collected evidence to show that fully 67 percent of the college's graduates had gone on to art or art-related careers. The result was a seven million dollar building that opened its doors to students in 1973. A year later Stan Perrott left to pursue, as he then believed, a new life in painting. More to the truth was that he was disillusioned and burnt out. The combination of too many students, not enough staff, and what were, to him, the unrelentingly mundane duties of educational administration, had done their job well.

Opening of the Alberta College of Art, February, 1974. Calgary, Alberta. Glenbow Archives, NA-2864-24626-16

Aside from his role as formal art educator, Perrott used what spare time he had furthering the cause of art in the province. He was president of the Alberta Society of Artists through 1956 to 1958. He taught summer schools at the University of Alberta, and community art classes in Lethbridge. Always mindful of the need to expose children to the joy of art, he was instrumental in establishing regular Saturday art classes for children. He was a perennial juror for the Alberta Visual Arts Board for formal art competitions and exhibitions, and also at the Banff School of Fine Arts. He judged at the annual Calgary and Edmonton Exhibitions and at innumerable art exhibitions in and outside of the province. An inspiring and entertaining speaker, he was in high demand at banquet tables in Calgary, Edmonton, and Banff – a forum he used to demythologize formal art as an elitist journey towards creative genius. By dwelling on its relevance and more significantly its open-endedness, Perrott led hundreds of people to art, most of whom would never had dared to take up the challenge. In time the public recognitions came. In 1971, he was appointed to the Senate of the University of Calgary and in late 1974, received the Alberta Government's Award of Excellence.

In retirement, Stan Perrott did not paint as much or as often as he would have liked. Other demands ate deeply into his spare time. Most were art related. He continued to teach regular art classes to amateur groups in Bragg Creek and Cochrane, and summer courses at Red Deer College. He also gave several weekend workshops at various venues across the province and found time to work extensively with seniors. In fact, in noting their enthusiasm for art, Perrott wished he had discovered them sooner. Juror and Committee duties, interspersed with a hectic public speaking schedule, also kept him away from the easel in his brightly-lit studio in Bragg Creek. Stan Perrott was also a knowledgeable and avid gardener. He once said that by judiciously planting windbreaks at his parents' farm, he could grow flowers only found in lower latitude climates. His Bragg Creek garden was a virtual cornucopia of color and design, and clearly reflected the patient hours laboring in its creation and tending. He also loved to travel and spent several vacations visiting places such as India and Japan which inspired his creative spirit. Finally, Perrott's extraordinary personality ensured that his house was rarely without visitors who just happened to drop in "for a cup of mud." In one 17-week period in 1981 he counted 542 visitors. Many were former students. Some came for advice; others to admire his house and garden; a few came for help; while others like myself were there to interview him. Most just wanted to talk with an old (or new) valued friend.

Other honors came his way. In 1987 he received the Alberta College of Art Award of Excellence, and a year later the Alberta Government honored him with its prestigious Frederick Haultain Prize. Three years later, in 1991, he received an honorary doctorate from the University of Calgary. In the mid-1990s, Perrott's health began to fail. But though he now tired easily, he continued to paint and maintain his garden. Although clearly unwell, he was present in April, 2001, at the launching of his biography, *The Chalk and the Easel: The Life and Works of Stanford Perrott*. There he mingled and spent over an hour patiently signing copies of the book. He died less than eight months later on December 6, 2001.

Though best known for his watercolors, Stan Perrott was a versatile artist both in terms of subject matter and mediums. Urban subjects and abstractions figured prominently in his portfolio. He worked in charcoal and oil and produced lithographs and etchings. However, he identified with, and is most recognized for his western Canadian landscape watercolors that convey his strong and abiding love for this land. His paintings hang in major galleries and collections around the world. If there is a failing in Stan Perrott's work, it is that he did not produce enough of it. His teaching "just got in the way."

It is interesting to conjecture just how far Stanford Perrott would have gone as an artist had teaching not come first in his life. Many of his students, some professional painters themselves, see him simply as *the best*. To them he was the equal if not superior to any western Canadian artist of his time, including Kerr. Typically, Perrott was always very modest about his painting, often referring to himself as "not being very good," or "ordinary."[6] Yet below this self-effacement was a firm belief that art was a lifelong journey which if followed with diligence and creativity would lead to "those accidents which by demanding solutions, force me to reach beyond myself."[7] Perrott's artistic life reflected this long pursuit of creative self-fulfillment.

Stan Perrott's formal training in art went well beyond his years at the Provincial Institute of Technology and Art. In 1947 he spent a summer at the Philadelphia Art Academy in Chester Springs, Pennsylvania. Seven years later he took a year's leave of absence to study under two of North America's most prominent Modernists. In Provincetown, Massachusetts, he was exposed to the internationally recognized German colorist Hans Hofmann, a formidable but inspirational teacher.

After a harrowing beginning when his artistic bonds would not release, Perrott responded well to Hofmann's teaching methods. By the end of the courses in Provincetown, he had impressed the not-so-impressionable Hofmann as an artist of great promise. In the fall of 1954, Perrott went to New York to study at the Arts Student League under the noted American printmaker and painter, Will Barnet. Before long, Perrott was filling in for Barnet, taking over his teacher's classes when other engagements took Barnet out of the city. Perrott learned a great deal from these two prominent abstractionists. Hofmann exposed him to the force of "unleashed order." The more humanistic Barnet taught him that the essence of true art lay in creating "one's own personal theatre." Most important, he learned to use color, composition, and size to free his work from the shackles of convention. While in New York, Perrott also studied etching and engraving with Leo Katz at Atelier 17, and Lithography at Blackburn's Graphics Studio. In 1957, he rejoined his friend Will Barnet when the latter conducted the very popular summer art school at Emma Lake, Saskatchewan.

The influence of Hofmann and Barnet can be seen in Perrott's singular successes and several exhibitions in the late 1950s and the early 1960s. While in New York, he was exhibited along with noted artists like Will Barnet, Cameron Booth, Harlan Jackson, and Robert Blackburn at the Young Men's Hebrew Association Art Gallery. In 1961, he was one of seven North American art instructors selected for the Finalists Exhibition, International College Art Exhibitor's Exhibition at the high-profile Pietrantonio Galleries in New York. In the same year his watercolor "Stanza I" was hung at the twenty-first annual Western Ontario Art Exhibition in London, Ontario.

Perrott took well to abstractionism despite the discipline and control that underlay his preferred approach to composition in much of his own work as well as in his teaching methods. The best Perrott abstractions indicate an enormous potential. With his superb sense of design he allowed his abstractions to offer many interpretations while standing on their own in expressing a single clear image. It was this duality that carried through in his subsequent return to realism. As one colleague has remarked, he "would fly," not knowing why he had incorporated an element of color or form to a particular piece of work.[8]

Stanford Perrott was a proficient and mature painter when he rediscovered realism in his retirement years. His western Canadian landscapes are personal statements in design, color, and composition.

A good example is reflected in his love of trees where his ability to capture the combination of delicacy and scar in aspen poplar trunks in the winter snow, or the twisted, timeless magnificence of limber pine trees on windy outcrops is unparalleled. His facility with mood is remarkable. He employed fine tonalities to portray the essence of fog, storm, or numbing cold in his winter paintings, or color juxtapositions in his summer mountain or foothill scenes. He once noted that he wanted to convey a feeling of being able "to physically walk in and tramp through the scenery." Color was vital to Perrott and he used it skillfully to convey depth, tone, and a sense of space. Its increasing use in his later years could be considered a metaphor for his own liberation of spirit.

While it is perhaps unfortunate that this magnificent painter did not leave more of his work behind, his is a wider legacy. When he began teaching, art in western Canada was still seen through Old World eyes. Stan Perrott helped shape new visions by teaching his students to approach their art with the confidence born of encouragement and discipline, and to rely on personal experience to see the uniqueness and possibilities of their own environments. This is true empowerment.

It is not easy to encapsulate a life in a phrase. Stanford Perrott may be an exception. But what phrase? I see him as personifying teaching as "the purest of the arts." To Jackie Graff, he was Alberta's "Apostle of the Arts." Les Graff saw him as being "always where the light was shining." As for Stan himself, he would probably have opted for the phrase he used in an address he gave at the sixtieth anniversary celebration of the Alberta College of Art in 1986: "I have thousands of kids." Yet, ironically perhaps, when the long passage of time allows more distant assessments, it might well be the sensitive and empathetic watercolors, those personal signatures of the western Canadian landscape, that will ultimately define Stanford's place in Canadian Art.

Notes

1. Interview with Stanford Perrott, 11 March 1994.

2. Recollections of Bob Hinman, 17 October 1996.

3. Written comments from Ed Drahanchuk to author, Fall, 1993.

4. Interview with Les Graff, 10 March 1997.

5. Interview with Stanford Perrott, 10 March 1990.

6. Stanford Perrott Files, Nancy Tousley, "Work Brings Outdoors Inside," *Calgary Herald* [u.d.], c1984.

7. Interview with Stanford Perrott, 3 April 1991.

8. Interview with George Wood, 3 July 1997.

A Warrior Among Businessmen
Arthur Child
by Brian Brennan

In 1966, the Burns meat-packing empire was in deep financial trouble – losing $350 000 a month, and on the brink of bankruptcy. Its corporate owners summoned Arthur Child to perform a salvage operation. He was a 55-year-old number-crunching specialist who liked to apply military analogies to business. He started off by unceremoniously dumping staff throughout the venerable company that legendary Calgary cattle baron, Pat Burns, had founded in 1890, and within three years Child had restored the ailing giant to health. He transformed Burns from a money-losing operation into a $1.5 billion corporation that – notwithstanding all the job cuts – reasserted itself in 1969 as Alberta's largest private employer and the leading industry in nine Western Canadian cities.

How did he do it? Child had been working in the meat-packing business for 35 years when asked to restore the Burns company to profitability, and he was happy to provide newspaper reporters with his formula for success. As a former reserve officer and an admirer of Julius Caesar's authoritarian approach, Child said he didn't believe in modern management-by-consensus techniques. "I found that Caesar's qualities of leadership applied equally well to business as to military matters. Orders had to be obeyed promptly, and no excuses were accepted for non-performance. Any challenge to my authority was met with immediate dismissal. Those who couldn't come up to my standards were gone immediately."

He didn't believe in keeping staff he considered redundant either: "I reduced the dairy division's executive from 10 to three and – all across the country – reduced the jobs of three men to two. Plus, I cut the head office staff from eighty to thirty. Like the government, there were too many people in that place with no concern for where the money was coming from."

Comments from former associates served to magnify his public image as a corporate bully. "When Art Child said 'jump,' you asked 'how high?' – on the way up!" said one Burns executive. But Child offered no apologies or excuses for his autocratic leadership style. "It was a pretty loose company," he shrugged. "I was used to just the opposite – a situation where orders were orders, and you carried them out immediately without any 'ifs,' 'ands' or 'buts.'"

His private image, by contrast, was that of an incurable romantic, a lover of languages and literature, whose only nod to vanity was a preference for impeccably tailored three-piece suits and an ill-fitting toupee that fooled no one. Born Arthur James Edward Child in Guildford, Surrey, on May 19, 1910, he grew up in the picturesque Thousand Islands area of southeastern Ontario, where his father, William, worked in a steel mill. During the First World War, William served overseas with the British army while his wife Helena instilled in young Arthur, a sense of pride in his British heritage. "It never occurred to me that anyone was equal to the British," he said afterwards. "I firmly believed that the British army had the best soldiers in the world." His mother also taught him the value of a good education. He spent six nights a week reading in the Gananoque library where she worked.

After finishing high school, Arthur won a scholarship to Queen's University in Kingston, earned a bachelor of commerce degree, and looked forward to pursuing a career as an academic. An interest in languages led him toward becoming proficient in French, German, Spanish, Russian, Latin, and Greek. At the same time, he pursued an interest in military matters by serving as a second lieutenant in the Royal Canadian Corps of Signals, and as a regimental sergeant major in the Canadian Officers' Training Corps. However, the economics of the depression dictated that he leave university and get a secure job after completing his under-graduate degree. Only a large company, he decided, could offer a promising financial future to a new college graduate. In 1931, after producing an 80-page analysis of the Canadian meat-packing industry for his Bachelor of Commerce thesis, Child joined Canada Packers in Toronto as an "office junior," responsible for filing correspondence and checking arithmetic on invoices. He would remain in the meat processing business for the next 65 years.

Child moved swiftly up the corporate ladder. His boss, J. Stanley McLean, was "a bit of a curmudgeon," but he liked the succinct, one-page memos that Child wrote offering suggestions for improvements in office procedures. In 1938, at age 27, Child was appointed chief internal auditor for Canada Packers. Three years later, in 1941, he was summoned to Ottawa to advise the government on wartime meat and gasoline rationing. Eleven years after that, in 1952, he was named vice-president of finance for Canada Packers. During the same period, in collaboration with accountant Bradford Cadmus, Child wrote a book about business fraud and economic waste that qualified him for a membership in the Canadian Authors Association. He served as treasurer of the CAA (Hugh MacLennan was secretary) and helped save the group from financial collapse.

In 1956, Child took a year's leave of absence from Canada Packers to fill some of the gaps in his education. He read early French literature at Laval, studied business economics at Harvard, and began work on a master's degree in economics at the University of Toronto (U of T) that he would complete in 1960 while back working full-time at Canada Packers. He spent his lunch hours, evenings, and weekends attending classes and writing papers ("I worked one hundred hours a week for two years") while simultaneously discharging his duties as company vice-president.

Child continued with his studies and completed the course work and thesis for a Ph.D. in economics at U of T. However, for reasons he never revealed publicly, he did not submit his finished thesis for adjudication. Instead, he included portions of it in a book of essays that he wrote about pre-1860 economics and politics in the U.S. banking industry.

Child wanted but never attained the presidency of Canada Packers. He discovered after 23 years with the family-owned firm that only a family member had any chance of making it to the top. Although he enjoyed a close working relationship with J. Stanley McLean, who controlled Canada Packers' stock during most of Child's time at the firm, he was disappointed to see the top job go to a McLean son upon J. Stanley's death in 1954.

In 1960, with no chance of further promotion in sight, Child left Canada Packers to become president of the troubled Intercontinental Packers in Saskatoon. His primary task there was to rescue the company from near bankruptcy, a challenge that he relished. "You lay everything on the line when you do a rescue operation," he said. "You risk your whole career. You'd find it difficult to live with yourself if you failed." Child spent five years with Intercontinental, tripled the size of the company, and then looked around for other challenges. That's when Burns Foods beckoned.

The Burns company had begun operations in 1890 when Pat Burns, a 34-year-old Ontario-born cattle trader, landed a contract to supply beef to construction crews building a rail line between Calgary and Edmonton. He established his headquarters in Calgary, built a small slaughterhouse and office shack that doubled as his sleeping quarters on Ninth Avenue East, and hired a full-time butcher. When the Calgary-Edmonton line was finished, he began supplying beef to the crews building the southern extension from Calgary to Fort Macleod. He also shipped beef into the Crowsnest Pass region, south into Washington state, and west to the East Kootenay region of southeastern British Columbia.

He suffered a few setbacks along the way. In 1892, the Burns slaughterhouse burned to the ground. In 1906-1907, Burns lost hundreds of cattle during a very cold winter. In 1913, his Calgary plant burned to the ground for the second time. But Burns bounced back from each disaster, determined to do better than before. He added pork and sheep to his cattle operations and established himself as the "meat king of Western Canada" when he bought out the extensive holdings of William Roper Hull, his biggest competitor. As part of that deal, Burns acquired an extensive chain of butcher shops in Alberta and British Columbia, and a 4 000-acre ranch property in what is now Fish Creek Provincial Park in Calgary. When a government commission investigated charges of a meat monopoly in 1907, Burns protested: "Without Pat Burns, the western country would starve in ten days."

The Fish Creek property was one of several southern Alberta ranches that Burns purchased during the first decades of the twentieth century. While he made his money as a meat contractor, it was as a cattle rancher that he wanted to be known. That's how he described himself in 1912 when he joined forces with ranchers George Lane, A. E. Cross, and Archie McLean (collectively known as the Big Four) to finance the first Calgary Stampede.

During the 1920s, Burns built his company into one of the world's largest meat-packing and food distribution businesses. His empire stretched from Seattle to Alaska, and from Vancouver to Halifax. He owned seven meat-packing plants, 100 butcher shops, 65 creamery and cheese factories, and 29 wholesale food supply warehouses. Additionally, he had interests in lumber, mining, oil wells, fishing, and real estate. His branch offices were located in London, Liverpool, and Yokohama.

In 1928, Burns sold his meat-processing operations for 15 million dollars through a public share issue that Child would later characterize as poorly conceived: "The spirit went out of the company when it was sold to the public." Burns continued to exercise a measure of control over the company until his death in 1937 at age 81. By that time, his nephew, Michael John Burns, had assumed the presidency of the company. Michael John remained in charge until 1950, when he retired at age 67. Control then passed to his son, Dick Burns, who had run the Burns packing plants in Regina and Vancouver after earning a law degree from the University of Alberta.

Dick Burns remained with the company for only one year after his father retired. In 1951, he joined a Calgary law firm specializing in wills and trusts, and thus finally severed a 61-year connection between his family and the company that bore its name. After that, in Child's words, "the company's financial fortunes drifted lower and lower until control was bought by eastern interests in 1964 at bargain prices."

The eastern owners included Toronto entrepreneur Alec Hill and Montreal financier Howard Webster, whose holdings then included substantial stakes in the Toronto Blue Jays baseball team, Quebecair, and the Toronto *Globe and Mail*. The owners hired six different consulting firms to restore the Burns company to health, but to no avail. "These consulting firms spent months telling them what an experienced meat man could have told them in half a day," said Child. He quickly established himself as the experienced meat man that the company needed. To demonstrate his commitment to making the company successful, Child sank all his savings into Burns shares. "I risked my whole future, my reputation and all my finances," he said. "By taking such a large risk, I was showing my confidence that things would work out."

As well as clearing the top management ranks of deadwood, Child achieved efficiencies by writing off packing plants in Regina, Prince Albert, and Medicine Hat, and diversifying into restaurants, catering, groceries, vegetable oils, tanning, and trading with Japan. By 1974, sales had tripled and profits stood at $4 571 000.

In 1978, Webster and Child decided to go private by forming a new company, WCB Holdings, to buy the public's shares for 50 million dollars, and escape the distractions that came with being publicly traded. "Being private means we can run Burns Foods like a family business, without Big Brother –the shareholders and regulators – looking over our shoulders," said Child. "We don't have to disclose anything to anybody, and we don't have stock-market analysts urging us to get into non-related businesses – which can be a bit of a bother." While the company's books were now closed to prying eyes, it was estimated by *Financial Post* writer

Richard Osler that Child's personal stake in Burns was worth at least 10 million dollars and growing.

In 1985, Child and Webster sold Burns to Union Gas for $125 million. A year later, Child and a minority partner, Ron Jackson, bought back two-thirds of the company for $52.5 million. Some investment analysts concluded that they got the least attractive parts of the Burns empire, including the company's then-floundering meat-processing division, but Child emphatically disagreed. "I know a lot about these operations that others don't know," he said. "I predict that 1986 is going to be a great year for all the divisions involved."

His prediction proved accurate. Although he would not disclose profit figures, Child did reveal in 1988 that Burns was profitable, with 2 500 employees and sales nudging $900 million a year. At that point, Child was 77, still working 10 hours a day seven days a week, and showing no signs of slowing down. "Business is my life," he said. "Nothing is as fascinating as business." His official company biography ran to seven pages of detail on his work habits, and claimed – somewhat disingenuously – that he had "no social or sports interests whatsoever. For the most part, his time is spent at his office, his home, or travelling on business."

While it was true that Child invested most of himself in his work, it was not true – as his biography asserted – that he had no life outside the office. He was active in both the Reform Party and the Canada West Foundation, a conservative think tank that produces analyses of Western Canadian economic and political issues. He flew his own vintage Tiger Moth, swam every day before dinner with his wife Mary (they had no children), collected art (mainly Robert Hurleys), piloted a 30-ton pleasure cruiser on voyages off Vancouver Island's west coast, wrote and published essays on such topics as public service strikes and the economic decline of his beloved Britain, held memberships in private clubs from Vancouver to Montreal, and built up one of the largest private collections of military history books in the country.

In 1993, when he was 83, Child told a reporter he planned to keep working until he died. His doctor had told him that his work seemed to be keeping him in good health and as a result, Child was developing a strategy for Burns to take over Intercontinental Packers, consolidate the Canadian pork industry as a national concern, and keep it out of American hands. His junior partner, Ron Jackson, joked that Child was "one of the few eighty-year-olds with a twenty-year game plan."

That same year, 1993, Child experienced one of his great thrills outside of work. As honorary colonel of the Canadian Armed Forces' No. 4 (Fighter) Wing in Baden, Germany, he was invited to take over the controls of an American F-16 fighter jet at Nellis Air Force Base outside Las Vegas. He thus became the oldest person ever to pilot one of the so-called Fighting Falcons. When his American host started to explain to him how the ejection seat worked, Child gently interrupted: "I won't need that. At my age, if I get into trouble, I just ride her down."

Child rode herd on annual food sales of one billion dollars until shortly before his death, at age 86, from pneumonia, on July 30, 1996. His death was the result of a common sequence: a fall, a broken hip, and subsequent infection. Six weeks later, Burns Foods was sold to Maple Leaf Foods (formerly Canada Packers) for an estimated $100 million, and the historic Burns name finally disappeared from the letterheads of corporate Canada. (It continued to grace the letterhead of a charitable trust fund established in 1937 with one million dollars from the Pat Burns estate.) A year after that, in 1997, Child was again in the headlines when it was revealed that he had bequeathed one million dollars to the Reform (later Canadian Alliance) party, and one million dollars to the controversial, anti-French, Alliance for the Preservation of English in Canada. Though bilingual himself, Child had no time for Canada's Official Languages Act or government-funded French immersion programs. While the APEC bequest caused some tongues to wag disapprovingly, it came as no surprise to those who knew of Child's Anglophile characteristics. "He was always strongly supportive of English Canada," said John Nalon, a local historian based in Child's hometown of Gananoque, Ontario. "I believe he was always humming in the back of his mind, 'There Will Always Be an England.'"

A Strong-Minded Woman
Ruth Gorman
by Frits Pannekoek

Ruth L. Gorman was one of the greatest advocates of Aboriginal rights in Alberta, and spear-headed efforts that made important changes to the Canadian First Nations legislation.

Born into a privileged Mount Royal environment in turn of the century Calgary, Ruth graduated from the University of Alberta with a Bachelor of Arts in 1937 and with a law degree in 1939, before going on to article in her father's law firm. Her father, M. B. Peacock, a key influence in her life, was a close friend of Banff's Norman Luxton, who had married into the famous McDougall missionary family of Morley, Alberta. Her father was easily persuaded to become involved with the Aboriginal communities between Calgary and Banff, particularly those connected to the work of the missionaries. He fought the famous Wesley case, which clarified the hunting rights of the Stoney, and worked through his Sunday schools classes at Wesley United Church in Calgary to build bridges.[1] They often went to the reserve to play hockey with their native neighbors hoping to develop closer connections between the City and the reserve. Because of her father's work and contributions, Ruth Gorman herself was made a Stoney "princess" well before any of her activism, an honor she admitted she did not appreciate until later.[2] Gorman paints herself as a somewhat shallow "girl" at University, who became quickly but reluctantly enlightened when she returned to Calgary from law school. Because she was one of the few women lawyers in Calgary, and perhaps because her mother had held the position, or more likely her father was a lawyer, when Ruth Gorman returned from university, she was asked almost immediately to be the Convenor of Laws for the Calgary Local Council of Women. She held the position for 23 years, and during much of that time she also served as the Honorary Convenor of Laws for the Canadian National Council of Women.

The Local Council of Women's membership reflected the better-off of Calgary, the wives of the professionals and the moneyed. It had been formed in Calgary during the 1895 visit of Lady Aberdeen, the wife of the Governor General of Canada. According to Ruth Gorman, these women, while the victims of a more restrictive age that frowned on work, assigned themselves the role of social reform and keeper of the country's morals. While Gorman herself did not necessarily agree with this role, she not only accepted it, she made the best of it.

One of the first causes put to her by the Local Council was the need for an amendment to Alberta's Dower Act. Her persuasions ensured that a wife's recourse was not only against her husband, but also to anyone who has subsequently acquired an inappropriately alienated family home or farm. To guarantee passage of the act, according to her account published in *A Leaven of Ladies*, she went directly to William Aberhart to get the law changed. He must have admired her, because according to Gorman, he asked her to become his attorney general, an offer she did not accept given her family obligations. This refusal to enter formal public life was always a struggle for Gorman who felt the tensions between her soul and domestic duty. As the Council's legal convenor, she also fought for the marketing of skimmed milk, and for women on the police force. She also worked to help create Calgary's Indian Friendship Centre and was active in the Calgary Rehabilitation Society for the Handicapped. Ruth Gorman also confessed to Marjorie Norris that the "most lasting and effective move for Calgary in the legal field of LCW's efforts"[3] was her (Gorman's) fight to prevent the move of the railway to current Prince's Island, now a park preserve.

This career was accompanied by several others: publisher of the *Golden West*, a key news journal that served as a vehicle for all of Gorman's various passions; legal advisor to the Western Canada Concept; and champion of Western rights in the repatriation of the Canadian Constitution. In all of these endeavors, her legal expertise combined with her law school contacts and her women's network were the foundations of her influence and success. She attempted to use the press in the repatriation of the Canadian Constitution in the 1980s. Her fame as a public figure ensured that she would get coverage, but she was unable to mobilize key power brokers to oppose the repatriation, which she believed abrogated property rights.

The work for which she received most of her awards was her career as the "unpaid lawyer" for the Indian Association of Alberta (IAA). In 1944, John Laurie, a Calgary school teacher, secretary of the Alberta Indian Association and champion of the Aboriginal peoples, persuaded her to become its unpaid solicitor. Why he approached her is not entirely clear, but it is likely because the Calgary Local Council of Women had

Ruth Gorman speaking at a meeting of the Indian Association of Alberta.
Glenbow Archives, na-4212-52

become involved in minor advocacy for Aboriginal peoples, and because as M. B. Peacock's daughter and a "princess" there was an "traditional" link. Whatever the reason, that role was to occupy much of the next 20 years of her life. She became the chief political and publicity strategist of the Association. Her support of John Laurie, her leadership in the Hobbema cases, and the securing of critical amendments to the Indian Act in 1960-1961, were her most important works. Her drive, her persistence, and her knowledge were almost solely responsible for finally securing for the First Nations of Canada the vote without the threat of enfranchisement.

In 1951, the Federal Liberal government passed bill 79 – the culmination of several attempts to impose limits on those who would have access to Treaty rights and live on reserves. Despite opposition from John Laurie and the Indian Association, it stipulated that any 10 band members could protest the membership of any individual based on, for example, their legitimacy or that of their ancestors, or whether they or they ancestors had ever taken Métis scrip. On January 15, 1952, 10 members of the Samson band on the Hobbema reserve protested the membership of 27 individuals who, with their children, numbered 103, or one-third of the band. The situation was a serious one and not necessarily understood by everyone. Some who protested individuals, themselves ended up on the list because of their relationship to the person protested. The initial hearings began March 29 in Hobbema, with the protestors represented by Ruth Gorman. This was the first of the seriously politicized First Nations legal cases in Canada and established a precedent for the future. While some believe that the Canadian courts would have never allowed the removals, even they concede that the case marks the beginning of the "political re-emergence of the Indian questions in post-war Canadian political life."[4] Although the government was unable, due to Gorman's clever legal tactics, to prove its allegations that two families and their descendants took scrip, the government searched for new evidence and reopened the enquiry July 7 and 8, 1955. This time the Crown persisted and on November 6, 1956, those who protested were ordered removed by the commissioner.

Gorman went into aggressive action and she and John Laurie gave over 81 speeches, securing support from the Canadian Bar Association, the churches, and literally hundreds of critical community groups. She ensured that *Time*, the *Calgary Herald*, and every national newspaper knew about the case. She used every political contact she knew and ensured that Douglas Harkness, Calgary MP, and a former teaching colleague of Laurie's, exposed the absurdity of the case. The government was hoping that Gorman would appeal the commissioner's decision to the courts as was permitted under the Act. She intended to do so but only at the last minute since the moment an appeal was filed, the federal Minister, Jack Pickersgill, could hide from making comment. Gorman made certain that she used every minute before the appeal deadline. For example, she drafted a petition to the Crown for First Nations leaders. The government refused to forward it to the Crown – unleashing the thunder of the leader of the opposition, John Diefenbaker.

The appeal was filed and heard in February and March of 1957. Gorman did not herself act as counsel at this last hearing, but enlisted the aid of her husband, and A. F. "Spud" Moir, possibly because she knew that she had become a media figure, and that the courts may not have reacted well to a "strong-minded" woman. But it was her victory, and she was honored at Hobbema with the title of "Mother" of the Cree, one that they celebrated by sending her cards and gifts throughout most of her life, particularly on Mother's Day.

While Diefenbaker was sympathetic to Gorman's political storms and communicated with her frequently, the repulsive section of the Act still existed. When Laurie died shortly after the Hobbema case, Gorman saw it as her mission to change the Indian Act. Section 112, compulsory enfranchisement, had to be removed. She worked hard to secure "grass roots" support both in the Alberta Aboriginal community and amongst Canadian decision makers to achieve her objectives. She would take the issue to the Joint Senate House of Commons committee struck in 1959 to investigate the conditions of First Nations. As always, she and the Indian Association of Alberta intended to be well-prepared. Her fact-finding mission took on the trappings of a political campaign – which indeed it was. The following months she spent touring Alberta's key native communities in 1959/60 were the highlights of her years with the Indian Association of Alberta. She was firm that the communities must support that change.

Ruth Gorman, legal counsel for the Alberta Indian Association, travelled to Ottawa where she presented a brief from Alberta First Nations people to the committee studying proposed revisions of the Indian Act. Glenbow Archives, na-2557-17

While removal of enfranchisement provisions were key, the Indian Association added concerns about education, welfare, and hunting and fishing rights – for a total of 57 resolutions. Although Gorman supported all of them, it is clear from her argument to the Joint Committee of the Senate and the House of Commons on Indian Affairs in 1960 that her own efforts were for the removal of Section 112. The resolutions were endorsed by the Friends of Indians in Calgary and Edmonton, a group of largely White women and their male supporters, who wanted to support political action by First Nations, and by the Canadian Bar Association.

This great trek throughout the province by Ruth Gorman and the executive of the IAA created incredible expectations. The executive first went to the Sarcee Reserve, and then to the Stoney Reserve. This was followed by meetings in Cardston with Chief Clarence McHugh, and Chief Shot on Both Sides, then on to Hobbema and then to Lesser Slave Lake and Cold Lake. These five large meetings elected representatives for a consolidated meeting at Hobbema to draft the final resolutions. The IAA correspondence on the preparation of the brief to the Senate and House of Commons Committee indicates how seriously the communities considered the process. Indeed the committee minutes are probably one of the best snap shots of the concerns of the reserves throughout Alberta. There was by no means consensus on all of the issues at the final Hobbema meeting orchestrated by Gorman, and in fact some of the delegates felt that where issues had not been fully dealt with by their communities, they should go back for further consultation. This tendency concerned Gorman, who felt that elected delegates should have the latitude to shape the resolutions. It also threatened any sense of unanimity. The degree of public consensus that the IAA managed to achieve is evidenced in the "Minutes of Proceedings and Evidence of the Senate and House of Commons on Indian Affairs," a copy of which was one of Ruth Gorman's most cherished possessions.

Particularly contentious was the discussion on the vote. Gorman put the matter to the First Nations representatives in Hobbema very succinctly. Individuals were to be for the vote, against the vote, or could reserve the decision. Peter Many Wounds felt that each band at home should settle the questions. He felt that the delegates represented only a fraction of the people – only all of the people should decide. Gorman strongly argued that the resolution could not be taken home. "You as delegates here today have the vote of your people." Fred Gladstone spoke in favor of the third option in that he didn't "want the IAA to commit itself one way or the other." Johnnie Samson, a close friend of Gorman's, was clear that

> By now we are all quite familiar with those resolutions and a lot of us should know by now the general feeling of the people on our reserves. As far as we are concerned at Hobbema we do not want the provincial vote at all.[5]

When queried by Fred Gladstone as to whether he meant the federal vote as well, he replied "None at all – no vote. There is no guarantee we would not lose any of our treaty rights." There was obviously doubt in the room that the vote would bring anything but anguish. Senator Gladstone did indicate that the vote would bring some benefits. He emphasized that their rights – particularly treaty rights – would not be diminished. Joe Jiroux was concerned that the vote might mean additional taxation, but he did concede that First Nations would likely have more say in their affairs. In the end the consensus was as Gorman wanted – they would oppose the vote until Section 112 was removed.

It was obvious that the meetings throughout the province, and particularly the final critical one at Hobbema, were guided by Mrs. Gorman's strong hand and voice. At Hobbema, someone commented, "for two days now it seems as though it is this woman's meeting."[6] At that point Mrs.

Gorman left the meeting, refusing to accept the insults. On camera the President said

> We would like Mrs. Gorman back. We do not want a new lawyer. Time is getting short. We have to meet the Joint Committee with someone who knows it and who can make a good job of the brief. I know some of you are confused. She has tried her best in her own way – she's helping us.

Mrs. Gorman was persuaded to return but remained resolute and unbowed. She stated that there were still,

> long legal questions of your brief which you have not okayed. I would suggest that you form a committee who can authorize the brief. I want you to take a vote whether you want me to stay as your lawyer or not. All the things I have done today, drawing the resolutions from your old minutes, new resolutions I talked on my tour to your various reserves and they were all approved by your own executive. I have never in my life done anything which was not passed by the IAA without the consent of your executive. I do understand what an effort you have made and it is that reason why I am glad to help you. I want to thank Hobbema ladies for their wonderful courtesy to me. I will go home now and I won't even cross a T until I have talked to your committee.[7]

The emphasis on "your" is not to be missed. Gorman was aware of the role of Whites and of women within Aboriginal society and fought to ensure their equal voice in their communities and in the Indian Association.

Howard Beebe, Peter Burnsstick, Albert Lightning, Mrs. Nora Matchatis, John Samson, and Ralph Steinhaurer as well as Hugh Dempsey, are given credit for authoring the final brief to the House of Commons Senate Committee that was going to look at the Act. However, in truth, much of it was written by Ruth Gorman. The Committee then resolved to send a committee to Ottawa to make formal representations. While there, Gorman dominated the discussions, although Howard Beebe, President of the IAA, and Chief Johnnie Samson, Northern Representative, spoke frequently in support. Gerald Tail Feathers was also there representing the Blood Indian Reserve Protestant Group. Senator Gladstone was the Senate Chair. The Hon. J. W. Pickersgill, on Ruth Gorman's most detested list to the end, was on the Committee although he did not speak, and there is no record of his attendance.

The presentation is an extraordinary document of which Gorman was extremely proud. The brief is clear that in the last years of the nineteenth century and the first years of the twentieth, individual First Nations were successfully making the transition to the capitalist economy. Whether this is something that Gorman got out of reading L. M. Hanks and J. H. Hanks's Tribe *Under Trust – A Study of the Blackfoot Reserve in Alberta* (Toronto: University of Toronto Press, 1950) for which she wrote an extensive eye-opening review for the *Calgary Herald,* will not be known. Gorman documents First Nations economic successes of the 1880s and 1890s. Black Horses, for example, owned a coal mine during the 1890s employing 128 Indians. Chief Moon, a Blood, was in the hay contracting business, successfully competing for contracts with White ranchers. Big Swan, a Peigan, and Coyote from Hobbema operated stopping houses. The brief suggests that changing attitudes in the Department of Indian Affairs in the early 1900s stifled the initiatives, forcing instead the sale of "unused" lands, and the breaking up of reserves. It was during this period as well that "trust funds" that resulted from these sales were used for the education and welfare of the respective reserves. Gorman felt, and strongly stated these feelings to the Committee, that this was in breach of the Treaties and normal conditions of trust. She saw the Department as engaged in ever tightening their control of the reserves with the amendments to the Indian Act in 1919 being particularly evil. The new amendments of that year encouraged enfranchisement by offering those who did choose it, 10 years of treaty payments in one lump sum. As she pointed out – if to 1919 only 102 First Nations had ever "chosen" enfranchisement, since 1919, only 487 "chose" it.

As a whole the brief was an extraordinarily powerful one – one that should have induced shame and did from some, although not all, of the committee's members. Senator Hugh Horner was hardly sympathetic and there were other members as well who were always careful to compare the rights of native people with those of the rest of Canadians. Gorman repeatedly pulled the committee back to the reality of the Treaties and the realities of marginalization. John Samson put it clearly

> We want our people to progress, but not at the expense of our basic rights as treaty [sic] Indians. We feel that it should be possible for use to be able to live on an equal footing with the white [sic] man, without having to give up

our right to live on our reserves if we so wish or to lose our
legal status as treaty [sic] Indians."[8]

The word "enfranchised" caused the committee, as it did many
Canadians, confusion. It meant "liberation" to some, forcible removal
from the reserve to live unsupported without Treaty in the White man's
world, but to many Canadians it meant getting the vote. In some
provinces, First Nations already had the vote, and in the Dominion
Elections Act, First Nations are allowed the vote provided they subject
themselves to the payment of taxes.[9] It became abundantly clear, however,
to the committee that First Nations would refuse the vote until Section
112 was removed. To them the word signified those clauses in the Indian
Act, that if enforced would cause them to lose the protection of the
Treaties, their homes, and their families.

While the whole enfranchisement issue was one that dominated the
discussions, another issue that preoccupied Ruth Gorman was the status
of Aboriginal women, who were marginalized by the Indian Act. Married
women were the responsibility of their husband's reserve, as were their
children. However, unmarried women and their children were the
responsibility of the mother's reserve. Decisions as to whether to marry
became economic. In the case of Hobbema, for example, the illegitimacy
rate was high simply because it would be to the economic benefit of any
Hobbema woman's children and husband to be able to continue to
secure her monthly trust income. Amendments were suggested to ensure
that the husband would continue to be responsible for the children upon
abandonment. Gorman was also concerned that Aboriginal women who
married White men should be able to return to the reserve should the
marriage fail. There was also a considerable discussion about the interest
of White men in marrying Aboriginal women for their share of the band
trust funds. What these discussions did for the Committee was to bring
into focus the pain of governing every aspect of a people's life through
irrational, contradictory, and poorly thought out legislation and
bureaucratic processes. Discussion of education, business financing, and
fish and game policies offered similar imponderables. The Department
had its bureaucrats out in full force at the committee meetings and they
protected their interests well. Some found joy in catching Gorman out in
small details – but for the most part they avoided jousting with the
voluntary legal advisor to the Indian Association of Alberta.

There is much of Gorman the lawyer throughout the document,
particularly in the language. The issue of "trust" is one that she held

dearly and referred to often. She believed firmly that any sale of reserve assets, including land, should not be used for the social and/or welfare issues facing so many reserves. She felt that these were responsibilities that should be fully funded by the federal government out of general revenues. Capital expenditures to generate new income might be eligible – but even here she felt that there was a considerable obligation in the Treaties to provide this kind of support. What was clear was that the federal government's responsibilities should not be foisted off on band trust funds. Education was a primary concern that was well articulated by John Samson, who said "we do not want education that will turn us into second class white [sic] people; rather we want to become first class Indians." But the education they wanted was community based, not residential school based, and that could be had at neighboring Canadian schools if desired. They asked for equitable treatment with Canadians, but Gorman more than once interjected that she felt they should have more than equitable treatment. They wanted changes to general school curricula to ensure respectful treatment of Aboriginal peoples – but they also wanted the skills not only to be healthy in their own community and culture, but also in the wider Canadian culture should they choose their future there. In the end this committee report caused amendments to the Indian Act removing Section 112.

To Gorman, this was the revolution. Once democratic rights were available, she believed they would be exercised and in time, the Aboriginal people of Canada would assume control of their own destiny. If in the end she had any regrets, it was that reform had not moved quickly enough.

Gorman's journey of reform was a public one and not easy. Sometimes she would use words of her generation that could offend. For example as "mother" of the Cree she would use the phrase "my children." Any thought that this reflected prejudice on Ruth Gorman's part was painful to her. In her papers she recounts an event in the late 1950s in Banff. She was to attend a gathering of lawyers and arrived early. In an effort to promote Aboriginal arts, she wore (something she did infrequently) her full native costume that had been given to her by the Stoneys in 1937. She must have looked the part, because when she sat down to wait for her party, she experienced what every one of her Indian friends had many times over.

> I said to the waiter – may I have a cup of coffee and he said "get it yourself in the kitchen." So there I sat and suddenly

> I felt the strangest thing. I can only describe it as a subtle drawing away from me. I was left in a small circle of aloneness. My attempts at conversation received only short and quick replies. The backs were there and all against me. Suddenly I knew how the Indians felt. It is something you can't put your finger on. This aloneness, this subtle you're here but not really included was what my Indians had often tried to tell me in halting words – we miss friends talk.

Her feelings as usual were open and honest. She realized that tolerance would always be a struggle for all human beings, but that tolerance could be learned.

> I was fortunate. I acquired the gift of tolerance. I don't believe any of us are naturally tolerant. We appreciate ourselves and anything that differs from us creates curiosity and even fear, and unconsciously intolerance enters our life . . . we can do little to prevent the original flashes of warning "they are different" that is the basis of all intolerance. It's the smell, the touch of a dark hand, the . . . hair, the laugh, a joke we can't understand that create a constant state of insecurity. . . . Fortunately I had a mother and father who practiced tolerance.[11]

She counted Walking Buffalo as one of her real friends – a teacher and a humanist. She was once at an event in Banff and heard some intolerant comments from Canadians at the CPR hotel about the smell of Indians. She was furious and left the hotel to join her friend Walking Buffalo. Just as she was to relate what had happened to her, Walking Buffalo said, "White savages smell so bad." Gorman was somewhat taken aback, but asked him why. He said he found the use of cosmetics offensive, and that Canadians smelled of gasoline – of cars. But despite this smell, it would not change their humanity. It was from frank encounters like this that Gorman learned her approach to tolerance. Any group can be intolerant if it focuses on differences.[12] She also believed that intolerance could breed exploitation and marginalization.

All of Ruth Gorman's projects were connected by a singular devotion to correcting a major injustice. This tradition of championing the disadvantaged was one accepted, and indeed sought after by Western Canadian women of strong spirit.[13] There are several characteristics that emerge in Gorman's writing and in her life. First, she was intent on making her world a better place. Like other strong-minded women, she did not reject the domestic sphere, but smoothed it out and arranged it so as to ensure that there was time for "the fight." She was always aware of the necessity to balance the needs of her child and husband with her most recent cause. In her papers, there is frequent mention of her inability to attend a meeting, or of the need to return to Calgary to care for a family issue. She was often on the threshold of resigning from her position as unpaid solicitor to preserve her marriage and family. However, as with many strong-minded women, they were successful in part because of at least the partial support of their husbands. Certainly in the case of her work with the Indian Association of Alberta, she was assisted by her husband, who sometimes acted as the lawyer of record when she could not. What Gorman shares with the female radicals of her time is her devotion to human rights, and to fairness and justice. What she also had in common with many strong-minded women of her generation is her strong drive to write and to share her experiences. One senses too in Gorman's writings, whether in her manuscript biography of John Laurie or in *My Golden West*, a continuous struggle to break out of the restrictions of class and convention. Her writings on marriage in *My Golden West*, for example, give a sense of "suffocating confinement."[14] But in the end the conventions were so strong, that she confided that the reason she did not write her own autobiography and chose John Laurie as her vehicle was that "it would seem to be boasting" and would seem to take away from a man's contribution.

Gorman was fully involved in a man's world; indeed she stands continuously on the "threshold of a man's world," always looking over her shoulder at what she doesn't want to leave behind. While Gorman certainly acknowledges the Calgary Local Council of Women, in her writings they are cast in a supportive role. It can be argued that Gorman herself was the ultimate "supporter." As unpaid solicitor for the Indian Association of Alberta, of which John Laurie was front and center, she had the supporting role. Yet there is considerable frustration in this self type-casting. She knew that it was her expertise, vigor, and sense of injustice that won the day. He had the need; she had the professional skills. There is no doubt, however, that she was the key strategist, frustrated at a number of points by the unwillingness of men to recognize her mind and support. She handled an Aboriginal anti-feminist outburst at a key Hobbema strategy session, as culturally-based. She put her own outspokenness to her training as a "lawyer." She was aware from her law school days that she was often a "token woman" amongst men, but knew that she would succeed because she was more able than they were.

Gorman was of that generation of women who, for the first time, did not have to rely on professional men as their advocates. Perhaps this tension contributed to her personal difficulties. Gorman did eventually break out of the mould set for her by the professional male patriarchs. After Laurie's death, she became her own advocate. She was the key spokesperson at the 1960 Parliamentary hearings for a group of men. It is in *My Golden West* that Gorman found her own distinct voice again, pushing what she thought were the boundaries of her community and culture. Her personal papers are rich and give incredible depth of the life of a Calgary professional woman living on the threshold of what was acceptable to her gender in her day, and the radical alternative. While she saw herself as pushing the boundaries, and the nation certainly recognized that through her many awards, these same awards were provided by the nation's establishment.

Notes

1. Douglas Sanders, "The Queen's Promises" in Louis Knafla ed., *Law and Justice in a New Land: Essays in Western Canadian Legal History* (Toronto: Carswell, 1986), 104.

2. Gorman Papers (private), 1937 newspaper clipping from *Calgary Albertan*. For a narrative autobiography, see Marjorie Norris, *A Leaven of Ladies: A History of the Calgary Local Council of Women* (Calgary: Detselig, 1995), 231-262.

3. Norris, *Leaven*, 197.

4. Sanders, *Queen's Promises*, 127.

5. Glenbow Archives (G. A.), Gladstone Papers (G.P.), M7811, File 2 Verbatim copy of Minutes 21-20 November 1959.

6. G. A., G.P., M7811, File 2, Verbatim copy of minutes 21-20 November 1959.

7. Ibid.

8. Canada, Parliament, Third Session – Twenty-fourth Parliament, 1960. Joint Committee of the Senate and the House of Commons on Indian Affairs, Minutes of Proceedings and Evidence, 131.

9. *Ibid.*, 132.

10. Gorman Papers (private), File Autobiography, "Tolerance."

11. Ibid.

12. Gorman Papers (private), Tolerance file, n.d.

13. C. Cavanagh and Randi Warne, *Telling Tales* (Vancouver, 2000), 21.

14. J. Conway, *In Her Own Words* (New York, 1999), xi.

Shall We Dance?
Jack and Wahnita Penley
by J. Kenneth Penley

From the J. Kenneth Penley Collection.

Wahnita Barker[1] had an early aptitude for music and was playing piano quite well by age six. Her teacher in Bridgeport, Connecticut, advanced her to accompany a violinist and cellist. When she was eight years old, a chance meeting at a school crossing was perhaps a turning point in her life. She and her friends were each handed folded notes which invited the holder to attend a dancing school class as an observer. Curious, Wahnita attended, was captivated by what she saw and asked her mother, "May I have dancing lessons?"

Thus Wahnita was launched on a career in dancing. Despite her youth, she proved to be adept at learning the lessons, and the teacher noted her ease in understanding as well as performing them. The social dances of the time were taught: the waltz, two step, polka, and some square dancing. Social etiquette, poise, deportment, and carriage were taught as well. Wahnita soon moved on to what was then called "Fancy Dancing," the foundation of which was based on ballet techniques. Exciting and exotic Spanish dancing with the full-skirted costumes

Wahnita Penley. From the J. Kenneth Penley Collection.

especially appealed to Wahnita. Soon she was assisting her teacher with some of the slower learners among the pupils. At age 11, Wahnita attended evening classes with her mother and took ballroom dance lessons. She was soon assisting her teacher with these as well.

Wahnita and a partner opened a dancing school in Bridgeport. This met with great success and confirmed for her that teaching dance should be her career. At just 16 years old, she enrolled in a summer school for ballroom dance teachers in New York city. She and her mother got a room and off to lessons she went. The school held a social dance to welcome the new students, with one of New York's best dance orchestras providing the music. Unfortunately, Wahnita didn't know anyone there and, although very anxious to be up and dancing, she didn't have a partner. Then a gentleman approached Wahnita and said, "My name is John Penley. Would you care to dance?"

John Penley[2] was the fourth of 10 children in the Penley family of Orillia, Ontario. In 1907 the family decided to try farming in Saskatchewan, so John, his father, and John's three older brothers left to find land and prepare a home for the rest of the family. With settlers effects they travelled by rail to North Battleford, then trekked with four oxen some 80 miles to a site near Kelfield. While living in a tent, they built a sod house 14 by 24 feet. Mother Penley and the rest of the family joined them the next year and they all lived in the sod house for the next four years. The older boys and their father filed on land and John proved up his quarter section, breaking the land behind a team of oxen. For extra income he worked in lumber camps in the winters as he had done in Ontario.

In 1912 John took a vacation, intending to go to Banff. His funds ran out when he reached Calgary so he took a job in Cashman's clothing store. Whether he had intended to return to Kelfield or seek a new life in Alberta, we do not know, but Calgary became his home for the next 44 years.

It was during his first year in Calgary that dancing began to figure prominently in his life. John took ballroom dancing lessons from a Professor Christopher Robinson. He progressed to become an assistant instructor, then later became Robinson's partner, and still later bought the business at 917 - 14th Ave. SW. He retained the Robinson name for the school for about a year, then moved to the downtown area, renting the Hickman Hall, located on the second floor at 334a - 8th Ave. SW. John changed the name to Penley's Academy. In addition to dance instruction, he held public dances in the 50 x 50 foot dance hall. These were evidently prosperous times in the growing city. John thought he should keep up-to-date with the latest dance steps and teaching methods, so in the summer of 1917 he enrolled in a dancer's normal school in New York city.

One evening at a social dance for the students, he approached a young woman who was not dancing, introduced himself, and asked for the pleasure of a dance. The woman was Wahnita Barker. They danced well together, not just that evening, but for the remainder of the course and thus became better acquainted.

John told Wahnita what a wonderful place Calgary was and asked her if she would come to work for him. Wahnita had little idea of where Calgary was, nor did she know much about Mr. Penley. The chief instructor spoke well of Mr. Penley but had only known him at the classes. However, a Mrs. MacDonald and her daughter Marie, who taught dancing in Calgary, were also in the class and gave Mr. Penley a high recommendation. This was reassuring but the fact remained that Wahnita was still in high school and felt she was too young to accept.

The two corresponded the rest of that year and in December, John proposed marriage in a letter. Wahnita replied that she was too young to consider marriage and thought a young woman should be 18 before taking such a step. John accepted that and while they continued to exchange letters, he explained that he was of the age to receive his call to the armed forces and was concerned that the business he had built would disappear if he left. In January 1918, Wahnita received a wire stating that John was sending two rail tickets and that she and her mother should come to Calgary so that she could take over the studio. He had his military call.

Wahnita and her parents thought it over carefully. Finally her father said he would stay with his job in Bridgeport while his wife and daughter accepted the offer in Calgary. If it didn't work out, they could return.

Wahnita said later she had so much to thank her parents for, as they more or less broke up their home to let their daughter advance her career.

After the long rail journey, mother and daughter disembarked at Calgary to find John on the station platform and some tall buildings nearby to reassure them that Calgary might be of some size. Rooms had been booked at the Palliser Hotel for a week until they could get settled. Wahnita was shown the Academy and introduced to some of the pupils and classes which she was to take over.

John again proposed marriage. He thought that it would be better in case he didn't return. Wahnita agreed to an engagement, so one day, while walking to the Academy, John met her at 8th Ave. and 2nd St. W., where the Lancaster building stands, and presented her with an engage-ment ring. The wedding took place in the manse of First Baptist church on March 25, 1918. That same evening they took the train to Winnipeg, where John was to have a test to see if he was suitable for flying as he had applied for Royal Flying Corps. He was accepted and Wahnita returned to Calgary.

The young bride, at age 17, was left in charge of the Academy and its public dances, and was eager to make a good job of it. She and her mother took a small suite next to the Academy. A bedroom window overlooked the rear of her place of business. One night, they were awakened by a loud crash, and saw glowing red through the window. Firemen urged them to vacate as the fire was next door in the premises beneath the dance hall. Before the fire was extinguished, it had burned a hole through the centre of the dance floor. Public dances and class lessons had to be cancelled and only a few private lessons could be held in another part of the building. Once again Mrs. MacDonald and her daughter Marie, although competitors, showed their kind friendship and offered Wahnita space in their facility, which was in the 900 block of 12th Ave. SW. Repairs were completed by the end of June, but during the summer season, public dances and most children's lessons ceased.

Things looked much better in September when the Fall season opened. Classes and public dances resumed and the young teacher felt she would be able to inform her husband how well the business was progressing when another severe setback upset her plans. The Spanish flu epidemic hit the country and Calgary. All public gatherings were cancelled and her income was effectively stopped.

John had been accepted and trained with the Royal Flying Corps at Camp Borden, Desaronto, and Toronto. He became a sufficiently skilled pilot to become a lieutenant instructor and the rest of the war was spent in that capacity in Ontario. He returned to civilian life in Calgary in December of 1918.

Nineteen nineteen was a busy year. The couple found a small bungalow on Sunnyside Boulevard, and after a motor trip to Saskatchewan to introduce Wahnita to his family, they began to establish their chosen profession and to make their mark together in Calgary. That year the Prince of Wales came to Calgary and they were among the guests who danced away the evening at the Prince of Wales Ball,[3] held at the recently built Mewata Armouries.

John and Wahnita again attended dancing school in New York during the summer of 1920, but two children born to them in 1921 and 1922 delayed any further such trips for a while.

Business was good in the 1920s. Jack Penley, as he was called by almost everyone except his wife, expanded to have a second dance hall on 1st St. SW between 12th and 13th Avenues, which he called the Central. Wahnita's father came to Calgary and managed that location. A disastrous fire closed that venture. Jack took over the Isis theatre nearby and installed a dance floor for a short period. It later returned to being a theatre.

Jack always closed the Calgary location during the hot summers but kept searching for good open air pavilions for cooler evening dancing. He operated such a dance at Bowness Park one summer, then had public dances and taught lessons in Banff during the summer of 1926.

At the same time, Wahnita was busy with her classes, instructing children and young women as well as helping with the ballroom dance lessons. Piano accompaniment for lessons was provided by Mrs. Bernard Choppen and then by "Ma" Trainor. Wahnita decided to perform this task herself, but Ma Trainor said she would not turn her job over until she heard Wahnita play. After a short audition, Ma said "You'll do." Wahnita thereafter played piano for her children's lessons with eyes on the students. She was often asked to have her pupils perform at public gatherings. A recital of her pupils' dancing skills was held each June for parents and the public.

The movie theatres in those days presented the public with live stage performances between showings of the feature films. The Capitol theatre often had the Penley's "Kiddies" dance on stage Saturday afternoons and the older girls' classes often performed during the evening shows. The manager of the Capitol, Mr. John Hazza, called Wahnita one day to say he had heard of a new dance called the Charleston and wanted it demonstrated during the evening show. Wahnita got about a dozen of her pupils together, they learned the new dance craze that day, and presented it with the accompaniment of a live orchestra. It was the first appearance of the dance in Calgary.

On another occasion, the movie "The Merry Widow" appeared at the Capitol and John and Wahnita were asked to dance the Merry Widow waltz on stage in the prologue. It was a hit and was remembered for years by many. Similar stage performances were also held at the Palace Theatre when manager Mr. Pete Egan desired to tie in a specialty dance with some movie. John and Wahnita were especially remembered for their fiery Spanish-style dances, replete with costumes. An example of this was seen on program at the Grand Theatre, sponsored by the Rotary Club. Mr. and Mrs. J. K. Penley performed the Espanita Waltz then the Argentine Tango,[4] Wahnita playing the castanets as they spun around the stage. They also introduced the Whoops-a-Daisy dance at the Crystal ballroom of the Palliser Hotel at the request of R. C. Thomas of the Wales Hotel who had seen the dance when he had visited England and Wales.

In 1929, a new larger building became available and Penley's Academy moved to 620 - 8th Ave. SW. There was a much larger dance floor with a full stage for the dance orchestra and several smaller rooms for private lessons such as tap dancing. A full size banquet room and kitchen were available in the basement. The Penley family had also recently moved into a larger home in the Belt Line district.

The Academy had some assistant dance teachers. They included: Robert Thoreau, Kathy McHugh, Irene McKinnon, and Peggy Smith. Jean Gauld had been one of Mr. Penley's assistants before Wahnita arrived. Mary Malcolm Forrest, a former pupil, later taught Scottish dancing. Daughter Nita Penley assisted her parents. Charlie Martin, a skilled tap dancer, taught at Penley's for several years. He and Wahnita often performed as a tap dancing duo.

Wahnita again went east to attend summer school classes and when she returned, John told her he had agreed that she and her pupils would collaborate with Jean de Rimanoczy and the Calgary Philharmonic Orchestra in an elaborate Russian Ballet. It was quite a task. Wahnita had to choreograph the dances, teach the pupils, design the costumes, buy the materials, and interact with the orchestral musicians. Jean de Rimanoczy had chosen music for the ballet in three scenes with "The Sea and Sinbad's Ship" from Sheherazade as the prelude and music from Tschaikowsky's "Nutcracker Suite" followed by Smetana's "Bartered Bride." The final scene was the "Ballet Russe" by Luiguini. The production was titled "One Thousand and One Nights." Wahnita had a cast that included all her young ladies, as well as pupils from other dancing schools in the city.[5] The performance was held at the Grand Theatre on three evenings plus a Saturday matinee. It was favorably reviewed and considered a success.

In the early to mid-1930s, Jack Penley rented the community hall at Chestermere Lake for summer jitney dances. They were well attended and quite popular except when the weather refused to cooperate. Several good Calgary dance orchestras played for the dances, but the best remembered was Vancouver's Mart Kenney and His Western Gentlemen, who attracted large crowds. One evening there were so many standing on the perimeter of the dance floor as Mart saw it, "the porch gradually sank out of sight with all the people on it."[6] Mart Kenney's orchestra then played for the Penleys through the fall season until New Year's Eve. The following year they attained national recognition, partly due to being heard on CBC radio.

The hard times of the Depression were felt. Some found that they couldn't afford to have their children take dance lessons and many adults stayed home from the public dances to save money. Lesson and admittance prices were lowered. The 1933 New Year's Eve frolic at Penley's, with the Mart Kenney Orchestra, horns, hats, other novelties, and a full-course hot turkey dinner, could be enjoyed for merely $1.50 per couple. The following night, New Year's Day, the same dance was offered, with a cold turkey dinner for just $1.00 per couple.[7] That same winter, the hall was rented to a club to sponsor a dance. The weather turned angry and not one patron showed up. The woman in charge was in tears. To his credit, Mart Kenney told her there would be no charge for his orchestra and Jack Penley followed suit with no rent for the premises. Times were tough.

Lessons continued. Many parents continued to send their youngsters for training. One wonders if they were hoping their daughter might be another Shirley Temple, or older children become as skilled as Mickey Rooney and Judy Garland. During the 1930s, the Hudson's Bay Company put on a Christmas show at the Grand Theatre which included a visit from Santa Claus. It was free to all children. Mr. Curll of the Bay asked Wahnita to supply her pupils for the stage show, which she did for several years. As well, the pupils entertained during Easter week for the

Children's Welfare arranged by Mrs. Harold Riley. Some of the stage shows combined the pupils of Penley's Academy and the Alice Murdoch School of Dancing.

About the mid-thirties, Jack Penley chose to have his summer dances at Sylvan Lake rather than Chestermere Lake. He rented the Varsity Hall and the venture was quite successful. He later purchased the hall, and his summer jitney dances and Sunday evening concerts were so well remembered that in 1999 the town named a new street *Penley Close* after him.

In Calgary, the Depression ended as the war started. The dance crowds and larger classes returned along with prosperous times. Jack bought the building that he had been renting. He later sold it to be developed as an office building, and perhaps he even meant to retire, but the young patrons asked, "Where will we dance? You can't close." So he reopened nearby at 609 - 7th Ave. for a while, until it too was sold as Calgary's business centre was moving further west. With his son-in-law Allan Bertram, who had the Al San Cabaret and lunch club, Jack jointly occupied a site at 5th Ave. and 3rd St SW previously used as the Packard automobile showrooms. Thinking of retiring, Jack was on Vancouver Island in 1956, considering a move to the warmer climate, when he died of a heart attack. He was 68 years old. His daughter 'Nita and her husband operated the public dances for a short time, but the days of the large dance orchestras and big ballrooms were over.

Wahnita continued to teach in her home, renovated for that purpose. As well, she went out to people's homes where small groups of six or eight couples wanted to learn new dance steps like the Cha Cha or Rumba. She wanted to teach until she had done so for 50 years, then stop, with memories of a wonderful career behind her.

Penley's Academy is remembered by many Calgarians for providing a venue with a reputation for a high standard of behavior. Proper dress was required and Jack kept a supply of suit jackets and ties for the gentlemen rather than have them suffer the embarrassment of being turned away. No alcohol was allowed and those seen by the doormen at the entrance to have a bottle, had it removed and checked for retrieval after the dance – much like a coat check. It was a carefree, yet safe environment for people of all ages. Parents were content allowing their young charges to attend dances at Penley's. Indeed, Wahnita and her children have often been told by former patrons that they met their future spouses at Penley's. One such meeting was described by Mary Mackay in her memoirs of Don Mackay, who later became mayor of Calgary:

"We met at Penley's, the fabulous dance centre which gave young singles the opportunity to meet under strict moral conditions and to have wholesome recreation. . . . Our church had their annual Ball and it was there that the Penleys introduced us."[8]

In 1990, The Calgary Exhibition and Stampede brought back the memories of those pleasant days by erecting a tent covered dance floor on the grounds and calling it Penley's Academy. As well, they had Mart Kenney and his Orchestra as one of three groups providing music for the dancers. Mart, who had said "Jack and Wahnita Penley were two of the smoothest dancers he had ever seen,"[9] attracted so many former and present fans that long line-ups resulted.

Jack and Wahnita Penley were an integral part of Calgary's early history. They were well known and respected in the city. Although not pioneers, they came to the city when it was young and made their mark. One was a farm boy who abruptly changed his life's direction and started a business with confidence in his own ability. The other was a teenaged girl who bravely crossed the continent to live in a strange country, a strange city, with a man she had only known slightly until then. They grew with the city and touched the lives of countless Calgarians.

From the J. Kenneth Penley Collection.

Notes

1. Autobiography of Wahnita E. Penley, audio cassette tape and written summary "The Dancing Penleys," Glenbow Archives, Calgary & Provincial Museum Archives, Edmonton, no. 87.309.

2. Ibid.

3. Wahnita's dance card and gloves worn, Glenbow Museum, Calgary; Rotary Club Minstrels program, 21-23 November 1921, Glenbow Archives and Library.

4. Glenbow Archives.

5. Photos of many Penley pupils may be seen at Glenbow Archives photography section.

6. Mart Kenney autobiography, *Mart Kenney and His Western Gentlemen*, Western Producer Prairie Books, Saskatoon, Sask. 1981.

7. Advertisement, *Calgary Herald*, December 1933.

8. Mary Mackay, Glenbow Archives.

9. Mart Kenney autobiography, 1981.

The Legend of Jimmy Smith

by Frederick Hunter

Many generations of Calgarians across the better part of a century have been familiar with or at least heard of the time-honoured chestnut concerning Jimmy Smith, which runs very much as follows:

In the autumn of 1890, so the story goes, an elderly Chinese coolie, discharged upon completion of the Canadian Pacific Railway some five years before, died alone and almost totally ignored in consequence of typhoid, in a room of the Royal Hotel. He was visited only by the Anglican Rector, the Reverend Alfred William Francis Cooper, to whom the dying man donated a good suit of clothes as a final gesture and token of gratitude, together with all his worldly assets. The amount, variously said to range anywhere from about $100 to some $600 or $700, was designated for the purpose of establishing a public hospital so that none again should ever have to suffer such hardship and neglect as he, or endure similar treatment and privation in future.

The traditional tale, however, leaves many additional questions unanswered, and in fact raises far more than it resolves.

For example, how could such an individual afford a hotel room, and, if he could, why could he not also obtain proper medical attention? Why would someone in his condition, afflicted with so dread a disease, be admitted to a hotel which, only four years earlier, had recoiled in horror at the prospect and refused admittance and entry to one of Calgary's most prominent citizens, barrister Fitzgerald Cochrane, when stricken with a fit of apoplexy, even though accompanied and personally brought to the hotel by one of Calgary's leading physicians, Dr. Andrew Henderson, with every assurance and promise of diligent care? What was a supposedly indigent resident of Calgary's Chinatown of that era doing with a fine suit worthy of an Anglican clergyman (who would probably not have worn secular clothing as a matter of course in any case)? Why was he known by an English surname and why is he buried in one of the most respectable parts of Union Cemetery (both most unusual occurrences at that period), despite the vehement anti-Chinese sentiments of the time – especially with his demise occurring just two years prior to the attempted armed extermination by Calgarians of the entire Chinese community for their spreading of another deadly malady, smallpox?

According to research requiring only a very few minutes on the sunny summer afternoon of Thursday, August 17, 2000, we can now confirm that in reality, the old account is essentially very nearly correct, (particularly in its main premise, that Smith did indeed die and did prescribe a bequest to the Hospital Fund), with distinct exception of the following few points: the event did not occur in the autumn of the year; he was far from aged; certainly not by any means disregarded or unvisited; did not die of typhoid or for that matter in a hotel room; and neither Canon Cooper nor any Anglican clergyman had anything whatever to do with the incident. The elements concerning the suit and the cash legacy also require additional clarification. Otherwise, the remaining details seem about right.

All such falsehoods being set aside, the real mystery lies in how, within such a brief span of time, so many peripheral distortions could possibly enter into the historic record short of, or without resort to, conscious and deliberate fabrication. In any event, the several circumstances described could scarcely be further from the truth.

James Smith, to accord him the name by which he was converted to the Christian faith, was a remarkably determined young man in his mid-20s with an uncommon desire to improve and prove himself, and to achieve success. He was Calgary's only Chinese settler of his time to fully adopt and embrace Western ways and styles, including surname, culture, and attire, as well as religion, whilst most of his countrymen preferred to keep to themselves in inscrutable isolation, which bred suspicion, mistrust, and contempt in the larger community.

For the past several years Jimmy had worked as a cook for "upscale" establishments at both Calgary and Lethbridge, including a stint at Calgary's famed Grand Central Hotel, and, with his engaging personality and excellent performance, had won high acclaim and regard, and gained much popularity and even more friends. With careful attention to personal affairs and finances, he had also managed to accumulate a fair nest-egg, and might even have been considered fairly well-to-do, especially by the standards of his own compatriots. This frugality was no doubt further facilitated and augmented by a significant lack of normal basic expenses, owing largely to his presumably receiving the customary, complimentary staff lodgings and meals at the hotel.

To a wide circle of Calgarians of the time, he was the exception to the rule, and the nickname or sobriquet "Jimmy the Chinaman" soon became a term of endearment rather than a derogatory epithet. Amidst all the tensions, with Orientals for the most part reviled, despised, and shunned, Jimmy Smith, by contrast, was truly respected and loved – indeed one might even say honoured – amongst his Caucasian contemporaries.

Taking ill with consumption (tuberculosis), it was to his trusted Occidental friends, and modern medical science and technology, as well as to his new-found God, that Jimmy chose to turn and adhere, rather than to traditional Oriental methods. This was quite unlike the reclusive smallpox carrier and his co-conspirators, who by their secretive conduct (regardless of efforts by modern apologists to whitewash the truth), directly spawned an epidemic which resulted in much misery and death and incited the infamous "Smallpox Riots" and the "Battle of China-town" only two summers later.

Jimmy's innocent faith in his friends was accordingly reciprocated and rewarded. He spent his final weeks at the home of Mr. and Mrs. Nelson James Hoad – Mrs. Elizabeth "Lizzie" Hoad being perhaps the earliest recognised practitioner of nursing skills in town. This couple (who themselves lie buried well within sight of Jimmy's final resting place, just across Spiller Road in Calgary's Burnsland Cemetery), eked out a modest living at many occupations along the way, she particularly at dressmaking, but they took on health care assignments whenever they could obtain them. Indeed, when the first General Hospital finally opened its doors a few months later, in November 1890, largely on the basis of Jimmy's legacy, it was the Hoads who were employed to administer it at a flat rate of $40 per month. They had complete charge of the primitive facility during its first four years of operation, with Mrs. Hoad as Matron and her husband as her assistant and, in effect, Orderly Officer.

Sadly, James Smith, despite this private nursing and the best available medical care by local physicians, succumbed at the Hoad residence on the sparsely-populated Section 16 in the extreme west end of the Townsite, expiring about 10:00 on Saturday morning, June 21, 1890. Jimmy was genuinely mourned by the general population of Calgary, a considerable host of whom turned out, despite the threat of rain, for his funeral at 3:00 the next afternoon. From the Hoad household, he was laid to rest on the hilltop at the old Calgary Town Cemetery at Shaganappi Point on Section 18, (now the site of Shaganappi Golf Course), then still slightly beyond the town limits. His high-quality casket supplied by Henry Yarlett, Calgary's original undertaker, was borne by six pallbearers, of whom three were Chinese and three were some of the little town's most distinguished men.

Ironically, although his interment was one of the last, if not actually the last, at the old Shaganappi Cemetery before its abandonment, one of those participating was a brother to his good friend the Reverend Angus Robertson, Calgary's first Presbyterian minister, who would himself – within barely more than two months – become the very first burial in the brand-new Union Cemetery.

Smith left a will executed by his solicitor, Senator James Alexander Lougheed, in which he devised the sum of $500 to a local friend and special gifts to three clergymen who had befriended him – two Methodists (George Jacques and John J. Leach) and a Presbyterian (James Chalmers Herdman). No Anglicans were included and contrary to popular legend, even the Reverend Canon Cooper (who was absent much of that summer) did not so much as figure amongst the beneficiaries.

After all medical, legal, and other expenses, however, the remaining balance was bequeathed by civic-minded and humanitarian Jimmy toward a more permanent Hospital Endowment. It was Jean Ann Drever Pinkham, the wife of the Anglican Bishop, who took a leading role in that enterprise and received the donation.

Initially the estate was estimated on a preliminary basis as amounting to perhaps some $1 500 to $2 000 in all. Later reports indicate it may have been valued somewhat substantially higher when all was said and done, with possibly as much as $1 500 or more being left over beyond other costs, clear and unencumbered, for hospital purposes alone.

Recipient of an expensive suit (which Jimmy probably possessed primarily for Sabbath services) was the Reverend George Jacques of the Methodist Church, father of Calgary's pioneer jeweller of the same name. However, Mr. Jacques felt disinclined to wear the suit until pressured by his wife into reluctantly donning it for a special gala dinner and lecture at the Opera House on Thursday, October 9, 1890, which he desired in particular to attend.

Once there, though, he quickly took exception and registered vociferous objection to the fact that smoking was not only permitted but actively engaged in by all save a half-dozen or fewer of the several hundred present. After excusing himself on several occasions to step outside for a breath of fresh air (consequently later complaining of having been forced to miss significant portions of the proceedings), the Reverend gentleman seriously considered prematurely leaving the function altogether. This threat he eventually carried out despite the substantial admission fee, lest the newly inherited outfit should become contaminated with the unsavoury odour of tobacco smoke – described by him as a "desecration!"

From this we may perhaps also infer that Jimmy Smith, like the Reverend Mr. Jacques, and unlike many of his own community, must have been a non-smoker of either tobacco or harder drugs.

Jimmy had further directed that his grave on the hill at Shaganappi should be surrounded by a stone fence. Given the closure of the cemetery at the Shaganappi site slightly over a month later, and his impending transfer to the new location, now Union Cemetery, it seems doubtful whether he ever received his wish. Certainly he has never had one in upwards of a century at Union, and now presumably never will, owing to present-day cemetery regulations. However, he did once have a tombstone, as might well be expected in view of his affluence and the size and extent of his estate.

In March 1922, the famous William Roland Reader, then Superintendent of City Parks and Cemeteries, reported that the marker was in such poor condition as to necessitate its imminent removal for safety reasons, and requested advice from the law firm of Lougheed and Bennett, successors to the original executors, as to whether they or the estate wished to have it repaired or replaced. Although we cannot now know precisely what form it may have taken, we may conjecture – and the implication appears to be – that the monument was fairly substantial, likely tall in nature with the potential of falling, or with precarious or fragile embellishments, typical of the era, which would be in danger of breaking and toppling. Sandstone, then so commonplace and popular but also so easily eroded, would seem the probable material, at least of the base if not of the superstructure as well.

The Honourable Sir James A. Lougheed himself replied the following month from his Senate office at Ottawa, with a response to the effect that all their old legal records and files had been destroyed in the disastrous fire in the Clarence Block some years earlier. Consequently Lougheed and Bennett had no official knowledge or recollection of Jimmy Smith.

Sir James, however, privately acknowledged personally recalling the case, and added that it was his belief that no funds had been left over or now remained in the firm's hands for such a purpose after final settlement of the estate, all having been properly allocated and disbursed according to instructions; therefore, with no finances on hand, there was nothing further he or his practice could do in the matter.

The result was the discovery that Jimmy Smith, recorded in the earliest Union Cemetery Register simply as "James Smith, Chinaman," lay, at the time of this original research, in an obscure gravesite, unmarked as well as necessarily unwalled, now in death truly alone and forgotten at last, as never in life. One was led to wonder, would not either the Civic or hospital authorities or the Chinese community in this day and age have thought it well to consider erecting a suitable memorial tablet or marker as a lasting tribute to one whose legacy formed the nucleus of an institution which has contributed so much comfort to so many ever since?

It seemed surely not too late in the Millennial Year of 2001, to regard this as yet another possible Millennial Project, or too early to consider planning it in commemoration of the Province's Centenary in the year 2005. With those thoughts in mind, approaches were made by an *ad hoc* group, the Calgary Cemeteries and Historical Commemorations Committee, to all those who might or should have had an interest in the subject, with surprisingly disappointing results. The City of Calgary, which had operated the original hospital, offered best wishes and neatly sidestepped the entire issue. The Provincial Department of Health, which administers the hospital's modern successor, the Peter Lougheed Centre, obfuscated by referring the question from one person to another within the Government of Alberta until the whole topic finally faded, then vanished into oblivion. The Calgary Regional Health Authority, the direct descendant of Jimmy's valiant efforts and inheritor of his heroic gift, callously and repeatedly made no response whatever.

The Chinese community, through its Sien Lok Society, generously volunteered the sum of $1 500, but in the end it was an entirely separate initiative by another independent group which led the way. Fittingly, the Alumnae Association of the Calgary General Hospital School of Nursing, likewise in a sense also heirs of Calgary's first hospital founded and funded by Jimmy's original bequest, ultimately took the principal role, inspired and spearheaded by an active member, Helen White.

Although the Nurses' Alumnae had first learned of the situation during a Union Cemetery tour also involving some of the same individuals affiliated or concerned with the original *ad hoc* committee, neither became aware of the others' plans for some months, and by the time the two groups finally discovered each other it was, unfortunately, far too late to pool resources, inasmuch as the nurses had already commissioned a monument and made tentative arrangements for its dedication. However, it was still possible to collaborate in other ways, all of which proved mutually beneficial and highly successful. Both groups breathed a collective sigh of relief that they had fortuitously come together with their co-ordination just in time to stave off a most embarrassing outcome – the *ad hoc* committee itself had been on the verge of ordering a marker of its own, and Jimmy had thus come perilously close and very nearly gone, almost overnight, as it were, from having no tombstone at all, to having two!

The memorial tablet, set in place in mid-July 2003, complete with Jimmy's name rendered in Chinese characters, was accordingly dedicated at a combined ceremony scheduled for 2:30 in the afternoon on Tuesday,

The official wreath placed by the Alumnae Association of the Calgary General Hospital School of Nursing, at the Dedication Ceremony, consisted of a band of red and a band of white, surmounted by flowers of gold. Red and gold were the colours of the School, and white signified a special symbolism in Chinese culture regarding death and funeral customs. Photo courtesy of the Alumnae Association, CGH School of Nursing.

September 9, 2003. A cloudy, cool day with a hint of rain was in the offing; however, forecasts notwithstanding, precipitation held off and even a slight glimmer of sunlight occasionally shone through, resulting in a splendid setting for the event after all. Some in attendance even remarked upon the appropriate nature of the weather for the occasion, reminding those assembled that the conditions at the memorial service were quite reminiscent of the descriptions of Jimmy's first funeral on a midsummer day some 113 years before.

At the cemetery yet one further surprise and cause for excitement was forthcoming. Amongst those present was Earl Joseph Salterio, retired banker, eminent numismatist and former president of both the Canadian Numismatic Association and the Canadian Paper Money Society. His great-granduncle, Joseph Salterio, had owned and operated the Grand Central Hotel during the time of Jimmy Smith's employment there, and had thus been Jimmy's employer. Joseph Salterio himself died only a couple of years later, on July 6, 1892, also of consumption, similarly at a very early and untimely age, and is buried not far away in Union Cemetery.

Joseph Lincoln Salterio perched on the lap of the Grand Central Hotel's Chinese cook, ostensibly Jimmy Smith. Photo courtesy of the late Earl Joseph Salterio, who died March 1, 2005.

Earl J. Salterio, to the amazement of all present, produced at the ceremony, an aged photograph in sepia tones extracted from his family archives. The photo depicted a baby boy on the lap of a nattily-dressed and distinguished-looking young man quite clearly and obviously of Chinese stock and stem. The child was Joseph Lincoln Salterio, born February 14, 1890, infant son to Joseph Salterio. He later became a Judge in Saskatchewan. The Chinese man was the cook at the Grand Central Hotel. According to family legend and tradition, the cook had requested permission to have the photo taken in order that he might send a copy to his relatives in China as proof of his success and the esteem with which he was regarded.

This rather irregular action would have been entirely characteristic of Jimmy, and the appearance of the individual in question further confirmed the truth of the legends. No doubt the suit in which he was photographed would have been the same which was afterward bequeathed to the Reverend Mr. Jacques upon Jimmy's premature and unexpected death only a few months later that very summer.

Until the publicity preceding the event, Earl Salterio had no real conception of the historical significance of the picture beyond his own family interest. Thus, remarkably, surfaced the only known likeness of Jimmy Smith, of whom it had been hitherto assumed no pictorial record remained in existence!

One final, equally intriguing point which came to light in the process, was that the photograph bore the imprint of the studio of "A. J. Ross." Alexander J. Ross (who is also buried nearby at Union Cemetery), holds claim to fame as one of Canada's most noteworthy pioneer photographers, owing to some of the other enduring historical works he happened to create in the course of his conventional business activities.

The same Alex Ross was responsible for arguably the most familiar and famous defining photo in Canadian history – that of the celebrated "Driving of the Last Spike" at Craigellachie on November 7, 1885. The renowned and oft-reproduced portrait of Chief Crowfoot represents yet another of his many credits.

Thus, accordingly, another popular myth bites the dust. Yet, by association, in more ways than one, and even in full light of the authentic facts now known, Jimmy Smith remains today all the more firmly entrenched and enshrined than ever as an intriguingly indelible part of the lore of old Calgary and of the Canadian West.

Jimmy, however, will perhaps be best of all remembered in perpetuity as the first member of the local Chinese community to make a significant and identifiable individual contribution to, and thereby leave his personal mark upon, the little settlement of Calgary and, by extension, the heritage of the entire Greater Calgary region.

Color Conscious
Racial Attitudes in Early 20th Century Calgary
by Donald B. Smith

Today Calgary celebrates its cultural diversity. Over the last few years the Calgary Multicultural Centre has organized many multicultural galas to promote understanding in the city. Other groups have sponsored similar events in our city, such as Asian Heritage Month, African Week, Native Awareness Week, Caribana, Latin American Week, and the One World Festival.[1] Today scores of ethnicities live side-by-side in Calgary, now a city of approximately one million, and one of Canada's most cosmopolitan metropolitan centres. What a contrast to look at Calgary nearly a century ago, when monoculturalism, rather than multiculturalism, prevailed. Putting the Calgary of the early twentieth century under a microscope reveals just how much change can occur over a nearly hundred-year span.

"The Coming of White Man." This sculpture portrays how the Indian was vanishing before the onrush of the 'superior' White Man with his agriculture, his railways, and his factories. While the Indian is represented as noble, he also appears incapable of surviving these new, life-altering conditions. Sculpture given by early Calgarian, T. J. S. Skinner to the Southern Alberta Pioneers; photo by Mel Gray; sculpture reproduced by permission of the descendants of T. J. S. Skinner.

The "kidnapping" of Mayor George Webster on the steps of City Hall, July 12, 1923. As part of the Calgary Stampede festivities, member of the First Nations in close proximity to Calgary "captured" City Hall. Chief Buffalo Child Long Lance holds the mayor's arm, while Acting Mayor Blackfoot Chief Running Rabbit stands to Webster's right. In an honorary adoption, the mayor was named Chief Crowfoot. Long Lance grew up in an African-American community in North Carolina, but presented himself as a Cherokee from Oklahoma when he first arrived in Calgary. Glenbow Archives, NA-2399-182

A century ago, race theory, a belief in the hierarchy of "races," enjoyed widespread support in North America. Many recognized scientists and social scientists initially endorsed the view that races varied greatly in innate intelligence and temperament. Race science was regarded as good science.[2] Only in the 1930s, as their disciplines further developed, did North American biologists and anthropologists come to reject race theory as an explanation of the character of peoples. By the mid-twentieth century scholars realized that social, political, economic, and geographical factors better explained human difference than biology.[3] "Race" has come to be seen as an "unnatural" category, one that is socially and historically constructed.[4]

Many individuals in early twentieth century Alberta accepted as self-evident the existence of "superior" and "inferior" races.[5] R. B. Bennett, leading Conservative politician, and law partner of Calgary's federal cabinet minister, James Lougheed, explained, for instance, in an address in 1914 why "we" ruled over other countries like India and Egypt:

> We are there because under the Providence of God we are a Christian people that have given the subject races of the world the only kind of decent government they have ever known . . . and you and I must carry our portion of that responsibility if we are to be the true Imperialists we should be. . . . An Imperialist, to me, means a man who accepts gladly and bears proudly the responsibilities of his race and breed.[6]

In the early twentieth century conventional wisdom, informed by the most advanced scientific opinions of the time, held that "races" were "evolutionary units, fixed in their physical and behavioural characteristics."[7]

Alberta historians, Don Wetherell and Irene Kmet, have concisely summarized the outlook of Alberta's dominant British Protestant community in the early twentieth century toward *foreigners*:

> Some 'foreigners' were judged to be less 'foreign' than others: those considered to be easily assimilable and willing to assimilate quickly, without fuss, were given conditional acceptance. It is true, of course, that those of non-European origin could expect no acceptance or access.[8]

Only one non-white group, in fact, enjoyed right of entry into the dominant society, those who were not *foreigners*: the original inhabitants of the country. But the Native peoples gained entry only if they assimilated totally.

Racial preferences were stated openly in early twentieth century Calgary. In 1911, for instance, the Calgary Board of Trade (now the Chamber of Commerce) pronounced themselves against Canada allowing African-Americans as immigrants to Western Canada.[9] That same year *The Albertan*, the Calgary morning paper, bluntly expressed its opinion of non-Whites: "We do not want a colored Alberta . . . shut out all colored people from homeland rights. Close out the yellow man, the red man and the black man. They are not good settlers. They cannot become good Canadians."[10] Bob Edwards, the famed editor of the *Eye Opener*, also repeated the message of racial superiority-inferiority. On December 6, 1913, for instance, the *Eye Opener* railed against Canada, "allowing anyone to enter in, irrespective of color, race, creed, or ideals. It is permitting races to enter which cannot assimilate with the white race, and in so doing is retrograding."

Some Calgary businesses openly practiced racial discrimination, even though very few people of African, Asian, and First Nation background lived in the city. In 1921, Calgary's population numbered 63 000, of whom 52 000 (82%), or four out of five Calgarians, declared they were of "British" background. The remainder were of various European backgrounds[11] with only slightly more than 1% of the total population, "non-White." Although only 729 Asians, 22 Native People,[12] and 66 African Canadians,[13] lived in Calgary in 1921, the racial barrier was up. In 1914 the Sherman Grand Theatre prevented a man of African descent from occupying a seat on the main floor of the theatre.[14] Three years earlier, *Calgary. Sunny Alberta. The Industrial Prodigy of the Great West* (1911), a promotional book, included an ad for the brand-new King George Hotel, which advertised its "Whites-only" policy. The hotel emphasized that, "their service is first class in every particular, none but the most skilled and experienced white help being employed in all departments."[15] Similarly the Empress Hotel in the World War One years hired "white help only" for their restaurant's kitchen;[16] as did the popular Tea Kettle Inn, which opened in 1922, on 7th Avenue, opposite the Hudson's Bay store.[17] Resentment against racial discrimination ran deep amongst its victims. Louie (or Luey) Kheong, a well-respected merchant who had established Calgary's first Chinese grocery store in the mid-1890s,[18] spoke out against racial discrimination in a letter to the *Herald* in October 1910: "You send missionaries to our homes in China, and we use them good; also English business men. If my people are no good to live here, what good trying to make them go to Heaven? Perhaps there will be only my people there."[19]

This wall sign, probably painted in the late 1910s, advertises the Gibson Cafe on Jasper Avenue, Edmonton. Note the benefits of the cafe: open all night, best service, and "White help only." This sentiment was echoed throughout Alberta at the time. Photo taken in late 1970s by Peter Macklon of Calgary.

Calgary's color-consciousness caused an unexpected controversy in early 1914. A local citizens' group began to meet to organize a bid for Calgary to host the International Sunday School conference in 1917. But discussion broke down on the question of the opening reception. Should there be one or two receptions for the visitors? George Dingle, chair of the council of 100, the organizing committee for the conference, recommended two separate receptions, one for Whites and one for the "Negroes, Filipinos, Indians, Mexicans, Chinese and Japanese." Committee member, Mrs. Maude Riley, then intervened with an appropriate question: "What will happen when we all get to heaven?"[20]

In all this racial cataloging in Western Canada, the First Nations occupied a special position. A remark by the Rev. Archibald MacRae, principal of the private Western Canada College and a Presbyterian minister, in his *History of the Province of Alberta* (1912), points to the dual image of the Aboriginal peoples. In his book the Calgary educator included this assessment of Native character: "The Red Man of the West has always been a difficult individual, he does not care to work, to beg he is not ashamed. In consequence he tends to become shiftless and vagrant. And yet, who can but sympathize with this passing race. The remorseless march of civilization demands his submission to its genius, or his disappearance."[21] As the American poet Longfellow described them in his "The Song of Hiawatha," these children of nature once had been admirable.

Unlike other non-White groups, however, First Nations people, as well as individuals of some North American Indian ancestry, might become White. In the United States individuals of any known African ancestry, regardless of how far back it was acquired, were classified as Black. No amount of White ancestry, except 100% European, permitted entrance to the White race. In contrast, in both the United States and Canada, one could admit distant North American ancestry and still be White. In Calgary it was well known, for example, that one of Father Albert Lacombe's great-grandparents was an Ojibwa from the Sault Ste. Marie area in Ontario.[22] But the public regarded the most famous Roman Catholic missionary in Alberta as French Canadian, not French Métis.

Non-Natives with distant genealogical links with celebrated First Nations people might also publicly declare them. During the Vice-Regal tour of Western Canada in 1900, Lady Minto made an astonishing declaration. On the Blood Reserve near Fort Macleod in September, 1900, the wife of Canada's Governor-General told the Bloods, in the words of Captain Burton Deane, "that she was descended from a famous Indian princess, Pocahontas." The Mounted Police officer continued: "They were not at all impressed by the circumstances, and as a matter of fact did not believe the story. An Indian is loath to believe what he cannot see."[23] On his subsequent visit to the Blackfoot Reserve Lord Minto, proud of the fact, apparently repeated that his wife was, "a descendant of Pocahontas, the Indian maid who saved the life of Capt. John Smith, the discoverer of Virginia."[24]

In the early twentieth century the First Nations lived apart from the Newcomers. The neighboring Sarcee (Tsuu T'ina) from Fish Creek immediately to the south of Calgary; the Blackfoot (Siksika) at Gleichen, 100 kilometres to the east; and the Stoney (Nakoda) at Morley 50 kilometres to the west; visited Calgary, but they resided on their reserves, not in the city. Conventional wisdom held that in the near future the larger society would absorb the First Nations. As Dudley McClean, a *Herald* reporter, stated in 1923: "It is a general belief that in the next two generations the inhabitants of the Indian reservations will be merely colonies of civilized people, principally farmers."[25]

Calgarians who believed in the possibility of assimilating the First Nations could point to the example of the handsome, well-spoken, well-dressed Sylvester Long Lance, a self-identified Cherokee from Oklahoma.[26] The World War veteran worked as a reporter for the *Calgary Herald* in the early 1920s and made many friends in the city. But his reception differed from that given to the First Nation people of the area. Those Native people who remained apart faced great prejudice. Diamond Jenness, the renowned Canadian anthropologist, visited Southern Alberta frequently after the First World War. He later recalled that farmers around Calgary in 1921 paid "$4 a day to immigrant harvesters of Polish and Ukrainian nationalities, but to Indians working in the same fields only $2.50."[27]

While few, if any, individuals recognized under the Canadian Indian Act as "Indian" lived in early twentieth century Calgary, a small number of Métis people did. The ancestors of these Calgarians of French and Native background had helped to build the original North West Mounted Police fort in 1875. But a number of the French, and some English Métis, or "Half Breeds," to adopt contemporary usage, remained separate. Standing apart, they felt the resentment of the majority, which included some of their own people. Mary Lee, a Calgary Métis woman, recalled years later her memories of attending the Midnapore public school in the mid- and late 1920s:

> We encountered racial discrimination from the students, but not from the teachers. I still remember the jeers of 'Nitches,' 'gawd damned Sarcees,' and other obscenities that were shouted at us by our tormentors, as well as the viciousness that goes with discrimination in its rawest form. Probably the most pathetic part of this whole horrible experience was the fact the children who tantalized us the most were themselves Scottish-French Half-Breed, who denied their Indian ancestry.[28]

A small number of those of British and Aboriginal parentage, individuals who belonged to old elite fur trade families, had fully adopted British Protestant values. They belonged to the centre, not the periphery of Calgary society. Belle Hardisty Lougheed, regarded as the first lady in early twentieth century Calgary society,[29] headed this group. As a Scottish traveller, Elizabeth B. Mitchell noted in her overview of the prairie provinces, *In Western Canada before the War* (1915), "in old-timer settlements, important citizens have often much Indian blood."[30] The daughter of a Hudson's Bay Company Chief Factor in the Mackenzie River Valley, Belle had North American Indian and British ancestry on both parents' sides. Her own mother, and several other family members, then living in Manitoba, applied in 1900 for Métis scrip, a cash or land payment, given to descendants of European and First Nation unions. In their applications they identified themselves as "Half Breeds."[31]

Belle's first cousins, Richard, Percy, and Eliza Hardisty, added a new layer of complexity to this story of racial self-definition. They were the children of Richard Hardisty, the English Métis chief factor of the Hudson's Bay Company at Fort Edmonton, and his wife, non-Native Eliza McDougall, the sister of the Ontario-born Methodist missionary John McDougall. On the basis of their father's ancestry, the Hardistys applied for, and obtained, Métis scrip.[32] Although they obtained scrip, they identified themselves as "White." Richard was known as "the first white child born in Rupert's Land,"[33] and his sister Eliza "the first white girl born in Alberta."[34] The veteran fur trader Isaac Cowie offered his own explanation for this choice of identity in his account of the Western Canadian fur trade, *The Company of Adventurers* (1913): "New-coming recruits from Scotland intermarried with the mixed offspring of their predecessors, and the prepotency of the strong Scottish strain soon tended to make the term "halfbreed" a misnomer in the case of those who were chiefly of British extraction."[35]

To add another nuance to the "racial" composition of Belle Hardisty Lougheed's family, she had a first cousin on the Hardisty side, Mary Faries Dokis, who was a legal Indian, a status Indian under the Indian Act. Belle's aunt, Hannah Hardisty, married Walter Faries. Their daughter, Mary Faries, Belle's first cousin, married William Dokis, a member of the Dokis Ojibwa band on the French River west of Lake Nipissing, in Ontario.[36] Through her marriage she gained legal recognition as an "Indian." Hence, Belle had biological first cousins who were White, and at least one who was a legal Indian.

Given what Calgary historian Jack Peach, who grew up in Calgary in the 1910s and 1920s, once called early Calgary's "unbridled racism,"[37] some individuals of Native ancestry who lived prominent lives in Calgary did not advertise their heritage. Edmund Taylor, Belle Lougheed's husband's chief investment partner, who joined him to form the brokerage firm of Lougheed and Taylor in 1911, was part North American Indian. Edmund's parents, like Belle's, both belonged to well-known "Hudson's Bay Company families." Edmund Taylor's family apparently felt comfortable with the description of English-speaking Métis as members of "Hudson's Bay Company families," (as the phrase appeared in his obituary). After receiving a good education, young Edmund entered the Hudson's Bay Company (HBC), and rose to become manager of the store in Calgary in the 1890s, and later general manager of the company's department store in Winnipeg. He left the HBC in 1906 for five years to explore the financial world in Toronto. The formation of an investment partnership with Belle's husband, Senator James Lougheed, brought him back west.[38]

According to the available documentation Belle Lougheed provides the best example of racial self-definition in the city a century ago. Belle Lougheed, the chatelaine of Beaulieu (the Lougheed's sandstone mansion), headed Calgary society. At the school she attended in the mid-1870s, the Wesleyan Ladies' College in Hamilton, Ontario, a fellow student believed her to be, "the daughter of an Indian chief."[39] In Calgary, Belle's Native background was well-known, in fact, the popular writer Chief Buffalo Child Long Lance, known before his honorary adoption by the Bloods in 1922 as Sylvester Long Lance,[40] included her in a list he prepared of prominent Western Canadians of some North American Indian heritage: "Some of western Canada's best citizens are of Scotch and Indian descent. Lady Lougheed, wife of Sir James Lougheed, minister of the interior, is a half-breed. So are Brigadier General H. G. MacDonald, CMG, DSO, and D. H. MacDonald, member of the Saskatchewan legislature. James McKay, chief justice of Saskatchewan, is of Scotch and Cree descent, as are many others holding responsible positions in Canada."[41] Yet Belle identified publicly with the European, not the Native, side of her ancestry.

The dominant society in Canada a century ago believed in a racial hierarchy. The 1901 census was quite clear about how federal enumerators should record racial background. Skin-color determined it. The "Instructions to Officers" noted that: "The races of men will be designated by the use of 'w' for white, 'r' for red, 'b' for black, and 'y' for yellow." The instructions expanded upon this point:

> The whites are, of course, the Caucasian race, the reds are the American Indian, the blacks are the African or Negro, and the yellows are the Mongolian (Japanese and Chinese). But only pure whites will be classed as whites; the children begotten of marriages between whites and any one of the other races will be classed as red, black, or yellow, as the case may be, irrespective of the degree of colour.[42]

No doubt here about who occupies the highest rank. White comes first. The adjective "pure" only describes the White race.

Belle listed herself in the 1901 census as White,[43] the group she identified with most. Understandably this influential and powerful woman who stood at the very top of the social hierarchy in Calgary, did not request inclusion under the fifth category: "Persons of mixed white and red blood – commonly known as 'breeds' – will be described by the addition of the initial letters 'f.b.' for French breed, 'e.b.' for English breed, 's.b.' for Scotch breed, 'i.b.' for Irish breed. . . . Other mixtures of Indians besides the four above specified are rare, and may be described by the letters 'o.b.' for other breed."[44]

In her lifetime Belle had seen the high-ranking fur trade families of mixed First Nations and European ancestry drop in status. Many descendants of Western Canada's old fur trading elite now kept silent about their Aboriginal ancestry. A racially-obsessed society now color-coded everyone. Obviously Belle knew that many Calgarians were aware of her mixed ancestry; but in conversation with writer Elizabeth Bailey Price, Belle did not mention it, nor did Price bring it up. Culturally, Belle belonged to White society, and that is how she identified herself.[45] Yet, if asked whether or not she knew the steps of the Red River, the dance so closely associated with the fur trade and the Métis people, she replied that she did.[46]

Thanks to her position as the wife of James Lougheed, early twentieth century Calgary's most powerful business and political leader, and her role as the leader of Calgary society, Belle Lougheed escaped being color-coded. Others of some North American Indian ancestry, like Edmund Taylor, also did so. Few Calgarians with any African or Asian ancestry were so fortunate.

Racial discrimination remains a major issue in early twenty-first century Calgary. Much work must still be done to fight it. But, in contrast to a century ago, Calgary has become a more tolerant society. Significant developments have occurred. Today one in every four Calgarians belongs to a visible minority.[47] Young Calgarians grow up amid diversity. A society free of hatred, prejudice, and discrimination remains a long way in the future, but certainly we have moved ahead from Calgary's color-coded beginnings.

Notes

1. Vettivelu Nallainayagam, "Festival Celebrated One City, Many Worlds," *Herald*, 23 September 2003.

2. Maureen K. Lux, *Medicine That Walks: Disease, Medicine, and Canadian Plains Native People, 1880-1940* (Toronto: University of Toronto Press, 2001), 7.

3. Constance Backhouse, *Colour-Coded. A Legal History of Racism in Canada, 1900-1950* (Toronto: University of Toronto Press, 1999), 6.

4. Thomas F. Gossett, *Race. The History of an Idea in America* (Dallas: Southern Methodist University Press, 1963): 373, 410; Elizabeth Jameson and Susan Armitage, "Editor's Introduction," in *Writing the Range: Race, Class, and Culture in the Woman's West*, eds. Elizabeth Jameson and Susan Armitage (Norman: University of Oklahoma Press, 1997), 6.

5. Howard Palmer, *Patterns of Prejudice: A History of Nativism in Alberta* (Toronto: McClelland and Stewart, 1982), remains the classic study of ethnic prejudice in Alberta.

6. R. B. Bennett, speech in Toronto, 24 May 1914; quoted in Carl Berger, *The Sense of Power: Studies in the Ideas of Canadian Imperialism, 1867-1914* (Toronto: University of Toronto Press, 1970), 230-231.

7. James W. St. G. Walker, *"Race," Rights and the Law in the Supreme Court of Canada: Historical Case Studies* (Waterloo: Wilfrid Laurier University Press, 1997), 14.

8. Donald B. Wetherell with Irene Kmet, *Useful Pleasures: The Shaping of Leisure in Alberta 1896-1945* (Regina: Canadian Plains Research Centre, 1990), xxi.

9. "Negroes Not Wanted In Province of Alberta. Calgary Board of Trade Endorses the Edmonton Resolution to Exclude Negro," *Albertan*, 20 May 1911.

10. "Keep the Negroes Out," *Albertan*, 6 April 1911; ; cited in David Bright, *The Limits of Labour: Class Formation and the Labour Movement in Calgary, 1883-1929* (Vancouver: University of Calgary Press, 1998), 44.

11. Max Foran, "Table VII: Ethnic Origins of Calgary's Population, 1901-1961," *Calgary: An Illustrated History* (Toronto: James Lorimer, 1978), 178.

12. *Ibid.*

13. Howard and Tamara Palmer, "Urban Blacks in Alberta", *Alberta History*, 29, 3 (Summer 1981), 9.

14. Howard and Tamara Palmer, "Urban Blacks in Alberta," *Alberta History*, 29, 3 (Summer 1981), 9; "A Colored Man Sues a Theater," *News Telegram*, 17 February 1914; "Will Discriminate against Negroes," *Albertan*, 10 February 1914; "Colored Man is Suing Theatre For Refusal to Grant Admission," *Herald*, 3 March 1914; "Negro Gets Damages from Local Theatre," *Albertan*, 26 March 1914.

15. "The King George Hotel," *Calgary, Sunny Alberta: The Industrial Prodigy of the Great West* (Calgary: Jennings Publishing Company, 1911), 182.

16. Fred Albright to Evelyn Albright, dated Calgary, 26 October 1915. The Albright Letters, transcribed by Lorna Brooke, available on the web: [http://ca.geocities.com/echoinmyheart@rogers.com]; for a contemporary description of the Empress see: "The Empress Hotel," in *The Albertan, Calgary, The 100,000 manufacturing, building and wholesale book edition of the Morning Albertan 1914*, 79.

17. Margaret Howson, undated manuscript on the 1920s in Calgary in the clipping file, Glenbow Library, no page numbers. The reference to the Tea Kettle Inn appears in the section, "Where We Dined." The manuscript has this title on the cover page, "Section 35. Topic 1."

18. "Louie Kheong Returns to His Ancestors: Calgary Chinese Mourn Old Friend with Ancient Rites," *Herald*, 27 April 1939.

19. Luey Kheong's letter to the Editor, dated 6 October 1910, *Herald*, 7 October 1910; cited in Brian Dawson, *Moon Cakes in Gold Mountain: From China to the Canadian Plains* (Calgary: Detselig Enterprises, 1991), 51.

20. "Will Calgary Draw the Color Line?" *Albertan*, 15 March 1914,

21. Archibald Oswald MacRae, *History of the Province of Alberta* (The Western Canada History Company, 1912), 430.

22. "Was Most Famous of All Catholic Missionaries," *Herald*, 12 December 1916.

23. Captain R. Burton Deane, *Mounted Police Life in Canada: A Record of Thirty-One Years' Service* (London: Cassell and Company, 1916), 89-90.

24. Edmund Montague Morris, *The Diaries of Edmund Montague Morris: Western Journeys 1907-1910* (Toronto: Royal Ontario Museum, 1985), 119.

25. Dudley McClean, "Ancient and Tribal Customs Are Still Clung to by Fast Declining Race in Sun Dance," *Herald*, 25 August 1923.

26. For details on Long Lance in Calgary, see: Donald B. Smith, Chief Buffalo Child Long Lance. *The Glorious Impostor*. Revised edition (Red Deer, Alberta: Red Deer Press, 1999).

27. Diamond Jenness, "Canada's Indians Yesterday: What of Today?," *The Canadian Journal of Economics and Political Science*, 20, 1 (1954), 95-100.

28. Mary Madeline Lee, *The New Nation-Christ's Chosen People* (Calgary: N.p., 1987).

29. Brian Brennan, "Sir James Lougheed," *Building a Province: 60 Alberta Lives* (Calgary: Fifth House, 2000), 14.

30. Elizabeth B. Mitchell, *In Western Canada before the War* (London: John Murray, 1915; reprinted, Saskatoon: Western Producer Prairie Books, 1981), 34.

31. See the following scrip files in R. G. 15, Dept. of the Interior, Series D-II-8-c, National Archives of Canada, for: Mary Louise Hardisty Hackland, vol. 1350, reel C-14972; Frank Allen Hardisty, vol. 1350, reel C-14975; William Lucas Hardisty, vol. 1350, reel C-14975; Mary Allen Hardisty Thomas, vol. 1369, reel C-15006; Mary Allen Hardisty Thomas, vol. 1369, reel C-15006. My thanks to Pat Cleary of Vancouver for these references.

32. See the following scrip files in R. G. 15, Dept. of the Interior, Series D-II-8-c, National Archives of Canada, for: Richard G. Hardisty, volume 1350, reel C-14975; and Richard G. Hardisty for William David Percy Hardisty, vol. 1350, reel C-14975. On the application for scrip for Percy Hardisty a handwritten note appears at the bottom, "see case 3214 of 1900 allowed for sister Clara Victoria Hardisty."

33. Archibald Oswald MacRae, "Richard George Hardisty," in *History of the Province of Alberta* (2 vols., N.p.p.: The Western Canada History Co., 1912), 2: 890.

34. Elizabeth Bailey Price, "The First White Girl Born in Alberta," *Lethbridge Herald*, 23 October 1926; clipping in the Elizabeth Bailey Price Papers, M 1000, Glenbow Archives.

35. Isaac Cowie, *The Company of Adventurers: A Narrative of Seven Years in the Service of the Hudson's Bay Company during 1867-1874* (Toronto: William Briggs, 1913; Lincoln: University of Nebraska Press, 1993), 65.

36. Biographical information supplied by Charlotte Woodley, Hudson's Bay Company Archives, Provincial Archives of Manitoba, 18 July 2003. My thanks to Jim Morrison of Winnipeg for his earlier help with this genealogical information.

37. Jack Peach, "'Innocent' Labels of Past Mocking Jibes of Present," *Herald*, 16 December 1990, B6.

38. "Edmund Taylor Dies Suddenly Following Brief Indisposition," *Herald*, 3 October 1929. The phrase "Hudson's Bay families" appears in the article. Henry Klassen provides background on Taylor's business career in his *Eye on the Future: Business People in Calgary and the Bow Valley, 1870-1900* (Calgary: University of Calgary Press, 2002), 285-287.

39. Mrs. Louise E. Ramsay Purchase, "A Sketch of Janet (Nettie) T. Coatsworth Ramsay. Mistress of English Literature, 1875-1879. Hamilton Ladies' College," Archives File, Wesleyan Ladies College, Hamilton Public Library. My thanks to Jennifer Bobrovitz of Calgary for a copy of this memoir by Nettie Coatsworth's oldest daughter, written in May 1962, Albright Gardens, Beamsville, Ontario, May 1962. The original is in the Reference Department of the Hamilton Public Library.

40. Hugh A. Dempsey, *Tribal Honors: A History of the Kainai Chieftainship* (Calgary: Kainai Chieftainship, 1997): 33-34, 139.

41. Chief Buffalo Child Long Lance, "Indians of the Northwest and West Canada," *The Mentor*, 12, 3 (March 1924), 6.

42. Quoted in Backhouse, *Colour-Coded* , 3-4, 283-284.

43. Canada. Census of Canada 1901. Alberta. District of Central Alberta, 13. Microfilm reel: T-6550.

44. Backhouse, *Colour-Coded*, 283-284.

45. In an interview with Calgary journalist Elizabeth Bailey Price, Belle apparently made this remark to distinguish herself from the Métis: "In Calgary's early days it was almost impossible to get help. The squaws and half breed women were all that were available. They could wash but could not iron, and they were never dependable," *Saturday Night*, 16 September 1922. This quotation appears in the longer version of the article (which is printed unsigned, but is clearly written by Elizabeth Bailey Price as the typed copy of the story appears in her papers at the Glenbow Archives, Manuscripts and Clippings, 1920s-1950s, biographies, L-Z, Alberta," M1000). The shorter version, which contains many of the identical sentences used in the *Saturday Night* article, appeared in the *Herald*, 20 March 1922, Elizabeth B. Price, "Alberta's Women Pioneers Will Form Organizations."

46. Elizabeth Bailey Price, "Preserving the Red River Jig for Posterity," *Toronto Star Weekly*, 7 April 1928.

47. Pearl T'sang and Kerry Williamson, "Immigrants Reinforce Calgary's Fabric," *Herald*, 30 December 2003, B1.

Calgary and the Tsuu T'ina Nation
The Early Years, 1877-1887
by Patricia K. Wood

Some say, a long time ago, the Dene were walking on the land when a sea creature poked its horn up through the ice. A grandmother looked down and saw it and pulled it up, breaking the ice. The split left part of the group on one side of the open water and the rest on the other side, too far apart to reunite. The Tsuu T'ina (formerly known as the Sarcee) were part of the group that broke away and eventually came to live quite a bit south of the Dene, in what is now called Southern Alberta, probably about 400 years ago. The Blackfoot, Blood, Stoney, and Peigan also inhabited this area. Although linguistically the Tsuu T'ina are Athapaskan, and in many other ways distinct from the Blackfoot bands, they joined them in the Blackfoot Confederacy.

Two hundred fifty years later, after the Tsuu T'ina settled in the area, give or take, the Royal Canadian North-West Mounted Police marched into the region, which was inhabited by Blackfoot, Blood, Stoneys, and Peigan as well, and established Fort Calgary at the confluence of the Bow and Elbow Rivers. Within a year, in September 1877, the police helped orchestrate the signing of Treaty 7 with all these bands, and settled them onto reserves in the area. Almost immediately following the signing of the Treaty, reports to the Department of Indian Affairs testify to the destitution and poor health, even starvation, of the bands, including the Tsuu T'ina. In 1880, the Tsuu T'ina are reported returning from Cypress Hills "in small straggling parties . . . most of them on foot and starving."[1]

According to the terms of Treaty 7, the Tsuu T'ina were initially settled onto a reserve with the Siksika (Blackfoot), but the two did not get along well. Each group accused the other of thefts and other wrongdoings, and the Tsuu T'ina took to coming in and camping near Fort Calgary, and sometimes travelling all the way down to Fort Macleod, which the Department of Indian Affairs did not like. But the Tsuu T'ina insisted on their own land closer to the city of Calgary and through the diplomacy of their chief, Bull Head, in 1882 the Tsuu T'ina claimed a rectangle of three townships, approximately 70 000 acres, above and including Fish Creek (or Wolf Creek, as they call it), approximately 10 kilometres to the southwest of the emerging White settlement on the Bow and Elbow Rivers. The Tsuu T'ina had done some trading with early White settlers to the area, had worked for at least one farmer in the area, and were able to continue to trade with Calgary, which was incorporated as a town in 1884 and a city in 1894.

As with earlier treaties, one of the central purposes of Treaty 7 and its amendments was to establish the boundaries between Natives and non-Natives. The creation of separate spaces was to open up safe areas within which Whites could develop the West as they saw fit. Even after the reserves were surveyed and delineated with precision, Whites discovered these two spaces were not as mutually exclusive as they had envisioned. For many reasons, Natives did not remain on their assigned territory, particularly as many bands interpreted the treaties to mean that their ability to travel outside the reserves had not been removed. In addition, Whites sometimes discovered that there were resources on Native land that appealed to them. The Native and non-Native communities, then, were difficult to keep entirely separate in practice. The relationship between Natives and non-Natives, particularly in the case of Calgary and the Tsuu T'ina, was, moreover, a mediated one, with heavy involvement by the federal government. Their actions often proved a powerful determinant of the existence, frequency, and nature of contact between the town and the reserve.

The federal government quickly observed that the Tsuu T'ina's settlement onto the reserve near Calgary would not be successful in the ways they had hoped. Sir John A. Macdonald, Superintendent General of Indian Affairs (as well as Prime Minister), reported in 1882 that the Tsuu T'ina Nation was "too near the Rocky Mountains to admit of reliance being placed on their producing good crops." He felt the Stoney, on their reserve near Morley, were more "favorably situated" in terms of climate, and more "industriously disposed" as well.[2] The Indian Agent at Winnipeg, C. E. Denny, similarly concluded that the Sarcee were not thriving. On his visit in 1882, he found, "Their flour had run out some time and they were in consequence much dissatisfied. They had done little or no work, not having tools, and the agency itself being almost without any. They had only a few houses built."[3] Some officials worried the Tsuu T'ina would never be successful at farming, that their land was too poor and the area too vulnerable to summer frosts.

Other officials, such as the Dominion Land Surveyor John Nelson, were more optimistic. From his observations from surveying the reserve, he concluded, "The soil is remarkably fertile, as shown by the richness of the growth of pea vine and grass. There is a good supply of spruce and poplar timber." An additional resource he noted was the good amount of dry timber, which he felt the Tsuu T'ina could chop and sell to the Mounted Police at Fort Calgary.[4]

Concerns about agriculture and climate notwithstanding, officials were principally troubled by the short distance between the Tsuu T'ina and Calgary. Year after year, agents and bureaucrats at all levels raised this issue as a central preoccupation. In 1883, Macdonald considered the Tsuu T'ina to be the "least promising of any of the Bands within the territory covered by Treaty No. 7." Why? "The proximity of this Reserve to Calgary operates detrimentally, to their improvement, as they are continually visiting the latter place and neglecting their fields."[5] A Sub-Agent in Treaty 7, William Pocklington, agreed. "The great trouble with these Indians," he wrote his superiors, "is that they are too close to Calgary, and take every possible opportunity of going there."[6] Pocklington successfully requested to be stationed at Calgary so that he might better manage the situation.

Pocklington took pains to explain that the Tsuu T'ina were not imposing themselves on a disinterested population. While many Calgarians complained to Indian Affairs officials about the Tsuu T'ina's presence and asked for the pass system that was already in existence to be enforced, many others actively sought the Tsuu T'ina. This reveals the complicated nature of the emerging relationship between the two communities. Many Calgarians gave Tsuu T'ina money and food in exchange for performing chores, such as chopping wood. These employers were sufficiently pleased with the low rate of pay and the work being done that they would send "presents of tea and tobacco" to the reserve to encourage the workers to return to town.[7] Pocklington felt the resolution to the problem rested primarily in the hands of Calgarians:

> If the people of Calgary do not want the Indians, they have it in their power to keep them out. If, instead of getting them to do their chores for a small sum of money and a little food, thus encouraging them to stay, they refused to give them any assistance, the Indians would see they were not wanted and would seldom go there.[8]

The following year, Agent Magnus Begg echoed the frustration: "The people of Calgary complain of them, but still they continue to employ them."[9]

Clearly, the Tsuu T'ina wanted to avail themselves of the resources of the emerging town of Calgary. Tsuu T'ina men had been warriors and hunters. Although they rapidly improved their abilities in farming, it was nevertheless unfamiliar to them as a practice and as a lifestyle. Moreover, their impoverishment made any opportunity to earn money or food a matter of survival. Their population went into serious decline following Treaty 7. Even into the early twentieth century, as Tsuu T'ina councillor Bruce Starlight explains, the Tsuu T'ina were "in bad shape . . . very weak in those years."[10]

On at least one front, the Tsuu T'ina presence in Calgary was a mutually beneficial and welcome one. Those who employed individuals from the band continued to find their work useful and encouraged them to return. However, these engagements remained in a relatively private and in many ways controlled area: some Calgarians hired Tsuu T'ina for work at their homes or on their farms, where they were easily supervised and largely out of public view. We should not necessarily read a broader acceptance of the Tsuu T'ina on the part of these Calgarians in these exchanges. For there was a bigger, more volatile issue about the Tsuu T'ina presence in the public spaces of Calgary that greatly strained the relationship between the communities.

For several years, one of Macdonald's prime complaints about the Tsuu T'ina's frequenting of Calgary was the women. A typical report in 1884 argued, "The reserve occupied by this band is situated too near Calgary. The Indians resort constantly to that place, neglect their work, and many of their women pass lives of depravity in wretched tents or wigwams, pitched in proximity to the town."[11] Tsuu T'ina and other Natives frequently set up camp in the town and some of these camps were known to be sites of consensual sex, including prostitution. Individual women also seem to have made their way into town on what Pocklington called "the worst possible errands."[12]

Indian Affairs officials took several steps to end these activities. In 1883, the Deputy Superintendent General of Indian Affairs from Ottawa met with Tsuu T'ina chief and councillors to discuss the matter and, by his account, they shared his concern. The chief said that "he had even gone with carts and forced them to return to their reserve; but that they would no sooner arrive than they would be followed by evil disposed persons from Calgary and induced to return to that place."[13] The Farm Instructor working with the Tsuu T'ina was subsequently instructed to disregard his own farm and devote his energies completely to the band, as well as withhold the rations of those who left the reserve. When this proved unsatisfactory, Pocklington's suggestion of a resident agent was taken up. As Macdonald argued, "close supervision . . . is necessary for the successful management of Indians settled upon reserves in such close proximity to leading centres of white [sic] population."[14]

Indian Affairs thus subjected the Tsuu T'ina to tight control, effectively managing their relationship with Calgary, and the concerns about their travels into town disappeared almost overnight. In 1886, Macdonald reported his pleasure regarding the Tsuu T'ina's visits to Calgary, as their purpose was to sell goods from their harvest: "The Sarcee band, occupying the reserve southwest of Calgary, made during the year better use than they had theretofore done of the advantages afforded them by the possession of a fertile tract in close proximity to a good market."[15] Similarly, Macdonald's successor at Indian Affairs, Thomas White, believed that the town's presence nearby was assisting the farming success of the Tsuu T'ina. As he put it, "their proximity to a good market at Calgary . . . encourages them to raise more produce."[16]

Their resident agent, William Carnegy de Balinhard, had shed many of his fears about the Tsuu T'ina venturing into town and was effusive in his description of the benefit of Calgary's proximity: "The neighbourhood of Calgary enabled the Sarcees, to get clothing, blankets, & c., by the sale of their surplus potatoes, & c. This is their only means of obtaining money lawfully, as they hunt but little, and the fish does not amount to much. They have made marked progress in their general conduct, and I find them attentive and obedient to the advice given them."[17] The 1887 report of Alexander McGibbon, Inspector of Indian Agencies and Reserves, testified to the financial benefit of Calgary to the Tsuu T'ina: "They realized about $200 this year, selling the privilege of cutting hay on the reserve."[18]

Policing the border between the two communities went both ways. Some Indian Affairs officials were concerned that the land granted to Tsuu T'ina be protected from careless or unscrupulous White settlers. Some issues were just troublesome, such as when cattle and other livestock sometimes wandered into the reserve from neighboring properties. Other incidents were more serious: some men crossed the line to cut wood, including one who chopped as much as 80 cords before turning himself in, claiming he did not realize he was on the Tsuu T'ina's side.[19] Denny felt that the railway in particular was going to increase population pressures on Natives in Southern Alberta and anticipated that competition over resources would worsen their relationship with Whites. He reported in 1883 that "so far, the settlers who have come in contact with the Indians have treated them well and kindly, but as they get more used to them this will likely change, and unless the interests of the Indians are well looked after, they will go to the wall altogether and many petty depredations will take place."[20]

Whether officials sought to protect the Tsuu T'ina from Whites or preserve the racial purity of Calgary from incursions by Natives, they were always trying to keep the communities separate and control inter-actions between them. The fears of incompatibility, immorality, and miscegenation only amplified what was a common belief of the time, that Natives and cities were antithetical. As the work of Evelyn Peters has detailed, non-Native ideas about who lives in cities conflicted with non-Native ideas about Natives.[21] In the late nineteenth and early twentieth centuries, the newly emerging modern Canadian city prided itself on its very modernity. Even though Calgary was small compared to Toronto or Montreal, it was nevertheless growing rapidly. Being modern meant industry; it meant ever-taller buildings that were not made from timber; it meant a middle class visibly acquiring wealth, demonstrating it through urban fashions, clothes that were intentionally unsuitable for manual labor, especially farm work. Natives, on the other hand were viewed as the antithesis of the modern. It was widely assumed, in fact, that they would die out. They did not belong in the city.

This attitude prevailed for a long time, and came to dominate the relationship between the Tsuu T'ina and Calgarians. By the time Alberta became a province in 1905, the Calgary Board of Trade was (repeatedly) petitioning the Minister of the Interior to remove the Tsuu T'ina to a greater distance from the city, and to open up some of their land for White settlement. In the early years, however, there was still room for a more ambivalent relationship, with its share of tensions, in which the Tsuu T'ina's interests in Calgary were welcomed by the town's residents and mutually beneficial exchanges took place.

Notes

1. Norman Macleod to Dewdney, Department of Indian Affairs (DIA) Annual Report 1880, 97.

2. John A. Macdonald, DIA Annual Report 1882, xvii.

3. C. E. Denny, Indian Agent at Winnipeg, DIA Annual Report 1882, 169.

4. John C. Nelson, D. L. S., Indian Reserve Survey, DIA Annual Report 1882, 220.

5. Macdonald, DIA Annual Report 1883, lii.

6. William Pocklington, DIA Annual Report 1883, 86.

7. Pocklington, DIA Annual Report 1884, 88.

8. Ibid.

9. Magnus Begg, Indian Agent of northern division of Treaty 7, DIA Annual Report 1885, 75.

10 Interview with Bruce Starlight, 28 January 2002.

11. Macdonald, DIA Annual Report 1884, xlix.

12. Pocklington, DIA Annual Report 1883, 86.

13. Macdonald, DIA Annual Report 1883, liii.

14. Macdonald, DIA Annual Report 1885, xlviii.

15. Macdonald, DIA Annual Report 1886, lii-liii.

16. Thomas White, DIA Annual Report 1887, lvi.

17. William Carnegy de Balinhard, DIA Annual Report 1886, 135.

18. Alexander McGibbon, DIA Annual Report 1887, 184.

19. Pocklington, DIA Annual Report 1884, 88; Pocklington, DIA Annual Report 1883, 86.

20. Denny, DIA Annual Report 1883, 81.

21. Evelyn Peters, "'Urban' and 'Aboriginal': An Impossible Contradiction?" in: J. Caulfield and L. Peake, eds., *City Lives and City Forms: Critical Research and Canadian Urbanism* (Toronto: University of Toronto Press, 1996), 47-62.

Role Models for Today
Chinook Country Métis
by Louise Crane

Recently, several school boards in southern Alberta joined forces in creating an Aboriginal Mentorship Program to encourage youth staying in school. Unfortunately, they have fallen short of one-to-one mentors for the number of students. Studying the Chinook Country's history can help supplement this program. We only need to look at their family trees and community archives to find a whole host of positive role models. This chapter will tease you with a sampling of Métis heroes, entrepreneurs, scientists, and community builders who lived and worked in the Chinook country.

What is a Métis? For this purpose, it is mixed heritage – part Native and part non-Native. In their journals, the Oblate missionaries described Métis as having strong observations skills, sense of humor, intelligence, warm-heartedness, love of family, and hospitality. They were congratulated for bravery, horsemanship, endurance, and patience. Sam Steel remembered the "Half-Breed" in his book, *40 Years in Canada*, as excellent marksmen and hunters, and recounted weddings and holidays where they demonstrated their joy of celebration and competition. The Métis here are just a few examples of the many men and women who influenced the growth and changes in Southern Alberta.

Marie Rose Smith

This fearless woman definitely makes the mentor list. Her father was Urbain Delorme, a trader from St. Francois Xavier on the Assiniboine River. Marie Rose recounted this trip in her memoirs, *The Fifty Dollar Bride*. With her great gift of storytelling, much of the Métis way of life was preserved through her writing. She was proud to tell of her grandma Vivia and how she could still do native dance steps at a "great age."

Marie Rose wrote about her own early childhood and gave us examples of what it was to be Métis in the late 1800s. In 1871, she travelled with her family on a fur-trading trip across the plains to Tail Creek (near Stettler). There she met her husband, Charlie Smith, who apparently paid 50 dollars for her. They travelled to St. Albert for the wedding and were married by Bishop Grandin. After sharing their first year together on the prairie in Métis hunting camps, Charlie and Marie Rose settled on the "Jughandle" Ranch near Pincher Creek. However, "settled" may not have been quite the right word for her husband, even if it had been for Marie Rose. Charlie Smith was a hunter and trader, so naturally spent months away at a time. Marie Rose stayed, raised 15 children, and ran the ranch. This was no easy task for a woman to bear alone in what was then rugged territory, but even travelling was often a test of strength. One of the events Marie Rose wrote of in her memoirs concerned a trip to Winnipeg when it was necessary for her to settle some family business.

> Thus I made ready for the trip, heading toward Winnipeg, with a covered democrat,[1] 5 head of horses, a tent, the necessary clothing and food enough to last until I would meet my husband, somewhere on his route back.

Marie Rose had the company of three of her children, and for the first part of the trip, a neighbor as well. At Duck Lake, she met up with her sister and her sister's two small daughters, and together the two women and five children went on unaccompanied for the last leg of the trip from Flat Creek to Winnipeg. Many mothers of today can relate to Marie Rose's words, "What a night that was! Our little ones cold and hungry, cried all night without ceasing. Five little tired bodies and two distracted, weeping mothers." This courageous woman did not meet her husband on the way, nor was he in Winnipeg, so she returned home with her sister as far as Batoche and from there, was escorted by her sister's father-in-law back to Pincher Creek through a fall blizzard.

Marie Rose lived to document many stories that were later printed in the Lethbridge and McLeod newspapers. She was resourceful, strong, articulate, patient, and full of joy. Her home at the Jughandle ranch made all travellers welcome. She opened her home to the Peigan families and fed them in tough times. With them, she learned to make leather goods and added to her beading abilities. She followed her trader husband through the Treaty days with most of the children in tow. Their daughter, Mary Anne died at residential school, so she home-schooled most of her children. When the CPR went through the area, the workers needed tents. Out came a sewing machine and Marie Rose entered yet another venture. With two other Métis women, she set up a cottage industry making three dozen tents, sewing from morning until night. She stopped only to cook the meals and feed the kids. Always busy living life to the fullest, and always there for her friends and family,

Marie Rose serves as inspiration to generations of young women. She ended her book draft with the following:

> "and now with my homestead days ended; my boarding house handed over to another, I plan to spend the remainder of my days quietly, near my children, along the foothills near my children, along the beautiful creek . . ."

Marie Rose was one who did get her story in print. Most Métis in the Calgary area did not. The stigma and racism that existed pressured many Métis families not to acknowledge their native blood. The 1881 Dominion Census for the Bow River show many of the Métis families listed as French, English, Irish, or Scot. In fact, Marie Rose Smith was listed as French. Families such as the Anoses, Bellecourts, Boiles, Gabriels, Gouins, Jarvaises, and even Kiskiwasises ("my child" in Cree), were listed as French. The Glen children who were Métis were listed as Irish, while the Gladstone family were all Scottish.

John L'heureux and Alex Cardinal

Métis carpenter and laborer, John L'heureux, along with Métis Alex Cardinal, built the original Lady of Our Peace Mission for Father Lacombe in 1872. They are listed as French in the census. Father Lacombe's journals praise his Métis brothers for their accomplishments. These gentlemen travelled with Father Lacombe from Lac St. Anne, built the Catholic Mission at St. Alberta, and then continued on to Calgary where they used their skills to build a Calgary Métis community. Both John and Alex were hard workers, faithful to employer and church, but Alexis was well-known for his brute strength. His extremely heavy axe is on exhibit in the St. Albert Musé Héritage.

Cuthbert McGillis

Another family that squatted by the banks of the Bow River was the family of Cuthbert McGillis. He was born at Fort Dauphine and was connected to the Métis Rebellion of 1869. Oblate Father Doucet was invited to accompany Cuthbert and a dozen Métis families to the Bow River in April 1875. The McGillis property was just north of the Calgary General Hospital to the Deerfoot Trail. His wife was a sister to Marie Rose Smith.

This family is an interesting example of how many of the Métis families in Calgary are family, cousins, and as they say in the Orkney Islands – definitely 52nd cousins. Cuthbert's son, Pascal, married Marie Brazeau who was related to Colin Fraser, a piper for governor George Simpson. George Simpson's "country born" wife was Margaret Taylor, aunt of Edmond Taylor who was Senator James Lougheed's business partner.

The McGillis clan were key transportation families for the Calgary area. Cuthbert's daughter, Melanie, married freighter Addison MacPherson, who established the MacPherson's Stopping House north of Airdrie. They provided freight and passenger services from Fort Benton to Calgary, Edmonton, Lac la Biche, and Winnipeg. Perhaps they were the Métis written about in the *Calgary Herald* around the time of the 1885 Métis Rebellion.

> Happy Half Breeds
>
> A number of half breeds in town at the present time have occasioned a certain amount of surprise to the citizens . . . There is scarcely one who is not worth $500 – $3 000 all made within the last few weeks freighting for the Hudson's Bay Company to Edmonton. Whatever the breeds may have done in other places, they are by no means backward in Calgary . . . They can afford to sell scrip cheap.[2] They make $8 – $10 a day in their ordinary business. Those who have a number of carts have reaped the benefit and several of them are making $100 a day out of it. A better method of dealing with their claims could not be adopted.

Crafty entrepreneurs of the time, one might say – Cuthbert McGillis, son Pascal, and the MacPherson families were definitely that. J. G. Macgregor in his book *Senator Hardisty's Prairies 1840/1889* states in his reports to the HBC that Richard Hardisty was made aware that free traders were indeed a strong opponent to the Hudson's Bay Company. "The McGillis' played us much the same trick as the Americans did you, went off with 4 to 500 robes from the Blackfeet."

While the MacPherson family had the foresight to create a freight and passenger service, the McGillis family knew the wagons needed a place to stop and they built it.

Members of the Kipling and McGillis families, 1904. Glenbow Archives, NA 4354-5

Clarence Kipling

The Métis are still benefiting from the McGillis clan. Mary McGillis was the mother of Clarence Kipling (1933-2001) and was instrumental in recording much of the family history. He became one of Calgary's first Métis genealogists. Charles Denny attributes much of his work success to the mentorship of Clarence. In 1967, Clarence Denny wrote:

> . . . though he did not travel at all, he had a great ability to gather information from numerous sources, and to assemble it into authentic families. I profited from that, and from several hundred index cards he made for me.

Many researchers today can find the results of Kipling's labor in the National Archives and throughout collections at the Glenbow Archives. Recently, Rod Macquarrie and a host of genealogists gathered a wonderful research tool from his works: the self-published book lists over 3 000 Métis connections and descendants from John Kipling (1724-1794), great-grandfather of Clarence Kipling. What makes this great reading are the stories that can be gleaned from the obituary notes, wills, scrip claims, and notes from person and the Hudson's Bay Company (HBC) journals, such as the following claim regarding Philip Bird:

> May 8, 1885 made scrip declaration at Calgary: Bird, Philip: His claim as HB child; Claim # 201; address: Calgary; Born: near Rocky Mountains; 1852; father James Bird(HB); Mother Sally Bird(Peigan Indian). I remained

constantly in the North West Territories until the year 1868 or 19 [sic] when I was employed as a freighter for the Hudson's Bay Company. I went to Winnipeg with freight there about 1869 or 1870 and remained there for several months during which time I married. I then returned to Saskatchewan and have lived since continually in the Saskatchewa [sic]. I never had any permanent residence in Manitoba and never applied for scrip there. Occupation: Interpreter for Rev. Mr. Davis at Blackfoot Crossing about six months ago.

The claim goes on to tell of his first wife, Louise Lussier, and her death, then continues to his marriage to Mary Kipling. He further notes his children and the fact that they died in infancy. Richard Hardisty, Uncle of Lady Lougheed, signed off the $240 document. In 1900, Bird claimed scrip in Prince Albert, Saskatchewan, for his remaining children. The collection of timely first hand documents provided an accurate record of this family. It acknowledges the many misspellings of names and provides historical linkages.

Louise King

Louise King was listed as French. In fact, this remarkable woman was the daughter of Métis free trader Felix Munroe. His father was frontiersman and trader Hugh Monroe (Rising Wolf), who lived with and married into the Montana Peigan tribe. When her father died suddenly near the Red Deer River, Louise came to Calgary and got a job as a housekeeper for the Mission House. In 1879 she married former Royal Canadian Mounted Police (RCMP) officer George C. King, who went on to become postmaster in Calgary in 1885. *Calgary Herald* news articles for their Golden Wedding anniversary described Louise as a "good looking, vivacious young lady. The extensive wedding dinner of buffalo meat, pies and cakes were all made by the little bride." Those who visited, praised her for keeping such an open and generous home. George went on to be Mayor of Calgary (1886-1887) and received an Order of the British Empire (OBE) in 1934. This put Louise in social circles that included Lady and Senator Lougheed.

Jane Livingston

Jane was a true Alberta Métis born at Fort Victoria (northeast of Edmonton) to HBC Factor Joseph Howse and his Métis wife Janet Spense; however, the 1881 census listed Jane, Métis wife of Sam Livingston, as English. Jane was another strong female role model raising her family while her hunter/trader husband worked away from the home. One story goes that in 1897, Mrs. Livingston had to get to town to summon the doctor to come visit a sick child. Because of the stigma many Aboriginals faced at the time, she floured her face so she would not be hassled enroute to the clinic. In a 1993 *Calgary Herald* news article, her daughter describes the family as Irish pioneers and mentions the grandfather as a Factor for the Hudson's Bay. Nowhere is there mention of Native ancestry or Métis blood. Fortunately, some of her Métis history was preserved in the book, *Tell me, Grandmother*, written by her granddaughter. The book mentioned the Métis Land Scrip they used to settle and how traditions of both cultures were handed down to the children. Jane Livingston was a pillar in the community in which she lived and a great model of dedication to her family, perseverance, and adaptability.

Laurence Clarke Junior

The Métis youth of today can look to the likes of Laurence Clarke Jr. (1859-1941) as a positive role model. Métis son of Laurence Clarke and Jane Bell, he attended St. John's College and went on to become a lawyer. His father was one of the first elected government officials in the west, and was a strong advocate for the Métis. In 1881 Laurence Sr. called for government action respecting the Métis claims. When the Métis were still disputing land claims during the 1885 uprising, Laurence Jr. was, according to his father, torn in many directions. By 1898, Laurence Jr. was the deputy registrar of Land Titles in Calgary, as involved with the land and its people as his father before him.

Edmond Taylor

Edmond Taylor was a partner of Senator James Lougheed. The HBC Archives show his parents as Thomas Taylor and Margaret Kennedy, yet the obituaries in the *Calgary Herald* list his mother as Elizabeth M. Taylor. A second marriage perhaps, but on the surface, this would be confusing to the novice researcher. Taylor was not a novice. He contributed a lot of data to the HBC archives about the old timers who lived in this area.

His ability to gather information as well as his ambitious nature made him a leader in the Calgary area. He was connected to the Turner Valley Oil Patch, president of the British Financial and Land Corporation, vice-president of the Drumheller Consolidated Colliers, and served as director with many other companies throughout Canada. He was also the president of Maclin Motors. A progressive role model, Taylor was an organizer and starting member of the Calgary Stock exchange.

James Owen Gresham (Pete) Sanderson

Pete Sanderson (1898-1963) was a Métis descendant of John Richard McKay and Harriet Ballenden. Educated in universities in Edmonton, Toronto, and Yale, Dr. Sanderson worked as a cowpoke and worked his way up the social and economic ladder as a geologist for Imperial Oil Ltd. He was president of the Society of Petroleum Engineers in 1938. At that time he also worked as a consulting geologist and went on to take over leadership in the Western Potash Corporation. He co-authored *Geology of the Red Deer River Valley* in 1945. He also knew the value of our country's youth. He gave sound advice to young people seeking professional guidance and pursuit of careers. He was a natural teacher as well as a doer. With all, he held a lusty view of life and a robust approach to living.

> Sanderson has attained a reputation as a consultant to high school boys. . . . "I ask them what they want to do and point out the sacrifices and needs of each profession. . . . I believe in the survival of the fittest. . . . Physical well being and mental equipment are the weapons. We should give these to our youth for the rest of life.[3]

General F. H. McDonald

F. H. McDonald was the son of infamous fur trader Archibald McDonald. His mother was Ellen Inkster. He worked hard to achieve status as a military general and didn't back down from a battle, even when it was in his personal life. His strength and courage led him to Ypres and the Somme in World War I, where he was severely wounded, losing one arm. But that strong spirit persevered. He continued to ski and play sports. More has been written about his MLA brothers, but his is a story of courage and determination.

Thelma Chalifoux

Métis role models are still making history. Senator Thelma Chalifoux was the first Métis woman to be appointed to Canada's Senate in 1997. This Calgarian and single mom of seven worked as a community developer for many years. She has modeled how one person can make change happen. She was one of the developers of the current Métis Association of Alberta, the Friendships Centres, and outspoken employee of the Alberta Family and Social Services. Ms. Chalifoux was the first to publicly state that the ills of today's society were not traditional in our cultures. At one workshop, she did an excellent job of dispelling the myth that family violence was an Aboriginal tradition. She listed the many stories and legends telling how our grandparents respected other people and how the community would band together to protect those who were victims of family violence. In 1995, she was recognized for her contributions through the Aboriginal Achievement Award.

These are but a few of the families who are possible role models. There are many more. The 1881 census is not the only source to start from. We can look at our own family trees that were once ashamed to include the mixed blood. We can thank people such as Geoff Burtonshaw, Charles Denny, Clarence Kipling, and his grandmother for providing our local archives with a wealth of information. We can thank the university for providing professors, such as Dr. D. Smith, who have encouraged many students to seek the knowledge of their ancestors and be proud of being Métis. Most of all we should thank the Creator for bringing people of many cultures together to create the unique world of the Métis. We, as Métis, should acknowledge and celebrate our role in building this nation and the communities in which we live. Let this be just the beginning.

Notes

1. Democrat. A wagon with both a front and back seat, some were open, while others had canopies. It is likely the canopied type that Marie Rose Smith referred to her in memoirs, [www.Albertacarriagesupply.com/vehicles_for _sale.php].

2. Scrip. Paper cash or land allotment provided to the Métis who did not live on reserves.

3. *Calgary Herald*, 10 August 1957.

My Home is Over Jordan
Southern Alberta's Black Pioneers
by Cheryl Foggo

Deep river – my home is over Jordan
Deep river, Lord
I want to cross over into camp ground.
– from a song the people used to sing

While I have never been blind to its faults, I have a deep love for my home city. For that reason, I've authored the piece that follows with a heavy heart. I expect that most who read it will feel the same. It's a cliché to say that racism is a poison, but it's true, and writing this article has been a little like drinking poison every day. I wish Canada had been the Home Over Jordan the people were looking for. But I can't change the past, I can only present what I know of it here.

I grew up inside a history that had no official status and a community that had no geographical place. My people were worthy, long-established residents of the city and province we called home, but our story was casually and precariously preserved – kept alive more by word of mouth amongst ourselves than by any canonical record or acknowledgment of our presence. According to the education I received in school, Black Calgary's history did not exist.

In recent years, John Ware has been designated the textbook representative of Calgary's Black history. That he was a former slave who came to the region now known as Southern Alberta in 1882 on a cattle drive is fairly well known. He was a tall, strong, legendary cowboy who won prizes in the local rodeos that led to the creation of the Stampede, and had a particular gift for taming wild horses. He had a great sense of humor; once when asked if he planned to take up this new mode of transportation known as the bicycle, he replied that he certainly would – as soon as the last horse was dead. He established his own ranch that was one of the most successful in the Brooks area. When his horse fell on top of him, killing him in 1905, he was widely grieved. His funeral at Calgary's Baptist Church was the largest the city had ever seen. All these things I have learned because they are a matter of public record.[1]

Strangely enough, it wasn't until my older brother went on a school field trip to the Glenbow Museum and saw his photograph that we learned John Ware was Black. My closest companion in those days, Richard, was obsessed with cowboys. We had heard the legendary cowboy's name, we knew that some called him the "greatest cowboy of all time." We just never heard that he was Black.

John Ware has since become more than a historical figure to me. His children were elders in my community. When I look at the familiar photographs of pre-1905 southern Alberta, I see them through John Ware's eyes. I look at Calgary's false-fronted log stores where he would have shopped, like Bannerman's Flour and Feed and I. G. Baker and Company where he first met his wife, Mildred;[2] the Sandstone structures like Knox Presbyterian Church, the Alberta Hotel, and the Bank of Montreal, that were erected in response to the terrible fire of 1886, and I imagine John Ware riding by in his wagon. He would have seen cows ambling by the bank, horses tethered to posts in front of the stores, and would have been intent on wrapping up his business as quickly as possible. He hated Calgary, where a Black man who may or may not have been guilty was the first person to be hung for murder,[3] where unlooked-for trouble, racist police, and drunken, fight-picking cowboys abounded. To Calgarians he was known as "Nigger John." The myth that he accepted the name, to his face, as a term of affection persists to this day. In 1960, after decades of enduring several landmarks in the Brooks area being named "Nigger John," two of his children, Bob and Nettie, wrote letters, cajoled, and finally worked the media in order to remove the offending word from the titles of the places named in his honor. "No one called my father 'Nigger John'," said Nettie. "Not to his face. The only time I saw someone do it was in Calgary – and that man ended up in hospital. But Father paid his bill."[4]

It is also a myth that John Ware and his wife's family, the Lewis's, were the only Black people in the region in the 1800s. Many less famous Black men and women lived in the territory during and prior to John Ware's time. Black fur traders, one by the name of Henry Mills, were present in the mid-1800s.[5] There was a whiskey runner named William Bond. Daniel and Charlotte Lewis came to the area in 1889 with their large family, and after first (unsuccessfully) trying their hand at ranching near Shepard, they moved to Calgary so that Daniel could return to carpentry, which had been his trade in Toronto. He specialized in building fancy staircases in Calgary's upscale homes, while Charlotte took in laundry to add to the family's income. Their oldest daughter, Mildred, married John Ware in Calgary in 1892. One of their younger daughters,

The Darby family at Vulcan, Alberta, circa 1904. Herbert Darby was the first cook in the Imperial Hotel when it was moved to Vulcan from Frank, Alberta, after the slide. Glenbow Archives, NA-748-83

Mary, met and married a Black cook by the name of William Herbert Darby, who worked for the hotel in Vulcan circa 1900;[6] then after Darby's death Mary wed Sam Carruthers and moved to Amber Valley.

At around the same time, in the southwest corner of Alberta, there was a well-known North West Mounted Police (NWMP) translator named Dave Mills, whose mother was Blood and whose father was the previously mentioned fur trader, Henry Mills. The younger Mills married Holy Rabbit Woman, and many of their descendants live on the Blood reserve near Cardston today.[7]

Also in the late 1800s, a Black man named Charlie Dyson operated a blacksmithing business in Pincher Creek. Later, he and his wife Eliza homesteaded near Grassy Butte.[8] Another Black Pincher Creek resident was an adventurous young cowboy by the name of Billy "The Kid" Welsh (or Welch). In 1902, after a night of drinking, he drowned in a Pincher Creek flood while trying to guide a friend to safety.[9]

An even earlier Black resident of Pincher Creek was a woman named Annie Saunders, who had previously worked as a nanny and housekeeper for the Colonel James and Mrs. Mary Macleod family. After leaving the employ of the Macleods, Annie, who was known around town as "Old Auntie," ensconced herself across from the skating pond, running a laundry service, a restaurant, and a boarding home for children. She played an active part in Pincher Creek life, appearing frequently in the *Macleod Gazette* after hosting choirs, the drama club, various parties, and several visiting dignitaries at her restaurant. She also apparently liked to amuse people – including the visiting Marquis of Lorne – by informing them that she had been the first White woman to live in Pincher Creek.[10]

The Canada census of 1901 lists two Black men named George and Louie Robinson who worked as a jockey and stable boy respectively, in the service of John Mclaughlin of High River. The same census found George Williams working as a shoemaker and photographer in Innisfail. There was also a Black cowboy named Lige Abel who worked for the Waldron ranch north of Lundbreck,[11] and another by the name of Green Walters, a ranching cook known for his singing. A Black woman named Flora Wolfe lived as the common-law wife of British nobleman De Laval Beresford on a ranch not far from John Ware's Brooks property. Beresford and Wolfe had come north looking for greater acceptance of their relationship than they had experienced in Mexico. Tom Rengald was a valued cowhand on the Chipman Ranch west of Calgary, Felix Luttrell rode for Little Bow, and Jim Whitford worked on ranches around Lethbridge for years until he was killed by lightning in 1908.[12] The 1901 census counted 27 as the total number of Blacks in the entire region that would eventually become Alberta, a figure that may have been too low, as my research into the time period has uncovered Blacks in excess of that number just in the southernmost regions of Alberta. For example, the census of that year and other sources make reference to six Black residents of Medicine Hat alone.[13]

In the years immediately following John Ware's death, two things happened that brought many more people of African descent to Alberta. The first was the merging of the Indian and Western Territories to create the state of Oklahoma, U.S.A.. The second was the plea from the Canadian government for hardy American farmers to settle the northern regions of Alberta and Saskatchewan. That the two events happened at around the same time in the early years of the twentieth century, seemed to many Black Americans to be a divine signal directing them northward.

My maternal great-grandparents had moved away from other southern states in pursuit of the relatively generous freedoms available to Blacks in the Indian Territory. They lost those freedoms when Oklahoma became a state. Whites who had pressed hard for the establishment of Oklahoma made it their first priority to attack the Blacks who had settled there, through politics and through violence. In his book, *Deemed Unsuitable*, Bruce Shepard quotes prominent Oklahoma citizen Roy Stafford, writing in the *Oklahoman*:

> The law is [as] powerless to curb the debased, ignorant and brutal negro [sic] as it is to restrain vicious animals that attack men. Does not this alone explain the hangings, burnings and horrible forms of mob violence visited upon those of the black [sic] race who shatter the law?

Lynchings frequently followed such tirades, which dominated newspaper editorials and election platforms of the time. Numerous towns saw the burning and dynamiting of Black homes and beatings of Black citizens. A racist mob descended on the town of Wairuka and gave its Black citizens 24 hours to leave. Politicians won seats by promising to introduce segregation in all aspects of public life, in elections where Blacks were denied participation through various and illegal means.

My forebears – the Glovers and the Smiths, were spiritual people who believed God had a place for them. Like hundreds of their Black neighbors, they had proven themselves willing to pull up stakes in the past, so when the Canadian government began placing ads in southern newspapers for farmers to come north and settle the wilder regions of Alberta and Saskatchewan, they were willing to move again. They held romantic notions of Canada, the legendary last stop on the Underground Railroad, which had been reinforced throughout their lives by the code names for Canada that had been passed down through spiritual songs. Canada's secret names were Canaan, Heaven, the other side of Jordan. Along with between one and two thousand friends, neighbors, and acquaintances, my great-grandparents thought they were setting out for the Promised Land.

Small numbers of these pioneers stopped in rural southern Alberta and Saskatchewan, or in the cities. The vast majority chose isolated locations much further north.

The communities formed by these settlers were in and around Maidstone (Saskatchewan), North Battleford (Saskatchewan), Keystone, (now Bretton, Alberta), Campsie (Alberta), Junkins (now Wildwood, Alberta) and the largest and best known, Amber Valley (Alberta). They lived in abandoned railroad boxcars, sod huts, or tiny log cabins with dirt floors and tar paper roofs. Some of the pioneers described enduring temperatures of 60 degrees below zero, in shacks where the wind and snow blew through the cracks. They ate moose and pork when they could get it, rabbit and squirrel when they had to. They struggled to clear their land and endured day-long walks or wagon rides through muskeg to buy supplies.[14]

Far worse than a challenging landscape and climate, though, was the immediate realization that their welcome was not what they'd hoped for. A sampling of newspaper headlines concerning their arrival include "Negroes Not Wanted in Alberta," "Canada Will Bar The Negro Out," "We Want No Dark Spots in Alberta," and "Colored Question Up in The House – Members Express Some Alarm Lest Many Should Come to Canada." Numerous petitions protesting their presence were also circulated. Both the Calgary and Edmonton Boards of Trade drafted resolutions demanding that Prime Minister Wilfred Laurier enact legislation to bar Blacks from entering Western Canada. The secretary of the Edmonton Board of Trade claimed that "ninety percent of the citizens who have been asked to sign the petitions against the negro [sic] immigration have complied without hesitation." Several downtown Edmonton offices, including those of the Merchants Bank, the Windsor and King Edward Hotels, and the Board of Trade rooms displayed the petition. The Edmonton Trades and Labour Council also passed a resolution, which read, in part "it was amply proven that an unlimited influx of negroes [sic] into the province would invariably lower the standard of living." Dr. Ella Synge, a spokesperson for a women's group, said, "the finger of fate [is] pointing to lynch law which will be the ultimate result, as sure as we allow such people to settle among us." Laurier responded to his western constituency by drafting the following Order-in-Council on August 12th, 1911:

> From a period of one year from and after the date hereof
> the landing in Canada shall be and the same is prohibited
> of any immigrants belonging to the Negro race, which race
> is deemed unsuitable to the climate and requirements of
> Canada."[15]

Owing to fears that anti-Black legislation would alienate Black voters in the east, the order-in-council was ultimately rescinded. Instead, the Canadian government hired Black preachers to travel throughout the south to warn Blacks not to come to Canada. This strategy proved to be effective, and the wave of Black immigration trickled off around 1912.

The northern pioneers chose to stick together, work their land, and keep their heads down. Survival for them depended more on how hard they were willing to work than on the good graces of their surrounding communities. Their counterparts who chose to settle in the cities of Edmonton and Calgary fared much worse. They were dependent on the established White community for every aspect of their survival, and hostility was a daily part of their lives. Employee unions demanded that only White labor be used and city newspapers frequently reported incidents of Blacks being denied service in hotels and restaurants. Other visible racial groups were experiencing similar treatment. Calgary's famous hospitality did not extend to brown-skinned people.

Calgary began to thrive in the 1920s. Industries of all kinds flourished, Calgarians began to prosper, and as they did so, theatres and leisure facilities abounded. Calgary benefited from increased train travel in Canada, and numerous hotels and restaurants opened to provide lodging and food for the travellers.

Those positive changes had little impact on the Black community. Restaurants, hotels, theatres, leisure facilities, and industry continued to limit Black participation. Canadians borrowed from American stereotypes in their dealings with Black women, but even more so with Black men. Calgary's newspapers of the day and the Rotary Club frequently featured cartoon depictions and minstrel portrayals of shuffling, hapless Black males, and William Aberhart delighted in sharing "Negro" jokes on his broadcasts.[16] The belief that Black men were inherently dangerous to White women proliferated after the arrest of an Edmonton Black man for an assault on a 15-year-old girl made headlines for a week in many prairie newspapers. Calgary's two major dailies, as well as the *Lethbridge Daily News,* all took a "we told you so" stance, and called for careful monitoring of Blacks, expulsion, and a slam-the-door immigration policy. Nine days after the first reports of the incident, it was revealed that the girl had, in fact, not been the victim of any crime. Having lost an expensive ring belonging to her mother, she had staged a robbery in her home and invented a story for her parents and the police that a Black man had been responsible.[17] Employment stereotypes also abounded – Black men shone shoes on many Calgary street corners. Other Black men were forced to accept low, menial labor; some of the women were able to find work as domestics or cooks.

Black men who arrived in Calgary from the east as porters on the railroads, often denied service in the hotels and restaurants, soon enough began to figure out where they could go. They were welcomed by the Chinese proprietors of a few cafes in particular in the twenties and thirties – the Crystal Café and the Canadian Café, and the White owner of another – the Palace Café. The early Calgary pioneers loved to reminisce about Hop Wo, who owned one of the cafés, and who fed many a hungry porter with recipes he adapted to their tastes. "We called him our brother," said Dick Bellamy. (People in my community continue to be extremely fond of Chinese food. Next to our own versions of soul food, Chinese food remains the meal of choice at many large gatherings.) Bellamy also used to delight in telling the story of how Mrs. Moulds, who owned the Palace, tore a strip off of two visiting Texans in 1932, who demanded to know why he (Bellamy) was allowed to eat in her establishment. "I'll throw you out of here before I ever ask him to leave," she told them.[18] Black people also tried to respond to the needs of their own community by opening barber shops and rooming houses, but establishments of this kind met with tremendous resistance by the White community.

City council records and newspaper accounts throughout the early decades of a Black presence in Calgary demonstrate that Blacks resisted and protested against racism, sometimes meeting with success and sometimes not. As early as 1910, an organization called the "Coloured People's Protective Association" existed in Calgary. Evidence that the organization was able to attract more than 150 Black residents of southern Alberta to a ball it held in October of 1910[19] supports the supposition that census estimates of Black residence in the area may have been low. An international organization called the "Universal Negro Improvement Association" also had a substantial Alberta membership. In March of 1911, a Black woman wrote a letter to the mayor of Calgary objecting to statements reported in the newspapers about "driving all Negroes out of Calgary," attributed to Calgary's chief of police. Acknowledging that there may have been bad eggs among them, she took exception to the many being punished for the actions of the few.[20] In 1914 a Black man named Charles Daniels brought charges against the owners of the Sherman Grand for refusing him admission to the theatre. He won his suit by default when no one from the firm of Lougheed and Bennett appeared in court to defend the case. In December of 1916, a group of Black citizens who objected to the advertising and showing of the films "Birth of A Nation" and "The Nigger" at the Bijou Theatre wrote to the mayor of Calgary, outlining their concerns. In his reply, Mayor Costello stated that although he was not able to persuade the theatre owners to cancel the run of the latter picture, they had agreed to make some changes to the advertising displayed in the newspapers and outside the theatre.

Disputes between police, the courts, and operators of rooming facilities for Black porters were common. In 1911 Harry and Bertha Palmer were referred to in newspaper headlines as "evildoers" and were both sentenced to six months hard labor, having been found guilty of operating a "disorderly house," on Second Avenue. Interrupting a vigorous defence of their right to provide accommodations to porters by their counsel, F. E. Eaton, Magistrate Sanders stated, "You are wasting my time, Mr. Eaton. I am satisfied with the evidence I have before me that the place is a disorderly house."

The issue of porter hangouts rose again in 1920, when a group of White residents of Victoria Park hired a lawyer to represent their concerns to city council about Blacks in their neighborhood. According to the *Calgary Daily Herald*, Mayor R. C. Marshall invited the White citizens to form a subcommittee to meet face-to-face with a subcommittee of the Black citizens. The White citizens claimed that,

> . . . aside from the general undesirability of colored residents in groups in a white residential section, the actions of some of the colored persons who have moved in make them undesirable among members of their own race . . . that in one instance what was termed a boarding house was virtually a club or gathering place for boarders and other colored men; that the house included a pool room fifty feet long and a bar where soft drinks were sold.

It would seem that the mayor was also dealing with other complaints of this kind. In a directive dated April 27, 1920, with the heading "Re Negroes," the following resolution was adopted:

> That petitions and communications re Negroes resident in certain sections of the City be referred to the Mayor & Commissioners for settlement, and if necessary, report back to Council.

Ultimately, 472 inhabitants of Victoria Park signed a petition to city council that read:

> We request that they be restrained from purchasing any property in the said district and any who may now be residing there will be compelled to move into some other locality.

City Council wrote to 16 other Canadian cities seeking a precedent for officially segregating or barring Blacks from living in those cities. After ascertaining that no precedent existed, council refused the petitioners' request. Informally, the mayor suggested to the Black citizens that one function of their committee should be to "persuade other colored [sic] people not to come into the district," which they agreed to do, although insisting that they could not be "held responsible for the actions of strangers coming in." He also suggested to the White petitioners that they pursue real estate agents who facilitated the transfer of property to Blacks in their area, stating

> . . . one of the best methods of preventing like trouble in the future was to get after real estate men who made such transfers under subterfuge, and that an aroused public opinion on such actions would accomplish more than any move the city authorities could make.[21]

These kinds of formal attempts to legalize bigotry against Blacks were sporadic, but informal discrimination and negative stereotyping continued to be widespread throughout the ensuing decades. In addition to encountering resistance in housing and employment, Blacks found that they were barred from many nightclubs, bars, swimming pools, and skating rinks. In 1948 the proprietor of a Calgary swimming pool was questioned by a reporter about keeping Blacks out of his facility. He replied: "That has always been the rule here. . . . If too many Negroes come to swim, no one else would want to use the pool and we would go out of business." He went on to say the same rule applied to the Chinese and Japanese.[22]

Black Calgary began to make its own spaces. Black businesses like the Chicken Inn, owned by Bob Melton and Florence Carter, and the Chicken Fry, owned by Louella and Dick Bellamy, cropped up. Both the Inn and the Fry were raucous party joints, and although Black patrons formed a core clientele, the restaurants attracted large numbers of White customers as well. A strong Black church was established in Calgary in 1947 by Andrew Risby, a son of early pioneers who had settled at Campsie, and who married my mother's older sister, Edith. Holding services at first in the railroad mission, occasionally at Utopia Hall, and finally at the Standard Church of America in Inglewood, the church provided a meeting place and support network for the Black people who didn't relish the atmosphere at the Inn and the Fry, preferring to submerge their sorrows in the scriptures. Andrew Risby also provided the much-needed service of marrying and burying. Prior to his arrival, weddings and especially funerals caused panic in a community that was both without a spiritual rudder and uncertain of who it could turn to when a clergyman was needed. Utopia Hall also served as a neutral space, for meetings where the church-going and secular Black factions needed common ground. Black events were held there so frequently that it became known in the community as "the hall" and eventually as "the hole," because, according to my Aunt Pearl, that's what it was.

During the 1940s Blacks in Calgary began to organize, and groups like the Brotherhood of Sleeping Car Porters morphed into the Alberta Association for the Advancement of Coloured People (AAACP). Well-known Black American labor activist A. Philip Randolph and Ontario activist Stanley Grizzle both spent time in Calgary working with influential Black citizens like Dick Bellamy, P. T. Clay, and later, Roy Williams, Melvin Crump, Burt Proctor, and Teddy King, to combat discrimination and try to present a more accurate representation of the character of the community. This unified voice found important allies in the White community, including city councillors, reporters, members of the Co-operative Commonwealth Federation (CCF – forerunner of the New Democratic Party, or NDP), members of B'nai B'rith, and Mayor J. C. Watson. Gradual progress was made, specifically against racial discrimination by proprietors of restaurants and hotels.[23]

The traditional avenues for Black success in North America – sports and music – were more open to Black strivers in Calgary as well. The high profile of Black athletes like Sugarfoot Anderson, who were also respected in the White community, began to act as a bridge between the communities in the forties and fifties. Black athletes and entertainers were seen to bring reflected glory on Alberta. But making a living as an athlete or entertainer was difficult, and by no means did it provide protection from racism. Anderson's wife, Virnetta, who later became an alderman, was surprised and appalled in the 1940s by the way some Calgarians performed an attitude about-face after learning she was married to Sugarfoot.[24]

The worst and most widely-publicized incident of hatred toward Blacks in Calgary took place in April of 1940. Soldiers from Currie Barracks sometimes frequented a dance hall owned by a Black musician named Lou Darby, son of the William Herbert Darby that had married into John Ware's family at the turn of the century. An argument between a White soldier whose girlfriend had shown interest in Darby's brother, a member of his orchestra, led to a fistfight. The private left the premises to round up a group of 200 of his fellow soldiers, who then stormed Lou Darby's residence at 133, 2nd Avenue East. Egged on by a large crowd of civilian onlookers, shouting that they were going to "bust up the nigger joints" and then go down to "Harlem" (8th Ave. and 4th St. East, where most of the Black people lived) to "run out the niggers," the mob destroyed the picket fence, heaved rocks through the windows and finally broke down the door. Inside the house were the terrified Lou Darby, his sister Eva and her husband, a White soldier named Private Thomas

Liesk. By the time police arrived, the soldiers were in the process of attacking Liesk and had stripped him of his uniform. The police were able to push their way through the crowd and guide the three inhabitants to safety, then spent the rest of the night corralling the soldiers and marching them back to the barracks.[25]

During the first half of the twentieth century, one of the most insidious aspects of life in Calgary for individual Blacks was being regarded as an undesirable, unsuitable citizen and associated with criminal activity, no matter how upstanding and determined to make a positive contribution they were.

When I read decades-old accounts of Black men and women in conflict with the law and with mainstream Calgary society, I can't help but filter those accounts through my knowledge of the impact racism had on the lives of those people. While not wanting to make excuses for those who were in fact guilty of destructive living, I often recall a file I came across while doing research for a project at the Provincial Archives in Edmonton a couple of years ago. The case concerned a criminal assault committed by a Black resident of the community of Campsie, circa 1924. The file detailed how the man had assaulted and injured the community's male teacher, in what it characterized as an unprovoked attack. Witnesses gave testimony on behalf of the teacher, and several important White town officials decried the lawless, vigilante spirit of the "Negroes" and their lack of desirability as neighbors. I recognized the name of the defendant from a description of that same event I had heard only weeks before from my uncle. I read every page of the file, looking in vain for some recorded acknowledgment of the behavior of the teacher that had led to the assault. My uncle, Andrew Risby, the revered and respected pastor of the Standard Church in Calgary, was a young boy growing up in Campsie at the time the incident took place. The teacher was an unrepentant, outspoken racist, who found ways to refuse admittance of Black children to the schoolhouse. Although Black residents protested through what they thought were the proper official channels, nothing changed. Frustration mounted, and when the teacher became verbally abusive toward the mother of one of the children, her husband punched him. The assault had taken place, but the greater crime remained unreported.[26]

There is no denying there were Black people in Calgary who did resort to crime. There was a divide between those who "lived right" and those who didn't. I used to listen to the elders describe people in our community who engaged in illegal activity in one of two ways. The first, and worst, in the eyes of those who lived right, were described as having chosen "the sporting life," being "bad actors," or "fools." The way Uncle Andrew always framed it was "they let the devil take hold." People who fell into that category were generally regarded as having made bad choices when they could have, and should have, done otherwise. Then there was another, more sympathetic categorization. These were people who were driven to do things they normally wouldn't, by a lack of other available options. They lost hope, or grew tired and bitter, or their kids were going hungry. Like Ray Charles sang in the song, "Now I am no thief, but a man can go wrong when he's busted . . ." The people who lived right didn't like to see anyone of their community walk down the path of ruin, whatever the reason. Firstly, they cared about the people, or at least knew someone in that person's family to care about. Secondly, it didn't matter if there were 500 Black people who lived right for every one who didn't. Step out of line and every Black man, woman, and child in the city would pay. Whatever the circumstances, whether they were no good or just desperate, the numbers who stepped over that line were small. Most of the people I knew would take any kind of job and work diligently at it, suffer, even go hungry, to stay on the "side of right." Because the racism they faced in Canada didn't usually amount to actual loss of life, a consequence they had regularly faced in the U.S., they were determined that prejudice would not push them off the path they had chosen to walk. Time and again, certain meager-hearted Canadians would attempt to enact legislation against them; time and again those attempts failed. From this, they drew encouragement.

When railroad travel to western Canada began to boom in the late 1920s, local Black men were hired in large numbers to work as porters, beginning a tradition of employment that lasted more than 50 years. Attracted by the security of railroad jobs, many families from the northern Black settlements moved to the cities as well. Every family I knew who had roots in the Black pioneering community had fathers, brothers, or uncles who worked as porters at one time or another. John Ware's sons, Bob and Arthur, both worked for the railroads. Through today's eyes, it's difficult to see why the job was prized. It took the men away from home for long stretches. It was hard work – porters were often on their feet from Vancouver to Winnipeg. The men were sometimes treated with disdain or contempt by the clientele whose beds they were making and meals they were serving. No porter ever became wealthy, although the living it afforded was superior to what pinning chickens or shining shoes could provide. But up to the early 1970s, Black families respected their porters. Porters wore clean shirts. They travelled, bringing back stories and an air of sophistication that few would otherwise have been able to afford. They were part of a brotherhood that sustained our community. Somewhere between the sixties and seventies, working on the road lost its prestige. There was a time of overlap between the days when portering was esteemed and the era when young Blacks were refusing to settle for service employment. They were able to afford to choose education and were taking advantage of doors that had been opened for them by people whose work they no longer honored.

I was born in 1956, about halfway through what has now been the first hundred years of an actual Black presence in Southern Alberta. The shift between the old and the new has taken place in my lifetime. I remember being a curiosity on a daily basis. To quote from the memoirs of Peggy Brown (nee Bowen), who grew up in Amber Valley but has lived in Calgary for 50 years, "I didn't have a problem with the colour of my skin – other people did." I recall praying that no one would call my brothers and sister and me names at the playground. I was around for sickening minstrel shows and racist advertising. I was both worried and proud when people from my community and family would face down bigots. I feared that the terrible things I heard of happening to Black people in the U.S. would happen here, to people I knew.

But there was more to growing up Black in Calgary than racism. We didn't cower in our homes. There were picnics at Bowness Park or the Zoo, where we would commandeer at least a dozen tables that would be laid out with food prepared by the best down-home cooks in the city. There were Christmas concerts and Watch Night services at church on New Year's Eve. There was a great deal of singing. There were gentle brown grandfathers who smelled like cinnamon, and spoke in a back-country, lyrical Canadian/American hybrid vernacular. There were bossy, confident Black women wearing aprons, women of extraordinary strength who somehow managed to create a sense of place and peace, raising children to love themselves in a world that didn't love them. There were many children for us to tear around with, whose faces betrayed that they were Lawsons, or Saunderses, or Lipscombes or Mayeses, or Bowens, or Browns or Williamses or Hayeses or Proctors or Sneeds. . . . There were cranky, sharp-tongued people, always outnumbered by those who practiced doubled-over, staggering-across-the-room, cackling laughter. My favorite outings were the ones to Banff. We travelled in a caravan of cars, Uncle Andrew always in the lead. Somehow, without ever having said a word about the gapes our large group of brown faces drew, he managed to communicate to us, the children, that we didn't need to concern ourselves with people who stared at us like we didn't belong. Banff, all of Alberta, belonged to us. We could see that by the way he strode around, tall and fearless. We learned to claim our place.

At around the same time that northern communities started to lose their young people to Calgary and Edmonton, Caribbean immigrants began to make their way to the two cities. When the vestiges of racist immigration polices were taken off the books in Canada in the late sixties, more people of African descent arrived in Southern Alberta. Human Rights legislation was introduced in Alberta in 1966. Trudeau's vision of Canada reflected a shift in societal attitudes, away from tacit acceptance of discrimination. The American Civil Rights movement and other world fronts raised awareness of racism in our own country. Local newspaper columnists like Eva Reid and Suzanne Zwarun, and later, Brian Brennan and David Bly, began to report regularly on the positive contributions of Black citizens like Vi King, who in 1954 became the first Black female law graduate in Canada and the second woman to be admitted to the bar in Calgary. Floyd Sneed's exploits as the drummer for one of the seventies seminal bands, Three Dog Night, and Oliver Bowen's work as the chief engineer for Calgary's Light Rail Transit (LRT), also received recognition.[27]

Despite these positive signs, the need to work for respect and fairness was ongoing. In the 1960s, Black organizations sought support from city

June, 1954, Violet King is the first Black woman called to the bar as a lawyer. Here she is presented with a purse by the Calgary local of the International Brotherhood of Sleeping Car Porters. Left to right: Violet King, Phillip Randolph, Bennie Smith and Roy Williams.. Glenbow Archives, NA-5600-7757a hall to have racist caricatures removed from public advertising on city streets, and to monitor continued discriminatory practices in the workforce. Throughout the 1970s, 1980s, and 1990s, myriad White supremacist organizations were active in Alberta, receiving the most attention for a cross-burning in Provost in 1990.[28] In the early eighties, a map showing parts of southern Alberta incorporated into a planned "Whites Only" zone surfaced during (former Calgary Stampeder Football Team Owner) Larry Ryckman's research for his film, *The Aryan Nation*. At around the same time, a Nigerian man was falsely accused of drunkenness and pimping, and was severely beaten by Calgary police.[29] In response to these alarming developments, the AAACP was briefly revived in the early eighties, and my sister Noel and I signed on as fundraising chair and newsletter editor respectively, our family having had our own experiences with stereotyping and racial discrimination. Noel and I, and a Black female friend of ours who was a geologist working for a downtown oil company, had been experiencing frequent embarrassing harassment from White men who assumed we were prostitutes. Between the three of us we hit on the idea of carrying briefcases whenever we were downtown, a plan which reduced, but did not eliminate, the provocation. At around the same time, our brother Richard was an outstanding student and basketball player for the University of Calgary Dinosaurs. A Calgary food company offered employment to every member of the U of C and Mount Royal College basketball teams; however, Richard and the sole Black player on Mount Royal's team were refused. Thinking it was an oversight, Richard applied a second time, but was informed all positions had been filled. Two days later, when another of his White teammates found employment with the company, there could be no mistaking the firm's racist hiring policy. One of Richard's teammates quit his job with the company in disgust over their actions.

In 2004, in the months leading up to the writing of this article, bar and nightclub owners in Calgary have made headlines for attempting to prevent Black men and men from other identifiable groups from frequenting their premises. Evidence of racism in other aspects of public life, including the work force and in local professional sports, have also made headlines.[30]

But Calgary is a more cosmopolitan city than it used to be. When incidents of racism are publicized, there is often an outcry, and not just from people who are on the receiving end of unjust treatment. Calgary is a complex place and sometimes it is impossible for people on the outside to see the layers. Although from the city's beginnings, there have been people working to create a breeding ground for intolerance here, those people have created an equal and opposite reaction. Just as Dick Bellamy had Mrs. Moulds to send the Texans packing from her restaurant and my brother Richard had the teammate who refused to work for bigots, I have had friends willing to stand up. The mythical, hope-of-the-world Canadians really do exist and one of the best ways to find them is to be Black.

In recent years, Black Calgarians have chosen to honor our history and counter racism by celebrating the achievements of Alberta's Black doctors, scholars, artists, peace officers, athletes, entrepreneurs, authors, educators, scientists, and philanthropists through organizations like the Black Achievement Awards Society of Alberta, the Black Pioneers Descendants Society, and through various activities during Black History Month in February of each year.[31]

Knowing what I now know about the hardships my ancestors and their people faced, both before coming to Canada and after they arrived, I'm amazed when I recall the lack of bitterness I heard in their voices, the sweetness of their beings. They remained optimistic and convinced that God had guided their feet to this "Promised Land" and that things would work out for the best. Like me, many of them found good friends among their White neighbors and didn't hold the treatment they received in their day-to-day lives against humanity in general. Most of the pioneers, including my ancestors, became fiercely loyal Canadians.

Our stories have started to creep into books, into courses taught at universities, and onto websites, for those who are interested enough to seek them out. Our history remains absent from Alberta's school curriculum and from the minds of the majority of people. It's November 9, 2004. I'm sitting here writing, you're sitting there reading. Let's see what the next hundred years brings.

Notes

1. *Calgary Herald*, September 1905; *Our Foothills Local History*, 226-227; *John Ware's Cow Country*, Grant MacEwan; *Canadian Cattlemen*, 6-7; Calgary Public Library, Local History Room, John Ware file; Glenbow Museum Archives.

2. *Passion and Scandal – Great Canadian Love Stories*, Barbara Smith, 148; *John Ware's Cow Country*, Grant MacEwan, 131.

3. Jesse Williams barely escaped a lynch mob. He was arrested, tried and sentenced to hang all in one day. Scholars debate the fairness of his trial. *John Ware's Cow Country*, Grant MacEwan, 62; *Calgary Herald*, 20 March 1995.

4. *Canadian Cattlemen*, 67, 82; *Albertan*, 25 August 1960; *John Ware's Cow Country*, Grant MacEwan, 62, 63, 76, 82-83, 110-112; *Legacy Magazine*, spring 2004, 24; *Calgary Herald*, 1 June 1970; *Albertan*, 16 August 1960; *Calgary Herald*, August 20, 1960; Information about the Ware family was also gleaned from the private papers and memories of good friend and executor of Mildred (jr.) and Nettie Ware's estates, Mr. Don Mallory of Kirkaldy, Alberta.

5. *Peoples of Alberta*, Howard and Tamara Palmer, 365; Hudson's Bay Company Archives.

6. From the private collection of Mr. Don Mallory, Kirkaldy, Alberta; Glenbow Museum Archives.

7. *Peoples of Alberta*, Howard and Tamara Palmer; Glenbow Museum Archives; From an interview with Charlie Crow Chief, November, 2004.

8. *Sixty Years in an Old Cowtown*, A. L Freebairn; *Prairie Grass to Mountain Pass: History of the Pioneers of Pincher Creek and District*, 628; *Rocky Mountain Echo*, Fred Stenson (pre-publication).

9. *The Golden Age of the Canadian Cowboy*, Hugh A. Dempsey, 54; *The Range Men*, L. V. Kelly; *Prairie Grass to Mountain Pass: History of the Pioneers of Pincher Creek and District*.

10. Collected files of Professor Sarah Carter, University of Calgary, department of History; *Macleod Gazette*, 13, 24 January, 5, 14 March, 14 April, 3-12 October 1883, 14 September 1884, 20 October 1885, 29 July 1898; Glenbow Museum archives: photographs and Macleod letters (1882/10, 1883/25); "Mary Drever Macleod: A Biographical Study," unpublished manuscript, Provincial Archives of Alberta; *From Home to Home: Autumn Wanderings in the North-West in the Years 1882, 1883, 1884*, Alex Stavely Hill, 220; 1881 Census of Canada, Bow River; *Lethbridge Herald*, 11 January 1952; "Eleven Miles of Prayer," from the

writings of Rev. S. Trivett; *The Range Men*, Leroy Victor Kelly; *Prairie Grass to Mountain Pass: History of the Pioneers of Pincher Creek and District*, 111, 175-176.

11. *The Range Men*, L. V. Kelly; *Rocky Mountain Echo*, Fred Stenson (pre-publication); Canada census, 1901, High River.

12. *Canadian Cattlemen*, Mary Terrill, June 1943; *Leaves From the Medicine Tree*, 314; *Lethbridge News*, 5 June 1908; *Before the Fences*, Frederick William Ings, 19; *The Golden Age of the Canadian Cowboy*, Hugh A. Dempsey.

13. *The Weather Factory: A Pictorial History of Medicine Hat*, David C. Jones, L. J. Roy Wilson, Donny White, 32; Canada census, 1901, Medicine Hat

14. For more information on the conditions that brought the 1905-1912 wave of Black immigration to Northern Alberta and Saskatchewan and the conditions they found when they got here, see my book, *Pourin' Down Rain*, Cheryl Foggo; *A Keystone Legacy*, Gwen Hooks; *Deemed Unsuitable*, R. Bruce Shepard; *The Windows of Our Memories*, Velma Carter and Wanda Leffler Akili; *The Peoples of Alberta*, Howard and Tamara Palmer; other sources include my family's personal archives, interviews with family members, deceased and living, and "The Story of My Father's Life," an unpublished manuscript written by my great-aunt Daisy Smith Mayes Williams.

15. Statutes of Canada, Debates, Sessional Papers, Parliament, House of Commons; *Deemed Unsuitable*, R. Bruce Shepard 71-85; *Albertan*, 24 March, 4, 12, 21, 27 April, 20 May 1911; *Calgary Herald*, March, April, 1911; *Edmonton Capital*, 5, 25, 27, 28, March, 11, 25, 27, April, 3 May, 14 November 1911, 9 April 1912; *Edmonton Journal*, 8 April 1911; *Edmonton Daily Bulletin*, 21-22 March, 30 May 1911, 27 June 1912; *Lethbridge Herald*, 21, 28 March 1911; *Lloydminster Times*, 30 March 1911; *Saskatoon Daily Phoenix*, 22-23 March 1911; *Winnipeg Free Press*, 17, 20 March 1908; *Manitoba Free Press*, 12, 28 March, 27 April 1911; *The University Magazine*, Vol. 13, 1914; *The Globe*, 4 April 1911; *Alberta History Magazine*, vol. 25, no. 4; Autumn, 1977 "Dark Spots in Alberta," Colin Thomson; *Alberta History Magazine*, vol. 29, no. 3, Summer 1981, *Urban Blacks in Alberta*, Tamara and Howard Palmer.

16. Glenbow Museum Archives photographic collection, Glenbow Museum Rotary Club Papers, Aberhart speeches transcriptions (Glenbow Archives Norman Smith papers); Racist charicatures of Blacks in Calgary's newspapers, from the 1800s to the 1940s are too numerous to list here. For a few representative examples see the *Calgary Daily Herald*, 4 March 1911 and the *Calgary Herald*, 8 April 1940.

17. *Deemed Unsuitable*, R. Bruce Shepard, 78-81; *Calgary Albertan, Calgary Herald, Lethbridge Daily News, Lethbridge Herald, Saskatoon Daily Phoenix, Regina Leader, Edmonton Bulletin*, 6-15 April 1911.

18. Glenbow Museum Archives, interview with Tamara Palmer, 1979; and from my own interviews conducted with family members and community elders.

19. *Calgary Herald*, 11 October 1910.

20. *Calgary Daily Herald*, 6 March 1911; City Clerk Papers, 10 March 1911.

21. City Clerk Papers, 10 March 1911; *Morning Albertan*, 11 December 1911; City Clerk Papers; 19 February 1914, 3, 5 December 1916, 31 March, 27 April 1920; *Calgary Herald*, 27, 29, 30 April 1920; *Albertan*, 27, 29, 30 April, 1, 21 May 1920; *Calgary Daily Herald*, 5 January 1920.

22. *Calgary Herald*, 17 December 1938, 22 March, 23 April, 1 December 1947, 24 August 1948, 8 May 1951.

23. *Calgary Herald*, 22 March, 23 April, 1 December 1947; Glenbow Archives, City Clerk papers, 17, 28, 31 March, 8 April 1947; Glenbow Archives, Howard Palmer fonds, interviews by Howard and Tamara Palmer with Andrew Risby, Dick Bellamy, Alge and Joan Armstead, Boadie Bowen; from my own interviews with Alge and Joan Armstead, 1980 and Edith Risby, 2004; *Calgary Herald*, 2 August 2004, interview by David Bly with Melvin Crump.

24. Glenbow Museum Archives, Howard Palmer fonds, interview with Virnetta Anderson, 1979.

25. *Albertan*, 8, 9 April 1940; *Calgary Herald*, 8, 10 April 1940.

26. From my interview with Andrew Risby, 2001; This incident was also mentioned in Howard Palmer's interview with Andrew Risby, 1979, Glenbow Museum Archives, Howard Palmer fonds.

27. *Albertan*, 30 June 1967; *Calgary Herald*, 3 October 1969, 8 June 1993, 9, 10 May 1994, 2 November 1996, 7, 21 November 1999, 28 June 2002, 2 August 2004.

28. *The Ku Klux Klan in Central Alberta*, William Peter Baergen; *Web of Hate*, Warren Kinsella; *Campaigning Against Hate*, Marcus Gee, John Howse, Maclean's, Sept. 1, 1986; *Tall Tales*, David Bercuson, *Saturday Night*, October 1987; "Rolling out a Not-Welcome Mat for Neo-Nazis," Cristine Bye, *United Church Observer*, Nov. 1990; *Calgary Herald*, 28 February 1989, 8-9, 16, 26 September 1990, 11 January, 17 August, 7 December 1991, 29 February 1992, 27 February, 27 April 1993, 28 April 1995, 9 February 1997, 23 February 2002.

29. *The Aryan Nation*, a film, Larry Ryckman, 1985; *Calgary Herald*, Nov. 5, 1980.

30. Global Television, 1 September 2004; *Calgary Herald*, 10, 21 March, 3, 30, September, 27 October 2004.

31. *Calgary Herald*, 11 June, 31 July, 10 September, 1995, 5 July 1996, 7 February 1999, 11 October 2000, 5 October 2003.

Calgary's Jewish Community
A Brief History
by Jack Switzer

In September 1884 several Jewish men met in a Calgary hall. They formed a *minyan*, the quorum traditionally required to form a prayer group, and held the *Rosh Hashanah* – Jewish New Year's – services. It was an early example of community formation, the development of communal institutions that would mark Jewish life in southern Alberta through to the twenty-first century.

The service was led by Jacob Diamond, Alberta's first permanent Jewish settler. He had come to Calgary from Russia (via Ontario) in 1888. The first Jew in the province may have been a Montana-based prospector, in 1869. Jews were known to have worked on track-laying crews that brought the CPR into Alberta in 1882. Winnipeg's Repstein brothers, following the railhead to Calgary in 1883, set up a tent store near the tracks but soon left.

Diamond was part of a mass-migration that saw over two million east-European Jews cross the Atlantic to North America between 1881 and 1914. Most went to the United States, but about 100 000 chose Canadian destinations, mainly Montreal and Toronto. A few ventured farther west.

Impetus for the huge movement were the anti-Jewish *pogroms* – physical attacks and restrictive laws – that followed the 1881 assassination of Tsar Alexander II of Russia. Increasingly dim economic conditions also spurred many to leave the overcrowded, fetid *shtetls* and cities of the Jewish Pale of Settlement in Tsarist Russia, an area stretching from the Baltic to the Black sea, and including much of present-day Lithuania, Poland, Byelorussia, and Ukraine, as well as rural western Russia. Romania and parts of the Austro-Hungarian empire also contributed to Jewish emigration.

Jewish philanthropists, notably Baron de Hirsch, attempted to settle immigrant Jews on farm communities, believing the rural life to offer more economic and spiritual potential than the ghettos of the cities. The 1880s saw several brief and unsuccessful

Jewish farming ventures in present-day Saskatchewan, with two notable failures in Alberta, near Pine Lake and Macleod.

Jacob Diamond was joined by his brother William in 1892, and by a few other Jewish families before the turn of the century. There were about 50 Jews in Calgary, in 1905. A few Jewish families ran country stores and there was a sprinkling of Jewish farmers in the area.

Most Jewish men worked in mercantile trades, ranging from peddling to retailing. The Diamond family followed in this tradition. Jacob Diamond became a liquor merchant; William Diamond ran a clothing store before moving to become an Edmonton Jewish pioneer, and another brother, Philip Diamond, opened a general store in Canmore. This small-business focus was to characterize Jewish bread-winning for several decades.

While some immigrants worked briefly in wage jobs – the CPR shops and the Burns packing plant were popular employers – almost all took up small business ventures as soon as possible. Work was often hard and dirty, but there were no sweat shops of the sort that characterized Jewish workplaces in the eastern cities and Winnipeg.

The very early Calgary Jewish community met frequently for social occasions, but in 1904 the community was forced to organize more formally. An infant girl, Goldie Bell, died. Her father and the community's *ad hoc* leader, Jacob Diamond, approached the City fathers to buy land for a Jewish cemetery. A small plot of land on what is now Macleod Trail on Cemetery Hill became the nucleus of a major Jewish burial area.

The Jewish burial society, the *Chevra Kadisha*, was not formally incorporated for several years, but it formed the base for more Jewish communal groups. In 1905 the burial society leaders formed a religious society, the House of Jacob congregation. Later that year, a Montreal merchant donated a torah scroll to the young community.

The Calgary group united with Edmonton's Jewish community in 1906 to share the services of Alberta's first rabbi, Hyman Goldstick. He traveled by train between the two cities to lead services, teach children, perform ritual animal slaughtering duties, and provide circumcisions. Goldstick soon settled in Edmonton, and left Calgary's rabbinical needs to be filled by lay persons and visiting clerics.

The early 1900s also saw the beginnings of Jewish communal life in Lethbridge and Medicine Hat. The Harris Goodman family was the first to settle in Lethbridge. There was rapid growth, and by 1909 the community had an organized congregation and its own cemetery.

Medicine Hat showed a similar growth pattern – rapid post-1905 settlement, with quick organization to meet religious and communal needs.

The year 1905 is another milestone; it was marked by major anti-Tsarist activity in Russia, again followed by anti-Semitic repression and major Jewish emigration. About 20 000 Jews entered Canada between 1900 and 1905. Another 40 000 came during the next five years, 1906 to 1910. The West attracted relatively few, but shared the growth proportionately.

We know that Alberta experienced explosive growth after the province's birth in 1905. Calgary's 1901 population of 4 109 grew more than tenfold, to 44 000 in 1911, and 56 000 by 1916. Jewish population growth kept step. The handful of Jews at the turn of the century became more than 600 in 1911. Edmonton then had about 200 Jews, Lethbridge about 50, and Medicine Hat about 20.

The very early Jewish pioneers had met some hostility – as had other east-European immigrants. Later immigrants recognized their alien, minority status, and worked hard to assimilate, while keeping their major religious and cultural characteristics intact. Almost all spoke Yiddish among themselves, but quickly learned English for their external dealings. Kosher butchers and bakeries catered to the needs of the religiously observant, although some Jews abandoned traditional rituals as part of the pragmatism required for prairie life.

Southern Alberta's Jews were busy with community-building during the decade preceding the Great War. In Calgary, the House of Jacob congregation bought land on 5th Avenue East and in 1909 erected a small building in the back of the property to house prayer and Hebrew school activities. In 1911, a large synagogue was opened on the site. It seated 500, and served the city's orthodox community until its demolition in 1968.

The Jews of Lethbridge started a cemetery in 1909 and established a congregation in 1911. Medicine Hat's Jews formed the Sons of Abraham congregation in 1912. The development of homesteading and the growth of rail lines early in the century brought Jewish families into many area towns, mainly to run stores and hotels.

Meanwhile, a second wave of Jewish farm settlement was underway. In 1905 and 1906 several Jewish families took up homesteads on either side of the Red Deer River near Trochu and Rumsey. A smaller group later (1910) established a block settlement near Sibbald, and called it the Montefiore colony.

The Jewish farm "colonies" formed strong communities. They built synagogues and hired itinerant religious functionaries when finances allowed it. Some farmers spent the winter months in Calgary, earning money to see them through the pioneering farm years. Loans from the Jewish Colonization Association also helped.

By 1914 the Rumsey/Trochu settlements numbered about 50 families, while Montefiore, a much less fertile area, had about 20 Jewish farmers.

Several very large and influential extended families set roots in Calgary during the years preceding World War I. A few young professionals and wealthy businessmen also chose to locate in the city. These (and other) second-generation, English-speaking young Jews helped move their community from the east-Calgary ghetto toward more integration with the greater society.

Most pre-World War I Jews did business and lived in East Calgary. Immigrant-owned second hand stores, confectioneries, tailor shops, and the like were largely located on 8th Avenue East and nearby streets. Most newcomers lived east and north of city hall, in Riverside, or across the tracks in Victoria park. The better off Jews moved west or south of downtown.

World War I slowed immigration, and allowed southern Alberta's Jewish community to consolidate its improving status. In 1914, the 900 or so Jews in Calgary had a small cemetery, a large synagogue, an afternoon Hebrew school, and a growing number of clubs. There was an active Zionist organization, a Workmen's Circle (socialist group), a Yiddish cultural society, and a Young Men's Hebrew Association, which sponsored social and athletic activities, including a baseball team.

A twelve-man *Vaad Ha'ir*, a community council, attempted after 1912 to coordinate Jewish activities and ensure provision of basic religious and educational services. It soon disbanded as the growing number of diverse Jewish groups competed for the community's resources. One success was the 1913 establishment of a regular Hebrew school, previously sporadic, but now operating after public school hours in rented quarters.

Several area Jews served in the Canadian army during the war, and two were killed in action. (Another died later of war wounds.) Jews actively raised funds for the relief of European refugees, and celebrated when the Balfour declaration – promising that Palestine would become a Jewish homeland – was announced.

Calgary's Jews were becoming increasingly more sophisticated. As early as 1912, wealthier, more-assimilated Jews were holding formal dances as charity fundraisers. Younger Jewish men and women were quick to adopt the customs and mores of their "Anglo" peers. Secularization and Canadianization were well underway.

The growing diversity of the Calgary Jewish community became obvious during the 1916 High Holy Days when four different services were held in Calgary. The established Orthodox community met at the House of Jacob Synagogue, while alternate congregations, one of them using American-style Reform rituals, met in rented halls. None of the new congregations lasted very long.

In 1917 a B'Nai Brith lodge – with "American" rituals and meetings conducted in English – was formed in Calgary.

Local Jewish charity work – helping needy Jews – had previously been the venue of ad hoc groups, but was formalized with the creation in 1918 of the Calgary Jewish Ladies' Aid Society, which later became part of the National Council of Jewish Women. The Daughters of Zion Hadassah chapter, a branch of the world-wide women's Zionist group, was formed in Calgary in 1921.

The end of World War I opened the immigration gates once more. Calgary's Jewish population rose modestly between 1920 and 1930, from 1 263 to about 1 600 persons.

Many of the new immigrants were *Yiddishists*, Jews who felt the Yiddish language and culture to be important aspects of the Judaic experience. They formed a strong Yiddish cultural group, with a busy schedule of speakers, concerts, and films. In 1927 club members formed the I. L. Peretz school. In 1929 the school opened its own building on Centre Street and 13th Avenue South; full-day classes began soon afterwards.

The opening of the Peretz School building may have delayed the campaign by a competing group to build a multi-purpose Jewish Community Centre. Fundraising began in 1926, but construction did not begin until 1929. A year later, only the lower level was complete, but the *House of Israel* building at 18th Avenue and Centre Street opened its doors to the Hebrew School and to social/cultural uses.

Calgary Jews were active in the local classical music scene. For a decade after 1927 the Calgary Symphony Orchestra was conducted by a Russian-trained Jew, Grigory Garbovitsky. His concert master was Jascha

THE HOUSE OF ISRAEL
בית ישראל

Kindergarten students of the Calgary Talmud Torah (Hebrew School) are seen in front of the House of Israel building where the school was located. The building also housed the Beth Israel congregation, as well as meeting room and social facilities. Calgary, Alberta, 1943. Jewish Historical Society of Southern Alberta Archives.

Galpern, also a refugee from the Russian revolution. Several Jewish men and women played in the symphony orchestra.

The 1931 census recorded 1 603 Jews in Calgary, about two per cent of the city's population. Lethbridge had 111 Jews, Medicine Hat 104. Twenty-five southern Alberta towns had Jewish residents; most had one or two families, but Drumheller had 44 Jews.

The depression years stemmed immigration, and saw Jews sharing the economic problems of other Albertans – unemployment, declining farm incomes, low credit availability, and shrinking business opportunities. Local Jews turned to self-help programs. Two Jewish *free-loan* societies operated, and several social organizations expanded their mandates to help needy brethren.

By the early thirties most Jewish farmers had left the land, opting for life in Calgary and other urban centres. Farm life was harsh and uncertain, while the cities offered opportunities for a fuller Jewish life, better jobs and schooling, and Jewish mates for their children.

Small-town Jewry also became a one-generation phenomenon; most small-town Jews moved to the cities as their children grew older or as the farm-based rural economy declined.

Several Calgary Jews were friends of Social Credit premier William Aberhart, but the community generally felt apprehensive about the ruling party's strong fundamentalist Christian base.

Despite hard times the Calgary Jewish community continued to evolve during the 1930s. A young men's group, Aleph Tzadik Aleph, was formed; Zionist youth clubs and a Jewish scouting group served children and teens.

Various adult Zionist groups operated, and a local branch of the Canadian Jewish Congress became active. It was headed for some time by Morris Smith, founder of the Smithbilt Hat company. Congress was able to counter local anti-Semitism, but could do little to promote its major agenda, the re-opening of immigration to allow victims of Nazi persecution into Canada.

The Lethbridge and Medicine Hat congregations moved into their own synagogue buildings during the 1930s, and in Calgary the Beth Israel Congregation, using "Modern Orthodox" ritual, began holding services in 1935 in the House of Israel community building.

An economic survey late in the 1930s counted 385 working Jews in Calgary; half were business owners, mainly of the mom-and-pop variety. Fifty-eight Jews ran groceries or confectioneries, and there were 26 second-hand dealers. Thirteen Jews ran clothing stores and 44 other stores were Jewish-owned. Thirty Jews were listed as cattle buyers.

Only nine Jews in the 1938 survey were professionals – six lawyers, two doctors, and one dentist. A major employment area was at the Calgary Film Exchange, where most studio distribution offices were headed by Jewish men.

Within days of the outbreak of war in 1939, a significant number of southern Alberta Jews joined in Canada's armed forces. In all, about 250 men and women, one in 10 of all local Jews, were in uniform. Twelve died in action, mainly RCAF bomber-crew members. More were wounded, some taken prisoner, and several won medals for valor.

On the home front, Jewish organizations did their part. They raised funds for international relief, helped equip recreation facilities at local bases, and sent packages to the "boys" overseas. War

These Jewish men enlisted in the Canadian Armed Forces within days of the outbreak of World War II. This photo was taken at their initiation into the Calgary B'Nai Brith Lodge in September, 1939, Calgary, Alberta. Jewish Historical Society of Southern Alberta Archives.

bonds were purchased, blood donated, and socks knit. Visiting Jewish servicemen were welcomed into local homes and synagogues for Jewish observances.

The returning soldiers were confident and able; they had proven themselves the equal of any Canadian serviceman. Jewish veterans took full advantage of training programs and the opportunities afforded by the post-war boom. They soon started new businesses or expanded old ones, opened professional practices, and took previously restricted jobs in universities and the civil service. Jewish teachers became numerous, and the post-war oil boom brought many Jews into the petroleum industry.

War's end also brought survivors of the terrible holocaust that had nearly destroyed European Jewry. Several hundred survivors came to southern Alberta, some of them teen orphans, some independent adults, and many to join established family members. They and their children now formed about 10% of the Jewish population.

Community development resumed after the war. The House of Israel community building was completed in 1949. It housed the Hebrew School, which had moved to day-school status in 1947, and the Beth Israel Congregation, which joined the Conservative movement in 1952. There were also meeting rooms and banquet facilities.

The years between 1956 and 1966 saw a massive Jewish building spree in southern Alberta. Medicine Hat Jews rebuilt the Sons of Abraham synagogue. (Jewish activist Harry Veiner served as the city's mayor for many years between 1952 and 1974.) Camp B'Nai Brith opened at Pine Lake in 1956. Lethbridge Jews opened a new community centre, Beth Israel synagogue.

The Calgary section of the National Council of Jewish Women celebrated its 30th anniversary in 1959. Past presidents are grouped around the table. Council had a busy schedule of social-service and community improvement programs, most reaching out to the greater community. Its members were largely second-generation, English-speaking women. Jewish Historical Society of Southern Alberta Archives.

In Calgary, Jews were moving from the west-central districts south along the Elbow Drive axis, first into Britannia, and gradually south as the suburbs spread. A member-owned Jewish curling rink, the Meadowlark club, operated for several years on 58th Avenue SW. The Hebrew School moved to its Glenmore Trail location in 1959; a year later Beth Israel Synagogue opened on a site next door to it. The Peretz School chose an Altadore location for its new building, opened in 1959.

A new congregation, "Modern-Orthodox" Shaarey Tzedec, built its synagogue in 1960 next to the old House of Israel building. And in 1961 the Chevra Kadisha finally built its own funeral chapel at a Scarboro location.

Physical development took a respite for several years, until 1979, when the current Jewish Community Centre was opened on 90th Avenue SW. Near it is the new House of Jacob – Mikveh Israel synagogue, built in 1982. This congregation sponsored the founding of an Orthodox day school, the Akiva Academy. The Orthodox community was augmented in 1988 by the opening of a Lubovich outreach facility in the Woodlands district.

A Reform congregation, Temple B'Nai Tikvah, was formed in 1979 and now shares use of a large Britannia-area building with a United Church group. During the 1980s the Hebrew School and the Peretz School merged, forming the Calgary Jewish Academy. Another merger saw the Beth Israel and Shaarey Tzedec congregations unite to become Beth Tzedec.

Population growth was spurred by the arrival during the 1970s of Jewish families from Montreal, fleeing what they viewed as repressive conditions in Quebec. Many were professionals, and the Montreal newcomers were quick to participate in community affairs.

Russian Jews emigrated to Calgary in large numbers (some via Israel) during the 1980s, and today one in 12 Calgary Jews was born in the former Soviet Union.

Israelis and South African Jews also joined the community in sizable numbers during the last three decades, and there has been continuing inter-provincial migration – Jews also come from Canadian centres, such as Saskatoon, Winnipeg, and Toronto. This in-migration has far exceeded the number who have left.

Calgary's Jewish population now exceeds 8 000, a four-fold increase from the approximately 2 000 counted in 1950. Regrettably, both Lethbridge and Medicine Hat have seen declines in Jewish population. Both cities still have small Jewish groups, but have had to close their synagogues.

Calgary's Jews may be the most successful of any of the city's religious/ethnic minorities. Proportionately, twice as many Jews earn high incomes than do Calgarians as a whole. Sixty percent of all Jews are either enrolled in university or have completed at least a bachelor's degree, more than double the general figures. Jews comprise one per cent of the city's population, but one out of 20 doctors and dentists in Calgary is Jewish.

Intermarriage rates are rising. About one in six "Jewish" marriages has a non-Jewish spouse, a bit higher than the national average. In marriages currently taking place, as many as 40% may involve intermarriage.

But there is also poverty, notably among recent immigrants and the elderly. The rate of affiliation with Jewish institutes is declining – more and more persons identify themselves as Jews but do not belong to Jewish organizations or donate to Jewish charities.

However, positive indicators also exist. Jewish day-school enrollment is strong – proportionally the highest in Canada. About 300 children attend the Calgary Jewish Academy and the smaller Akiva Academy. Synagogue membership is high. Affiliated Jews continue to support the community's annual United Israel Appeal, which distributes funds to local organizations as well as Israeli charities. Holocaust remembrance events are well attended, as are the many other events that regularly mark the community's social, cultural, and religious calendar.

Calgary's Jews have, in just over 100 years of continuous effort, managed to achieve what few other local minorities have done. They have become fully integrated into the fabric of the greater society while developing and maintaining very distinct ethnic/religious identities.

The next century will be as challenging. There will be Jews in Calgary in 2105. They will be in every way Calgarians, but they will also continue to be Jews.

Muslim Presence in Alberta:
Contribution and Challenges
by Karim-Aly S. Kassam

The Ismaili Jamat Khana and Centre, Calgary, Alberta. Photo by Navroz Mitha, provided by Fiaz Merani.

Muslims are being represented in the North American media through a myopic stereotypical lens that lacks both breadth of understanding and depth of knowledge that Muslims comprise some 1.4 billion souls who live in almost all habitable corners of the world among diverse cultures (Kassam *et al* 2002; Karim 2000). It is not surprising that this 1 400-year-old faith has a history of contact with the Americas. Recent scholarship indicates that Zheng He, the Chinese Admiral of the Ming Emperor Zhu Di and a devout Muslim, made a voyage of exploration to the Americas in 1421 when he circumnavigated the World. He predates Christopher Columbus to the Americas by 70 years (Menzies 2002). The historical connection and dependence of Christopher Columbus or Giovani Caboto (John Cabot) on science and navigation of Muslim civilizations remains virtually unexplored in most textbooks used in schools. For instance, the reliance of Columbus on the astronomical, geographical, maritime, and philosophical sciences of the day came primarily from scholars who were Muslim. Despite being a Christian living during the intolerance of the Spanish Inquisition, he openly acknowledged his dependence upon Muslim intellectuals for his knowledge (Chapman 1992; Colón 1992). Nonetheless, this is largely unknown to most Canadians, leaving us in relative ignorance of the contributions of Muslim civilizations to humanity in general and the settlement of the Americas in particular.

There is an even more direct link between the indigenous peoples of the Americas and Muslims caused by the ostensible discovery of the "New World" in 1492. When Columbus "sailed the ocean blue" and landed in the Americas, he thought he had found India. He maintained this belief till his death. The diverse Native peoples of the Americas suddenly were cast into one monolithic rubric called the "Indian," much like Muslims in the media today. The cultural and linguistic diversity of the Aboriginal peoples of the Americas was largely ignored. The year 1492 precipitated cultural genocide of staggering proportions on the peoples of the Americas (Casas 1971; Wright 1993). However, these events had a previous history across the Atlantic in Spain. After living there for 800 years, Muslims and Jews were being expelled. The ingredients of cultural genocide began in Spain with the burning of books (entire libraries), followed by restrictions in religious practices, use of language, clothing, and even bathing (because it was considered sensual). The stereotype of the savage infidel sodomite Moor (Muslim) was then transposed onto the variety of indigenous peoples of the Americas. Having initiated the recipe of cultural annihilation in Spain, it was soon implemented in the "New World." We have our residential schools, in Canada, as more recent examples of this recipe. Aboriginal peoples in the Southern Americas were even tried as Muslim or Jewish heretics despite no knowledge of Moses or Muhammad. As Spanish and Portuguese power waned, but not soon enough to prevent the brutality, the French and British in North America followed suit. Except now the model of cultural cleansing had been perfected in the Americas and could now be applied to another "savage" in Africa and South East Asia. In fact, the signs on British social clubs in the 1930s in East Africa read "No dogs and Asians allowed." The negative image of the Moor applied to the North American Indian was now applied to Muslims and others in Africa and Asia. As long as the Moors or North American Indians were thought to be savage sodomite infidels, they were worthy of domination and to be "civilized" if possible (Matar 1999). Many of those who lived under British rule in Africa and Asia later immigrated to Canada and Alberta in particular. They carried with them a memory of this history.

In 1854, 13 years before Confederation, the first Muslim, James Love, named after his father, was born in Ontario to a teenage bride, Agnes, of Scottish descent. The Loves went on to have seven additional children, the youngest, Alexander, born in 1868, one year after Confederation. Similarly, another couple, Martha and John Simon, described in government documents as *Mahometans,*[1] settled in Ontario in 1871 coming from the United States. Like Agnes, Martha and John were of western European extraction. Martha was French and John, English. The first national census in 1871 counted 13 Muslims in Canada (Hamdani 1997; 1999).[2] Muslims began arriving in Alberta at the turn of the twentieth century.

The length of Muslim presence in Alberta spans approximately the age of this Province. The early Muslims in Alberta originated from the Levant (modern day Lebanon, Syria, and occupied Territories), which was then part of the Ottoman Empire. Their arrival in Alberta was facilitated by a small but resourceful network of previous immigrant Arabs of both Christian and Muslim background who had settled in Quebec, Ontario, Manitoba, and parts of the United States. These early immigrants to Alberta in the 1900s also sought to avoid being drafted into the Ottoman army. They began as laborers laying tracks for the Canadian Pacific Railway, building grain elevators in southern Alberta for the United Grain Growers, and working in sawmills to eke out a living (Baker 1976; Fahlman 1995; Hamdani 1996). As soon as they had saved enough funds to set up small enterprises, they quickly turned to work as *peddlers* – a term used at that time to indicate a social class of peripatetic merchants who sell easily transportable goods (Duncanson 1978, 1970; Fahlman 1995).[3] In fact, self-employment through peddlery was well-suited to the early immigrants from the Levant as their homeland was geographically the bridge between the east and west and the centre of mercantilism in the Mediterranean (Abu-Laban 1980). As they became more established and proficient in the English language, these pioneers began to engage in the fur trade – buying and selling fur, and trading in dry goods and food. They travelled Northern Alberta, Saskatchewan, and the Northwest Territories bartering for fur to be sent to southern markets (Baker 1976; Duncanson 1978, 1970).

Harold Adams Innis, the eminent Canadian economic historian, observed that in order to survive in the environment of the New World, the early European settlers had to seek the help of the indigenous peoples of this land. This meant the Europeans had to adapt their cultural traits to suit the cultural and geographic terrain. The fur trade could only succeed with Aboriginal support. Their thorough knowledge of animal habits and close connection to the land, their ability to traverse a vast geography, and their capacity to secure sources of food for the Europeans, all speak to fundamental and often ignored roles the indigenous people of this land played in facilitating European settlement (Innis 1995, 2001).

Similarly, early Muslim pioneers in Alberta depended entirely on the Aboriginal peoples of Northern Alberta and Northwest Territories. They learned Native languages such as Chipewyan and Cree to become skilled at and thrive in the fur trade. Many of them travelled by dog team to Aboriginal camps and settlements loaded with dry goods and food items to trade (Baker 1976; Duncanson 1978; 1980). Sam (Esmeil) Jamha, who emigrated from the Levant to Canada at the tender age of 14 and began fur trading in 1907, before his 16th birthday, relied on and was trusted by Aboriginal peoples. An unpublished biography at the Glenbow Museum Archives describes his relationship with them:

> He spent considerable time with the Indians. . . . He spoke Cree like a native and had no difficulty with other Indian dialects. The natives are his friends, they delight in teaching him and show genuine affection for him. Furs begin to fascinate Sam and the learning process of his future as a fur buyer begins as he learns the difference between a rat [Muskrat] and a mink and the various other pelts of otter, beaver, fox, martin, skunk, weasel, fisher, squirrel and rabbit. How to distinguish prime from poor pelts and many native secrets of catching and preparing the skins. (Duncanson 1978: 29)

Sam Jamha not only lived amongst indigenous peoples for the purposes of trade but learned to sing with them in their language. In later life he describes with almost lyrical reverie, a passage of love with a beautiful young Aboriginal woman on a spring afternoon during his youth. He searched but could never find her again, as if she had vanished with mythical splendor (Ibid: 82).

However, survival in the fur trade was not easy. Often jealousy from white fur traders led to considerable difficulties. The success of individuals like Peter Baker, a Muslim from the Levant who emigrated after Sam Jamha, caused the Hudson's Bay Company to take notice. He was in direct competition with them. At Fort Smith the manager, with the help of the District Inspector, conspired to spread rumors about Peter Baker in order to stop Aboriginal peoples converted to Christianity from trading with him.

When [Willy] Lyall moved over he started talking nasty and mean . . . he told people all about the 'Jew' and made up a name for my place, the 'Jew's store.' The people, Indian, Metis, and whites [sic] came and told me that he was spreading false propaganda about me. Along with Lyall, a young Scotch policeman, McIvor, was also annoying me. Before Lyall came to [Fort] Smith I had never heard anybody mention such a word as 'Jew'. . . . In those days, when anybody was called a 'Jew', it meant outcast and despised, because a 'Jew' was a 'Christkiller'. I was called that most often. (Baker 1976: 38)

It is noteworthy that Peter Baker, a Muslim Arab, does not deny being a 'Jew.' In fact he accepts it (Baker 1976:38-39). The conflation of Muslim with the Jew is revealing. The prejudice against being a "Muslim" probably meant nothing in the north but being a "Jew" had currency particularly as a result of the work of missionaries.

Peter Baker's religious identity mentions his birth name, Bedouin Ferran, only once early in his posthumously published autobiography. In 1909, he was given the name Peter Baker by a Catholic priest at the Holy Cross College where Peter worked as a laborer before immigrating to Alberta (Baker 1976:12). While he indicates that he had been described as a "Moslem infidel" (Ibid. 144), Peter Baker's Muslim identity was established through the obituary notices in the *Edmonton Journal* which indicated that his funeral took place at the Al-Rashid Mosque in Edmonton on November 13, 1973.[4] Indeed the majority of early Muslim settlers Anglicized their first names or changed them altogether (Awid and Haymour 1973; Ali 1999). A lot of pressure must have been exerted on these early Muslims to fit in (Abu-Laban 1980). While winning friends and engaging in trade, prejudice in business, at times motivated by outright jealousy, was always prevalent and took on legal manifestations. Baker relates how the Minister of the Interior, Charlie Stewart, in 1926, at the urging of the President of the Northern Traders Company, amended Territorial Trading and Trafficking Laws at ministerial discretion without an Order-in-Council. In order to obtain a Territorial Trading and Trafficking License, merchants like Baker would no longer be able to travel to the camps of the trappers but fur trading would have to be confined to permanent posts. When Baker confronted the Minister in Edmonton, Stewart replied: "It wouldn't be necessary for the new rule if it was not for those damned Syrians and Jews going around fooling the poor Indians!" (Baker 1976: 192).

Peter Baker later went on to represent a mostly Aboriginal constituency in the Legislature of the Northwest Territories (1964 to 1967) and produced a serialized version of his life as a fur trader in "News of the North" in Yellowknife.

The story of Muslim settlement is not limited to men in the fur trade. Women, too, played a significant role in Muslim settlement in Alberta. Their contributions were not limited to their families, rather they extended to all those who were their neighbors irrespective of creed or color. For instance, Mary (Rikia) Saddy's family homesteaded and ranched in Southern Alberta and she fed the crews that worked in their fields (Ali 1999). The early roles of Muslim women were affected by their arrival and adaptation in a new land and their contributions were fundamental to community building in Alberta. In addition to their reproductive roles of child care and domestic labor, early Muslim women were also involved in community management that included the collective aspect of organization, production, and consumption of resources (Moser 1993; Kassam 1997). A prominent example of the contribution of Muslim women is the establishment of the first Muslim place of prayer in Canada to be built for that purpose alone: a Mosque located in Alberta.

In the 1920s, the Muslim community in Alberta began to think of a place for congregational prayer (Duncanson 1978, 1980; Ali 1999). The idea of a mosque was a major milestone in the thinking of these early settlers as it represented a sign of their permanence and confidence in Alberta. The province would be their definitive home now and into future. In this home they needed a place that marked the births, deaths, and marriages of members of the community in addition to observing religious obligations and meeting their spiritual needs. These early Muslim pioneers were now becoming citizens contributing to the common good of Alberta. While the founders list names both women and men, it was really the women who were the prime movers behind the Al-Rashid Mosque through fundraising (Lorenz 1999). In 1938, a mosque was finally built in the City of Edmonton with the support of Muslims from across Alberta and Saskatchewan. In keeping with the cooperative sentiment of the prairies that "we are all in it together," Christian and Jewish Albertans also contributed. (Ali 1999; Duncanson 1978, 1980; Lorenz 1999; Khattab 1969). A Ukrainian Albertan architect drew up the original plans for the mosque. The thirties were a difficult time to raise funds as the country was in the ravages of an economic depression. Fundraising from shopkeepers on Jasper Avenue, dances, teas, dinners, and card parties gradually raised the $5 000 necessary to build the Al Rashid Mosque. These early Muslim women established the organization infrastructure that sustained a fledgling community of Muslims in Alberta.

Al Rashid was not just a place of prayer but contributed to the life of the Alberta Muslim community. Some of the Muslim women who contributed both to the establishment of, and the cultural life of the Alberta Muslims at the mosque were Margaret Ailley, Hilwie Hamdon, Vera Jamha, and Miriam Teha (Awid and Haymour 1973). Some of these women were converts to Islam, born European Christians and married to Muslim men, but they supported the religious and cultural well-being of the community. The mosque was home to religious festivals such as Idd, community gatherings, music and traditional dances, visiting church groups, and cultural clubs (Al-Ati 1963; Khattab 1969; Lorenz 1999).

In the late 1980s, as the fiftieth anniversary of the Al Rashid Mosque approached, it was threatened by imminent demolition to make way for a parking lot for the Royal Alexandra Hospital. A group of Albertan Muslim men failed to raise the funds needed to save the first Canadian Mosque. The Canadian Council of Muslim Women stepped in, led by the granddaughters of the pioneer women. Karen Hamdon, granddaughter of Hilwie Hamdon; Mahmuda Ali, granddaughter of Mary Saddy; and Lila Fahlman, descended from Sufi healers and staunch English Methodists, engaged in a vigorous campaign much like their women kinfolk before them. They successfully raised the money needed, restored the mosque to its original glory, and had it located among other historical buildings at Fort Edmonton Park. This was achieved at a time when there was pronounced anti-Islamic sentiment spurred on by the Gulf War. On May 28, 1992, the restored Al Rashid was officially opened (Ali 1999; Fahlman 1995, 1999; Lorenz 1999).

According to the Statistics Canada 2001 Census Data, there are 49 045 Muslims in Alberta. Muslims comprise 1.7% of the total population of Alberta. Between 1981 and 1991, the population of Muslims increased by 84% in the Province. The percentage increase in the decennial period 1991 to 2001, slowed to a 58% increase in the population of Alberta Muslims. The population of Muslims in the city of Calgary is 25 900, representing nearly three percent of the City's total population. Between 1991 and 2001, Calgary's Muslim population increased by 86.5%. The population of Muslims in Alberta is significant. Following the various Christian denominations, Alberta Muslims comprise the largest non-Christian religious group in the Province.

Unlike the early Muslim settlers in Alberta who were largely from the Levant, post-war Muslim immigration to Canada is noteworthy for its cultural and linguistic diversity. Between 1991 and 2001, 15% of immigrants to Canada were of a Muslim background (Statistic Canada 2003b). The cities of Calgary and Edmonton respectively have the fourth and fifth largest proportions of visible minorities in metropolitan centres in the country. In 2001, Alberta was home to 11.2% of Canada's visible minorities (Statistics Canada 2003a). The ethnic origins for Canadian Muslims ranges from Africa (especially East and North Africa), China, Central Asia (including the southern States in the Russian Federation, the newly formed republics and Afghanistan), Europe (both Eastern and Western as well as the Balkans), Iran, the Indian sub-continent (Bangladesh India, and Pakistan), the Middle East (particularly Lebanon, Jordan, Palestine, and Egypt), Philippines, Turkey, and so on (Abu-Laban 1983, 1995; Buchignani et al 1985; Palmer 1985; Rashid 1985; Hamdani 1999; Statistics Canada 2003a). While some of these post-war immigrants fled political, ethnic, and religious persecution, many migrated seeking gainful employment based on their professional skills or entrepreneurial opportunities (Abu-Laban 1983; Nanji 1983; Rashid 1985; Hamdani 1999). Thus, unlike the early Alberta Muslims, who began as peddlers and then expanded their entrepreneurial functions into the fur trade, the relatively more recent Muslim immigrants have a diversity of skills and professions.

Alberta Muslims are not only ethnically diverse but represent a plurality of interpretations of Islam (Abu-Laban 1983). Among the early Alberta Muslims religious diversity was present. The family of Sied Ameen had a strong Sufi heritage (Fahlman 1995). The Sufi tradition tends to focus on the spirit of the Quran rather than its literal interpretation. At the heart of Sufism is the tendency towards the inner and mystical aspects of the faith (Lings 1975). It is therefore not surprising that one of the sons of Sheikh Sied Ameen, King Ganam, grew to become Canada's uncrowned King of Fiddlers, inspiring and being a mentor to the likes of Billy Jones and Tommy Hunter. Music is closely linked to Sufism. Sheikh Ameen, in typical rural Canadian fashion, ordered his five-year-old son's first violin from an Eaton's catalogue (Fahlman 1995). Today in Alberta the various schools of Sunni Islam are found. The variety of Shia interpretations such as Ithna'ashari, Ismaili, and Druze are also present. For example, the Ismaili interpretation of Islam makes up approximately a quarter of the total Muslim population in Alberta and a third of the population in the City of Calgary.

Ismailis vary in ethnic origin from Arab, African, Central Asian, Indo-Pakistani, Persian to European. Muslims in this province, like their fellow Albertans, are heterogeneous in terms of their ethnicity, professional background, and religious interpretations.

The Mosque and Jamat Khana, both places of assembly, prayer, and cultural life of the community, are symbols of the definitive presence of Muslims in Alberta. These are the physical manifestations of institutions that support the life of the community (Abu-Laban 1983; Nanji 1983). In addition to being sacred places of prayer, these institutions enable religious solidarity, provide religious education, facilitate performance of marriages and funeral ceremonies, give space for mediation and dispute resolution, act as points of reference to interact with fellow Albertans on important events, are a focus of religious festivals, and are an architectural feature of Muslim permanence and commitment to this land. Based on online searches and counts in telephone directories, there are at least 25 Jamat Khanas, Mosques, and Muslim centres in Alberta.

Like the early Alberta Muslim women and men who came to this Province as young people seeking to make a better life, today's median age of Canadian Muslims is 28 years, lower than any Christian or non-Christian religious group in the country (Statistics Canada 2003b). With youth comes the opportunity to build anew based on a strong heritage. The tradition of Muslims in Alberta is one of hard work, where women play a prominent role in the life of the community overcoming racial and religious prejudice. It is a tradition of religious and ethnic survival and adaptation with strong linkages to the Aboriginal peoples of this land. Finally, it is a heritage of ethnic diversity and variety of religious interpretations. Muslims in Alberta are a microcosm of Canadian society, mirroring the desires and needs of a multi-cultural nation. Canada's multicultural history began with the diversity of First Nations. Cultural and religious pluralism are the foundations of Canadian society. Institutional structures and civil society in Alberta offer Muslims opportunities to practice Islam with a plurality of interpretations suited to the twenty-first century and with a security perhaps not found in any other nation in the World.

The challenge for Alberta Muslims will be to produce leaders who are as comfortable with their faith as they are with the cultural ecology of Canada. The historical adaptation of Muslims to Alberta is an opportunity for Muslims to break down facile media representations of a global community that spans 1.4 billion people living in diverse lands and cultures. Soon, Alberta Muslims may be able to export leaders that are raised in a civil society that both represent the humanistic values of Islam as well as Canada.

References

Abu-Laban, Baha. 1980. *An Olive Branch on the Family Tree: The Arabs in Canada.* Toronto: McClelland and Stewart.

Abu-Laban, Baha. 1983. "The Canadian Muslim Community: The Need for a New Survival Strategy." In *The Muslim Community in North America,* edited by Earle Waugh, Baha Abu-Laban, and Regula Qureshi. Edmonton: University of Alberta Press, 75-92.

Abu-Laban, Baha. 1995. "The Muslim Community of Canada." In *Muslim Minorities in the West,* edited by Ziaddun Sardar and Syed Z. Abedin. London: Institute of Muslim Minority Affairs, 134-149.

Ali, Alia Mohammed. 1999. "Amina and Rikia." In *At My Mother's Feet: Stories of Muslim Women,* edited by Sadia Zaman. Kingston: The Canadian Council of Muslim Women, 27-38.

Al-Ati, Hummudah Abd. 1963. "The Imam's Message." In *Al Rashid Mosque Twenty-Fifth Anniversary Celebration,* 30 June, A faded copy of a booklet available from Fort Edmonton Park Library.

Awid, Richard, and Jim Haymour. 1973. *A Salute to the Arab Pioneers of Northern Alberta.* Edmonton: Canadian Arab Friendship Association.

Baker, Peter. 1976. *Memoirs of an Arctic Arab: The Story of a Free-Trader in Northern Canada.* Saskatoon: Yellowknife Publishing Company.

Buchignani, Norman, Doreen M. Indra, with Ram Srivastiva. 1985. *Continuous Journey: A Social History of South Asians in Canada.* Toronto: McClelland and Stewart.

Casas, Bartolomé de las (1474-1566). 1971. *History of the Indies.* Translated and edited by Andrée Collard. New York: Harper & Row.

Chapman, Paul H. 1992. *Discovering Columbus.* Columbus, GA, U.S.A.: Isac Press.

Colón, Fernando (1488-1539). 1992. *The Life of the Admiral Christopher Columbus by his son Ferdinand.* Translated, annotated, and with a new introduction by Benjamin Keen. New Brunswick, N. J.: Rutgers University Press.

Duncanson, Mildred. 1978. "This, Canadian, Uncle Sam." Unpublished Manuscript. Calgary: Glenbow Museum Archives.

Duncanson, Mildred. 1980. "Uncle Sam Jamha." *Alberta History,* 28(1), 7-17.

Fahlman, Lila. 1995. *Fiddler with a Wink.* Edmonton: Purple Wolf Publishing.

Fahlman, Lila. 1999. "Lila." In *At My Mother's Feet: Stories of Muslim Women,* edited by Sadia Zaman. Kingston: The Canadian Council of Muslim Women, 51-69.

Hamdani, Daood H. 1997. "Canada's Muslims." *Hamdard Islamicus,* 20(3), 1-5.

Hamdani, Daood H. 1999. "Canadian Muslims on the Eve of the Twenty-first Century." *Journal of Muslim Minority Affairs,* 19 (2), 197-209.

Innis, Harold. 1995. *Staples, Markets, and Cultural Change: Selected Essays of Harold Innis.* Montreal: McGill-Queens University Press.

Innis, Harold. 2001. *The Fur Trade in Canada.* Toronto: University of Toronto Press.

Karim, Karim H. 2000. *Islamic Peril: Media and Global Violence.* Montréal: Black Rose Books.

Kassam, Karim-Aly, George Melnyk, and Lynne Perras (editors). 2002. *Canada and September 11th: Impact and Responses.* Calgary: Detselig.

Kassam, Karim-Aly. 1997. "Gender Analysis: Its Strengths and Weaknesses, and Requisite Skills for Effective Gender Planning." *Social Development Issues,* 19(2/3): 189-202.

Khattab, Abdelmoneim. 1969. "The Assimilation of Arab Muslims in Alberta." A Thesis submitted to the Faculty of Graduate Studies in partial fulfillment of the requirement for the degree of Master of Arts. Edmonton: University of Alberta.

Lings, Martin. 1975. *What is Sufism?* London: George Allen and Unwin Ltd.

Lorenz, Andrea. 1999. "The Women of Behind the Al Rashid." *Legacy,* November – January, 17-20.

Matar, Nabil. 1999. *Turks, Moors and Englishmen in the Age of Discovery.* New York: Columbia University Press.

Moser, Caroline. 1993. *Gender Planning and Development: Theory, Practice and Training.* New York: Routledge.

Menzies, Gavin. 2002. *1421: The Year China Discovered the World.* London: Bantam Press.

Nanji, Azim. 1983. "The Nizari Ismaili Muslim Community in North America: Background and Development." In *The Muslim Community in North America,* edited by Earle Waugh, Baha Abu-Laban, and Regula Qureshi. Edmonton: University of Alberta Press, 149-164.

Palmar, Howard and Tamara (editors). 1985. *Peoples of Alberta*. Saskatoon: Western Producers Prairie Books.

Rashid, A. 1985. *1981 Census of Canada: The Muslims of Canada, A Profile*. Ottawa: Minister of Supply and Services.

Statistics Canada. 2003a. *Canada's Ethnocultural Portrait: The Changing Mosaic*. Ottawa: Minister of Industry.

Statistics Canada. 2003b. *Religions in Canada*. Ottawa: Minister of Industry.

Wright, Ronald. 1993. *Stolen Continents: The "New World" Through Indian Eyes*. Toronto: Penguin Books.

Notes

1. This is a term used especially by the British to describe Muslims as the followers of Muhammad (Mahometans) like Christians are followers of Christ. A term considered offensive by many Muslims as they do not follow an individual but a message conveyed to him by God.

2. In the period 1911 to 1931, 22 percent of Canadians were foreign-born immigrants entering the country to settle in the Western provinces (Statistics Canada 2003a).

3. The Hudson's Bay Company referred to independent traders as "peddlers." In a society that stressed sedentary life as a mark of Godliness, at a time when Aboriginal communities were forced into settlements, peddlers were seen as a threat particularly to established businesses.

4. It is noteworthy that in the Notices of Deaths in the *Edmonton Journal*, Saturday, 17 November 1973, Peter Baker was identified as Faron Ahmed, 62.

Calgary's Early Courts
Establishing Our Justice System
by David Mittelstadt

I am not prepared to hear that verdict, gentlemen. You will be taken back to reconsider it.

Thus spoke Justice Charles Borromee Rouleau of the Supreme Court of the Northwest Territories, banging his fist on his table. He was addressing the jury in the trial of Jumbo Fisk, accused of murdering a young Aboriginal girl. Faced with a mountain of evidence implicating Fisk, the jury still chose to acquit him. Rouleau declared a mistrial, and Fisk would face six of his peers again.

The Fisk affair was only one of many sensational courtroom dramas played out in Calgary's early history. The courts of Calgary were a busy place, for the peaceable Canadian West still had its rascals, as well as disputes between rancher, farmer, merchant, and laborer for the civil court. While many notorious trials are remembered, the history of the courts, and their organization in Calgary, is less well known.[1] The following pages present a sketch of the evolution of the courts from the city's founding up to the 1970s, when major reforms took place.

The first courts arrived in Calgary with the North West Mounted Police (NWMP). Before 1873, there was no system of justice for the vast lands of the Northwest Territories.[2] The Dominion of Canada made three provisions for the administration of justice in the newly acquired Territories. The 1869 North West Territories Act allowed the Lieutenant Governor to appoint civilian justices of the peace. In keeping with English tradition, they were magistrates who could try less serious criminal offences. The 1873 Act for the Administration of Justice established the NWMP and also stipulated that paid judges, called Stipendiary Magistrates, be appointed.

The government was initially reluctant to appoint paid judges, and few people were available to serve as justices of the peace in the Territories. To make it easier for the NWMP to bring malefactors before a judge, the officers of the force were made *ex-officio* justices of the peace. They could try minor offences where summary convictions and sentencing was allowed. It was a development without precedent for English jurisprudence: the same police who arrested a criminal prosecuted and convicted him! Given the practical difficulties of transporting prisoners to the nearest judge – Manitoba – it was an expedient solution. It functioned remarkably well – allowing the police to deal with whiskey traders and other petty criminals. Fines were collected on the spot, and jail time served in the guardroom of the nearest mounted police barracks. Police superintendents would conduct courts in Calgary for well over a decade.

Mounted police officers only looked after minor offences. To allow the trial of more serious crimes, the first Stipendiary Magistrate was appointed in 1876 and the commissioner of the NWMP was given some judicial powers. Colonel James Macleod of the NWMP acted in this capacity as commissioner until 1880, when he quit the police to become a judge full time.[3] The magistrates' authority was initially quite limited: any offence with a maximum sentence of more than seven years had to be tried in Manitoba's superior court. The Stipendiaries were quickly given more power, until they could even try a capital crime in association with another magistrate or a justice of the peace. Only qualified lawyers of five years standing could be appointed to the position.

The Territories was divided up into three districts: Calgary was in Bow River (later renamed Alberta), which included all Alberta south of the Red Deer River. Colonel Macleod, the judge for the district, had his headquarters in Fort Macleod, and until 1885 Calgarians waited for his arrival on circuit for the administration of higher justice. He only began making regular visits in 1883, when the arrival of Canadian Pacific Railway (CPR) made Calgary one the most important centres in the Territories.[4] After 1883, court was scheduled for twice a year. Macleod held court in the fort until proceedings outgrew the barracks, and then rented space where he could find it.

As Calgary grew, there was much resentment at the lack of a judge resident at the town. Along with the judge, the sheriff and clerk of court for the district were based in Fort Macleod. All applications to the court had to be sent there, sometimes at considerable extra expense, or submitted when the magistrate came to town, which usually meant missing that session of court. Mindful of expenses, the Department of Justice stubbornly refused the appointment of additional magistrates, despite the demands throughout the Territories.[5] It left the magistrates stretched thin and Territorials unhappy. When court was cancelled on one occasion in 1884, the *Calgary Herald* was moved to complain:

The witnesses in criminal cases were under bonds, and as their bonds are now discharged, in all probability the prisoners will now escape, because their[sic] will be no evidence against them. The lawyers are disgusted and held a meeting to consider the matter . . . We have three Stipendiaries, there ought to be six, and one of them should reside at Calgary.[6]

Calgary attempted to solve the problem by petitioning the government in the Spring of 1885 to move Colonel Macleod, arguing the town was now the dominant commercial centre of the judicial district.[7] Fort Macleod countered with a petition demanding that the judge stay. The government responded by finally increasing the number of Stipendiary Magistrates, appointing Jeremiah Travis, a lawyer from New Brunswick, to Calgary on July 30, 1885.

Calgary no sooner had a judge than they wanted to get rid of him. A teetotaller and supporter of the temperance movement, the stiff-necked Travis tried to rigorously enforce the unpopular Territorial prohibition of liquor. After Travis learned that the town constable, the mayor, and the town solicitor were taking kickbacks from saloon owners to turn a blind eye to the liquor trade, he declared war on the town's so-called "whiskey ring." The arrest of hotelier and town councillor Simon John Clarke for obstructing two undercover officers began the showdown. Outraged at Clarke's sentence of six months of hard labor, his supporters sent a deputation to Ottawa to ask for the removal of Travis. The judge retaliated by disallowing the result of the 1886 municipal election, charging that the incumbents, including Mayor Murdoch, were improperly elected.

Travis, however, had sown the seeds of his own destruction. The affair had been seized upon by the Liberal press as a chance to embarrass the government. Worse, one of the rowdy element, Hugh Cayley, who Travis had jailed for contempt of court, had an uncle who was a former Conservative cabinet minister. The government appointed Judge Thomas Taylor of Winnipeg to investigate the situation, and he found that the magistrate had exceeded his legal authority. Taylor's report was not released until June of 1887, by which time the Dominion had undertaken a thorough overhaul of the courts in the Territories and quietly got rid of Travis.

The Travis affair helped bring about the reorganization of the courts for the Northwest Territories in 1886, which was welcomed in Calgary. A Supreme Court was constituted to replace the Stipendiaries, which could try any criminal and civil cases and also take appeals when sitting in a quorum of three. Less popular was the size of the bench: there were only five justices for the territories. Calgary, however, was the headquarters of the new judicial district of Northern Alberta, stretching from the immediate area around the town north to include Edmonton. Calgary would have a resident judge, court officers, and could look forward to three sessions of court each year.

Charles B. Rouleau was elevated to the new bench and appointed as resident justice of the district. Originally stationed in Battleford as a Stipendiary, Rouleau fled to Calgary during the Riel Rebellion. A staunch supporter of the Conservative Party, Rouleau was also a legal scholar whose decisions were the product of meticulous research. Along with Rouleau, Calgary received a new courthouse. In 1890, the Dominion government finished building a proper courthouse, arguably the most impressive in the Territories, to replace makeshift quarters in the town's immigration building. Built of rough-hewn local sandstone, it was an impressive pile for the little frontier town.

The workload in Calgary was too much for just one judge, and complaints continued about delays in the courts. Calgarians again cast their eye about for a handy judge. Over protests from all of Southern Alberta, they successfully lobbied for Colonel Macleod, who had remained in Fort Macleod as the justice for the Southern Alberta judicial district. Macleod joined Rouleau in Calgary in 1894, while still remaining

1914 Courthouse, the Land Titles building, and an old Territorial Courthouse, 7th Avenue, Calgary, Alberta. Postcard from The Camera Products Co.; Calgary Public Library.

responsible for his old district. This may have hastened his death: Macleod, worn out from years of travel as a judge and suffering from Bright's Disease, died in September. He was belatedly replaced by David Lynch Scott, a Regina lawyer. After Rouleau's death in 1901, it was over six months before he was replaced by Justice T. H. McGuire, who was also named Chief Justice of the Territorial bench. Calgary lost Justice Scott to Edmonton soon after and found itself again down to a single judge. Arthur L. Sifton, prominent Liberal, former city solicitor, and future premier of Alberta, replaced McGuire in 1903. Although his appointment was greeted with scandalized outcry in conservative Calgary, he soon earned respect for his no-nonsense campaign to stamp out livestock rustling. Finally, bowing to the constant lobbying, another justice was stationed to Calgary in 1906, just as the new province of Alberta was sorting out a judicial system.

When the new Supreme Court of Alberta was inaugurated in October 1907, it was a major shake-up for the courts of Calgary. A whole new bench, the District Court, was added. The province was divided up into five judicial districts: Calgary was named headquarters of an eponymous district that initially stretched as far as Medicine Hat and the eastern border of Alberta, and as far north as Innisfail. The Supreme Court Justices, five in number, resided in Edmonton and Calgary. The personnel of the Territorial court were divided between Alberta and Saskatchewan. Sifton remained chief justice with his seat in Calgary, joined by Horace Harvey and Charles Stuart, one of the 1906 appointments. Appeals were handled by a quorum of three judges sitting alternatively in Calgary or Edmonton.

A great part of the workload of the Territorial Justices was given to the new District Court. It handled criminal offences with maximum sentences of seven years and civil suits under $500. Each district had its own judge, who also had a circuit court, with regular sittings at points throughout the district. Calgary's first District Court judge was C. R. Mitchell of Medicine Hat, who left for politics in 1910 and was replaced by A. A. Carpenter. The business for the District Court generated by Calgary soon proved too much for a single judge. Carpenter was joined by Roland Winter in 1913, a cultured Englishman known for his impromptu cello performances. Calgary saw the size of its district bench increase to three by 1921.

The provincial courts lagged behind the growth in Calgary, and overloaded dockets and long delays continued. The federal government appointed and paid the salaries of the judges, and was always reluctant to incur more expense. Calgary's resident bench eventually expanded and also took on a more conservative tone. William L. Walsh and Maitland McCarthy, partners in a prominent law firm that was well known for its support of the Conservative Party, were named to the Supreme Court in 1912 and 1914 respectively, joined in 1921 by Arthur Clarke. Sifton had left the bench to become Premier of Alberta in 1910, succeeded by Horace Harvey as Chief Justice. The province was more generous than the Dominion, building a new courthouse that opened in 1914.

The Supreme Court went through another major change in 1919. The province had experimented some years earlier with having the justices rotate between trials and sitting as appeal judges. It worked so well that the province decided to set up a separate appeal court. It took until 1921 to organize it, and the bench was divided into the two courts. Justices now were either part of the trial division or the appeal division. The appeal court sat in both Calgary and Edmonton, while the bench for the trial division was also divided between the two cities. As far as the District and Supreme Court were concerned, Calgarians were accustomed to the same faces on the bench for years at a time. The judges themselves mostly took up housekeeping in the districts of Mount Royal or Elbow Park.

One aspect of the courts in Calgary which seems curious today was that there were no permanent crown prosecutors until the fifties. Instead, the Attorney General of Alberta would hire local lawyers to act as prosecutors in the higher courts, while police officers would prosecute minor offences before justices of the peace or police magistrates. Some law offices and lawyers, such as James Short, received the lion's share of the prosecuting work, but the crown would often just hire the city's best legal talent. For the controversial Picariello-Lassandro murder trial in 1921, A. A. McGillivray was hired as the prosecutor – but eight years later, in the Salloway-Mills stock fraud trials, he was the defence counsel. This was not uncommon among the city's best trial lawyers. A crown prosecutors' office was finally established in Calgary in 1953, with three lawyers as full time government employees.[8] They initially took over police court prosecutions, but within several years represented the crown in all the city's courtrooms.

The real workhorse of the justice system in Calgary was the Police Court. During the 1920s, the higher courts in Calgary dealt with about 200 cases a year – the police court dealt with over 4 000. It was aptly named: the arresting police officer generally acted as the prosecutor of the offender. The police court was established in the Territories by the appointment of Justices of the Peace. In their role as magistrates, the justices could try minor criminal offences where summary conviction and sentencing was allowed, such as public drunkenness, vagrancy, brawling, or petty thefts, and also municipal bylaw infractions. Stiff sentences could be handed out in police court, including the lash, which was allowed as a punishment until the fifties. Civilians with no legal training, the work of the justices was uneven and the source of many complaints. In one possibly apocryphal story, a Justice of the Peace tried a petty thief for piracy, because he stole goods off a barge on the North Saskatchewan River. Calgary's first Justice of the Peace was the notorious George Murdoch, saddle maker, first mayor, and nemesis of Jeremiah Travis. By 1886 there were five more JPs in Calgary.9

Aside from concerns about their competence, it was also difficult for the part-time Justices to deal with the workload in busy jurisdictions. To address this, in 1886 the position of police magistrate was formally created in Canada. The police magistrate was a paid judge who had to be a qualified lawyer, although limited to trying summary offences. Calgary was the first jurisdiction in the Territories to appoint a police magistrate, who replaced the civilian justices of the peace. The 1893 city charter for Calgary included a provision to pay for a police magistrate.10 Although the city footed the bill, the Dominion government made the appointment.11 The first magistrate in Calgary was Thomas Ede, appointed in 1895. He was not a success, showing up drunk for court and allegedly pocketing fines, and was fired in 1897.12 Crispin Smith, another local advocate, replaced Ede and also resigned under a cloud 10 years later.

To denote its lowly position on the judicial totem pole, the police court did not sit in the provincial courthouse, but made do with space in various civic buildings. In Calgary, the police court sat from the first in city hall. When a magnificent new civic building was designed in 1908, the architect included a courtroom in the basement. It was a popular venue, especially as most prostitution-related offences were tried there, much to the salacious interest of press and spectators.

Some critics, defence counsel in particular, felt that the police magistrates acted more as an arm of law enforcement than as impartial judges. In Calgary, the presence of an ex-policeman on the bench may have had something to do with this. From 1911 to 1932, Calgary's chief police magistrate was Colonel Gilbert E. Sanders, a former Mountie and soldier. Although not a lawyer, Sanders had judicial experience from his mounted police days. His accent, monocle, and military bearing made him the very picture of an English gentleman, but Sanders was actually born in Yale, British Columbia. His monocle was the source of some amusement and derision among the local bar. It had a tendency to pop out when the Colonel was surprised, adding a nicely dramatic effect to the courtroom. Both admired and derided as a "common sense" judge, Sanders had a long-standing and legendary feud with R. B. Bennett. Tough and no-nonsense, Sanders's justice tended to be harsh and displayed most of the prejudices of the Edwardian upper middle class.

In 1913, not long after Sanders's appointment, a juvenile court was constituted for all towns in Alberta of more than 500 people. It was intended to enforce the 1908 Juvenile Delinquency Act and get children out of the adult courts. In 1916, the province decided to appoint a female magistrate in Calgary to look after the new court and also hear cases in the police court that involved women. Alice Jukes Jamieson, a leading Calgary suffragist, was made the first female magistrate in the city, sharing with Emily Murphy of Edmonton, the honor of being the first women judges in the British Empire. The validity of Jamieson's appointment was soon challenged on the grounds that she was a woman and not legally competent to hold the post. The Alberta appeal court upheld her appointment, setting an important precedent for the famous Persons case of 1928. If critics worried that a woman would be too lenient, they needn't have wasted their energy: Jamieson soon established a reputation for strictness.

The courts of Calgary did not change much until the 1970s. Additional magistrate courts were added, including a Family Court in 1952. The size of the Supreme and District Court benches increased and the latter underwent a 1933 reorganization that saw the judges centralized in Calgary and Edmonton. The phenomenal growth after World War Two eventually brought about a radical reorganization. The province began reforms of the lower courts in 1970, and eight years later created the Provincial Court, with expanded criminal and civil jurisdiction, and incorporated the police court, family court, juvenile court, and all the other minor courts. The District Court had been assuming more and more of the prerogatives of the Supreme Court, so in 1978 it was eliminated and the Court of Queen's Bench and the Alberta Appeal Court were established. New facilities were created: the old Territorial courthouse was torn down in 1957 and the current Court of Queens Bench Building erected in its place. A new building was opened to house most of the Provincial Courts in 1983.

This account is only a brief outline of the courts of Calgary. It does not capture the vibrant and sometimes controversial personalities of the bench and bar, or the dramatic, tragic, and sometimes absurd goings on in the courtroom. There are also many minor changes not addressed and complexities left unexplained. A fascinating aspect of Calgary's history awaits further exploration.

Notes

1. Most works on the legal history of Calgary focus on specific trials or personalities. Neil Watson and Thomas Thorner in 'Keepers of the King's Peace: Colonel G. E. Sanders and the Calgary Police Magistrates Courts – 1911-1932," *Urban History Review*, 12 February 1984, present some structural information on the police courts but focus more on the ideology of one magistrate, Gilbert Sanders. *Lords of the Western Bench,* Louis Knafla and Rick Klumpenhouer, gives some background on the courts in Alberta as well as judicial biographies.

2. The Hudson's Bay Company, in its original charter, had been given the power to form courts to "enforce the laws of the kingdom" but set up its first court for the Selkirk colony in 1839. The courts of Upper Canada were given jurisdiction over Rupert's Land in 1821, but their authority was entirely nominal in the absence of enforcement.

3. Bowker, Wilbur F., *The Stipendiary Magistrates and Supreme Court Justices in the North West Territories – 1876-1907*; Bowker, Wilbur F., *A Consolidation of Fifty Years of Legal Writing: 1938-1988,* Edmonton: University of Alberta, Faculty of Law, 1989. Macleod left the police in 1876 to become a magistrate, but within six months was appointed commissioner of the NWMP, and simply retained his role as a judge.

4. Glenbow Archives, James Macleod Papers. "My Darling Mary" – letters, 1883-1884, correpondence dated 9 August 1883.

5. *Calgary Herald,* 26 October 1883.

6. *Calgary Herald,* 25 June 1884.

7. Glenbow Archives, James Macleod Papers. Correspondence ,4 March 1885 to Colonel James F. Macleod. Petitions attached.

8. *Architypes, Legal Archives Society of Alberta Newsletter,* Volume 8, no. 1, Summer 1999, 5. Probation officers carried out prosecutions in juvenile court until 1975. There are now almost 50 crown prosecutors in Calgary.

9. *Northwest Territories Gazette,* vol. 3, no. 1: 1-12, no. 2: 33.

10. It is unknown whether this was inserted by the drawers of the charter to give the city more control over this aspect of civic administration, or by Territorial officials so as to offload the expense onto the city. It was standard practice for cities to hire and pay their own magistrates, although the appointment was made by the Dominion Government.

11. Changed in 1939 to the provincial government. See Statutes of Alberta, 1939, c.83. s. 2.

12. Ede ended up in Blairmore where he practiced until his death in 1937 at the age of 87. He was the fifth lawyer enrolled on the list of the Law Society of Alberta, and had joined the Territorial bar in 1886. GML, Clipping file, "Ede, Thomas." Undated *Calgary Herald* clipping.

Some Things Remembered
Churches in the Chinook Area
by Kate Reeves

I was standing in the narthex of Wild Rose United Church in Calgary looking at two large paintings of Jesus. In one he was a shepherd. In the other, he was knocking at a door. Both were popular images from a former era but because of changing sensibilities, I knew that they would not be there much longer. But then I noticed a small plaque at the base of the painting. Rats, they were memorials. So now what were we to do with them?

Later while researching the history of the church, I saw a photo of the interior of a Methodist Church which had been a few blocks away. There were the two paintings, front and center. When that congregation, which joined the United Church Union in 1925, had eventually amalgamated with the former Presbyterian-based one (whose building I now work in) they had brought their paintings with them. They were not only a memorial to their founders, Mr. and Mrs. Alfred Maberley, but a piece of home.

This episode got me thinking – how do we remember these original congregations that were part of the fabric of early Calgary and district? Some have survived nearly intact, some have evolved, some have disappeared. And what does this say about how we view the past?

As an Irish Catholic from upstate New York, I found Calgary in 1970, did not have a lot that was familiar to me. The brave little St. Francis church, surrounded by urban renewal, was definitely not Holy Rosary Church where I was married. But there is certainly a strong Catholic presence in the city.

A cairn erected in 1939 stands as a memorial to the first church in the area. The cairn is at the end of a road which branches off from Highway 22 on the way to Bragg Creek. It was erected by the provincial government at the site of the Catholic Mission, Our Lady of Peace. An inscription reads:

Our Lady of Peace

In 1872 lay helper Alexis Cardinal built a crude log cabin surmounted by a cross on this site. Thus began the mission of Our Lady of Peace in the country of the Blackfeet, the first church in Southern Alberta. Father Constance Scollen, OMI, took up residence here in 1873. A zealous servant of God, he ministered to the dwellers of the plains during the hard times that saw the passing of their old way of life. His name is affixed to Treaty No. 7, signed by the Blackfoot Confederacy in 1877.

Our Lady of Peace was moved to the junction of the Bow and Elbow rivers when the North West Mounted Police built Fort Calgary there in 1875. This old mission was used infrequently until 1882 when it was abandoned.

The base of the cairn is built of the chimney stones of the original mission building. In 1974 a capsule was inserted into the cairn containing the story of the Mission. The cairn is fenced off where the road terminates and although I have never seen anyone else when I arrive there, the road seems well travelled.

Another cairn north west of this one lies just off the 1A Highway to Banff. Built in 1927, it stands near the entrance gate to a simple carpenter's gothic style church. It is the oldest Protestant church in southern Alberta, built by Rev. John McDougall and his father in 1875.

The cairn reads:

To the Glory of God and in Memory of Rev. George Millward McDougall and Rev. John Chantler McDougall. D. D. Father and son and their devoted wives. Combined ministry 77 years Pioneer missionaries of the Methodist Church to the Indians in Canada.

McDougall Memorial Church was built in 1875. This depiction was created by John Brook of the Chinook Country Historical Society.

The church was abandoned in 1921 after a new church was built farther west in the town of Morley on the Stoney Indian Reserve. The buildings at the mission site were demolished, but for some reason, the church was left, a haunt of youthful visitors who left their names on the walls and beams. Some of the names can still be seen despite the restoration in the early 1950s. The church is used for weddings and bi-annual commemorative services. Its front door bell tower, added after the builder had left Morley at the turn of the century, coincides with how we think a church should look. It has been used as a movie set as well as the subject for painters and photographers. Its image graces calendars, plates and jig saw puzzles. I am glad it was not demolished. Even non-church-goers are attracted to the site, using it as a source of refuge from the city.

It is said that Mrs. McDougall suggested the new settlement at the Bow and Elbow rivers needed a church and logs were sent down the river for the first Methodist Church. Several buildings have evolved into Central United Church at 7th Avenue and 1st Street across from the Hudson's Bay Department store. It stands today as a legacy of the Methodist tradition. A contrast to the McDougall Stoney Mission church, this one is at Calgary's busiest corner and serves the city's street people.

The Anglican tradition came a bit later to the area. In 1883 Rev. J. W. Tims arrived to work on the Blackfoot Indian reserve near Gleichen. He was asked to take a service which probably took place in Fort Calgary. The following year a church was built just east of the present Cathedral, Church of the Redeemer. The design of the wooden church was copied on a miniature scale in 1885 with the construction of the church of St. Paul, Midnapore-Fish Creek. This church building still stands and a society exists to maintain it. The Calgary church (Midnapore was outside the town of Calgary) was selected as the Bishop's "temporary" cathedral in 1889 and was thereafter known as the "Pro-Cathedral." The frame church was replaced with a more elaborate sandstone structure in 1905.

The original church has been memorialized in a stained glass window over the north door. It is one of my favorite windows. It was designed by the Very Rev. David J. Carter and I have used it to tell the early history of the area to tourists. There is the fort at the confluence of the Bow and Elbow Rivers, a 10 minute walk from the present church. Next to the first Church of the Redeemer is a teepee with an authentic Blackfoot design. Early forms of transportation shown in the window include a Red River oxcart, canoe,

To the Glory of God and in Thanksgiving for the Pioneers in every age.

Pioneer Window at the Cathedral Church of the Redeemer, Calgary, Alberta.
The Kate Reeves collection.

horse, and railroad. The bison are there (perilously close to the church) and in the sky, Franklin gulls represent the Holy Spirit. In one corner is Alberta's official flower, the prairie rose. A window is a particularly lovely way to remember those who came before. This congregation will be celebrating 100 years of the sandstone building's ministry in Calgary in 2005.

Across the street is the Calgary Urban Project (CUP) building with a wall mural depicting another dove. Margaret Waterchief, a native Anglican minister, treks from CUPs to the church when she occasionally takes the service in the chapel on Thursdays. Her presence, and the native people who sleep on the benches in the park beside the church, remind me of those who were here first.

Just to the west, at Centre Street and 7th Avenue, was the site of the first stone building in Calgary. The Presbyterians built Knox Church after moving their wooden structure across the Elbow River in 1884. When the site was sold some of the stones became part of Lindsay's Folly. This was a mansion begun by the purchaser of the lot, Dr. Lindsay, and it overlooked the Elbow River. The building was never finished and the ruins themselves have all but disappeared. Their subsequent church, now Knox United at 6th Avenue and 4th Street SW, has photographs of their previous buildings in the narthex. Knox has a living link with its past, as the granddaughter of its founder member, Col. James Walker, is an active member of the present congregation.

The Baptists lost their early Calgary church to fire in 1905 but rebuilt it within months. Then, needing a larger building, they purchased six lots from Richard Bedford Bennett at the corner of 13th Avenue and 4th Street SW, out of the downtown district. It stands across from Central Memorial Park and its handsome tower can be seen as one approaches the downtown along 4th Street. This congregation started a mission in 1903 on what was then Scarth (13th) Avenue and 2nd Street E. In 1905 this mission was organized as Westbourne Baptist Church.

This church is connected to another institution which was once downtown. As I pass by the Sears building (on what was the new Eaton's site), I stop to look at two newel posts in a display case. A plaque explains:

> *Calgary Prophetic Bible Institute was opened on this site in 1927. As the unofficial minister of Westbourne Baptist Church near the Stampede Grounds William Aberhart had operated a religious night school since 1923. When the activities outgrew the old church, Aberhart founded the Calgary Prophetic Bible Institute. The Institute would train young people as ministers and missionaries of his version of Baptist fundamentalism. The building also served as an auditorium for his public meetings, a studio for his radio broadcasts, and a new sanctuary for Westbourne Baptist Church.*

The move was reversed, however, when the Westbourne Baptist Church broke with Aberhart and left the institute building. The Westbourne Church building is now the Victory Outreach Centre and is looking for a new home as the Stampede grounds move north, will require its demolition.

The only physical remains of the Prophetic Bible Institute are these two newel posts but Aberhart's influence was felt throughout Alberta. Perhaps the work of the Victory Outreach Centre is fulfilling the Prophetic Bible Institute's mandate in a different way.

The Lutheran legacy is also part of downtown Calgary. The cornerstone of the Eau Claire Scandinavian Lutheran Congregation, now Historic Trinity Lutheran, is stamped 1899. The building itself was erected on the basement in 1924. The homestead-style church building is one of the last remaining buildings of the original Eau Claire district and its quaint shape reminds us of times past. Sometimes all we have is the shape of a building to remind us of the past. The Hillhurst Baptist

Church on Gladstone Road in Hillhurst closed in the early 1970s, but it is obvious to all who pass by that it once was a church.

When no longer needed, a building can be moved and used as a museum, thus commemorating the original congregation. The Anglican Church in Calgary's Heritage Park was St. Martin's in Livingston, near Pincher Creek. It was opened in 1896. Copies of original documents of the parish are shown inside the church. The church with many of its furnishings was obtained through the parishioners of Lundbreck. The pews were donated by the parishioners of St. Paul's Church in Midnapore. Headstones in the churchyard are original markers assembled by the Glenbow Foundation.

This is a storybook recreation of the past. I make a point of stopping at the church during Heritage Park's Twelve Days of Christmas. The wood stove is on, a lady in bonnet and shawl plays the pump organ and carolers in period costume stop by during their rounds of the park to lead the singing.

Many people who no longer have an affiliation with a church still want to be married in one. Often an old church building fits the bill. The Davisburg Presbyterian Church was built in 1899 near the confluence of the Bow and Highwood rivers. The church, which became Davisburg United after church union in 1925, closed in May 1958. It was restored a few years ago by the Davisburg Cemetery Society, which owns the property. It no longer has a congregation, but those who are married in it, and those who maintain it, are perpetuating its memory.

Sometimes a church building can be reused in another place. Most Holy Trinity Catholic Church was completed in Bankhead, near Banff, in 1908. The mine closed in 1922 and the town was abandoned. In 1927 Bishop Kidd had the materials of the church moved to Forest Lawn in Calgary where it was rebuilt as the first church in the community. The title of the original was retained in its new location.

Churches have a long history of recycling. When the new Holy Name of Mary Roman Catholic Church was completed in 1959 in Cochrane, the stained glass windows of the former St. Mary's Cathedral were donated to the new church. In the case of St. Gabriel's (Anglican) in Calgary, the beginnings of the parish were remembered by the inclusion in the new church of many objects from the original building. A small chapel was built as a miniature perpetuation of the old church. It contains the altar, altar rail, missal stand, candlesticks, lectern, sanctuary chair, and carpeting from the first St. Gabriel's.

Calgary's first Jewish congregation was the House of Jacob and their synagogue was built in 1911 at 323 - 5th Avenue E. (For a full history see the article on the history of Jews in Alberta.) A community centre built at 18th Avenue SW also had synagogue services that evolved into Congregation Beth Israel. Beth Israel's new synagogue on Glenmore Trail was dedicated in 1960. Meanwhile, the Shaarey Tzedec Congregation was established in 1959 and their synagogue was built adjacent to the House of Israel Community Centre. These two congregations amalgamated in 1987 and built at the Glenmore location. A Heritage Room was constructed that tells the history of the congregations. A sign explains:

Who We Were and Who We Are.

The individuals, organizations and activities of the Beth Israel and Shaarey Tzedec Congregations have been recorded in photographs, artifacts, and other documents. Such a picture of the past helps us to gain an image of ourselves and our participation in all aspects of community life.

As inner city demographics change and congregations are faced with dwindling numbers, many have faced closure. Remnants of various churches can be incorporated into one new one. St. Albert the Great in McKenzie Town installed windows and Stations of the Cross and pews for St. Johns Catholic Church that was once on 10th Street NW in Calgary. The tabernacle is from St. Francis Xavier parish in Crossfield. The altar was made by two parishioners and has an inlaid marble top made from the altar stones of many of the closed parishes in the diocese.

As I write this, another Anglican congregation, Holy Cross, is struggling with how best to incorporate the stained glass windows of an amalgamating congregation, that of St. Michael's and All Angels, once on 16th Avenue in northwest Calgary, into their present site.

St. Anne's Roman Catholic Church in Hussar was built in 1928 and was officially closed in 2001. Most of the contents, including a few pews, a statue of St. Anne, a full set of vestments, and the altar, which contains a relic of St. Anne, have been donated for use in the chapel of Sacred Heart Academy in Strathmore. "We're very fortunate," said one of the parishioners. "It's not like we're locking the doors and putting everything in storage and leaving it. We'll be remembered."

United Church inner city congregations such as St. Paul's, Trinity, and Wesley have disappeared and one wonders how they will be remembered. Will their plaques and memorials remain on the walls when the buildings are reused?

The stories of many congregations are contained in their written histories or in compilations such as *From the Buffalo to the Cross* by M. B. Venini Byrne. This is the history of the Catholic Diocese in Calgary. It has recently been updated with *Winds of Change: A History of the Roman Catholic Diocese for Calgary Since 1968* by Norman Knowles. Many Calgary authors contributed to *The Search for Souls: Histories of Calgary's Churches,* that was compiled as a Calgary Centennial project in 1975.

A charming way of remembering the past is found on china plates and paintings. Many congregations have plates made to commemorate anniversary dates. Some even have tea cups.

The comforting architecture of church buildings with their tower, spiral, or cross has attracted many artists. My husband and I delight in our collection of prints by Margaret Shelton that depict churches. St. Mary's in Banff is one. It was a simple wooden structure which has since been replaced.

I was pleased to be in attendance at the last service of the Okotoks United Church in their brick and sandstone building which they had outgrown. I took a photograph of a painting by Gena Thompson. The winter scene shows historical buildings of the town and right in the middle is the United Church. I imagine the congregation has taken that painting with them as they embark on their new journey.

Okotoks United Church. Painting by Gena Thompson. Photo from the Kate Reeves collection.

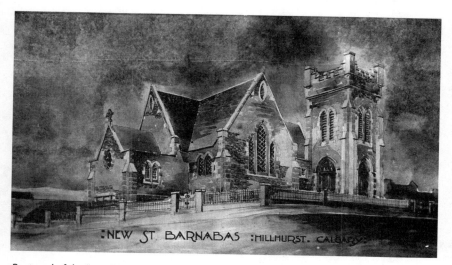

:NEW ST BARNABAS :HILLHURST. CALGARY

Postcard of the "new" St. Barnabas in Hillhurst, Calgary. The Kate Reeves collection.

Old postcards often depicted impressive buildings in a town or city. There are many hand-colored postcards of Calgary's St. Mary's, a church that was planned by the famous Father Lacombe. In some of the post-cards the domes of the twin towers are red, and in others, green. A model of that church is in the present St. Mary's Cathedral. A modern postcard of the model shows the domes as blue! Another of my favorite post cards shows the "New St. Barnabas: Hillhurst Calgary" which was built in 1912. The church itself was destroyed in a fire on a cold winter night in 1957, however the tower remained and was incorporated into the new building. The original church was erected by E. H. Riley in memory of his mother, father, and daughter whose graves are in the churchyard on the east side of the church.

The best way to remember a former congregation is by using and caring for their building. An admirable example of this is the relocation of the 112-year-old All Saints Anglican Church, which was moved in 2004 from downtown Cochrane to the Bethany Cochrane Care Centre to be used as a chapel. Ironically it is "a stone's throw" from where it was originally built in 1892 in the settlement of Mitford. When the town was overshadowed by nearby Cochrane, the congregation had moved the church there. It will now be used and cared for by the staff and residents of the care centre.

A cairn, a restored church building, a stained glass window, some photographs, a plaque, a plate, or a painting: there are myriad ways we remember. Remnants of former congregations are all around us. It seems to me we remember churches the same way we remember other pieces of our public life. Some things that should be remembered are probably forgotten while some, by chance or design, are memorialized.

And what of the two large paintings at the beginning of this article? They were moved to a chapel in the building. But their significance will only be remembered if we tell the story that goes with them. That is why I am particularly pleased the historical society has chosen an anthology to commemorate our province's centennial. I hope it will continue the tradition of "some things remembered."

Gateway to the Rocky Mountains
The Kananaskis Gate
by Bill Yeo

The G8 Summit Conference of June 2002 drew the world's attention to the Kananaskis Valley, Kananaskis Country, and Kananaskis Village. While the news media reported on the conference with the by-line "Kananaskis, Alberta," they simply followed what has become commonplace usage among many Albertans. Skiers, hikers, and golfers planning an outing or a holiday in the mountain playground west of Calgary tell their friends they're headed for "Kananaskis." Many people are probably unaware that there is another Kananaskis, somewhere else.

The hamlet of Kananaskis can be found just east of Exshaw, along Highway 1A, north of the Bow River: a few houses, the lime plant, and a railway siding. The Canadian Pacific Railway named the siding shortly after 1883, probably for Kananaskis Falls, situated some five kilometres downstream on the Bow River. Kananaskis post office opened in 1888; the first postmaster, John Walker, managed the Bow River Sawmill. The Loder brothers owned the other local industry. They made quicklime from stone quarried at the foot of Door Jamb Mountain. Lime is still being made there, but the sawmill is long gone, the post office closed in 1940, and the new Trans Canada Highway was built on the other side of the Bow River.[1]

Kananaskis may have slid into obscurity, but for 14 years it was the Eastern gateway to Canada's first national park. Established in 1887, the Rocky Mountains Park of Canada was renamed Banff National Park in 1930. In its early years visitors to the Park travelled to Banff by train, but after 1910, a growing number began arriving by automobile. The Calgary-Banff motor road crossed the park boundary just to the east of Kananaskis, so it was here that the first national park highway gate was established in 1916. It was a monument to Western Canada's early adoption of the automobile for leisure travel, to an era of pioneer road building, and to their considerable impact on the mountain national parks.

The new highway gate was one means of implementing amended Motor Vehicle Regulations approved in 1915. Over the previous decade the Department of the Interior had moved from an absolute prohibition of the use of "automobiles of every kind" within the park, to permitting entry into the park with regulated use of its roads. The first superintendent of Rocky Mountains Park had reported in 1888 that he had built several miles of road. By 1910 this network had been extended as far as the eastern boundary. For most of this period the Park's roads would have been used only by horses and horse-drawn vehicles, but the ban on automobiles was eventually challenged as cars were brought to Banff by rail and others made their way over the rough track from Calgary.[2]

In 1909, members of Senator James Lougheed's family drove to Banff in the Senator's new Pope-Toledo car. On the return trip the primitive state of the road brought the car to a halt near Kananaskis, so the party returned to Calgary by train. In September the following year the prohibition of automobiles was relaxed. Despite the damage to his new car, Senator Lougheed is said to have been instrumental in bringing about this change. He may have had a cordial relationship with Senator R. W. Scott, the Minister of the Interior. Lougheed was in opposition in the Senate until after the first Motor Vehicle Regulations were approved in April 1911. This step coincided with the completion of the Banff-Calgary motor road, which could have been the reason for the timing of these changes in policy.[3]

National parks historian W. F. Lothian has remarked that "of all the regulations established for the control and administration of national parks, none was subject to more frequent amendment than the Highway Traffic Regulations."[4] The fact is that Western Canadians took to the automobile with enthusiasm. The number of miles of motor road increased steadily, especially in the national parks. The regulations not only addressed entry into parks and the use of roads: they also instituted registration and the payment of fees and imposed speed limits. As roads lengthened and improved, and as the automobile grew in power and numbers, so the regulations were amended as needed.

The 1915 regulations enlarged and expanded the earlier ones, and continued the requirement that all vehicles entering the Park should be registered with the superintendent. A vehicle could be registered for the fee of five dollars a year, or one dollar for a maximum one-week single visit. The new gateway made it possible to register vehicles at the point of entry. Visitors arriving at the gate were issued *transient* motor vehicle licences. In September 1915 these regulations were extended to the other national parks.

By this time, enough Park residents had acquired cars to make it necessary to establish separate registration procedures for them. When the province of Alberta established its own licensing requirements for motor vehicles, an attempt was made in 1916 to licence those belonging to national park residents. This step led to an agreement being reached in 1918 with the Minister of the Interior, concerning the sharing of fees and the issuance of *resident* licences. A similar arrangement with the province of British Columbia formed part of the Banff-Windermere Road Agreement of 1919.

This 1919 agreement called for the Dominion of Canada to complete the construction of a trans-mountain all-weather road from the interprovincial boundary to a point where Radium Hot Springs is today. In exchange the province conveyed to Canada a large parcel of land which became Kootenay National Park. The new road branched off near Castle Mountain from an existing road that had reached Lake Louise from Banff in 1920, and was completed in 1922. The official opening the following summer marked a major step in the formation of Western Canada's highway network. By the beginning of World War II, road construction had reached Golden (1927) and Jasper (1939).[5]

Prior to 1922, British Columbians drove on the left-hand side of the road, unlike their neighbors in adjacent parts of North America. In the 1920s the province undertook an ambitious road-building program. The change to driving on the right was probably made in anticipation of improved connections with roads in Alberta and Washington State. A few intrepid motorists had already been venturing into British Columbia over the few drivable roads but, with the opening of the Banff-Windermere Road in 1923, their numbers increased. A second national park highway gate was built that year at Radium Hot Springs, and 4 500 automobiles passed through it the first season. Auto tourism had arrived. Promoters invented a Grand Circle Tour, or "Blue Trail," an extended travel route that went south from Calgary to various places in the western United States, returning by way of Spokane through the Columbia Valley to Windermere, and back to Calgary via Banff.[6]

Access by automobile radically altered the character of Rocky Mountains Park. Not only did it increase the number of tourists, it also broadened the social and economic profile of the visitor population. One symptom of this change was the development in 1916 of the Park's first official campground. By 1922 it was being advertised by Banff merchants as the "auto camping ground," a headquarters for do-it-yourself sightseeing excursions. Most of these auto tourists were from Southern

Alberta. A 1928 sample of vehicles entering and leaving the Kananaskis Gate revealed that only 10 percent were from outside Alberta. After 1926 those who did not own a car could ride a Brewster bus between Calgary and Banff.[7]

By today's standards a road trip from Calgary to Banff in the 1920s may appear to have been a leisurely affair. The 1922 issue of Calgary's City Manual describes the experience as "an extremely interesting and picturesque motor drive of about four hours."[8] This may have been the case when the weather, the condition of the road, and the durability of one's car were all favorable. Travellers often lingered at the gateway when they reached it, to chat, ask directions and of course to perform the ritual of registration. Some may have felt it a relief to have arrived, even if they were still a considerable distance from Banff. Few motorists travelled the road in winter, so the gateway office was closed from the end of October until April.

There was a public telephone and a supply of motor oil in the gateway office. Drivers might have topped up their fuel tanks at the Bowfort Garage to the east, near Old Fort Creek, but some neglected to check their oil levels. Tender tires were also a great hazard to motoring in this era. The unpaved road and inadequate rubber conspired to maroon motorists from time to time at Kananaskis Gate until help could be called from Zeller's Service at Exshaw. Road washouts and other calamities could mean a longer stay. Mrs. Staple, the gatekeeper, would take the stranded into her home and sometimes feed them. A chain across the roadway and a lighted red lantern greeted any who arrived after dark. Years later her daughter recalled how Mrs. Staple would get out of bed and go with her dog to the gate, to admit late arrivals.[9]

Arriving at the gate also meant an opportunity for taking snapshots. There are several surviving period photographs of contemporary automobiles, the office, and Mrs. Staple in the uniform she was issued in 1925. A favorite subject is the picturesque arch made of poles which straddled the road and acted as a formal entryway to the Park. It was built in 1917, but by the late 1920s the strong westerly winds through the Gap had taken their toll, and its deteriorating condition made it necessary to cut it down.

Annie Staple and her three children had joined her husband, Warden Tom Staple, at Kananaskis in 1916. The Park had begun construction of a house for them, to be known as Gateway Lodge, but it was not completed until late fall. Meanwhile the family lived in a tent.

When she accepted the position of gatekeeper in July, Mrs Staple's office was a table under a tree. There she registered incoming motorists, issued them licences, sealed any firearms they might have, and collected returned licences from those leaving the Park. There was a space provided for these functions in the new house, but the growth of road traffic soon justified the construction of a small separate office beside the gate. When her husband died in December 1919, Mrs. Staple was kept on as gatekeeper and allowed the year-round use of Gateway Lodge, where her fourth child was born the following May.[10]

The family was not isolated. They lived only a mile west of Kananaskis post office, which served eight families. Mrs. Staple's children attended school at nearby Exshaw. In summer they could assist their mother with her routine duties at the gate and meet the travellers passing through. One of their chores was to take wheelbarrow loads of grimy returned number plates to the nearby creek for washing. These plates were transient licences that had been issued to motorists when they entered the Park, and strapped onto the bumpers of their cars. They were removed and handed in as the cars left the Park. Life became much simpler when the plates were replaced by stickers, and later by the metal "buffalo" badges now so beloved of collectors and antique car buffs.[11]

As part of the Natural Resources Transfer Agreement of 1929, the boundaries of certain national parks in Alberta were to be redrawn to exclude lands "of substantial commercial value."[12] These changes came into effect in 1930, when the National Parks Act prescribed new boundaries, and a new name for Rocky Mountains Park. Banff National Park, as it became known, lost large areas to the east and south, including much of today's Kananaskis Country and Peter Lougheed Provincial Park. The Park boundary now intersected the highway near Duthil, some 29 kilometres west of the Kananaskis Gate. There, on the first of June 1930, a new temporary gate opened for business and Mrs. Staple's family once again moved into a tent.[13]

Today Banff National Park's East Gate is the busiest highway entrance in Canada's national park system. Its "Tudor Rustic" gateway kiosks strung across the incoming roadway are surely the most familiar national park structures. When the three oldest of them were built in 1936 they had gates between them, and they controlled both incoming and outgoing traffic. The most westerly building was originally the gate attendant's residence. It replaced the wooden-floored tent that had served for six years. Tight budgets, combined with a location problem, had delayed the construction of a new permanent gate.[14]

Albert Staple, who was born at the Kananaskis Gate 79 years before, visited his birthplace with his son and granddaughter in 1999. All he could find of Gateway Lodge was its concrete foundation, not far from the little creek where his older siblings had washed licence plates. Apart from his family's connection with this place, he felt it must have a story to tell.[15] Indeed it does. This is where those early motorists, who set forth to experience that "extremely interesting and picturesque" journey, would pass through the Kananaskis Gate and know they had almost made it to Banff. For better or worse, this is where Canada's first national park symbolically embraced the automobile.

Notes

1. National Archives of Canada Website, Archivianet "Post Offices and Post-masters," Kananaskis, Alberta. Aphrodite Karamitsanis, *Place Names of Alberta* Vol. I, "Loder Peak."

2. W. F. Lothian, *A History of Canada's National Parks* Vol. II, 31.

3. Jennifer Cook Bobrovitz, "From the Research Files," *Landmark*, October 2003. Lothian, Vol. II, 31.

4. Lothian, Vol. II, 31.

5. W. F. Lothian, *A History of Canada's National Parks* Vol. I, 38.

6. John Nichol, *The All-Red Route: From Halifax to Victoria in a 1912 Reo* (Toronto 1997). Lothian, Vol. I, 60. City of Calgary, *City Manual,* 1922, 3.

7. Donald G. Wetherall with Irene Kmet, *Useful Pleasures: The Shaping of Leisure in Alberta 1896-1945* (Regina 1990), 193-195. Lothian, Vol. I, 38.

8. *City Manual* 1922, 3.

9. Joyce Cole, "Annie Staple," in Ann Dixon's *Silent Partners: Wives of National Park Wardens* (Pincher Creek, 1985). Interview with Albert Staple 23 June 1999.

10. Joyce Cole.

11. Joyce Cole; Albert Staple. Jerry Svencicki, "Canadian National Parks Motor Vehicle Permits," unpublished manuscript on file, Calgary Service Centre, Parks Canada.

12. CANADA, Department of the Interior, *The National Parks Act and an Indexed Summary of Laws and Regulations Etc.* (Ottawa 1934).

13. Joyce Cole, Albert Staple.

14 Edward Mills, *Rustic Building Programs in Canada's National Parks 1887-1950* (Ottawa, 1994), 311. Lothian Vol. I, 37.

15. Albert Staple.

Our Prairie Origin
St. Andrew's Heights
by Verna MacKenzie

My earliest recollections of St. Andrew's Heights go way back – to the late twenties and early thirties; between the time when it was a golf course and today, when it is a lovely, thriving, single-family residential district, separated from the busy city of Calgary by the Trans Canada Highway (16th Avenue) on the North; 29th Street, Crowchild Trail, and University Drive on the East; and the lovely escarpment of Shawnee Slopes on the South. It is more like a small town than just a part of a busy city, but is only about a 10-minute drive from the city centre. This is St. Andrew's Heights.

A view from an east window of the Foothills Hospital today shows a small, beautiful green island of tall trees and bright shining house tops – all of which have developed since about 1954. In 1929, a view from 16th Avenue and 14th Street looking southwest showed a vast expanse of bald prairie – no trees, no homes – just the odd farm building off in the distance and the remains of the old St. Andrew's Golf Club buildings down near the escarpment. There was also a slough southwest of 16th Avenue and 14th Street complete with frogs splashing about. This prairie expanse of waving grass and wild flowers was one of my favorite places to go for walks.

St. Andrew's Golf Club as it looked in 1914, Calgary, Alberta. St. Andrews Heights Community Archives.

I lived with my family in Pleasant Heights on 20th Avenue in a small bungalow about a block and a half west of King George School. In 1926, about two years after my father's death, Mother enlarged our house and opened a small general store. She was lucky enough to obtain permission to operate a sub-post office at this location. It was known as Tate's General Store. In the early days, Calgary had a Wednesday afternoon early closing by-law, and if it was a bright and sunny day, Mother and I would lock up the store, each stuff a sandwich into our pockets, put our lovely, big Airedale dog, Rusty, on his leash and hike across the prairie down to Shouldice by the Bow River. In those days there was no park there, just a two-story general store by the bridge and a few other buildings behind it. Across the river from where we usually sat to eat our lunch, we could see the buildings of the old *Calgary Herald* Club House where we had attended many picnics and dances when my father was alive and worked for the *Herald.*

In those days, 16th Avenue was not the Trans Canada Highway but a dusty road, and the northeast corner of what was to be the North Hill Shopping Centre was a slough, with tall weeds and pond creatures. We avoided all this and went along 16th Avenue to about 24th Street and then cut across the open prairie – usually with Rusty running free. We enjoyed walking through the prairie paradise of waving grasses and wild flowers with the magnificent view of the mountains off to the west. It was so open and free. However, somewhere in this wonderful paradise was a small farm and on this farm were two nasty dogs who did not appreciate our Airedale invading their territory. We knew the farmer well, as he picked up his mail at the Post Office, and if he saw us hiking across the prairies he would call off his dogs. But all too often the dogs dashed out and tried to engage Rusty in a fight – which he would have enjoyed. Our strategy was for Mother to run ahead and call to Rusty to follow her, (which bless his heart he did, as he was Mother's special pal) and I would stay behind to persuade the big dogs to go home. Believe it or not, we never had to separate a dogfight! I shall always remember those trips through the prairie paradise with so many wild flowers and the magnificent view of the mountains. It was a long walk and quite an adventure for us, as we had not yet acquired a car.

My next brush with St. Andrew's Heights was in the early fifties when the district was just opening up and friends were building on Toronto Crescent. We were back and forth a great deal watching the development of the lovely homes in the district. What I really remember is the wet, sticky clay roads we ploughed over to get to St. Andrew's

1954 – a "new" housing development under construction on 12th Avenue NW, St. Andrews Heights, Calgary, Alberta. St. Andrews Heights Community Archives.

Heights. We came straight across on 14th Avenue with the district of Briar Hill to our south and the now-built North Hill Shopping Centre (then a strip mall) to our north. We went down across 24th Street and up a slippery mud hill into the district and through more mud and building debris to Toronto Crescent. We were always afraid of getting stuck there, but it was all just a form of progress. Later we watched the half-finished skeleton of the Foothills Hospital arise to the west and stand patiently waiting until the powers that be solved their problems and finally finished this wonderful hospital.

The hospital was not the only attraction for new residents to this district. In 1955, the Jubilee Auditorium opened to celebrate the 50th Anniversary of the creation of the province of Alberta and I had the thrill of singing in the One Thousand-Voice Choir at the Sunday afternoon dedication service. It is a magnificent building and added greatly to the appeal of St. Andrew's as a place to live. Also, the University of Calgary turned its first sod in those days and I was present at that. That area was another vast prairie space on the north side of St. Andrew's and when I attended the sod-turning ceremony, I wondered why they had to build it so far beyond the city. But it was another great attraction to this district – to live close to the University.

Anther asset for St. Andrew's was the almost instantaneous building of the McMahon Stadium – a huge attraction for the sport enthusiasts of Calgary. Surrounded on three sides by such attractions, St. Andrew's Heights was scheduled to become quite a desirable residential district.

Many people who have lived here have worked at the hospital, the university, surrounding banks, or in the offices of some of the big oil companies in downtown Calgary, which is only a 10-minute drive away.

It was a real thrill to me, an onlooker, to see this district evolve from bald prairie to a lovely, tree-lined residential district with a school and church and lots of playgrounds – not to mention a community centre. The wonderful view from Toronto Crescent of the mountains and the downtown area was certainly in its favor too.

My final introduction to St. Andrew's Heights was when I came here as a bride in 1972. My husband was one of the original owners and I now have the privilege of living in this lovely home. Perhaps I am living on land across which I once raced with my Airedale dog when I was in my teens. It has been exciting for me to see St. Andrew's Heights evolve from a prairie landscape into a vibrant, wonderful community. Today we are going into another state of change – we are growing up. Our quaint bungalow type homes are being replaced by two-story mansions on reclaimed property. Who knows what a difference another 50 years will bring?

The Nanton Lancaster
FM159

by Dave Birrell

Lancaster FM159 is a lucky Lancaster. One of 7374 built to help vanquish the Nazis, it was fortunate to have arrived for battle after the war in Europe ended, thus avoiding the flak and fighters that destroyed 3932 of its cohorts.

Saved from the scrap yard, the aircraft enjoyed a fulfilling career with the Royal Canadian Air Force, travelling widely from bases on both coasts to play a valuable role during the Cold War.

Replaced by a more modern aircraft, FM159 again escaped the scrap yard to become a town's landmark, watching the highway traffic pass by for thirty-one years.

Finally, FM159 found itself dedicated to a Canadian war hero and the centerpiece of a museum telling the story of those who served in aircraft like it during the Second World War.

During the early years of the Second World War, the British and their Allies were building as many aircraft as possible. In a surprisingly short time, thousands of aircraft of several types, including four-engined Lancaster Bombers, were being produced in Canada. For a country still largely agrarian and just recovering from a decade of depression, the challenge that was met was immense. Eventually Lancaster production reached the level of one aircraft per day and the project employed 10 thousand people. A total of 430 were built and 105 were lost in action.

Strangely, as the Canadian-built Lancasters that had operated during the war were returning home, newly built aircraft such as FM159 were being flown to England, even though the war in Europe had ended. After spending four months in England, FM159 returned to Canada, arriving safely at Yarmouth, Nova Scotia, to join others in temporary storage. However there was concern that the damp, salty climate of the Maritimes was beginning to cause corrosion and it was decided to fly hundreds of the bombers to a drier climate.

Lancaster FM159 airborne with the No. 407 Squad. Nanton Lancanster Society photo. Photographer unknown.

Residents of Western Canada must have been shocked to hear the roar of the huge warplanes as they travelled across the prairies. The aircrew aboard knew the horror of war, but they had beaten the odds and survived and were understandably elated. As they crossed the prairies and before landing their aircraft for the last time, they buzzed towns and farms at extremely low level, frightening both residents and livestock.

Numerous Lancasters, including FM159, landed at the former training base at Pearce, Alberta, northeast of Fort Macleod. Many were sold to farmers. A Lanc could be purchased for a few hundred dollars and its parts put to many uses on the farm. To begin with there was lots of oil and hydraulic cylinders that could be adapted to various uses around the farm. The aircraft also provided a seemingly endless supply of wire, metal tubes, and sheet aluminum. Some of the more novel ideas were placing Lancaster tail wheels on threshing machines, using crew door ladders for checking the level in grain bins, placing bomb-bay doors as borders of flower gardens, using propeller spinners as plant pots, and incorporating escape hatches (with windows) into the construction of outhouses.

Being a low-time Lancaster, FM159 was saved from the fate of becoming a farmer's hardware store, made a short hop to the former training base at Fort Macleod, and was placed in storage.

FM159 was recalled for duty as a result of the international situation in the early 1950s. Following the increase in tension between East and West, the Royal Canadian Air Force ordered the modification of 70 Lancasters to become maritime reconnaissance aircraft and play an anti-submarine role. The modifications included upgraded electronics and auxiliary fuel tanks fitted in the bomb bay. A silver paint scheme completed the conversion and FM159 emerged as a modern maritime reconnaissance aircraft.

From October, 1953, until early 1955 it served with No. 103 Search and Rescue Unit based at Greenwood, Nova Scotia. Then there were more modifications, including the installation of a new radar system that enabled a snorkelling submarine to be detected at a distance of 20 nautical miles and FM159 was transferred to the west coast to begin service with No. 407 Squadron. The threat posed by Soviet submarines in Canada's Pacific waters was being countered by Lancasters based at Comox on Vancouver Island. As well as maritime reconnaissance, the squadron was also tasked with search and rescue and other duties.

Almost immediately, FM159 was off on what was one of its most exciting adventures. Flying over Canada's high Arctic, an ice observer charted the colors, cracks, leads, and movement of the sea ice so that the Dew Line radar sites could be re-supplied. The flights were lengthy, some as long as 10 hours.

FM159's longest flight concluded with an unscheduled visit to the northernmost point in Canada, Alert, on the northern tip of Ellesmere Island just 490 miles from the North Pole. While returning from a long patrol to their base at Resolute Bay on Cornwallis Island, Captain Harry Addison received word that the airfield was experiencing a "white out." He was advised to fly to Thule, Greenland. Then about half an hour out of Thule, Harry was told that they were experiencing zero visibility. He then asked for another alternate and was advised that the weather at Alert was forecasted to improve. But Alert only came on the radio every four hours, so they didn't know for sure.

It was a 500-mile flight and the navigator's maps didn't go that far north. According to Harry Addison,

> Freddy Pineau, the flight engineer, was frantically doing all sorts of engine configurations to increase our flying time as we were getting critically low on fuel About forty miles out of Alert they came on with their regularly scheduled weather broadcast and we were relieved to hear that Alert was practically clear. Never having landed a Lancaster with so little fuel on board, we must have floated two-thirds of the runway before touching down. After a few 'Hail Mary's' the pale faces returned to colour and, as we turned off the

runway, number four engine died from lack of fuel. We had landed after a flying time of 12 hours 25 minutes. Needless to say we were all relieved to be on the ground.

FM159 had another close call in 1956 when an engine exploded and burned one foggy night over the Pacific. Then, while returning to base, all electrics and navigation was lost. Pilot Bert Clark recalled, "It's a strange feeling to be moving along at 180 knots into a black void not knowing where you are." Eventually they followed another aircraft home, passing through the Straits of Juan de Fuca at 300 feet without being able to see the lights of Vancouver.

During 1956, FM159 participated in an exercise designed to test the capability of Canadian and American interceptor squadrons. After leaving Comox and travelling north into the interior of BC, pilot Fred Burton dropped down into the valleys of the Rockies to avoid detection by radar. He recalled,

> The Canadians did catch us and we were jumped by CF-100 fighter jets. We continued on our southerly track and crossed into Washington State with no further interception. We then climbed to about 20 000 feet and began our simulated bomb run over the city of Spokane. We made three passes before a USAF F86 came up to see who we were!

Later that year, FM159 searched for a Trans Canada Airlines North Star that went down after leaving Vancouver with 60 people aboard included many players from the western all-star football team.

FM159 travelled widely during those years, including trips to Alaska and to the British Isles to take part in anti-submarine exercises. Flight engineer Duke Dawe recalled a problem while flying near London.

> The crystals for the radio were kept in a nice metal box with the frequencies labeled next to them. All went well on the first crystal change, but then the radio operator opened the box upside down, and all the crystals fell to the floor. What a mess! Needless to say we flew right through London control without talking to anyone. They must have had to divert all the traffic away from us.

The Lancaster era at Comox drew to a close in 1958 and it was with some nostalgia that F/L Brooks and flight engineer Duke Dawe left Comox, flew across the mountains, and parked FM159 at RCAF Station Calgary. The aircraft had acquired a total of 2 068 hours since its overhaul

Lancaster FM159 fording the Little Bow River, September 27, 1960. Nanton Lancaster Society photo. Photographer unknown.

in 1953. Duke recalled that leaving Lanc159 was a "rather moving experience." He had flown in the aircraft 62 times, accumulating a total of 224.5 hours and he, "always had a very great feeling for her." Later a civilian crew flew the aircraft to the former BCATP base southwest of Vulcan, where its engines and props were removed and the aircraft was to be scrapped.

But luck was with FM159. In 1960, George White of Nanton had the idea of acquiring an aircraft as a war memorial and tourist attraction for his town. After hearing that FM159 was to be scrapped he, together with Howie Armstrong and Fred Garratt, purchased the bomber for $513.

George recalled that they realized that the Lancaster's main wheels were too far apart to permit travelling along the roads. So the Nanton volunteers waited until the crops were all harvested, put the tail wheel in the back of a truck, and towed the bomber backwards across the fields. Two fencing crews were organized, one to take down the barbed wire fences ahead of the aircraft and a second to put them back up again. One of the more interesting challenges was easing the aircraft down the banks of the Little Bow River, through the ford, and up the other side.

Late in the day, FM159 passed between the south end of Connemara Lake and Mosquito Creek and reached the CPR tracks where the strange procession stopped for the night. Early the following morning the aircraft was pulled across the tracks and up onto Highway No. 2. It was smooth sailing from there and triumphantly, but likely somewhat uncomfortably, Lancaster bomber FM159 entered the Town of Nanton and was parked by the side of the highway.

When FM159 arrived in Nanton, it was complete and could have flown had the engines and propellers not been removed. Two years later it was a gutted shell, thieves having removed the instruments and interior equipment and vandals having broken the cockpit, turrets, and bomb-aimers perspex, and torn the fabric of the control surfaces. The aircraft was on the edge of town at the time and despite efforts by Fred Garratt and others, there was no stopping the vandalism.

In 1962 volunteers began to put FM159 back on the road to recovery from its sorry state. Engines and propellers were purchased and installed. The aircraft was placed on steel mounts, its tail high in the air to limit access. Fortunately those in charge took the time to ensure that the aircraft would not be damaged. Steel mounts were fabricated and the aircraft continued to rest on its landing gear.

Harry Dwelle fabricated aluminum "windows" to cover the broken perspex. This was most important as bird droppings cause rapid corrosion in an aluminum airplane. Ray McMahon, together with his family and friends, repaired the exterior as much as possible and painted the aircraft.

The trio who purchased FM159 then donated the aircraft to the town. Over the following 20 years volunteers and service clubs did what they could to keep FM159 looking its best as millions of people drove by on Highway No. 2 and the "Nanton Bomber" became a symbol for the town.

During the 1980s, there was interest from outside of Nanton. Offers to acquire the aircraft had been received from several individuals and even from her previous owners at Comox. However, the town rejected these advances and in 1985 looked again to George White for leadership, asking him to see if he could form an organization to, "take care of the bomber."

George wrote an article in the *Nanton News* asking if anyone was interested in helping. He was overwhelmed with the response and the Nanton Lancaster Society was formed.

At this time no one had been in the aircraft for 25 years and virtually no one in Nanton knew anything about Lancasters in general, or FM159 in particular. But soon related artifacts were on display and Lancaster T-shirts and caps were for sale in the local tourist information booth. The Society had also made the decision that the best way to, "take care of the bomber" was to restore it to its wartime configuration as the centerpiece of an air museum – a rather ambitious undertaking for a community of fewer than 2 000 people. "Open Bomber Days" were held featuring tours through FM159. These were most successful, with long lines forming at the ladder leading to the cockpit. The aircraft's role in the education of future generations had begun.

In 1991, through the co-operation of the three levels of government, Legion Branches, corporations, and thousands of individuals, a museum building was completed. On a bright Saturday morning, FM159 was rolling again, this time towed by a farm tractor into her new home.

FM159 is dedicated to the memory of Ian Bazalgette, a Lancaster pilot who was awarded the Commonwealth's highest award for valor, the only Albertan to be so recognized during WW II.

Ian was born in Calgary, educated in Britain, and joined the Royal Air Force. After completing a tour of operations, "Baz," as he became known, volunteered for additional service with the Pathfinder Force.

Bazalgette's Lancaster was hit by flak while approaching a V-1 Rocket site. Both starboard engines were knocked out and fires started. As the Master Bomber and Deputy Master Bomber were out of action it was up to Baz to mark the target for the remainder of the force. This he did but then the aircraft went into a violent dive. He regained control but soon the fire spread and a third engine stopped running. He ordered four of his crew to parachute but chose to remain on board in an attempt to save the others who were injured and could not jump. Baz managed to land the aircraft but it exploded and all aboard were killed. The surviving crew members evaded enemy soldiers and made their way to the allied forces. The story was told and the Victoria Cross awarded. The citation reads that, "His courage and devotion to duty were beyond praise."

Larry Melling served with Ian. He recalls being impressed by him on his first day at the squadron when he walked into the Flight Office,

> He had a tremendous sparkle in his eye is the best way to describe it. He stood out amongst the people who were there. He was an inviting sort of a person, a person that you wouldn't hesitate to approach. He was always the first to volunteer for a job, no matter what sort of job it might be.

A Dedication Ceremony was held in 1990. Mrs. Ethel Broderick, Ian's sister, unveiled a plaque and the markings of the Bazalgette aircraft (F2-T) were unveiled by two of Baz's crew members, Chuck Godfrey and George Turner.

FM159's friends from No. 407 Squadron were represented on this special day as well. The squadron's c/o, Lt. Col. Terry Chester, spoke at the ceremonies and a squadron Aurora performed a fly-past together with a CF-5 jet.

Early in the history of the Nanton Lancaster Society, a decision was made to restore FM159 to its wartime configuration as a memorial to those who served with Bomber Command. The aircraft has been inspected by engineers and found to be in very sound condition. With this in mind, restoration has proceeded with the goal of having a fully restored, static display aircraft that is capable of engine run-ups.

Society members have scoured Southern Alberta, visiting the barns and junk piles of farms whose owners had purchased Lancasters after the war. This has resulted in an extensive collection of parts that are used in the restoration of the aircraft and for trading with other museums

The first major restoration project involved the pilot's instrument panel. Jon Spinks acquired the instruments in England and by late 1987 had completed the beautifully restored panel. Extensive work has been done to restore the aircraft's three gun turrets. Following three years of work, the rear turret was made fully operational. The perspex in the cockpit canopy and bomb aimer's position has been replaced, as has that in the front and rear gun turrets. After suffering from water damage over the years, the navigator/wireless operator's table was removed and rebuilt. Considerable work has been done on the engines towards the goal of bringing FM159 to life again.

Restoring a World War II bomber is a huge undertaking, particularly when the museum itself has been under constant development. Numerous other aircraft have been acquired and restoration projects completed. Major building and expansion projects are frequently underway.

FM159 now enjoys a fulfilling role as the centerpiece of the Nanton Lancaster Society Air Museum. The museum features a dozen other aircraft as well as artifacts, aviation art, and interpretive displays that tell the story of Bomber Command and Canada's contribution to the air war. Hundreds of thousands of people have visited and all have left knowing more of the sacrifices that were made by the aircrew of Bomber Command.

FM159 remains the only Lancaster in the world that welcomes supervised visitors to its interior. During one of the "Open Bomber Days," two Lancaster veterans who had not seen each other since WW II met and embraced inside the aircraft. Over the years, FM159 has witnessed countless other memorable moments as aircrew have relived their memories. These include both the horrors they went through as well as happier times that forged lifetime bonds with their fellow crew members. Some Bomber Command veterans freely tell of their experiences as they visit, others quietly keep their memories to themselves. Some are brought to tears and others have just walked around the aircraft, unable to bring themselves to step inside.

Ground crew, women who served with the RCAF, and others who played important roles with Bomber Command have toured the museum. Men and women who worked for Victory Aircraft have visited FM159, some pointing to a particular part and saying, "I built that," or "I riveted those pieces together." Former aircrew who flew aboard FM159 during her postwar service are regular visitors and recall their valuable service during the Cold War.

Each year classes of school children sit under her wing to be told what freedom means and the role of Canada's Airforce in the past and today. Air Cadet Squadrons and veterans' and seniors' organizations visit regularly as well.

Dozens of special events have been held under FM159's wings. The bomber hears moving speeches of remembrance and presides over solemn ceremonies. Guests seated on her wing have heard the stirring RAF March-past during band concerts, a choir has sung, "Coming in on a Wing and a Prayer" from her cockpit, and a couple was married on the starboard wing.

But most importantly, the aircraft has been host to thousands of aircrew and their families as they visit the museum to honor, to learn, and to remember. In many cases the families have heard, for the first time, of a father's or grandfather's role in Bomber Command. World War II

Lancaster FM159. On display at the Nanton Lancaster Museum. Nanton Lancanster Society photo.

238 Remembering Chinook Country

touched the lives of all Canadian families and the Royal Canadian Air Force will always be a significant part of many family histories.

Each year thousands of visitors come to the museum knowing that the Lancaster played a crucial role in the life of a parent, grandparent, uncle or aunt.

FM159 and its museum tell their stories well. Visitors are often in awe of both the aircraft and those who served. They leave the museum with increased appreciation of the successes and sacrifices associated with Bomber Command.

From the Heart and Pocketbook
Philanthropy and Charity in Calgary
by Faye Reineberg Holt

A history of philanthropy in Calgary should be a simple thing. Who were all the wealthy men and what were the causes they supported? Sounds easy, but it offers a limited view of charitable hearts in Calgary. Charity might come from the heart, but philanthropy is only possible for individuals – traditionally males – with wealth. Addressing Calgary's charitable spirit over the decades means valuing women's contributions, too. Few were considered philanthropists, even though their husbands might be credited with the honor, and money donated came from family coffers. In addition, low- and middle-income families donated to some of the same causes supported by philanthropists. So, charity and philanthropy are two sides of a coin, with stories that are inseparable.

Even donations took many forms. Some people have volunteered tirelessly for their causes. Others provided the financial support needed by one individual or by large and small charitable societies. Some individuals with generous hearts have donated a few dollars to a cause. Others wrote cheques for millions to ensure a community need was met. Philanthropists even donated land for building sites, parks, or protected areas.

The face of charity and philanthropy is unbelievably diverse, but so are charitable groups. Today, the United Way is one of Calgary's largest charitable organizations. In reality, it is the umbrella organization for many smaller charities, but very significant registered charities exist independently of the United Way. In terms of big-league, organized donors, to many people, the Calgary Foundation represents philanthropy in the city. Once again, it is an umbrella organization made up of many charitable foundations. Some have been set up by the very wealthy. Others have been established by middle-income individuals and families. But the Calgary Foundation is really one of the new kids on the block.

Of course, when it comes to charity, money may be the bottom line, but gifts of time or talent have always been appreciated. For decades, Calgarians have made toys for needy children at Christmas; they have delivered Meals on Wheels; and they have volunteered to help stage the Stampede.

Nevertheless, charity and philanthropy are clearly different on some levels. The *Oxford Canadian Dictionary* claims *charity* is "giving voluntarily to those in need . . . help, especially money, given; an organization for helping those in need; a kindness." *Benevolence* has the related meaning of "doing good"; it involves being "actively friendly, helpful." *Philanthropy* is defined as "a love of human kind; practical benevolence, especially charity on a large scale." Perhaps not all philanthropists are actually focused on love of human kind, but they offer gifts of financial support on a large scale.

For someone earning a minimum wage, donating a few dollars to a cause may have more financial impact on the donor than the impact of donating thousands of dollars on wealthy individuals. Still, philanthropists often donate more than money or objects of great financial value. Some offer countless hours and valuable expertise to causes. At times, the gift of their time is geared to administering their foundations, those vehicles through which donations are made available to causes and individuals. They may have little, if any, direct contact with the individual or charitable society "in need." However, the philanthropist's time, effort, and expertise deserve recognition, just as the time and effort of other volunteers deserves acknowledgment.

So, philanthropy, charitable groups, good causes, and volunteering became virtually inseparable stories. Over the years, all have had a significant impact on the city. Important causes to receive support have addressed educational, cultural, health, social service, and recreational needs of Calgarians. A few early "causes" were absolutely crucial to quality of life in the young community.

When the railway began bringing thousands of people to the Calgary area, the needs of the community were basic, seemingly without end, and diverse. Those needs led to countless acts of charity by both men and women from diverse economic backgrounds. The story really begins with these well-meaning people, their commitments of time and effort, and fundraising that targeted anyone and everyone willing to donate a few hours time, a nickel, or a buck.

In the decades before any form of medicare, providing adequate heath care to citizens was a priority. Many charitable individuals and groups, especially church groups, were willing to pay the medical bills of sick children and even their parents. But Calgary needed a general hospital. The wealthy and wage-earners – of both sexes – supported the initiative. Land was donated for a building site. Other funds for the hospital came from public subscriptions, municipal reserves, and government coffers.

Not surprisingly, given traditional expectations for women at the time, the hospital became one of the causes where women played a very significant role. By 1890, men sat on the voluntary Calgary General Hospital Board and made large financial donations. Women with similar concerns formed the Women's Hospital Aid Society to raise money for services needed. Some of those women were wealthy or married to wealthy spouses. But the traditional roles of women meant the help they provided was generally defined as an act of "charity." Donations of money, time, and effort made by middle- or low-income men were considered the same. In contrast, donations to the hospital by wealthy men helped create their reputations as philanthropists.

Fundraising for the hospital was never a one-time effort, and over the years such well-known Calgarians as William and Margaret Pearce were actively involved in supporting an ever-larger and better equipped hospital. Early, well-known philanthropists who donated to many good causes and supported various local charities included the Big Four: Pat Burns, A. E. Cross, Archie MacLean, and George Lane. In fact, the Big Four, who each contributed $20 000 in order to stage the 1912 Stampede, had hoped to make money on the venture. So, they had promised to donate $500 each from their profits on the rodeo to the Calgary General Hospital fund. Despite good attendance, the Stampede did not register a big profit. The bills were many, including pay-outs for the competition purses and countless other expenses. However, Burns convinced his fellow sponsors to live up to their commitment to the hospital fund. Not only were the donations good deeds, the men's generosity garnered respect from the community.

Certainly, Burns became one of the most significant philanthropists in early Calgary. Settling in the community in 1890, he made his initial fortune from meat-packing and ranching. Later, Burns became a major stockholder in petroleum companies and countless other business ventures. It was well known that employees could expect turkeys as bonuses at Christmas. On his 75th birthday in 1931, when his appointment to the Senate was also announced, Calgary citizens enjoyed complimentary birthday cake. More importantly, Burns once again donated meat for the tables of needy families. This time it was 2 000 roasts of beef, and at least for a few days, poor children ate well.

Burns's acts of generosity and kindness were varied. Any number of circumstances involved his providing temporary or long-term financial assistance to people he knew and individuals who contacted him regarding their circumstances. Unrelated to Burns's support for the Stampede, he gave Guy Weadick financial help. In addition, he helped others with everything from mortgages to sponsoring the music career of Isabelle de las Giroday. Sometimes, he expected to be repaid and drew up the appropriate paper work. Sometimes he was repaid; sometimes he wasn't, but throughout the years, Burns's donations proved significant to many individuals and charities.

During those same years, women's charitable work continued to receive little recognition other than from their church-related societies. Commonly, women were considered more dependable as volunteers and fund-raisers than many of their male counterparts. However, given their limited involvement in money matters, their monetary donations to community were often small and seldom recorded. Their work for charities was a different story.

The Young Women's Benevolent Club focused on helping "distressed gentlewomen." In 1910, women from the Anglican Church organized the society. It raised money using the traditional methods of women: bazaars, bake sales, rummage sales, teas, and craft sales. By 1916, the name of the group was changed to the Samaritan Club. In the following years, the club offered financial assistance not only to individuals in need but also to a wide variety of social and community service organizations.

Another of the well-known women's charity groups in Calgary was the Young Women's Christian Association (YWCA). Intent on helping needy women, by 1907, the local YWCA had rented a building. Under the leadership of women such as Mrs. G. W. Kerby, Mrs. Thomas Underwood, and Mrs. A. B. Cushing, members were soon raising money for a much-needed new building.

Requiring a substantial sum to buy the lot and to erect the structure, the society turned to 120 men who controlled business and family finances. The women requested donations of $100 from each man. As well, the women raised money through Tag Days and refreshment booths at the fair. They operated the *Calgary Herald* for a day, and they petitioned the city for a day's profits from the street car system. By 1911, they had their new YWCA building.

With the city experiencing phenomenal growth, volunteers met every train coming into Calgary. They sought out those women who needed help and took many to the new residence. Those dedicated volunteers showed love for the broader group, for "human kind." They were "doing good" in an active and friendly way. They made gifts of their time and talents, but their acts were charity, not philanthropy. In contrast, some of the 120 men who donated to their causes were considered philanthropists. Once again, philanthropy and charity were two sides of the same coin.

Some philanthropists preferred to remain anonymous, but others became widely known for their financial contributions to community. William Roper Hull supported countless cultural endeavors and social services in Calgary. Born in England in 1856, Hull earned his wealth as a result of his ranching, meat packing, and other businesses. Despite his business acuity, he funded the building of Calgary's Opera House, thereby demonstrating the same interest that later-day philanthropists would have in culture.

Hull died in 1925. His wife passed away in 1953, and their estate totaled more than $5 million. Charity was an important component of Mrs. Hull's will, and she recognized the special needs of "at-risk" children within the city. She earmarked funds for William Roper Hull Home, re-named in 1962 as Hull Child and Family Services. Her own philanthropic commitment had created a service for troubled children. Yet, the facility's original name had commemorated her husband, and few would remember the name Emmeline Hull.

Other early and wealthy Calgarians to play important roles in supporting good causes included the Cross families. Another of the financially successful men in the Calgary area, Montreal-born A. E. Cross had extensive ranch holdings, and, in 1892, he founded Calgary Brewing and Malting Company. As well, he made money in Alberta's early petroleum industry, which would add name after name to the rolls of the city's philanthropists. By 1912, Cross had launched Calgary Petroleum Products, but also, he became a director of Canadian Western Natural Gas. The family supported many worthy causes. After Cross Sr. died in 1932, his sons took over their father's businesses. Eventually, the Cross families would be among the founding members of the Calgary Foundation.

Many other city philanthropists made fortunes in the oil and gas industries. Born in Ontario in 1892, Eric Harvie accrued a fortune as a result of payments from mineral rights, but he also owned several companies related to the oil industry. In addition, his professions as a lawyer and rancher created significant wealth for himself and his wife, Dorothy Jean Southam. By the 1950s, he had founded numerous charitable foundations, including the Harvie Foundation, Riveredge Foundation, Ace Foundation, and Devonian Foundation. In 1966, Harvie's Glenbow Foundation became the Glenbow-Alberta Institute.

Royalties from mineral rights helped create the wealth of Eric Harvie, whose phil-anthropic contributions to Calgary were extensive and diverse. Here he is seen at Meridian #1 well near Ribstone, Alberta. Glenbow Archives, NA 700-1

Through it, his contributions to the cultural fabric of Calgary and Alberta were some of the most significant in the province's history. Harvie's cultural legacy to the city included the diverse and valuable historical and art collections housed at Glenbow Museum. As a result of those local, national, and international art and history collections, the museum garnered an international reputation. Yet the collection would reflect the sometimes quirky and always diverse interests of the man. The legacy included First Nation's artifacts, world-class art works, Samurai armor, and unique curiosities of little financial value.

As well as gifting the city with the museum and collections, Harvie's philanthropy funded the Devonian Gardens, a beautiful garden escape in the midst of downtown yet, seemingly, a world away from the hustle and bustle of business. Without a doubt, the contributions he and his wife made showed a "love of human kind; practical benevolence, especially charity on a large scale." In 1968, an appreciative nation acknowledged that philanthropic vision when Harvie was given the Order of Canada.

Another of the city's important philanthropists, Max Bell, didn't actually move to Calgary until 1935. He came to take over the debt-ridden

Calgary Albertan from his dying father, and by the late 1940s, he had turned the paper around. However, on his way to status as a media magnate, Bell invested in Imperial Oil. When the company struck black gold in the Leduc field, Bell became rich. In addition, he was a major shareholder in the CPR and had investments in natural gas explorations. When he died in 1972, Bell was worth about $22 million. Most of that wealth went to the Max Bell Foundation, which has funded an addiction treatment centre, a theatre, an arena, and countless worthy causes in Calgary and across the nation.

In fact, the city's philanthropists have come from all walks of life and ethnic backgrounds. At times, significant philanthropic acts have been directed towards specific ethnic and religious groups within the community. A wealthy member recognized a need and came up with the money required to support the cause or achieve an important objective for the group. For instance, in the 1950s, one of the many charitable acts of George Ho Lem was to donate $120 000 to build the Chinese United Church in Calgary's Chinatown.

However, as Calgary became a large city where it was no longer possible to have reasonable access to individuals with reputations for philanthropy, increasingly, both charities and philanthropists had to adopt new organizational methods. The wealthy and even middle-income families wanted to support causes that meshed with their own values and priorities. Aware of that inclination, volunteers for charities realized that they had to publicize their causes, launch well-organized and large-scale fundraising campaigns, and/or make a case for their causes by formally applying to the various foundations for funding.

Already, by 1920, the concept of uniting charities under one umbrella to raise money for the needy and for various good causes seemed to be an answer. The first such charity umbrella group was the Community Chest. Although it lasted only one year, that year of operation allowed fund raisers to recognize the wisdom of such a unified approach. By 1939, an Inter-Service Club Committee and the Council of Social Agencies became the resurrected versions of the "umbrella" group. That year, 15 member organizations participated in fundraising, and the money raised was used for both operating and capital projects. Over the next 20 years, the name reverted to Community Chest and numerous organizations joined. By 1962, that umbrella organization again changed its name, becoming the United Fund.

Eleven years later, it was the United Way. Even in the 1940s and 1950s, the association included such big name charities as the Canadian Red Cross, the Salvation Army, and the Canadian Cancer Society, all with local chapters or branches. By the 1970s dozens of other organizations – including the Canadian National Institute for the Blind (CNIB), Elizabeth Fry Society, emergency shelters, health-related societies, boys and girls clubs, the Calgary Native Friendship Society – were added. Religious as well as lay groups were represented, and with the success of the United Way fundraising ventures, the needs of countless Calgarians were addressed. Thousands and thousands of charity-minded citizens without huge bankrolls at their disposal made small donations.

Large scale donations were very much in evidence, too. To make the process easier from their own perspective, many philanthropists adopted new ways of doing things. Beginning in 1955, The Calgary Foundation united the charitable foundations of 20 founding donors under one umbrella. Included were foundations funded by the Cross and Nickle families, Fred Mannix, Harry Cohen, Peter Bawden, Max Bell, and others. Dr. Gertrude M. Lange was the only female among the founding members.

That umbrella organization provided a template for planned, long-term giving. Member foundations still focused on the priorities or values of the individual donors, but they shared an administrative base. Also, together, they could more effectively communicate information about funds available to those individuals or organizations that needed financial help. Grant MacEwan was the first chairman of the Calgary Foundation's board, and he served from 1955 to 1963.

Eventually, his own charitable foundation would support many valuable causes, not all administered through the Calgary Foundation. The Grant MacEwan Award for Writing – valued at $25 000 – would become one of the most significant such awards for writers in Alberta. As with most philanthropists and their families, MacEwan – perhaps the most important and prolific writer of Alberta and western Canadian social history – wanted the award to acknowledge writing and writers that reflected his own interests. But his interests were broad! As a result, the award and other charitable works in his memory demonstrate how history, the arts, community, and culture can be enriched by one individual's philanthropic vision.

Esther Honen's foundation, administered through the Calgary Foundation, was to have a major cultural impact on the city. In 1908, at age five, Honen came to Calgary with her parents. As a young adult, she worked for 25 years at Henry Birks and Sons, Jewelers. From childhood and her own days of music lessons, she learned to love music. Ultimately, that passion for piano led her to create a $5 million dollar foundation that has funded the Kiwanis Music Festival, the Calgary Philharmonic Orchestra, the music program at Banff Centre, and other selected music programs.

Not all was easy in her life. In fact, she suffered from Parkinson's disease. But, like others, she created a lasting legacy in Calgary. The Esther Honen International Piano Competition was first staged in 1992, the year Esther died. The winner of the annual competition receives $50 000, and the competition has brought pianists from 17 different countries in Europe and North America to Calgary's doorstep. As a result, Honen enriched the music scene in Calgary, but also, she supported the development of talented musicians from around the world.

Independently administered philanthropic foundations funded by Calgarians have continued to have an enormous impact on the city, province, nation, and international communities, too. The Kahanoff Foundation is not part of the Calgary Foundation, but it is among the largest and most important charitable foundations in Canada. In about 1950, Sydney Kahanoff (1922-1980) moved with his family from Saskatchewan to Calgary. Although he had a degree in physics, his first job in the city was working at the Calgary brewery. Eventually, he owned Voyageur Petroleum.

At his death, the Kahanoff Foundation was established from his estate. With assets of about $100 million, not only does the foundation fund worthy causes in Calgary, the province, and the nation, it sponsors worthwhile programs in Israel.

Despite his phenomenal success in the oil industry, Kahanoff, like many early Alberta oilmen, had humble beginnings. His parents, Minnie and Ab Kahanoff, were Russian-Jewish immigrants. Although Ab was politically conservative, Minnie was a social activist. When the Canadian Commonwealth Federation (CCF), with its socialist leanings, was on the rise in Saskatchewan, Minnie campaigned for the party.

So, in a fashion, Syd Kahanoff's support for social causes was not surprising. However, business, the arts, community initiatives, and education have all benefited from funding. In Calgary, many charitable groups received much-needed support from the Kahanoff Foundation when the foundation provided them with a home – or at least office space. Recognizing the desperate need of charities for inexpensive, centrally located office space, the foundation purchased the Trans-Alta Building. Renamed the Kahanoff Building and extensively renovated, by 2003, it provided space to charities at a subsidized and reasonable rent. According to a United Way representative, it was "a godsend to us."

Also in the city, the foundation provided one million dollars in start-up funding to the Oakley Centre for the Gifted. Provincially, the foundation has partnered with programs such as the Alberta Performing Arts Stabilization Fund, and Science Alberta. It has funded various higher educational programs in Canada and Israel, including a chair for Israeli Studies at U of C.

Although Kahanoff was Jewish, in partnership with the Israel Association of Community Centres, his foundation has helped to fund community centres serving Moslems, Christians, Druze, and Bedouins, as well as Jews in Israel. There, it has also funded vocational schools, a school for the blind, and a hospital wing.

The Kahanoff Foundation has sponsored numerous educational programs and workshops focused on business – whether approaches are practical or theoretical. As well, in 2000, the foundation funded a tour of the Middle East and Europe by Canada's National Arts Council Orchestra. In hundreds of instances, the larger community has been enriched by support from the foundation.

Making large-scale financial donations to serve the local and greater community – and thereby showing "a love of human kind" – has always been a central concept in philanthropy. But simply supporting needy individuals in whatever way people can, "doing good," and being "helpful" in an "actively friendly" manner are equally important to community. Both have had a phenomenal impact on the quality of life in the city during the past. Both will continue to have an impact on the directions the city takes in the future. And both are dependent on the hearts and pocketbooks of Calgarians who care.

References

Avenue Magazine. Retrieved May 2003 from [www.avenuemagazine.ca/May 2003].

Bolton, Ken et al. *The Albertans.* Edmonton: Lone Pine Publishing, 1981.

Brennan, Brian. *Alberta Originals: Stories of Albertans Who Made a Difference.* Calgary: Fifth House, 2001.

Brennan, Brian. *Building a Province: 60 Alberta Lives.* Calgary: Fifth House, 2000.

Calgary Foundation. Calgary: Advertising Special, Feb 27, 2001; Annual Report, 2003; Funds & Grants, Pamphlet Files: Esther Honens.

Calgary Foundation, The. Retrieved from [www.thecalgaryfoundation.org].

Canadian Centre for Philanthropy. Retrieved from [www.ccp.ca].

"Home Sweet Home- Hull, William Roper." *Electronic version.* Retrieved from [http://collections.ic.gc.ca/calgary].

Stallworthy, Bob. *The Old Y Centre 1911-1991.* Calgary: The Old Y Centre for Community Organizations, 1991.

Kahanoff Foundation, The. Retrieved from [www.kahanoff.com/who.html].

Max Bell Fonds; Eric Harvie Fonds; Pat Burns Fonds; William Roper Hull Fonds; Calgary Hospital Board Fonds; United Way of Calgary Fonds; Samaritan Club of Calgary Fonds: Retrieved from [www.glenbow.org/museum.htm].

To Market, To Market
From Market Stall to City Hall
Carol Stokes

One of the many pleasures of summer in Calgary is the opportunity to shop at various Farmers' Markets around the city. While typically there are about a half dozen markets to choose from, citizens in Calgary's early years purchased directly from farmers at the Calgary Public Market. The market's early and rather sketchy history, from its establishment in 1884 until it found a permanent home in 1910, can be traced through records created by the Town and then the City of Calgary.

The Committee on Markets & Health[1] was formed on December 17, 1884. Composed entirely of Town Council members, Chairman Dr. Neville J. Lindsay served with Simon J. Clarke, Simon J. Hogg, Joseph H. Millward, and Mayor George Murdoch. The committee drafted By-law No. 20 to establish the Public Market, to regulate the public weigh scales, and to set the scale fees. Council passed this bylaw on February 11, 1885, and the Calgary Public Market was created.

By-law No. 20 states that "from and after the passing of this Bylaw, the vacan space lying between Byers Blacksmiths Shop and Drink-water Street in the Town of Calgary is hereby declared to be the Public Market of the Municipality of the Town of Calgary."[2] Using current street names, the Market would have been located on 8th Avenue SE near Macleod Trail.[3]

The bylaw also outlined the duties of the Market Superintendent. The market always had a superintendent or a market clerk, and the two terms appear to have been used interchangeably in both Town and City documents. Unfortunately, there is not a complete list of appointees to this position, which has had a very colorful history of its own.

On February 18, one week after passing By-law No. 20, Council approved the motion that "the vacant space lying between Byers Blacksmiths Shop and Drinkwater Street be a Public Market ground until arrangements can be made for a permanent ground."[4] Meanwhile, the Town Clerk was instructed by Council on February 25, to prepare notices to the public that the market bylaw establishing a market in Calgary was now in force and the chief constable was directed to post these notices in public places in the municipality.[5]

The effect of this bylaw was that all hay, straw, coal, and firewood brought into the municipality of the Town of Calgary by wagon, cart, sleigh, or other vehicle to be sold or offered for sale, had to first be exposed for sale in the public market. The by-law also stipulated that live-stock must be first offered for sale in the public market before being sold on the street; that the Market Superintendent had the authority to demand and receive fees, as stated in the by-law, from the seller of any article; and that any person convicted of an infraction of this by-law could be fined up to 50 dollars for each offence plus the costs of prosecution.

At the same time as they were developing a public market, Council was attempting to resolve the problem of the lack of a town hall. In December, 1884, the Hall Committee proposed that Council rent space on a monthly basis in The Far West Hotel at a fee of 20 dollars per month.[6] Council approved this plan on January 7, 1885, but there was growing concern that rental costs would eventually exceed the cost of building a hall and the town would have nothing to show for the money spent.

On February 11, 1885, Council was informed that Mr. William B. Scarth, Director of the Canada Northwest Land Company (CNLC), was offering lots for Town purposes through agent, Mr. William T. Ramsay.[7] The Committee on Public Works & Property recommended lots 1, 2, and 3 on Block 63 to Council as the most advisable location for the town hall and other town buildings such as a fire hall.[8] These lots were located at the corner of Stephen Avenue (8th Avenue) and Scarth Street West (1st Street SW) where the Alberta Hotel stands today.

Council referred this recommendation back to the committee with the request that they determine the cost of the buildings and whether or not there were any other suitable lots for this project.[9] One month later on March 11, the Committee on Public Works & Property reported that the CNLC would not grant these particular lots to the town, but instead had offered some other lots for Council's consideration.[10]

The Town Council was still committed to securing a permanent loca-tion for the public market. On March 18, 1885, they were informed that the CNLC intended to grant the Town of Calgary land for market purposes. To that end, the Committee on Public Works & Property was instructed to meet with Mr. Ramsay and to report its findings to Council.[11] The committee requested six lots for a market ground.

The lots on McIntyre Avenue between McTavish and Osler Streets were deemed suitable by the committee. Today this location is known as 7th Avenue (McIntyre Avenue) between Centre Street (McTavish Street) and 1st Street SE (Osler Street), approximately where the Hyatt Regency Hotel and the Centre Street LRT Station stand today. In addition to the lots for the market grounds, the Committee on Public Works & Property also requested four lots to be used for two fire halls in the future.

Later in April, the CNLC approved the six lots for the market, as well as one site for a fire hall rather than two sites as Council had requested. The CNLC also refused to grant Council any lots west of Osler Street (1st Street SE) so the Town did not receive lots for the town hall and other town buildings. The committee recommended that Council select lots for the market grounds and fire hall in one place, in particular Block 53, lots one to nine inclusive,[12] where the sandstone City Hall and grounds are located today. On April 22, 1885, Council approved this recommendation and instructed the Committee to apply for conveyance of these lots as soon as possible.[13]

Although Council now had land for the market grounds and a fire hall, there was still a great need for a town hall. On May 20, 1885, the Committee on Public Works & Property asked Council to "authorize them to procure plans, etc., for the erection of a Town Hall in the market grounds, the downstairs to be made a Police Office and 3 cells, the upstairs to be a Council Chamber and Police Court."[14] Council approved this request. The work proceeded quickly, and by September 1885, the town hall was complete.[15] The Town Hall now sat on land originally acquired for the market grounds while the market was still located at the vacant space between the blacksmith's shop and Drinkwater Street.

Meanwhile, 16 months passed before the market was mentioned again in the Town's records. On December 22, 1886, Council approved the recommendations of the Committee on Markets & Health that the hay scales purchased in 1885 be received and placed on the market square and that the Town ask for tenders to rent the market and the scales. The committee further recommended that the market be established, the scales placed in position at once, and that By-law No. 20 be amended.[16]

This was accomplished on March 12, 1887, when By-law No. 55 was passed, changing the market location so that "the Roadway on Atlantic Avenue from Bain Bros. Stables to Osler Street, in the Town of Calgary is hereby declared to be the Public Market of the Municipality of the Town of Calgary and that the Public Weigh Scales of the said Municipality and of the said Market should be the Weigh Scales owned by the Corporation on Atlantic Avenue opposite the Livery Stables of Bain Bros. in the said Town of Calgary."[17] This moved the public market approximately one block south and west from 8th Avenue SE near Macleod Trail to 9th Avenue and 1st Street SE.[18]

Later that month, on April 30, 1889, Council granted the Committee on Markets & Health 1 000 dollars to ensure the establishment of a regular market.[19] On June 25, the motion to instruct the Chairman of the Committee on Markets & Health to ask for tenders to build a market house according to the proposed plan, was lost.[20] It was over four years since By-law No. 20 established the Calgary Public Market, yet there was no permanent market building.

On August 6, 1889, the Committee on Markets & Health reported that the revenue collected from the market scales for the first six months of the year was 94 dollars. However, not all of the payments for loads weighed had been collected; there was still 147 dollars in outstanding receipts. The Committee stated that the Town could derive greater revenue if a market was established and the by-law was fully enforced.[21]

By September, the committee had received tenders and decided to accept the lowest bid, that of D. J. McLachlin, for 675 dollars. "We would state that it is absolutely necessary that this work be done at once as the CPR officials intend starting and fencing the whole right-of-way through the Town, so that no market place will then be available but the above."[22] Council adopted this report, allowing work on the market building to proceed.

On October 15, the Markets & Health Committee reported that the Market Building had been completed to the extent of three payment installments totalling 405 dollars and as of yet the contractor had not received payment. The committee recommended that the Treasurer make payments to the contractors and further recommended that the well in the centre of the grounds be cleaned out at once and a pump installed as well as a drinking trough for the use of the horses on the grounds.[23] On October 29, Council approved the committee's request that they be empowered to have the public weigh scales on the market grounds.[24]

By November, 1889, work on the market was complete and had been passed by the architects, Child and Wilson. The total cost for the market building – 793 dollars and 50 cents – was higher than the original bid, but this included moving the scales, work on the well and drinking trough, and the architects' inspection.[25] However, it was determined that further work on the building was required and two weeks later, the Committee on Markets & Health was authorized to enclose a small space at one end of the market shed to protect the market clerk and others from inclement weather.[26]

At the same meeting in November, Council passed By-law No. 113, an amendment to clause number 1 of By-law No. 20. The amendment stated that lots numbers 1 to 9 on Block 53 "in the Town of Calgary are hereby declared to be the Public Market of the Municipality of the Town of Calgary."[27] This was an official location change from Atlantic Avenue (9th Avenue SE) to the market grounds owned by the Town of Calgary. The bylaw also prohibited any person from infringing on the market rights.

At the end of 1889, on December 31, the Committee on Markets & Health submitted the following report to Council regarding the grant they had received in April:

Amount paid for Market Building	$675.00
Removal of Scales, etc.	75.00
Architect's Commission	37.50
Repairing pump	3.00
Cleaning well	3.00
Filling hole, Re. Atlantic Avenue	4.00
Removing dead dogs	1.75
500 weigh bills	6.50
Enclosing part shed	70.50
Chimney	18.00
Stove pipe, etc.	18.50
	$912.75[28]

In August 1890, Council approved the motion that "the Mayor proclaim Saturday of each week a market day for the convenience of the farmers in the surrounding community in compliance with the petition addressed to this Council in relation to this matter."[29] This motion was made in response to a petition from Whiggan, et al. on August 12, 1890.[30]

Other than the regular presentation of accounts, there is no mention of the public market in the Town's records until 1892. While the market building was far from elegant, it must have been a nicer space than others available in the town because on January 20, 1892, Council approved the motion that "in view of the miserable accommodation existing for holding the Police Committees and public meetings about

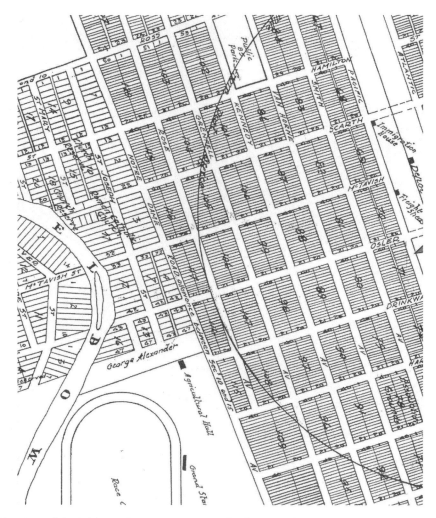

Locations of the Public Market in 1885, 1887, and 1889. Map of the Town of Calgary, 1891.

Town matters, the Chairman of Police and Relief and the Chairman of Public Works are hereby appointed a Special Committee to enquire the cost of and report on the advisability of fitting up the end of the Market Shed next to the town Hall for a court room and other public purposes."[31] Six days later the Special Committee reported back to Council "that a commodious room can be fitted up without a very large outlay."[32]

Over another year passed before the market was mentioned again in the Town's record. On April 18, 1893 Council approved the Chairman of the Committee on Markets & Health's request that the small office at

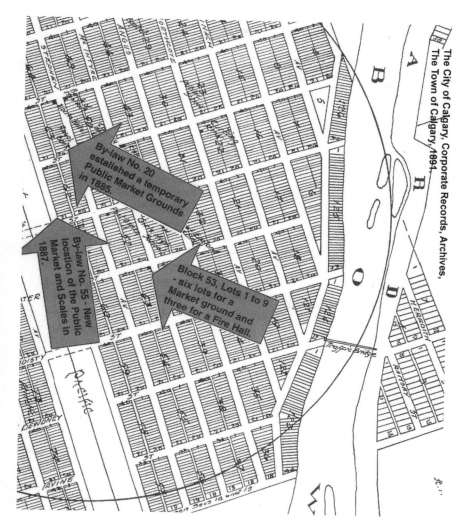

By-law No. 20 established a temporary Public Market Grounds in 1885

By-law No. 55 - New location of the Public Market and Scales in 1887.

Block 53, Lots 1 to 9 - six lots for a Market ground and three for a Fire Hall.

The City of Calgary, Corporate Records, Archives, The Town of Calgary, 1894.

The City of Calgary, Corporate Records, Archives.

the south end of the market shed be fitted up for the use of the Market Clerk and that a suitable stove be installed.[33]

One month later discussions focused on market access. On May 2, 1893, Council approved the motion that Mayor Lucas and Councillors MacLean and Orr "be a Committee to ascertain the best terms on which land can be purchased to make a road from Stephen Avenue into the Market grounds, and report to this Council."[34] However, over two years passed – and the Town of Calgary had been incorporated into The City of Calgary – when Council, on July 8, 1895, approved the purchase of

Lots 37 & 38, Block 53 (Stephen Avenue) Section 15 for a roadway into the market grounds.[35]

The following one sentence report was made to Council and adopted on July 16, 1895.

> Your Committee on Market and Health beg to report that they consider it necessary that the market grounds should be cleaned up and the shed cleaned out and be put in order for people bringing produce for sale and the by-laws governing Pedlars [sic] and Hawkers license be enforced, and compel all parties bringing produce to the City for sale to go on the Market and pay a market fee, and also that all parties who are in the habit of making a feeding corral of the market be not allowed to do so unless they have some produce to sell and have paid their fee, and that two days per week be considered Market days, viz: Tuesday and Saturday until one o'clock p.m. when all parties who have paid their fees, and had their wagons marked be allowed to dispose of their produce any place through the city they can.[36]

A month later, the Committee on Markets and Health reported that

> the Market has been cleaned up and the shed will be ready by the first of September and would advise that a notice be inserted in each of the papers, notifying all parties having produce to dispose of that unless they go on the market and comply with the by-law they will be prosecuted and that a fee not exceeding ten cents be charged all parties bringing produce, not necessary to weight on the Market Scales.[37]

The Market does not appear in The City's records again until May 31, 1898, when Council passed By-law No. 359 to establish a public market and public weigh scales in the city of Calgary. The bylaw states, once again, that Lots 1 to 9 inclusive in Block 53 are to be the public market of the city of Calgary and that "Friday shall be the market day for the City of Calgary and the said Market shall be open on such day all the year round, from the hour of 8 o'clock in the morning until six o'clock in the evening except when the said day may be a statutory holiday."[38]

By-law No. 359 further states that only producers "shall have the privilege of exposing goods for sale in the public market."[39] This bylaw stipulated that the only goods which could be sold in the market were meat, fish, grain, roots, vegetables, hay, straw, and other produce.

Meat could only be offered for sale when the quantity was less than a quarter of a carcass. However, "no person being the holder of a license for and keeping a butcher stall or shop within the City of Calgary shall sell or offer or expose for sale, outside the Public Market premises, any meat in quantities less than a quarter or fish without having first obtained a license so to do from the City Clerk and a certificate from the market Clerk that such fish or meat has be inspected by him nor shall such fish or meat be sold offered or exposed for sale outside said market premises before the hour of ten o'clock in the morning, provided that no such license shall be required from any person selling offering or exposing for sale fish or meat not oftener than once in any month."[40] The licence fee was 25 dollars and each certificate, valid only for the day it was dated, cost 10 cents.

This bylaw also outlined the duties of the Market Clerk, which included providing the certificates described above, weighing all articles brought to the market for sale, determining where animals (such as horses and oxen) and vehicles (wagons, carts and sleighs) would be stored, and collecting all fees as stated in the bylaw.

During the next few years there was sporadic mention of the Market in The City's records. On March 22, 1900, Council approved the recommendation from the Police & Relief Committee that the pump in the market yard be repaired.[41] (The Public Market had become the responsibility of the Police, Relief, Markets, Health, By-laws & Licence Committee, which included the Committee on Markets & Health, from 1900 to 1902.)

On September 6, 1900, Council approved the recommendation of the Public Works Committee that the south part of the market building be turned into a warehouse at a cost not to exceed 10 dollars.[42] This was done to store the large quantity of cement and sewer pipe recently purchased by The City. At the same meeting Council approved the recommendation of the Public Works Committee that "the present Coal Shed be turned into an office for the City Engineer."[43] The City's increasing requirements for space was outgrowing its facilities.

Five years later, on September 14, 1905, Council approved "That Mr. Dodd be requested to prepare plans for proposed Market and Police Buildings."[44] This resulting new bylaw was By-law No. 620, to raise $23 000.00 for the new police station, city offices, and a market building on City lots in Block 53, Section 15.[45]

A reporter from *The Weekly Albertan* reviewed the plans for the proposed municipal building, which would run along 2nd Street East (Macleod Trail). "The north end of the building will be given over to stalls and other furnishings for a market. The accommodations for that will be very limited."[46] According to *The Weekly Albertan,* the police station and market building were to be used for some time as a city hall.[47]

The proposed police station and market building were caught in the ongoing imbroglio of selecting a site and building a new city hall for Calgary. People were not so much opposed to a new police station and market building as desirous of a new city hall that reflected well on Calgary. As a result, it was recorded in Council on September 28, 1905, that By-law No. 620 was lost on September 25, 1905.

On February 19, 1906, the Commissioners reported to they had "an option to buy Lot 10, Block 53, Section 15 next to Market Square for $1 400.00."[48] Purchase of this lot would increase the size of the market square. Council approved the purchase by adopting the Commissioners' report. Council also approved the establishment of a produce market on Market Square which opened as of April 20, 1906.[49]

A few months later, on June 28, Council passed By-law No. 687 which stated that every

> Wednesday and Saturday shall be a Market day of the city
> of Calgary and the Market shall remain open on such days
> from the hour of 7 A.M till 1 P.M. for general produce and
> during such hours, no one bringing into the City fowls,
> butter, cheese, eggs, vegetables or other similar farm produce
> for sale, shall sell or offer the same for sale except at the Pub-
> lic Market; on every other day in the week the Public Mar-
> ket place shall be open from 8 A.M. till 6 P.M. unless such
> Wednesday, Saturday or other day shall be a Statutory or
> Public Holiday.[50]

There is very little mention of the market in the records for approx-imately another four years until March 14, 1910, when Council requested that the Board of Commissioners submit a report on other potential sites for the market as soon as possible. On April 25, they reported back to Council "we have looked into the question of a market site and would recommend as the most economical locations giving suf-ficient room, that to the west of 4th St East including 17 lots in block 124, 3rd St East, where weigh scales and dog pound are now located, and 10 lots of varying length to the west of 3rd St East along the river."[51] The

Commissioners also advised purchasing block 121, which contained 16 lots. This was an irregular shaped piece of land which had frontage on 4th Avenue, a street car route. They did suggest other sites as well, but felt this one suited the city's needs best.

On May 25, 1910, Council reviewed the Commissioners' report, which reiterated the purchase of lots 1 to 16 on Block 121

> ... being a triangular piece of ground near the present hay market which ground can be joined with the lots owned by the City along the Bow River. 3rd Ave can also be utilized if necessary in this site making a large area of ground, and we believe the property can ultimately be served by a spur track from one or other of the new railways coming to the City.[52]

The Commissioners further reported that it would be possible to purchase an additional five lots immediately east of the lots owned by The City, just west of the Langevin Bridge. Council approved the recommendations for purchase.[53]

On June 20, Council discussed the Commissioners' report regarding other available land for market sites and adopted their report, which concluded that the sites "be submitted to a vote of the people, including $50,000 for a market building."[54]

On August 5, 1910 the Council room was open at 5 p.m. "for a meeting of those interested in selection of a market site to assemble and prepare for a mass meeting to discuss the merits of the different proposed sites."[55]

Although there is no report in the records regarding this meeting to select a market site, on August 18, 1910, Council approved the motion that "the Birnie site be purchased and that a temporary market building be provided until the railway terminals are definitely decided."[56]

On April 24, 1911, Council approved the Commissioners Supplementary Report #2, which recommended accepting the tender of Doyle, Thomas & Christensen for the erection of a market building be approved.[57] The Calgary Public Market was on the move again to its new home and building located on 4th Avenue and 3rd Street SE, where another phase of the market's history would unfold.

Unfortunately for the Calgary Public Market, this new location would not ensure its success, and the City's operation of the market was plagued with difficulties during the ensuing years. In December 1945, The City sold the building to Mr. Sam Sheinin, who remained its owner until the building was destroyed on December 23, 1954, in a six-alarm fire.

Notes

1. Appointments to the Committee on Markets & Health were made annually from 1887 until 1908, after which time the Committee was no longer active. In 1894 and from 1900 to 1902 this committee was part of the Police, Relief, Markets, Health, By-laws & Licence Committee.

2. By-law No. 20, 11 February 1885, The Town of Calgary.

3. Byers Blacksmith's Shop, according to the 1886 Henderson's Directory, was located on Stephen Avenue, now also known as 8th Avenue. Drinkwater Street is now called Macleod Trail.

4. Council minutes, 18 February 1885, Volume I, 92.

5. Council minutes, 25 February 1885, Volume I, 98.

6. Council minutes, 24 December 1884, Volume I, 45.

7. Council minutes, 11 February 1885, Volume I, 84.

8. Ibid.

9. Ibid., 87.

10. Council minutes, 11 March 1885, Volume I, 106.

11. Council minutes, 18 March 1885, Volume I, 110.

12. Council minutes, 22 April 1885, Volume I, 123.

13. Council minutes, 22 April 1885, Volume 1, 124.

14. Council minutes, 20 May 1885, Volume I, 133.

15. Council minutes, 23 September 1885, Volume I, 186.

16. Council minutes, 22 December 1886, Volume I, 313.

17. By-law No. 55, 12 March 1887, The Town of Calgary.

18. Bain Brothers Livery was located on the west side of Osler Street (1st Street SE) facing Atlantic Avenue (9th Avenue SE).

19. Council minutes, 30 April 1889, Volume 2, 330.

20. Council minutes, 25 June 1889, Volume 2, 351.

21. Council minutes, 6 August 1889, Volume 2, 367.

22. Council minutes, 17 September 1889, Volume 2, 395-396.

23. Council minutes, 15 October 1889, Volume 3, 12.

24. Council minutes, 29 October 1889, Volume 3, 17.

25. Council minutes, 14 November 1889, Volume 3, 29-30.

26. Council minutes, 29 November 1889, Volume 3, 34.

27. By-law No. 113, 26 November 1889, The Town of Calgary.

28. Council minutes, 31 December 1889, Volume 3, 59.

29. Council minutes, 26 August 1890, Volume 3, 156.

30. Council minutes, 12 August 1890, Volume 3, 142.

31. Council minutes, 20 January 1892, Volume 3, 489.

32. Council minutes, 26 January 1892, Volume 3, 496.

33. Council minutes, 18 April 1893, Volume 4, 302.

34. Council minutes, 2 May 1893, Volume 4, 313.

35. Council minutes, 8 July 1895, volume 5, 386.

36. Council minutes, 16 July 1895, Volume 5, 392.

37. Council minutes, 27 August 1895, Volume 5, 411.

38. By-Law No. 359, The City of Calgary, 31 May 1898.

39. Ibid.

40. Ibid.

41. Council minutes, 22 March 1900, Volume 7, 3.

42. Council minutes, 6 September 1900, Volume 7, 92.

43. Ibid.

44. Council minutes, 14 September 1905, Volume 10, 102.

45. Bylaw No. 620.

46. *The Weekly Albertan*, Volume 24, No. 274, 31 August 1905.

47. *The Weekly Albertan*, Volume 24, No. 284, 21 September 1905.

48. Council minutes, 19 February 1906, Volume 10, 255.

49. Council minutes, 19 March 1906, Volume 10, 280.

50. By-law No. 687, 28 June 1906, The City of Calgary.

51. Council minutes, 25 April 1910, 80.

52. Council minutes, 25 May 1910, 97.

53. Council minutes, 25 May 1910, 95.

54. Council minutes, 20 June 1910, 131.

55. Council minutes, 4 August 1910, 176.

56. Council minutes, 18 August 1910, 194.

57. Council minutes, 24 April 1911, 127 and 135.

Live, on the Air
The Story of Early Radio in Calgary
by Bob Pearson

What had started out as a means of wireless telegraphy had
become radio. For the first time in history, one person with
a microphone could speak to many, influence them; perhaps
change their lives. The concept borrowed the metaphor of
a farmer scattering seeds across a field. Now a single speaker
could scatter seeds of information, propaganda, entertainment, political and religious fervor, culture and even hatred
across the land. The farmer's phrase, the new metaphor
for radio, the metaphor that changed the nation was
broadcasting.

In his groundbreaking documentary film *Empire of the Air*, Ken
Burns was referring to the introduction of radio broadcasting into life in
the United States. One cannot help but believe, however, that this
"metaphor that changed the nation" is even more apt in Alberta. In the
first half of the twentieth century, Alberta was still a predominantly rural
and agrarian province. So much so, that the United Farmers of Alberta
were the governing party from 1921 until 1935. In that year, a dynamic
preacher turned politician used radio broadcasting alone to unseat the
farmers' party. However, radio was more than a tool of political power. In
a province where many did not receive newspapers, radio was their only
window on the wider world. Voices coming to them through the ether
told of what was happening in the world, brought sports, music, laughter,
drama, suspense, and romance – allbeit vicariously – into the lives of
Albertans.

From radio's inception as a practical medium following World War
I, the people of Calgary began to play a major role in its development.
The enterprising spirit of men such as W. W. (Bill) Grant and Thomas
Alfred Crowe was instrumental in establishing Calgary's first radio
stations. Some of Calgary's early radio performers, such as Woodhouse
and Hawkins, would not only entertain the entire province from their
studios but would go on to national prominence as well. It is their stories
and a few others besides that we will tell in this short account of early

radio broadcasting in Calgary. We will see how these pioneers shaped the history of Alberta and, in fact, the entire country and how radio helped to bring Calgary to the forefront as a major metropolitan center.

As early as the 1880s, inventors were beginning to experiment with radio waves. At first, the concept was thought of as a means of wireless telegraphy. When Guglielmo Marconi made his historic transmission of the letter S from Cornwall on the English coast to Signal Hill at St. John's, Newfoundland, on December 13, 1901, he used Morse code. He was not interested in the idea of transmitting the human voice. Several minds were at work on the idea of transmitting sound. Among them was Canadian Reginald Fessenden. The notion of broadcasting sound to a mass of people instead of a single receiver had come to him in the late 1890s. On Christmas Eve, 1906, Fessenden made the first voice broadcast to the ships of the United Fruit Company from his laboratory at Brant Rock Massachusetts. He wished all a Merry Christmas, played some music by Handel on an Ediphone and a few seasonal selections on his violin.[1] Although those listening from the ships had been told, using the traditional Morse code, that they were in for a surprise, one can only imagine the wireless operators' astonishment when, for the first time ever, they heard speech and music through their headphones.

People were becoming interested in radio as a hobby, but the use of radio rapidly grew in importance and frequency. On April 14, 1912, it was used to save lives when the passenger liner Titanic sunk after striking an iceberg in the North Atlantic. Some, such as David Sarnoff, who later became the head of the Radio Corporation of America (RCA), understood the vast potential of radio as a medium of information and entertainment.

Although The First World War held up the licensing and development of the new invention, its effects were not all bad. The major powers all used telephony and wireless telegraphy extensively. Those who were trained in their use received a good grounding, one that would serve them well as civilians. One such was W. W. Grant. Following the war, he returned to Canada and landed a job as a radio operator with the Federal Government Forestry Service. He soon became bored with the routine of sending messages between pilots and began playing an hour or so of musical selections in the evening. The broadcasts could be heard as far away as Hawaii, since in those early days, there was little else on the air to interfere with them. The station was not licensed for civilian broadcasting and so, Grant was forced to return to transmitting authorized messages.[2] That was not for him.

Grant built a small experimental station at High River in 1921. A year later, he moved the station to Calgary and opened it using the call letters CFCN. At that time, most people were still listening to Grant's 100 watt station using crystal sets. All you needed was a cigar box or breadboard to use as a base, a crystal, a coil of wire, a pair of headphones and something called a "cat's whisker" with which to probe the crystal in order to tune in the different stations. Store bought radios were beginning to sell in large numbers. Bill Grant not only owned

William (Bill) W. Grant, radio broadcasting pioneer, Southern Alberta. Glenbow Archives, NA-4763-1.

and operated his own station, but built radios which he sold under the brand name "Voice of the Prairies." The name "Voice of the Prairies Ltd." encompassed Grant's radio repair and manufacturing shop and his broadcasting station as well.[3]

Bill Grant was certainly a pioneer in the field of radio, but his small station was by no means the first. Many accounts of the history of broadcasting will tell you that KDKA in Pittsburgh, Pennsylvania, broadcast the first program in the world, the returns of the 1920 U. S. presidential election. In fact, XWA, a station opened in Montreal by the Marconi Wireless Telegraph Company and licensed in 1919 as CFCF, was first on the air. In May of 1919, the station broadcast a musical program to Ottawa.[4]

Grant's technical genius left him with a problem. He operated a station and built radios. Now he needed something to broadcast. Here again, he provided at least part of the solution himself. In the early days at CFCN, Grant was not only the manager and engineer, but the disc jockey as well. He took requests and played records, even claiming on occasion that he was the singer. One thing was apparent from the first: request programs were popular. This led to one of the most popular

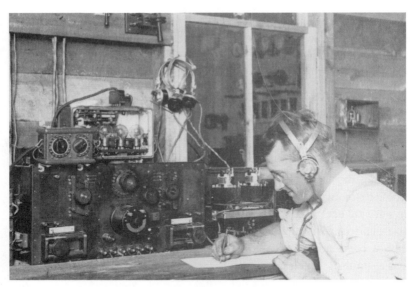

Bill Grant, setting up communications for Forestry Patrol aircraft that flew into the mountainous areas of Southern Alberta, circa 1924. Glenbow Archives, NA-4763-2

programs in the history of local radio. It started in 1924 as "Cy, Ebenezer, and the kid" but by 1927 went by the name that it would keep until it finally went off the air in the 1970s: "The Old Timers." The show featured a live orchestra in the studio and played requests phoned in by listeners. In fact, the show was not, at first, financed in the usual way. There was no commercial sponsor. Listeners would call in and offer to sponsor the band for an hour or two. The group was scheduled to be on the air from 9:00 to midnight each Friday night, but they would play as long as the requests came in. The Old Timers have received letters from most of the United States and every province in Canada. They have been heard in the far north, Hawaii, New Zealand, and one listener even wrote from Alcatraz Island, truly a captive listener. At the community of Great Slave Lake in northern Alberta, a dance was held to the music of the Old Timers each Friday night. One listener recalled, "It was a big event indeed when my father, in sort of a reckless mood I guess, put in a long distance phone call to Calgary, a good two hundred and fifty miles from our farm at Vegreville, and requested a special old time number for a neighbor couple who were having a wedding anniversary."[5]

The two men who were most instrumental in starting the show were George Smith and his son Bob. George stayed with the show until 1948. Among the myriad musicians who made their radio debut on the Old Timers was Wilf Carter. He was paid five dollars a week to perform on the program. As so often happens, he was heard by the right people and moved on to a recording contract with Victor records.[6] The rest is history. Wilf went on to become one of the most famous cowboy singers in the world. The show's announcer for a good many years was Cal Trainer, who gave his life for his country when he was lost in the mid-Atlantic during World War II.[7]

Like Bill Grant, Thomas Alfred Crowe gained experience in the use of wireless technology during the First World War, though he'd been experimenting with radio transmission at least as early as 1914.[8] He operated a radio shop and built radios during the early twenties. On December 14, 1926, private broadcasting license No. 71 was issued to Thomas Crowe. He operated his station using the call letters CJTC. The following year he changed the call sign to CJCJ. This was done because the previous call letters could not be distinctly heard given the nature of early transmitting and receiving equipment. With he and his wife the only regular employees of the station, Crowe had to be innovative with regard to programming. They did some remote broadcasts, including boxing from Stampede Park and live performances of the house orchestra from the Alexandra Hotel. They played records on the air which they borrowed from Clarke's Record Store on 8th Avenue. CJCJ also held contests to keep listeners interested in tuning in.[9]

In 1928, through stock purchases, the Albertan Publishing Company Limited (publishers of *The Albertan*, one of Calgary's two daily newspapers) acquired complete ownership and control of both CJCJ and Crowe's Radio Service and Repair Shop Ltd.[10] Shortly thereafter, Thomas Crowe moved to Lethbridge where he went to work at CJOC in 1929.

One of the most popular programs offered by CJCJ while it was under the control of *The Albertan* was Woodhouse and Hawkins. In real life the pair were Frank Deaville and Art McGregor. Frank was an actor who came from Victoria in search of work. He found a job in Calgary doing window displays for Ashdown's Hardware Store on 8th Avenue West. Art McGregor was a clerk in the store. The two soon got a reputation as a pair of lunchroom comics. One day in 1931, the manager of CJCJ made a remark about the bare shelves in the hardware store. Frank and Art made a retort which must have been a witty one indeed, because by the end of the day the duo had their first on-air engagement at three dollars per show. The program's original title was The Ashdown Funsters but the name was soon changed to Woodhouse and Hawkins. They soon began writing dialogue comedy and came up with Nitwit Court, an imaginary apartment building populated by some 20 colorful characters, all of whom were played by Deaville and McGregor, complete with accents. There was Lord Percy, a refined and genteel English aristocrat; the Major, a no-nonsense military type; and Egbert, a less than quick-witted character, not unlike Mortimer Snurd, one of Edger Bergen's wooden sidekicks. In Canada, the popularity of the program compared favorably with Jack Benny, W. C. Fields, Fred Allen, and even Amos and Andy.

The usually zany comedy offered by Woodhouse and Hawkins was an instant hit in the Calgary of the early thirties. The depression had hit the city of 84 000 hard. Unemployment reached 25% of the work force. Migrant workers were banned from the city and breadlines and soup kitchens were an everyday reality for many. The radio show's humor reflected much of that reality, as this excerpt from the 1930s illustrates:

> Now for just a few seconds I'd like to talk about nothing. Nothing has no moveable parts to wear out, keeps indefinitely, and is the most inexpensive commodity available today. A great many people have nothing because it's so easy to acquire. It's a great favorite with husbands as you ladies are well aware. Many times your husband has said to you 'when you go shopping downtown today dear, buy nothing.' Yes, no other product enjoys such general use. A recent survey proved that 75 percent of homeowners questioned replied 'I've got plenty of nothing.' Get nothing today and you'll have nothing tomorrow.

Woodhouse and Hawkins stayed with CJCJ from the time they went on the air in 1931 until 1933. They then moved over to CFCN in order to gain some network exposure. CFCN was part of the newly formed Western Broadcast Bureau, a small network operating on the prairies. Soon after, the station became an affiliate of the Federal Government's newly formed Canadian Radio Broadcasting Commission (CRBC). Woodhouse and Hawkins were on the network from the first and this gave them national exposure. In time, the two moved the show to Winnipeg and then to Toronto. They continued with the CRBC until 1936. In that year, the network was dissolved by the newly elected Liberal Government of MacKenzie King and a new network, the Canadian Broadcasting Corporation (CBC) was formed. Woodhouse and Hawkins survived the change. In 1941, they moved their show to the RCAF Manning Depot in Toronto. Like many performers they traveled the country for the Government during the war to help with the sales of Victory Bonds or to assist with recruitment drives. In 1942, they left the CBC.[11] The two continued their career in broadcasting. Eventually they formed the Woodhouse and Hawkins Advertising Agency in Toronto.[12]

In the early twenties, everyone from breweries to churches recognized the potential of radio to assist in furthering their cause. Many newspapers owned radio stations. At the end of 1926, nine of the 40 or so stations operating in Canada were owned by newspapers.[13] On May 5, 1922, the *Calgary Herald* opened a station using the call letters CQCA. One week later, the letters were switched to CHCQ and in August of the same year, the station became CFAC.[14] Like the other Calgary stations, and for that matter, most stations everywhere, CFAC relied on local talent to provide much of its programming. A glimpse at the evening program schedule from May 1, 1923, provides a clear illustration:

> 8:32 "The Waggle O' The Kilt"
> Comic song by G. Ramsay.
>
> 8:35 "Carissima" Mrs. Ellison, Soprano; Mrs. Jones, Piano.
>
> 8:39 "Love's Echo" Mrs. F. Young, soprano; Mr. Gates
> piano.

There were poetry readings, an announcement about an essay contest, an address on CFAC by the head of the *Calgary Herald*'s advertising department and a livestock report, always a staple on early Calgary radio.[15]

The Calgary Hillbillies play live in the radio station's studio, Calgary, Alberta.
Glenbow Archives, NA-856-3

CFAC had a couple of shows built around recorded music as well. "The Blighty Show" featured English music hall numbers and even used recorded applause. "Café Franz-Josef" was a program of Viennese waltz music. For this one they even hired an announcer with a German accent. According to one veteran broadcaster, his accent was so thick that most people could not understand him, but the ethnic audience loved it.

Radio before the days of tape delays and pre-recording had many embarrassing moments. On one memorable occasion, the owner of a shop that sold rugs and drapes was persuaded to sponsor one of CFAC's programs. He decided that he wanted more than the usual spot announcement. He desired a half hour broadcast with an orchestra and a singer similar to those being produced in the United States. The entire staff, particularly the announcer, was nervous. To add to their jitters, the sponsor and his family arrived to watch the program. When the red light came on, the announcer turned to the microphone and said; "Ladies and gentlemen, the following program comes to you through the courtesy of the Calgary Drug and Papery Shop."[16]

By the mid-thirties, CFAC was producing some quite sophisticated variety and dramatic shows. Club Thirteen ran through the winter of 1935-1936. The program purported to follow the life of a young couple, out for an evening's entertainment. They chatted about current goings on in Calgary. A record provided the night club sounds and a five piece band and the Belle Sisters, a popular local singing trio, provided the music. Mary Cairns wrote for and acted in the series. She also wrote a series of 38 plays based on events in Western Canadian history. She received no pay but, like many early local radio performers, did it for the enjoyment alone. Dick Tragillus, CFAC sound effects man at the time, recalls that although many effects were available on records, he was still obliged to produce many himself. Banging two coconuts together while jingling a key chain in his mouth would recreate the sound of harnessed horses pulling a buggy. The sounds didn't have to be too exact since broadcasting equipment and home radios were unable to reproduce sounds accurately.[17]

CFAC was important for another reason. It was part of the first radio network in North America. In 1923, Sir Henry Thornton, president of Canadian National Railway (CNR), was looking for ways to increase the number of riders on passenger trains. He hit upon the idea of providing radio programming for people riding in the observation car. On June 1, 1923, the CNR radio network was launched. It only owned three stations, CNRO in Ottawa, Ontario; CNRA in

Moncton, New Brunswick; and CNRV in Vancouver, British Columbia. In other cities, the network rented time on local stations to broadcast their programs while the trains were passing through. CFAC was the affiliate in Calgary. When the network's programming was being broadcast, the call letters became CNRC (Canadian National Railways Calgary).[18] Those riding the trains, as well as those Calgarians listening in, were treated to live classical and light classical music, opera, Canadian historical dramas, hockey, and even programs in French.[19] On July 1, 1927, The CNR network broadcast a nine hour celebration from Ottawa in honor of the Diamond Jubilee of Confederation. A children's choir sang patriotic songs, O' Canada was played on the Carillon of the Peace Tower, and actress Margaret Anglin read an original poem entitled "Dominion Day, 1927" by Canadian poet Bliss Carman. This broadcast was a major undertaking due to the complicated system of telephone and telegraph hook-ups that were required to feed the broadcast to the stations from coast to coast. It is estimated that five million people heard the broadcast in Canada, the United States, and Europe.[20] In 1933, the entire CNR radio system was purchased by the Canadian Radio Broadcasting Commission to be used as the basis for the Federal Government's first coast to coast network.[21]

But what of those great programs from the United States that we all associate with the "radio's golden age?" They were popular in Canada too. In fact, some listeners in the early twenties considered the Calgary stations a nuisance because they interfered with their efforts to bring in the big American stations such as KOA from Denver. Some listeners even went as far as to write to the authorities asking that the local stations be closed down so that their reception from the United States would be uninterrupted.[22] With more listeners and more dollars, radio grew much faster south of the border. By 1925, there were over 600 American stations, while in Canada, there were only 44.[23] Canadian listeners continued to tune in to hear their favorites from the United States. Eventually the CBC carried a good many of them, such as "Ma Perkins," "Jack Benny," "Lux Presents Hollywood," "Fibber McGee and Molly," and the "Shadow."[24] Through its affiliation with the Dominion Network of the CBC, Calgary listeners could hear these programs over CFCN.[25]

One of the most important elements of radio broadcasting today is sports. Thomas Crowe may in fact have been the first in Western Canada to do a remote, live broadcast of a sporting event with his broadcasts of boxing on CJCJ from Stampede Park in 1927. Fred

Kennedy, longtime reporter for the *Calgary Herald,* recalls doing the play-by-play of the Calgary Altomahs football team's final league game over CFAC from Taylor Field in Regina in 1932. There was no press box and the broadcast was done from the open bleachers. Kennedy and Bob Mamini were surrounded by the fans whose language provided most of the color. During the last play of the game, a fan disgusted at his team's loss, pushed Kennedy's head forward so that his mouth came in contact with the frozen steel of the microphone. "I lost an inch of skin from my lower lip," Kennedy later wrote.[26] Veteran broadcaster and local historian Jack Peach recalls CJCJ's first hockey broadcast from the early thirties. A Calgary team was scheduled to play a crucial league game at Vegreville, a town without a radio station of its own. Al Millican, the station manager and a skilled salesman, blanketed the town with a successful sales pitch. Al and technician "Mac" McKenzie took their equipment up to Vegreville. "From beside the rink Al did the play-by-play commentary which was sent by telephone wire to Calgary where we voiced and inserted the commercials. Team boosters in Calgary, and back in Vegreville, followed every hockey play!"[27] Of course, Calgarians listened to Hockey Night in Canada, which was broadcast over the CBC every Saturday night.

Two Calgary sports reporters who made quite a name for themselves were CFCN's Henry Viney and Doug Smith. Viney did some of the first live hockey broadcasts. He even did a guest appearance on Imperial Oil's Hockey Night in Canada in 1937.[28] Doug Smith was so well respected that he was chosen as the voice of the Montreal Canadiens on Hockey Night in Canada beginning in the early forties.[29] When four sports reporters were chosen from across Canada to bring the latest sports news to servicemen overseas during the Second World War, Doug Smith and Henry Viney were among those selected.[30] Viney remained in Calgary, becoming a local legend in sports broadcasting.

Another of modern radio's mainstays is news. Surprisingly, news was not a major factor in radio broadcasting until quite late. News, like sports, was not reported daily. Special events such as the birth of the Dionne Quintuplets in May of 1934 were reported by radio stations from coast to coast. The newspapers feared that radio was a threat to their very existence. It was felt that if people could hear the news on the radio for nothing, they would not buy newspapers. Many papers reacted to this perceived threat by purchasing radio stations so that they might gain some control and influence in the new medium. As mentioned previously, the *Calgary Herald* owned and operated CFAC, while CJCJ was the

Morning Albertan's station.[31] In March of 1935, H. Gordon Love, who purchased and assumed active direction of CFCN in 1928, began offering the first sponsored newscast in Canada. It went on the air on April 1, 1935, and was sponsored by Texaco. Leo Trainer was the first announcer, Dan Campbell was the first news editor, and Carl Nickle, the first reporter. Carl was not paid a salary but, like so many in early radio, worked for the experience only. Some longtime Calgarians remember the Texaco News and the siren that introduced it. At first, the newspapers were suspicious and listened in to try to catch the station pirating news. To save them the trouble of eavesdropping, Dan Campbell sent them copies of the newscasts. Soon, the papers realized that the reporting of news on radio would not put them out of business and that it could be carried out on an ethical level.[32] The growth of radio news reporting was rapid indeed. The same year that CFCN went on the air with the Texaco News, CJCJ also began offering news. By 1945, they were doing 13 newscasts per day.[33] Dan Campbell sums up the importance of radio news to the people of Southern Alberta: "The newscasts filled a most urgent need, especially in a country like ours where so many seldom got the news until the papers arrived through the mail, a day, or perhaps several days late."[34]

There is no better example of the influence and appeal of radio than the story of William Aberhart and the Social Credit Party. Aberhart, the principal of Crescent Heights High School, began doing a Sunday afternoon religious program over CFCN. The "Back to the Bible" broadcasts started in November of 1925 and were done live from the Palace Theatre on 8th Avenue. As Aberhart's biographers, Davis Elliott and Iris Miller, noted, "He did not yet know, but was soon to discover, that in radio he had found his greatest single means of influencing the public."[35] For several years the program was similar in character to the multitude of other evangelical broadcasts then on the air. It featured a combination of hymn singing and preaching by Mr. Aberhart. Through a fund-raising campaign, largely conducted over the air, enough was raised to build the Calgary Prophetic Bible Institute at 516, 8th Avenue S. W. The Institute was opened in October of 1927. Aberhart eventually moved the show to the institute. The First student to enroll was Ernest C. Manning, who would replace Aberhart as premier of the province following Aberhart's death in 1943. Manning had first heard Aberhart over CFCN in the fall of 1925, while Manning was still on the Saskatchewan farm where he grew up. Shortly thereafter he made the religious commitment that brought him to Calgary.[36] This alone is a powerful testament to the power of Aberhart's broadcasts.

At first, Aberhart's broadcasts seem to have steered clear of politics altogether. In the early thirties, troubled by the plight of his fellow Calgarians and of his graduating students in particular, he happened to read the theories of C. H. Douglas as set forth by Maurice Dale Colbourne in a book titled *Unemployment or War*. Douglas' Social Credit Philosophy was first introduced into the Back to the Bible broadcast on August 21, 1932.[37] From that point on, the program was never the same. Aberhart believed that Social Credit was the key to economic deliverance for Albertans. Soon Social Credit became a movement which gained official status with the formation of the Social Credit League. The League became a party in early 1935 and on August 22 of that year, won 56 of the 63 seats in the Provincial Legislature. William Aberhart had become premier, but how did he do it?

Social Credit had no friends in the press. The *Calgary Herald's* cartoonist Stewart Cameron practically made a career lampooning Aberhart and Social Credit. It was not until the Social Credit party purchased *The Albertan* that they were able to gain a voice in the press. Aberhart mixed the doctrines of Social Credit in with theology to such an extent that the *Herald's* Fred Kennedy was moved to ask if Aberhart was calling the people "to prayer, or ultimately, to the ballot box."[38] Aberhart did more than simply promote Social Credit on the Back to the Bible Hour. In November of 1934, a series of broadcasts entitled "The Man From Mars" began.[39] The programs were sponsored by the Social Credit League. The premise of the show was that a man from Mars came to earth and asked questions concerning the current economic woes of Albertans and why there should be so much poverty in the midst of plenty. In all his broadcasts, Aberhart used oft repeated themes and phrases; "poverty in the midst of plenty" and the "fifty big shots" who run the country. His mix of economic and political language with that of the Bible was also effective. He often talked of "economic deliverance" for Albertans, often referring to Social Credit's struggle as a "crusade." This was a new system of government but Aberhart's comforting analogy of a vote for Social Credit being like turning on a light switch, was something that at least those who had power could relate to. The crowning glory was the promise of a 25 dollars per month dividend for every Albertan.

William Aberhart's evangelical preaching and drama, his use of powerful and familiar phrases and analogies, and his understanding of inflection and tone of voice made him an irresistible radio presence.

Because many of his broadcasts were recorded, they still exist in the archives of the Glenbow Alberta Institute. Only by listening to them is it possible to gain a true understanding of their appeal. In 1935, the "Back to the Bible Hour" had over 300 000 listeners. That was more people than listened to Jack Benny's comedy program which followed it.[40]

In the latter years of the 1930s and during the Second World War, technology made radio a much more powerful means of relaying entertainment and information. Soon it would be much easier to record and rebroadcast programming. As a result, stations – and increasingly, networks – would share material more and more. Gone were the days when local station owners such as Bill Grant and Thomas Crowe would have to cast about for something – anything – to put on the air. As radio became more sophisticated, Calgarians such as Jack Peach and Henry Viney would play a part internationally. With this came a growing uniformity among broadcasters. The distinctively local sound of radio began to disappear. Gone too were the days when hobbyists would listen for the sheer thrill of bringing in a station from as far away as possible on their home-made crystal sets. They quickly came to depend on radio. For many it was a necessity. Radio was often the only link many isolated farm families had with the outside world.

Bill Grant, Thomas Crowe, and the multitude of Calgary's other radio pioneers, through invention and necessity, revolutionized the infant medium of radio. They created programs that remained on the air long after their names were all but forgotten. Because many of the broadcasts Albertan's heard came from Calgary, the importance and influence of the city increased. Here we have been able to cover only a small part of these stories, but we have seen how the early broadcasts sowed the seeds of things their creators could never have imagined.

Notes

1. "Media File" program broadcast on CBC Radio, 27 April 1991.

2. T. J. Allard, *Straight Up: Private Broadcasting In Canada 1918-58,* Heritage House Publishers Ltd., Ottawa, 1979, 7.

3. Interview conducted by Thomas W. Kirkham, with Hugh Craig, Fort Macleod, Alberta, 22 July 1981, for the Glenbow Alberta Institute.

4. Interview conducted by Vicki Gabereau, with Greg Gormick, Broadcast on CBC Radio, 6 June 1991.

5. CFCN Historical broadcast on the occasion of the opening of their new studios, 1953, available at the Glenbow Alberta Institute Archives, Calgary.

6. Terese Brasen, "Pioneer Radio: Cowboys, Hoedowns and Old-time Jamborees," from *Alberta Magazine*, November-December, 1981, 7.

7. CFCN Historical Broadcast, 1953.

8. "Crowe Takes Helm At Local Radio Station," from The *Lethbridge Herald*, 20 February 1929.

9. Interview conducted by Sue Baptie, with Mrs. Thomas A. Crowe, 7 November 1969, for the Glenbow Alberta Institute.

10. Letter from F. G. Nixon, Director, Telecommunications and Electronics Branch, Department of Transport, Ottawa, to J. E. Crowe Esq., 10 October 1962, available at the Glenbow Alberta Institute Archives.

11. Morningside, Special Feature on "Woodhouse and Hawkins" broadcast on CBC Radio, March 1996.

12. CFCN Historical Broadcast, 1953.

13. Sandy Stewart, *From Coast to Coast: A Personal History of Radio in Canada,* CBC Enterprises, Montreal, Toronto, New York, London, 1985, 31.

14. Jack Peach, "Early Radio Stations Reflected Voice of Community," from the *Calgary Sun,* 29 November 1986.

15. CFAC Program Schedule, 1 May 1923, Glenbow Alberta Institute Archives, Calgary.

16. Bill McNeil and Morris Wolfe, *Signing On: The Birth of Radio in Canada,* Doubleday Canada Ltd. Toronto, 1982, 136.

17. Bob Mclelland, "Performers Loved Craft When Radio Was King," from the *Calgary Herald,* 19 September 1981.

18. Bill McNeil *Signing On*, 183.

19. *CBC: A Brief History of the Canadian Broadcasting Corporation* (Public Relations, CBC Head Office, Ottawa, July 1976), 2.

20. Morris Wolfe, *Fifty Years of Radio: A Celebration of CBC Radio*, CBC Enterprises, Montreal, Toronto and London, 1986, 2.

21. T. J. Allard, *Straight Up*, 92.

22. *Ibid.*, 16.

23. "Media File," 27 April 1991.

24. *CBC: A Brief History of the Canadian Broadcasting Corporation*, 8.

25. CFCN Historical Broadcast, 1953.

26. Jack Peach, "Radio Cays Looked Bad On Paper," from the *Calgary Sunday Sun*, 25 October 1992.

27. Fred Kennedy, *Alberta Was My Beat: Memoirs of a Western Newspaperman* (The Albertan, Calgary, 1975), 204.

28. Don Seel, "Calgary's Favorite Fella: Biographical Notes on Henry Viney," unpublished, available at the Glenbow Alberta Institute Archives, Calgary.

29. The Canadian Sports Network "Hockey Night in Canada," 2-record set produced by The Longines Symphonette Society, New York, 1972.

30. CFCN Historical Broadcast, 1953.

31. Peach, "Radio Days Looked Bad On Paper."

32. CFCN Historical Broadcast, 1953.

33. "Ideas Make a Calgary Radio Station:How CJCJ Does It," from *Western Business and Industry*, Vol. 19, No. 5, August 1945, 70.

34. CFCN Historical Broadcast, 1953.

35. David R. Elliott and Iris Miller, *Bible Bill: A Biography of William Aberhart*, Reidmore Books, Edmonton, 1987, 73.

36. *Ibid.*, 82.

37. *Ibid.*, 108.

38. Kennedy, *Alberta Was My Beat*, 207.

39. Elliott, *Bible Bill*, 151

40. *Ibid.*, 191

McClelland & Stewart West and the 'Regional Publishing Problem'

by David Scollard and Lynne Thornton

McClelland & Stewart West began business in Calgary in August 1973 as a creative solution to one of the more vexing dilemmas of Canadian publishing. It closed up shop, having failed in its quest, in March 1976.

The "vexing dilemma" is the difficulty of publishing professional quality books that can reach readers across the country and beyond, on subjects that primarily deal with just one interest group or region. As summarized with perhaps a touch of central-Canada chauvinism, this is "the regional publishing problem."

And it is a problem. Every publisher knows of books waiting impatiently to be born, books that have every valid reason to be published and to succeed, that never appear, not because they lack in interest, or because the writer is not skilled, or because of other deficiencies, but simply because the publisher does not have a mechanism for matching books with readers.

One solution is the *regional publisher*, who turns out books by local authors, intended for local readers. Companies of this type tend to follow a predictable life cycle: enthusiastic, dedicated inception; early successes from the one or two books the founders genuinely know and care about; frustration as the hardships of limited-scale production take their toll; greater frustration as attempts to expand beyond the regional base encounter the realities of larger-scale business operations; disillusionment, disinterest, and exhaustion; and the winding-up of business. It's not always like this, but that's the way the story plays, far more often than not.

It was to solve this problem that McClelland & Stewart West was created. The concept was ingenious, unique, and came very close to working.

The two founding forces behind MSW were McClelland & Stewart Ltd., the self-proclaimed "Canadian Publishers", of Toronto; and Glenbow-Alberta Institute of Calgary.

The story begins, so to speak, when Pierre Berton was preparing his wildly successful histories on the building of the CPR: *The National Dream, The Last Spike,* and *The Great Railway Illustrated.* During the research stage, one of Berton's western Canadian assistants, Lynne Thornton, was greatly impressed by the unique selection of documents, manuscripts, photographs – many of which were used in *The Great Railway Illustrated* – and other assets that she found in the Glenbow archives. Enthusiastically, she passed this information on to Berton.

Berton in turn mentioned this discovery to his publisher, Jack McClelland, the president of McClelland & Stewart, with whom Berton had a close personal, as well as professional, relationship. McClelland, who relished his reputation as "the godfather" of Canadian publishing (a reference usually made with the ominous, not the benevolent, connotation) was, at that time, the dominating figure in the industry. Charismatic and mercurial, he was that rarity in Canadian publishing circles: an entrepreneur who instinctively thought in new approaches and wide horizons.

Intrigued by the possibilities, McClelland contracted Lynne Thornton to pursue further studies analyzing the suitability of the Glenbow materials for a publishing program. Thornton wrote a proposal confirming the initial impression: Glenbow did indeed have a superb collection of material on Western Canada.

But the real surprise was what was found in *other* areas of the Glenbow collection. In addition to an extensive art gallery and a wide range of Western Canadiana, Glenbow included some genuinely astonishing international pieces, such as a complete replica of the crown jewels of Great Britain and possibly the largest collections of two-dimensional shadow puppets outside Indonesia. The surprising – some would argue bizarre – eclecticism of the Glenbow holdings was largely attributable to the collecting mania of Glenbow's founder, Eric Harvie, who had indulged a lifetime passion for acquiring virtually anything that caught his fancy. As a result of Harvie's singularly eclectic approach, Glenbow possessed a non-pareil treasure trove that in many ways surpassed the results that a more systemic acquisitions program might have yielded. The very eccentricities that bedeviled the collection as a research tool made it a veritable mother lode of publishable material.

At this point, a key role in the coming together of McClelland & Stewart and Glenbow was played by Glenbow's Executive Vice-President, Allan Hammond. Up until this time, Glenbow had been a rather low profile operation, in large degree because its collections were scattered throughout an unappealing melange of offices, warehouses, courthouses, and libraries throughout Calgary. This was about to change, however – plans were already underway for a move to an attractive, modern consolidated centre (the present Glenbow Museum in downtown Calgary). To Hammond, it was axiomatic that the move to the upmarket new quarters was inseparable from enhancing public awareness and appreciation of Glenbow and its collections. The convergence seemed perfectly timed.

McClelland and Berton travelled to Calgary to discuss various publishing ideas with Hammond in 1972. Both sides recognized that some intriguing synergies might be possible. McClelland, with his disdain for any modest venture, was keen on the widest possible implementation of the program.

As always, the key would be to find the money. M & S, like every Canadian book publisher, lived in a world of financial chaos. Only the previous year M & S had been rescued from the brink by an Ontario government bailout; the price of the rescue was the acceptance of two government members on the M & S board. Glenbow, for its part, functioned on the proceeds of an annuity created by Eric Harvie; at one time the revenue appeared adequate for funding operations, but in the inflationary world of the 1970s, it was clear that emoluments from other sources – primarily the Alberta government – would be needed.

McClelland, Berton, and Hammond devised a genuinely creative solution to the cash problem. Glenbow had a membership organization, the Friends of Glenbow. The members paid an annual fee. The benefits of the fee, however, were questionable. Members didn't save on admission to the museum or the art gallery – the public was admitted free anyway. There was a newsletter, but it was a bit on the dowdy side. There were no glamorous openings to attract the beautiful people – certainly not to the old warehouse settings, anyway.

Suppose the whole operation could be shifted upscale – way upscale? The *objets d'art* would be so outstanding, and displayed so attractively, that the public would happily pay to see them. Openings would be so alluring that everyone would clamor to attend. All the prestigious art tours would put Glenbow high on their fixture list. A glossy Glenbow magazine would replace the little newsletter. A publishing program would turn out book after top-quality book on Glenbow treasures and related subjects – books that no one could resist buying. The benefits for the members would be irresistible: free admission to the shows, members-only invitations to the openings, special lectures, and fat discounts on all the books that Glenbow would publish through McClelland & Stewart. With such a program, a membership of 15 000 persons was projected. And here was the clever touch – *the fees from the membership list would be used to finance the publishing program.*

On paper, it seemed like the perfect arrangement. The Friends of Glenbow, almost by definition, would be interested in the books that Glenbow produced – the only sales tool needed to reach them would be a mailing list. At one stroke, the whole regional publishing dilemma of connecting publisher with reader would be circumvented. Glenbow's books would also be sold and distributed by McClelland & Stewart – arguably the most sales-oriented publisher in Canada – on a far wider scale than Glenbow could have managed by itself; this would enhance Glenbow's prestige on a national, even international scale, which in turn would bring in more opportunities for associated publishing ventures. With the sale and continuing development of books thus assured, sales revenues would be used to develop additional programs to make membership ever more attractive. It was a perfect self-sustaining loop.

By August 1973, McClelland & Stewart, and Glenbow had completed their negotiations, and prepared to launch their program. A new Calgary-based company, McClelland & Stewart West, was created as a wholly owned subsidiary of McClelland & Stewart for the specific purpose of working with Glenbow. Start-up costs were to be borne by McClelland & Stewart; as part of the arrangement, MSW would be Glenbow's exclusive publisher, not only for books and the magazine, but for all art catalogues and any other publications, and would also handle all Glenbow advertising and public relations functions. MSW would operate on an arms-length basis vis-à-vis Glenbow, although Glenbow had two members on the MSW board. Lynne Thornton was appointed MSW's Business Manager, with the additional mandate of developing the Glenbow membership program. David Scollard, the Managing Editor of McClelland & Stewart in Toronto, was transferred to Calgary as MSW's Editorial Director, with responsibility for developing the publishing program.

The "exclusive publisher" clause irritated a number of local critics, who felt the intrusion of a Toronto publisher, especially one as unapologetically commercial as McClelland & Stewart, constituted not just an affront to Alberta sensitivities but a bad deal for Glenbow. Some critics articulated rather forcefully their preference for putting each successive book up for bid, thus preventing MSW – at least in their view – from acquiring an exploitative control of Glenbow's publishing assets.

Bruised sensitivities notwithstanding, there was a valid reason for MSW's blanket publishing arrangement with Glenbow – the fact of production synergies. The whole publishing program was designed to be "modular," so that separate components could be re-used in different formats with minimal adjustment. As an example, Glenbow launched an exhibit of paintings by the frontier doctor R. B. Nevitt, and at the same time published (through MSW) a book based on Nevitt's diary of the 1874 March West by the NWMP. The book and an exhibition catalogue were designed with the same trim size, and the color illustrations for the two were produced in a single print run; by this means, an exceptionally handsome catalogue was produced for actually less money than would have been spent on a relatively plain one.

By 1974 the publishing side of the operation was in full operation. About a dozen art catalogues had been produced, and four full-scale books: *A Winter at Fort Macleod,* by R. B. Nevitt, referred to above; *The Mountains and the Sky*, by Lorne Render, Glenbow's art curator; *Calgary Many Years Hence*, a reprint of an old commercial catalogue; and *Men in Scarlet*, edited by Hugh Dempsey and published in conjunction with the Alberta Historical Society.

The Mountains and the Sky, an extensively illustrated coffee table presentation of Glenbow's Western landscape collection, was Glenbow/MSW's flagship book, intended as the jewel of the membership list for the Friends of Glenbow. It was in many ways, a remarkable book. For one thing, it demonstrated, as nothing before, the astonishing depth and breadth of the Glenbow art holdings. For another, it was an impressive publishing feat, with the entire body of writing, designing, photographing of the art, and printing having been completed in just over nine months, from New Year's Day to September 15, 1974. While the book generally received a good reception both from the market place and from critics, a price was paid for the rush schedule. Errors of fact crept in, which, while no more egregious than could be found in many comparable histories, were not helpful to the book or the publishing program.

Much more serious, the publication of *The Mountains and the Sky* revealed a fundamental, and potentially fatal, error in the underlying theory of the Glenbow/MSW publishing strategy. The essential concept of the formula was that Friends of Glenbow would purchase books and pay membership fees to cover overhead and operating costs. But what no one seemed to have planned for was that Glenbow was becoming virtually invisible to the public. At the very moment the membership was most needed to float the publishing venture, Glenbow had closed its museum, gallery, and library, and curtailed all public activities, to concentrate on the complex logistics of moving to the new downtown quarters.

Apart from the books themselves, there was literally nothing to offer Glenbow members. With nothing happening, the magazine was delayed, then delayed again. Nobody wanted to pay money to be a Friend. No funds came in to underwrite the publishing activities.

The result was the one thing that MSW had been designed to protect against, and that McClelland as well as Glenbow had dreaded the most – a negative cash flow.

Two strategies were devised to counteract the problem. The first was to publish commissioned books from outside sources that would bring in cash infusions through subsidies. This worked fairly well, with the publication of three commissioned titles in 1975. Two of the books were unqualified success stories: *Calgary, a Century of Memories*, by Bob Stamp, published in conjunction with the Calgary Board of Education, was praised as the best book of Calgary's centennial year; and *Cowtown*, by Tom Ward, a popular anecdotal history published through the City of Calgary Electrical System, was MSW's most commercially successful book (after a sold-out first printing, the Electrical System went on to publish four more printings on their own).

As a sidelight, the publishing of *Cowtown* rather nicely illustrated the problems of operating a publishing house with editorial offices in Calgary and the executive office in Toronto. In an exquisite demonstration of misplaced sensitivity, Toronto vetoed the putatively crude title *Cowtown* for fear that Calgarians might sniff out insensitive Eastern condescension; in its place they ordered *Cattletown*, which they thought would be more politically correct. Lynne Thornton put her job on the line in defence of *Cowtown*. Fortunately for MSW, she prevailed – no easy task when facing down the likes of Jack McClelland and Pierre Berton.

While *Century of Memories* and *Cowtown* brought in substantial revenue, this was partially offset by a book of photographs published for the City of Calgary, which suffered unanticipated production problems and ended up draining money instead of contributing.

The second strategy for attacking the cash flow problem headed in a totally different direction – a plan to re-launch Glenbow in its new quarters through a publicity extravaganza so dazzling that the public would buy Friends of Glenbow memberships in previously unimagined numbers, thereby curing the membership/cash flow crisis by going right to the root of the problem.

To accomplish this, Jack McClelland prepared to play one of his best cards. Through his publishing activities, McClelland had developed an almost unparalleled network of worldwide contacts. High on the list was the internationally famous photographer Rolof Beny, who published his prestigious studies of exotic locales through M & S. Beny closely resembled McClelland himself in his preternatural talent for getting along with senior politicians, heads of state, and similar celebrities of the power elite. At about the time Glenbow was searching for ways to establish its high profile in the public eye, McClelland and Beny were in Tehran to meet Farah Diba, the Empress of Iran, who was underwriting Beny's sumptuous book on the treasures of Persia, *Bridge of Turquoise*. Thanks to her generous financial support, all stops could be pulled out on printing and design; the resulting book was a visual masterpiece, and the Empress communicated her considerable satisfaction with the results.

Moreover, this satisfaction was a negotiable instrument. Would McClelland & Stewart be interested in developing additional projects with the Peacock Throne?

McClelland relayed the offer to Glenbow: would they be interested in hosting a special exhibition of the treasures of Persia as the main attraction for their grand opening? With the Shah and Empress in attendance to open the show?

The concept was stunning in its potential, not only as a stellar museum event, with an over-the-top book to go with it, but as a publicity-gathering blockbuster.

Allan Hammond visited Tehran to study the feasibility of the project. The conclusion was that the undertaking was indeed possible. Negotiations were initiated for the myriad details of bringing the Persian treasures to Calgary.

They almost pulled it off. What went wrong was the rapidly souring political climate – not in Iran, where the threat posed to the Pahlavi dynasty by the Ayatolla Khomeini, then languishing in exile in France, was still unimaginable – but in Canada, where relations between Alberta and Ottawa were undergoing rapid and serious deterioration.

The famously divisive National Energy Plan was still more than five years in the future, but already the animosity between the Alberta government and the federal government had reached a seriously disruptive level. The significance of this development for Glenbow and the Persian exhibition revolved around the thorny problem of protocol. The Shah and Empress of Iran were royal heads of state; a visit to Canada would have to obey the most unyielding strictures on a wide range of protocol matters. This meant, among other things, that many senior representatives of the Alberta government, including the Premier, would be ranked at a lower level than various (and in their minds "junior") federal representatives. This thought was galling to the Albertans, especially since Ottawa had refused all funding requests from Glenbow.

This was not a problem that could be shrugged off. The Iranian exhibit, far from augmenting Glenbow's income, threatened to jeopardize the main source of income altogether. There was no alternative. The project was quietly and irrevocably shelved.

McClelland & Stewart West was now in a serious cash flow dilemma. The main projected source of income – the membership list – had failed to materialize. The emergency resort to contract publishing had helped but not enough. Publishing activities in the company's first two years of operations had left a net deficit of approximately $80 000. While this might not seem like a monumental amount, in the cash-strapped economies of Canadian publishing it was life-threatening. Glenbow, while helping as much as possible through various retainers, was not in a position to alleviate the problem.

This meant that the debt load fell to McClelland & Stewart in Toronto. Even in the best of times this sum would have been a serious burden to the company. But these were not the best of times for M & S – far from it. The near-meltdown of 1971, along with the Ontario government bailout that staved off disaster, was still a vivid and painful memory. With the undoubted exception of Jack McClelland and one or two staff members on the financial side, no one was more conscious of the company's financial vulnerability than the two board members appointed by the Ontario government. Their role was a clear one: to protect government interests by ensuring the financial well-being of the company.

In this light, the MSW burden took on an increasingly onerous prospect, especially since there didn't seem to be any imminent signs of improvement. More serious still, the debt hadn't even been incurred for publishing activities in Ontario, but in Alberta, on behalf of a cultural institute in that province. Worst of all, the governments of Alberta and Ontario were in a period of distinctly frosty relations, the result of a dispute over the price that Ontario should pay for Alberta oil.

Beyond the general outline presented here, neither Scollard nor Thornton had access to deliberations at the McClelland & Stewart executive level. We of course knew about the rumors, but the first notification we received came on Friday, February 13, 1976, with a phone call from Toronto that MSW was to be dissolved. Four weeks later, on Friday March 13, McClelland and Berton arrived in Calgary to close up the office for good.

McClelland & Stewart West has now virtually vanished from memory. Scollard works for an oil company in Calgary. Thornton teaches at SAIT. MSW's only other employee, Molly Milvain, died of cancer shortly after the closing of the office. Allan Hammond left Glenbow in 1978 to take a federal government position in Vancouver. Pierre Berton moved to another publishing house, and Jack McClelland retired from M & S in 1987. Both men died in 2004. McClelland & Stewart itself was sold to a real estate speculator, Avie Bennett, who later donated 75% of its assets to University of Toronto Press. A phone call to their office reveals that no one on the current staff has heard of McClelland & Stewart West.

The Canadian landscape is haunted by the ghosts of vanished publishing companies. Even McClelland & Stewart – the best and most valuable publisher this country has ever seen, in the adamant view of both Scollard and Thornton – has changed so unrecognizably that it could be counted as one of the casualties itself. Since 1976, the year of MSW's demise, many other publishing companies have disappeared, the recent death-throes of General Publishing being undoubtedly the most spectacular. But offsetting this, an astonishing number of vital and energetic publishers have sprung to life, many of whom are showing encouraging signs of permanence. Undoubtedly, book publishing in Canada is an enterprise born of foolhardiness and passion. God bless those who try it anyway.

Polo Anyone?
A Legal Fraternity of Polo Enthusiasts
Brenda McCafferty

Take any aspect of Alberta's history, and the Legal Archives Society of Alberta (LASA), by virtue of the prominent role played by lawyers in the social, political, and economical development of our province, is bound to have something to contribute to the story. Connecting the LASA records from three historical files provides an interesting connection to the sport of Polo, which enjoyed a social prominence in early Alberta. A review of archival legal files provides the following history on Alberta polo and its connection to the legal fraternity.

In 1994 the Legal Archives received papers and photographs from the estate of the late Chief Justice of Alberta, the Honorable J. Valentine (Val) H. Milvain, QC. Found amongst those papers, and seemingly unrelated to Milvain, were three early (1899) photographs depicting polo scenes. Stories emanating from the images brought to life the colorful early years of this prominent lawyer and his family. His father, James Milvain, following in the footsteps of his brother Robert, arrived in Canada from England in 1888, and settled in the Pincher Creek district. After working for a time as a ranch hand he joined in a ranching partnership with Harold Mackintosh. Both men shared a passion for the game of polo and in 1901, James married Mackintosh's sister, Winnifred. Their first son, James Valentine Hogarth Milvain was born on Valentine's Day in 1904. Winnifred delivered the baby at home during a severe snowstorm with the sole help of a nurse, and good friend and neighbor, Isabelle Lynch-Staunton. The Lynch-Staunton's were another prominent pioneering family, who like the Milvain's, had connections with both polo and law in Alberta. (Alfred H. Lynch-Staunton is one of the players depicted in Milvain's photographs.) Val studied law at the University of Alberta and rose to become the first native-born Chief Justice of Alberta. The years growing up around polo had a profound effect on him and his fond childhood memories lingered throughout his distinguished life.

Isolated as they were from the rest of the province, a small group of Pincher Creek polo players formed several teams of varying combinations of players, each one developing its own distinctiveness. In 1895, rancher Allan Kennington organized a team from the Pincher Creek core that came to be known as the "North Fork Polo Team" (the group practiced on Kennington's ranch located on the North Fork of the Oldman River – the source of their team name). This small group of players collectively became recognized as one of the strongest clubs in the southwest. The core members included James Milvain, William "Billy" Keys Humfrey, W. E. Smith, and Allan Kennington. After Humfrey's departure from the area, Harry Gunn completed the foursome. The "Freebooters" were another North Fork pick-up assemblage of senior players captained by Louis Garnett, and comprised of retired North West Mounted Police (NWMP) staff sergeant Sam Heap and A. H. Lynch-Staunton.

May 24, 1899. Members of the North Fork polo team from left to right: James Milvain, Sam Heap, T. R. Miles, and Allan Kennington. James Valentine Hogarth Milvain fonds, LASA, 47-G-6.

Another strong polo presence in the early Alberta tournament scene were the teams from the High River area. From the start, High River and its players established a remarkable record of top-flight tournament play. Much of that success is attributed to the wealthy rancher, remittance man, and polo booster, George Ross. The first games and practices were held on Ross's ranch and he alone managed to attract a number of young cowboys to the game. Remarkably, it was the Alberta-raised players who became the backbone of the great High River teams who went on to dominate the next two decades of polo matches. An offshoot of the High River team developed as the sport grew in popularity. This offshoot team was mainly composed of players from the Sheep Creek-Millarville district southwest of Calgary.

James Milvain and Justin Deane Freeman met and played against one another during the annual fall exhibition held in conjunction with the Calgary tournament in September 1899, the same year the featured photographs donated by the Milvain estate were taken. The four-team roster assembled in Calgary included the North Fork Team (James Milvain and Harry Gunn both made the trip to Calgary), and the Sheep Creek-Millarville team that was a pick-up collection. Sheep Creek's fourth player in the 1899 tournament was 16-year-old Justin Deane-Freeman. It was the first documented appearance of this young man who, in the course of a brief, brilliant career came to be considered perhaps the greatest polo player ever to emerge from Southern Alberta.

After making a name for himself at the 1899 Calgary tournament, the young Justin Deane Freeman continued to build his reputation and quickly emerged as one of the finest players in Canada. In 1909, George Ross, Deane-Freeman's financial supporter, offered to take the young man to California to play polo professionally. Justin's wife of six years, Gertrude, along with their two small children and Justin's parents, also intended to make the move south.

Tragically, on March 12, 1910, while playing in a practice match at a club in Coronado, California, Deane-Freeman collided with an opposing player, fell from his horse, and died instantly on the field. The young father of two was not yet 30, and there remains little doubt that his best years of polo playing had yet to come. Gertrude Taylor, Justin's wife, was heartbroken and the shock of her husband's death brought on a lingering illness which culminated in her death less than a year later on January 14, 1911.

Before her death, Gertrude had returned to her home in Blackpool, England, leaving behind her two children – Justin, aged five, and May, an infant – in the care of a sister-in-law. The subject of the legal guardianship of the two orphaned Deane-Freeman children is at the heart of legal files acquired by the Legal Archives. The client file in question was found abandoned at the Hollingsworth Building (now part of Bankers Hall) and belonged to early Calgary lawyer J. P. J. Jephson (firm of Muir, Jephson, Adams & Brownlee). Included within the Deane-Freeman estate file is a commissioner of oath statement by Leonard Brockington (former City Solicitor and War Correspondent for Prime Minister Mackenzie King during the D-Day invasion of WWII), and an oath made by Patrick Burns of Big Four fame (Justin Deane-Freeman's former employer).

William Roland Winter was the Justice who presided over the guardianship case of the Deane-Freeman children and who awarded custody to their aunt and uncle residing in Midnapore.

Many are aware of the historical sites within Alberta that were flooded as a result of power dam construction. Sam Livingston's (one of Calgary's earliest residents) property was flooded by the construction of Calgary's Glenmore dam and the early town remains found under the water of Lake Minnewanka near Banff. Few, however, are aware of the presence of the Ghost River Polo Ranch incorporated on June 4, 1924, once situated on the site of what is now the Ghost River Dam.

The third and last historical legal file in possession of LASA and relating to the game of polo is found within the client files from the Lougheed, McLaws, Sinclair & Redman firm. The file belonging to Daniel Lee Redman will likely cause you to take a second glance next time you drive by the Ghost River dam west of Cochrane.

The 1920s dealings relate to a land investment in Alberta made by Captain M. R. Mortimer. In this case, lawyer Daniel Lee Redman acted as an advisor on a land purchase located between Calgary and Banff for the establishment of the Ghost River Polo Ranch. It was intended to be a tourist draw but met with very limited success, operating a mere four years.

The Ghost River Polo Ranch started with money willed to Malcolm R. Mortimer in trust from his father's estate in England. Mortimer purchased the land from the CPR. A man who had the flair and charm similar to the polo remittance men of this era, Captain Mortimer was experienced in raising and training polo ponies. His aim was to sell ponies to his contacts south of the border. In addition to his polo experience, Mortimer had knowledge of running a roadhouse. His idea was to run a guest ranch for U.S. and British visitors wanting training in ranching with a little polo offered on the side. His ranch was equipped with a hotel and barn, and the business was advertised in prominent British newspapers. Unfortunately, the funds obtained from the trust were inadequate to carry out business and his lack of capital forced him to sell to the Calgary Power Company, which had designs on the property for the purpose of building the dam. He moved to New York with his wife and young daughter in 1924. His wife was a well-known actress and studio director in New York's Madison Square Garden Broadcast Corp. Sadly, Mortimer suffered physically from war wounds. For a time he worked as secretary to a U.S. Senator and some years later he started another business in New York that was destroyed by fire, leaving Mortimer a broken man.

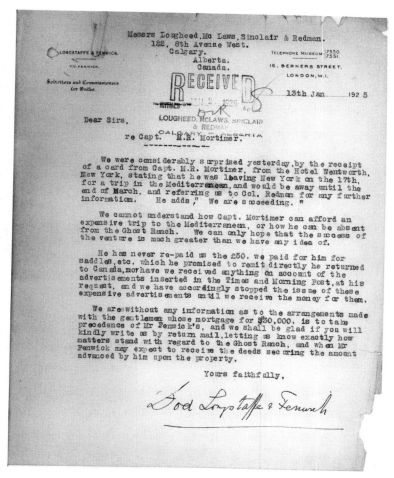

Letter written by Mortimer estate lawyers in England (financial enablers of the Ghost River Polo Ranch) to Daniel Redman, Capt. Mortimer's lawyer in Calgary. The ranch, more or less abandoned by Mortimer a year after its establishment, was doomed from the start. While not a remittance man in the classic sense, the Captain possessed many of the attributes commonly associated with remittance men of his time. McLaws, Redman, Lougheed, and Cairns fonds, LASA, 37-00-00, Vol 6, file 35.

By the year 1924, a lot had happened – Justin Deane-Freeman was gone, James Milvain had long since passed his polo-playing prime, and the game of polo, although continuing to remain popular, was not as it had been two decades earlier. Perhaps the absence and enthusiasm of Justin Deane-Freeman and Milvain had an impact on its demise. Unfortunately, Captain Mortimer arrived late on the scene and one wonders if his polo ranch may have been successful if the venture was started a decade or two earlier.

Notes

Polo, The Galloping Game – An Illustrated History of Polo in the Canadian West, by Tony Rees, provided much of the background information on the game of polo for this article and his thorough research was instrumental in linking two of LASA's acquisitions together. Tony's book not only serves as a history of the game of polo but also documents the important role polo occupied socially in the early development of Alberta. Most of Alberta's earliest and most prominent citizens were connected with the game.

Urban Planning in Calgary

A History

by Sally Jennings

In 1881, when Frank White stood on North Hill, he counted 16 log shacks, nine Indian tepees, and the Mounted Police Fort.[1] Today Calgary has a population of 933 495[2] and a downtown crowded with mirror-glass high-rise buildings. The story of how it grew from 16 log shacks to several hundred head offices is an interesting roller coaster ride.

Before 1875 there was no permanent settlement. Indians camped in the area, to hunt in the river valley and take shelter in the winter. In 1875, the North West Mounted Police rode west and established Fort Calgary at the confluence of the Bow and Elbow Rivers. I. G. Baker and the Hudson's Bay Company (HBC) set up shop, while the Roman Catholic Mission was founded one kilometre (km) south of the fort. The framework of a settlement was in place – the law, commerce, and the church. Now the new settlement awaited people. In 1877 Treaty Seven, signed at Blackfoot Crossing, allowed non-Native settlement to take place[3] and settlers began to move west to build a new life.

In the small town of about 400 people, rumors were circulating that the Canadian Pacific Railroad (CPR) was coming to Calgary, so in 1883 a Mr. Penny pre-empted a tract of flat land east of the Elbow River and opposite the fort in Section 14, which he thought was likely to be the centre of town. He sold it to Col. Irvine and Capt. Stewart who surveyed it into town lots for the first site of Calgary. Land speculation was rife and tents and log cabins were erected without delay.

Indeed, on August 11, 1883, eight years after the arrival of the Mounted Police, the CPR did arrive. "The rails were laid to the east side of the Elbow River and the construction train, called the 'front train' came to a stop in what is now East Calgary."[4] The CPR crossed the Bow River, passed the town site and went to Section 15, jointly owned by the CPR and Northwest Land Co. A boxcar served as the station. Calgary would be the 20th Siding.

Calgary's population doubled in a day. The shelves of the Hudson's Bay and I. G. Baker's stores were cleaned out by nightfall. Although everyone had rushed to get good locations on the east side, the CPR had other ideas. The railroad company had been given claim by government charter to the odd-numbered sections within a certain belt of land. The Elbow River was bridged and they quietly began to lay out a new town-site on Section 15. The settlers were shocked. Those with tents could move to the new area, but log cabins and more substantial buildings either had to stay or have their buildings moved while the river was frozen in the winter of 1883-1884.

The first lots on the new town site west of the Elbow River were made available in December 1883. W. T. Ramsay was in charge of the sales and customers drew lots from a hat to determine the order of choice. John Glenn of Fish Creek drew first choice. James Lougheed bought as much as he could on 8th and 9th Avenues, "so much that some spectators wondered if the man was completely sane."[5] It was said that he had a dream that Calgary would take the place of Ottawa as the national capital.

The CPR townsite was put on the market by the Canadian North West Land Company, a subsidiary of the CPR. The best lots cost $450. For 15 years, the CPR sold their township through a company known as the Canadian Pacific Townsite Company. Lots on 9th Avenue (between 1st Street W and 4th Street W) sold for $100 each: 10% cash down with payments over four years.[6] By the end of 1884 there were 180 buildings in Calgary.

Civic matters now needed to be attended to and James Reilly organized a public meeting on January 7, 1884, "to consider location of the townsite, bridges and other local matters.... It was Calgary's first election and neither pony race on the main avenue nor Sarcee war dance at the riverbank could have aroused more interest."[7]

On January 14, 24 candidates stood for election and seven got in to form a committee of citizens. "Every eligible voter voted and not more than a few voted twice."[8] Major Walker was named as chairman and agreed to take no bold action on other matters until a conference was held with Lieutenant-Governor Dewdney to discuss four issues of immediate importance: an allowance for a school, an increase from $300 to $1 000 as a grant for a bridge, incorporation as a town, and Calgary district representation in the Council of the Northwest Territories.

The CPR proved a major influence in creating the new township. It determined the location of downtown and the areas for industrial and commercial development. It subdivided areas for residential use, from Mount Royal for its managers to Bridgeland and Ramsay for its workers.

Stockyards, freight yards, and the Ogden Repair Shops established the industrial areas on the east side of town[9] and the CPR became a major employer in the new town.

The census now showed 428 residents, but somehow the population of 1884 went into the official records as 506 – it sounded better that way.

With a population of around 500, it was decided to apply for incorporation as a town. This process cost residents $500. On April 15, the full amount had been collected and was sent to the seat of Territorial Government at Regina. Finally, by November 12, 1884, it was announced through the press that the booming of Mr. Murdoch's gun on Monday afternoon indicated the telegram from Regina had come through, notifying the citizens of the proclamation creating Sections 14, 15, and 16 a town.[10] An election followed and on December 3, 1884, George Murdoch was elected mayor, with four councillors. The new council met in Councillor S. J. Clarke's saloon to appoint a town clerk and draw up draft bylaws. "At that time, too, the first official mention of the disagreeable word 'taxes' echoed ominously above the clink of glassware ... and the rattle of wagon wheels on the stony street outside."[11]

On August 27, 1884, a reporter wrote for the brand new *Calgary Herald*: "Two years ago, Calgary consisted of two stores, the old Fort of the Mounted Police and a few log houses. The gay monotony of city life was unknown, and the refinements arising from the visits of paleface ladies were few indeed." The possibility of an Indian uprising unsettled the town in 1885 but such civic duties as organizing a school district went ahead. Classes were begun in a frame building on 9th Avenue E and in the same year, Roman Catholic nuns opened separate school classes east of the Sacred Heart convent.

In 1886 the tax rate was 10 mills – with everything still to be done: sidewalks, schools, land development, and roads.[12] In 1886 a bridge was built over the Elbow costing $1 240. In 1887, the Eau Claire and Bow River Lumber Company built the first traffic bridge over the Bow River near the present site of the Louise Bridge. In 1888 a bridge was built across the Bow at 4th Street E.

Jack Campbell had been the town constable and now had a force of three men. By 1909, the police force was 52 strong. The first fire brigade with buckets and ladders was formed and after the fire of 1886, the first fire hall was built. A decision to build in sandstone rather than wood resulted in the first big sandstone building, Knox Presbyterian Church, on Centre Street and 7th Avenue in 1887.

Between 1885 and 1890, Calgary was growing in fits and starts. Boosterism* brought immigrants but crop failures and the extreme climate meant that many settlers moved away again. The arrival of the CPR had assured the survival of the town but as a distribution centre rather than as an agricultural community.[13] In the 1890s, it was ranching money that subsidized the new sandstone buildings and by 1911, Pat Burns, rancher, owner of a meat company, and Calgary's first millionaire, was declaring he "had made Calgary," which was probably true enough.[14]

Booming real estate opportunities. Glenbow Archives, NA-1380-7.

From the 1890s to 1902, the centre of the town covered one square mile: from 2nd Street E (Drinkwater St) to 4th Street W (Ross St) to 6th Avenue N (Angus Ave) and 12th Avenue S (Van Horne Ave).[15] In addition to the development around the CPR station, the original settlement remained east of Fort Calgary, now Inglewood. In this period, property values went up ($500 to $2 500 in the business district) and fortunes were made. The first moneyed class built big houses, but the houses were not in separate areas. Everyone wanted to live close to work, which was downtown. By 1905 fine houses were established along 12th and 13th Avenues, separated from the commercial centre by the warehouse district but within walking distance of town. James and Isabella Lougheed's "Beaulieu" (1889) and Pat Burn's mansion (1900) were examples of the palatial houses that showed the prosperity of Calgary.

---

* *Advertising with enthusiasm.*

With the introduction of streetcars and autos in the early 20th century, the rich were able to live further away in suburbs like Elbow Park.

Travel between Calgary and Edmonton had been by stage coach until 1890-1891, when the railway was constructed. It seems there were still complaints about local transport. T. H. Braden, editor of the *Prairie Illustrated*, writes on January 24, 1891:

> The Mission Bridge is full of holes,
> Yet no one cares a speck,
> That some poor horse might break his leg
> Or some poor man his neck.
> What is the best course to pursue,
> It is, we must consider,
> Cheaper to mend the bridge at once
> Than compensate the widder.[16]

City building slowed with the stagnating economy after 1891. The City Council provided incentives like a free land site, cash bonus, and extended tax exemption to any "prospective manufactory."[17] Council thought its mandate was the promotion of economic growth, not the provision of social services. Inefficient private water and electric companies were tolerated even in the 1890s.

Perhaps to pick up people's spirits, Mayor Wesley Orr, writing to his daughter Adelaide in 1893, said that he would choose the plain English word "Onward" for Calgary's motto.[18]

In the same year, the Belt Line area and Victoria district were added to the town site.[19] By now, Mayor Thomas Underwood could boast about waterworks, sewers, electric lights and a population of approximately 4 000[20] but Calgary's growth had slowed down and the contractors for a street railway system asked permission to postpone it. Many property owners wanted to sell but the cost of keeping real estate was so low that "some absentee owners . . . found it convenient to remit tax money in the form of postage stamps."[21] James Lougheed, Calgary's first lawyer, was steadily buying more property despite the downturn. He paid about half of all the taxes in the Corporation. At his death on November 2, 1925, it was said that "No other individual played as large a part in the actual building of this city."[22] Optimism about the future was still part of Calgary's philosophy and in 1893, Hull's grand Opera House was opened as another ornament to the city.

On January 1, 1894, Calgary was incorporated as the first city in the Northwest Territories, with a population of 4 000 and W. F. Orr as mayor.

Elections were considered opportunities to bet on the results, rather than elect the best officials for a new civic government. In general, the city was organized by the businessmen who paid the most taxes and had the greatest stake in the community. The party politics were indicated by a local saying that "Calgary skies and Tory blue went together."[23]

The economic slide was continuing and farmers were leaving to go north. In 1895, Mounted Police Sergeant A. F. M. Brooke wrote: "The population of Calgary is 3 207, which is correct . . . in 1891 there was hardly a vacant house in Calgary, or in the district, and there are at least fifty vacant houses in town at present."[24]

The shape of the city indicated its continued reliance on the CPR. Stretched out along the railway tracks were a mixture of clapboard stores, vacant lots, and sandstone buildings. The parks and treed boulevards the immigrants had left behind in Europe had not yet made an appearance in this frontier city. Boardwalks and mud roads indicated that Calgarians were less concerned with city beautification than with earning a living. Calgary's principle function was the centre for the ranching industry. Bob Edwards, as always, had something to say about the matter: "Stephen Avenue is not a street at all, as it is one big gravel heap, full of sand mounds, mortar beds, pipes, barricades and street-corner loafers."[25]

The City purchased the waterworks system operated by the Calgary Gas and Waterworks Company in 1900. In the same year, Wesley Orr left politics, but by then Calgary had quite a number of paved streets, bridges, public buildings, and industries.[26] W. H. Cushing took over as mayor and extended the city's ownership of public utilities by buying the Calgary Gas and Waterworks Company.

City Council was trying to attract industry and move away from reliance on unstable agricultural prices. Free sites and 10-year exemptions from taxes were some of the inducements but farming and ranching still overshadowed the limited urban industry.[27] The severe winters of 1881-1882, 1886-1887, and finally 1906-1907, were huge setbacks for ranchers and deterred American ranchers from moving to the Calgary area.[28] The open range industry never recovered. The 1912 First Calgary Stampede was thought to be a last hurrah for the ranching industry, but with the development of Marquis wheat and oats, the West finally came into its own. Calgary became the distribution centre for its hinterland.

Calgary's focal position as a railroad centre had promoted settlement and the building of the warehouse district along 9th and 10th Avenues. The building of stock yards and grain-handling facilities in 1887 and 1903 reinforced Calgary's position as a distributing and collecting centre.[29] The railway promotion of 1908 was not without reason.

Slowly, a new sense of pride in Calgary was emerging.[30] It was shown in a new concern for the appearance of boulevards and fences and front yards. A citizen was fined 75 cents for having a stack of hay on the street. Central Park was laid out for horticultural development and tree planting was being encouraged as never before. Aldermen and citizens had a vision of a city beautiful. From Caldwell Company of Virden, Manitoba, the city ordered a carload of young trees, mostly Manitoba maples and ash. A supplementary order for 2 000 seedlings and 1 000 cuttings of Russian poplar was made. Trees were planted on boulevards and in parks and many more were sold to private property owners at 10 cents a tree. Calgarians had found a new hobby: building for the future. William Pearce was the man behind this planting. He was an engineer, a surveyor, an advocate of irrigation and tree planting, and a devoted conservationist.

In 1904, named streets in downtown Calgary were changed to numbers (from names of CPR officials). The fact that the CPR refused to pay municipal taxes on the land it owned downtown might have been a factor. On those streets, the first cars were seen in 1904. In 1905 the Province of Alberta was created, separate from the Northwest Territories, with Edmonton named as the capital.

Calgary began to creep beyond its one square mile. Patterns of land-use were established by 1905, dependent on the CPR, the terrain, and the manufacturing area in the east, anchored by the stockyards, abattoir, and brewery.[31]

The business centre grew between 1906 and 1914, with many downtown buildings reaching the maximum height of six stories. This bylaw was based on pragmatic reasons – water pressure would not allow fire fighting beyond that height.[32] The retail area was now established along 8th Avenue, with residential districts south and west. Apart from Crescent Heights, development was slower to the north.

As the city grew, transport was needed. Bob Edwards wrote in 1907,[33] "The most distinctive attributes of a large, bustling city are streetcars, crooked gamblers, confidence men, and a 'complacent' police force. Hurry up with those streetcars, will you?" Two years later, on July 5, 1909, Mayor Cameron and aldermen were the first passengers to ride on the Calgary Municipal Street Railway. From downtown it went to Victoria Park and returned via 8th Avenue and 1st Street W. It was known as the "Rubberneck Special." Eight miles (13 km) of track were needed to serve the whole of Calgary. Within three years, 50 cars were negotiating almost 60 miles (97 km) of track. The street car served as a boost to suburban development and Calgary stretched more than 10 miles (16 km) from the city centre. Commercial areas began to develop where rents were lower along 17th Avenue S, Kensington Road, 10th and 4th Streets N and 11th Street S. Developers often built spurs and donated the lines to the city, leading to sprawling growth and residents of new houses waiting for utilities to be provided.

The building bylaw of 1912 encouraged the 25 foot lot (7.6 m), which allowed for dense settlement. Few regulations dictated the size or placement of the building on the lot, and subdivisions were sometimes of poor design. The demand for housing, however, led the city to approve them anyway. The Town Planning Act of 1912 was intended to control speculation but the city councils, looking for tax revenues, encouraged growth.

Interestingly, the banks of the Bow River were considered suitable for railway construction and low land prices reflected this attitude. In 1910 the proposed city market was located by the tracks and Chinatown was allowed to remain in this area. When the Grand Trunk Pacific ran its rails along the river bank through the site of old Fort Calgary in 1912, the city gave its approval. Some citizens protested that the area had scenic potential but these considerations were brushed aside.

The Industrial Policy of 1911 directed industries to areas where they could expand. The City provided utilities and transportation to low-rent areas, which influenced trends in land use. Industrial areas were located along the railway tracks and low-cost housing was built nearby, a policy encouraged by urban planners.

The concern for the beautification of Calgary was given a boost on November 13, 1911, when Mayor Mitchell authorized a committee "to prepare a comprehensive and extensive scheme of City Planning which will meet the requirements of this city for its future development."[34] The population had quadrupled in the previous six years. The downtown was congested, builders were building on the riverbanks, and real estate promoters were selling lots in areas which could never be serviced with sewers and water mains. The spirit of free enterprise needed to be reigned in. Bob Edwards described the city philosophy in the *Eye Opener* on October 25, 1911:

Come to Calgary, the Aquarium City. Full of sharks! Boozorium Park! Seize your opportunity! Do not delay! Come early and avoid the future residential district of Calgary, beautifully situated in the midst of the unparalleled scenic beauties of the bald-headed prairie, on a site famed for its badger and gopher holes and renowned in song and story for its entire absence of water. A pleasant place for a murder. Rural mail service promised before the turn of the century.

The bald-headed prairie, however, was about to be beautified. A Planning Commission was appointed and began to prepare plans for street lights, tree planting, cleaning up vacant lots, and improving garbage collection, but it seemed unwilling to tackle the major planning problems. Calgary in 1912 covered 36 square miles (50 sq. km).[35] Thomas Mawson was sponsored (by the Women's Canadian Club, the IODE, and the Planning Commission) to come to Calgary to give a public lecture on October 4, 1912. He had a good reputation as a planner and had carried out planning assignments for big European cities. He was from Liverpool University, was enthusiastic, and spoke with authority. R. B. Bennett was the chairman of the large meeting at the high school.

Mawson urged immediate planning to ensure that Calgary be "the point from which will radiate an incentive in commerce and industry and some day in arts, letters, music and science." The citizens were enthusiastic. One realtor said, "We'll build a New Jerusalem right there on the banks of the Bow."[36] Instead, circumstances intervened and Calgary continued in its entrepreneurial way to look "Onward."

The economic situation was changing – the real estate business was experiencing a downturn and the advent of World War I exaggerated the trend. Mawson's plans were shelved, to end up lining the interior of a garage until they were rediscovered in the mid 1970s. They are now housed in the Canadian Architectural Archives at the University of Calgary.

In 1914 both the Grand Trunk Pacific Railway and the Canadian Northern Railway built stations in Calgary.[37] By 1914, enough land had been subdivided to cover a city the size of Chicago.[38] After 1915, however, Calgary's vision of big city status vanished as rural Alberta went into decline with drought, inflation, and collapsing agricultural prices.[39] World War I ended the immigration boom. The City Clerk said 1923 was Calgary's worst year ever. There were no jobs in construction or real estate and the area remained depressed until World War II. By 1926 it was agreed that the Good Old Days had gone forever.

By 1924 autos outnumbered horses and wagons. The first traffic control on 8th Avenue and 1st Street W was a stop-and-go sign. "Constable Dan Finlayson was in charge of directing traffic. To sustain the constable from the bitter cold of a winter's day, he would sip a frequent nip from a flask hidden in his inside pocket."[40] The Calgary Municipal Railway was replaced in 1946 by the Calgary Transit System's trolley and diesel buses; the last street car ran in 1950.

Concern for beautification did not end with the boom. In the rush of expansion, Calgary did not neglect its parks such as Memorial Park and St. George's Island. Newer parks were created round the Glenmore Reservoir, in Confederation Park, the Brewery Gardens, the Burns Memorial Gardens, and Heritage Park.[41]

From the collapse of the construction boom in 1913, Calgary experienced no expansion until the housing shortage during World War II. Land prices fell and rents stabilized. The downtown core, served by the streetcar, continued to be the focus. The population was concentrated in the inner city area, encouraging multiple land use in the inner city and depressing land prices in the outer suburbs. So much land was reverting to the City for non-payment of taxes that the City initiated a policy of growth restriction in 1920. In 1929 a house-moving fund was established to help people move their houses to lots nearer the downtown.[42] Outlying property reverted to agricultural uses while the City sold off inner-city lots at a fraction of their value.

1914-1915, crowd reading war news on 8th Avenue. Glenbow Archives, NA-1447-10

The Alberta Town Planning Act (1929) empowered cities to appoint town planning commissions whose mandate would include the preparation of a zoning bylaw. The new bylaw allowed for four districts instead of two, and single family, two-family, and multiple dwelling districts, but it applied only to the inner city area.[43] In 1934, the first Calgary zoning bylaws came into effect and encouraged multiple uses for larger buildings as well as for land use. A transportation study was made with major arterial routes to relieve congestion downtown.

Oil and gas helped Calgary when agriculture could not. Calgary's economy has relied on both ranching and oil from the early days of its settlement. Oil had been discovered as early as 1910, with drilling at Cameron Brook (near Pincher Creek) reporting a flow of 300 barrels a day. Unfortunately, Canada had no oil refinery and transportation was a problem. Natural gas and coal were also discovered and began to boost the economy. On May 14, 1914, oil was struck at Dingman Number One in Turner Valley – the first major oil field in the British Empire. Every vehicle in the city was requisitioned to visit the oil field the next day and it looked as though another boom was on the way. Eighty-two days after the discovery, however, headlines announced "Great Britain declares War against Germany" and the boom collapsed. Wheat and cattle prices increased during the war, but oil had to wait. The oil boom did not return until 1924 when Royalite Number Four (also in Turner Valley) was drilled, indicating huge reserves. Bob Edwards wrote in 1922,[44] "Calgary is fortunate for having had all its real estate and oil scandals while young, as children have the measles and other diseases while young and are then shed of them forever." He was a little optimistic.

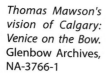
Thomas Mawson's vision of Calgary: Venice on the Bow. Glenbow Archives, NA-3766-1

Calgary experienced seemingly unlimited prosperity after 1947. Less reliance on agriculture and a booming oil industry created a new city. In the 1960s Calgary began to expand in the northwest and southeast. Downtown, new skyscrapers were being filled by the head offices of companies in the oil business. Calgary grew to 155 square miles (250 sq. km) by 1965.

To cope with this rapid growth, the City established a more powerful planning department with a mandate to specify the nature and scope of Calgary's growth and to co-ordinate this growth with regional interests. In 1966, City officials introduced the Downtown Master Plan, principally to restore the residential aspect of downtown as 98% of the population now lived in the suburbs while 40% worked downtown. The downtown had become an island, separated by the river, the railways tracks, and deteriorating areas to the east and west of the commercial core. Its isolation was increased by the policy of establishing neighborhood units with self-sufficient suburban services. Continued annexation fostered the idea that the city was limitless. Calgarians chose single-family houses and the automobile over the streetcar or walking to work. Between 1948 and 1965, over 60 000 houses were constructed.[45] Apartments were going up between the railway tracks and 17th Avenue S, contributing to multiple land use.

In 1967 a $21 million *Urban Renewal Scheme* for downtown was unveiled.[46] In the next 10 years, scores of buildings were razed to make way for school board complexes, the Glenbow Museum and Calgary Convention Centre, banks, and oil company offices. Husky Tower (now Calgary Tower) and Palliser Square (now Tower Centre), were built on the site of the old CPR station. The Centennial Planetarium was completed at Mewata Park. The Eau Claire and Bow Valley lumber mill at Prince's Island, which had cut much of the timber for Calgary's houses, was demolished in 1946. Peter Prince's mansion and the village of workers' houses were all gone, some to Heritage Park.

While old Calgary was being demolished, the oil and gas community grew steadily. A new and striking city skyline was being created. High-rise offices were established downtown, as well as an industry based on the by-products of oil. The Husky Tower (1968) reached 626 feet (190 m): a symbol of growing city stature. By 1971 there were 400 oil companies, and companies related to oil and gas. Five hundred million dollars worth of businesses and houses were under construction. In 1972, the city area was enlarged to 159 square miles (256 sq. km). Paved streets, sidewalks, and sewer systems were extended to hundreds of miles.

Highways began to divide the city. The Deerfoot Trail was begun in 1975. The Blackfoot and Sarcee Trails diverted traffic from downtown. In the early 1960s, Calgary grew to include Forest Lawn, Montgomery, and Bowness, which had long been outside the city. Control through corporate land ownership gave way to private development.

In 1978, the population of Calgary reached half a million and suburbs spread in all directions. The majority of jobs were still downtown, but people tended to live in the suburbs and shop in local malls. Downtown became less vibrant after work. Increased traffic meant that traffic lights on every block, one-way street systems, and parking buildings were changing the landscape downtown. Vacant lots reminiscent of the grass-covered lots of early Calgary, but now the result of demolition, were turned into parking lots.

Oil and gas enabled Calgary to extend its sphere of influence beyond the province and its agricultural base and become involved in international business. Calgary began to resemble Houston, Texas, another oil centre, rather than the European city that Thomas Mawson had in mind.

Since the 1950s, the UniCity approach has been a cornerstone of growth management. Calgary and the adjacent municipalities constituted one urban area, but were under the control of four local governing bodies. The 1956 McNally Royal Commission outlined the key principles of the UniCity, and Calgary continues to adhere to these, voluntarily collaborating with the municipalities.

Investment in city infrastructure continued in the 1980s with the building of the Calgary Municipal Building adjacent to the old City Hall. Tiers of blue-grey mirror glass contrast with the old sandstone building. The Calgary Centre for the Performing Arts, created from a series of buildings opposite the Municipal Building, created a backdrop for the 1988 Olympic Plaza that had become the heart of the city. The Olympics added significantly to the city in terms of sports buildings as well as city spirit and was so successful that Calgary instigated a winter festival in subsequent years. This celebration of the city continued when Calgary turned 100 years old in 1994, and will be celebrated again when the province reaches a century in 2005.

Awareness that Calgary is a winter city has been growing since the 1980s with the building of Plus-15s,[47] enabling Calgarians to traverse the city indoors. Also indoors are interlinked shopping malls and the Devonian Gardens, giving the city an inward-looking aspect which contrasts with the summer strollers on the historic Stephen Avenue

Mall. Sandstone buildings still line Stephen Avenue (8th Avenue) downtown but while the city preserves its past, it is looking to the future. In 1989 City Council approved "Calgary 2020" as a vision for Calgary. The guideposts are:

- Investment in education, training, strong communities, and quality work environments;
- The best choices for the future are based on our heritage and values;
- Hard work, innovation, and entrepreneurship has built Calgary; it will continue with modern, aggressive approaches;
- The natural environment is our greatest asset;
- Wellness is the basis for a healthy community;
- Interdependence and volunteerism remain the key to the future;
- Multiculturalism has great potential;
- Social services must be provided to all;
- Safety and security are important; and
- Citizenship and involvement are assumed in Calgary.

The vision statement of the Calgary Municipal Development Plan (1998) based on the Calgary Transportation Plan (1995) guides city growth with these principles. By the year 2024:

- The population will be 1.25 million (in 2004, it was 933 495);
- We live closer to where we work; we walk, cycle, and use transit;
- The outward growth of the city has slowed and density and diversity are increasing;
- Downtown is still a centre for employment and has kept in step with market demand;
- We have a user pay system as a funding source for the transportation system;
- Air quality remains at 1990 levels because we have cleaner cars and we car pool;
- Telecommuting and flex-time have reduced traffic congestion at rush hour;
- We are protecting our river valleys, our environment, and our communities; and
- Mobility needs, community and environmental impacts, and costs are carefully considered before decisions are made.

As Thomas Mawson said in 1912:

> City planning is not the attempt to pull down your city and rebuild it at ruinous expense. It is merely deciding what you would like to have done when you get the chance, so that when the chance does come, little by little you may make the city plan conform to your ideals.[48]

Notes

1. Leishman McNeill, *Tales of the Old Town*, 1966.

2. City of Calgary Census, 2004.

3. Donald Smith (ed.), *Centennial City, Calgary 1894-1994*, 1994.

4. Grant MacEwan, *Calgary Cavalcade: From Fort to Fortune*, 1975.

5. *Ibid.*, 79.

6. Leishman McNeill, *Tales of the Old Town*, 25.

7. Grant MacEwan, *Calgary Cavalcade*, 39.

8. *Ibid.*

9. Max Foran, in *Centennial City, Calgary 1894-1994*, 16.

10. Grant MacEwan, *Calgary Cavalcade*, 44.

11. *Ibid.*

12. Herb Surplis (editor), *Past and Present, Century Calgary*, 1975.

13. Max Foran, *Calgary: An Illustrated History*, 25.

14. Max Foran, in *Centennial City, Calgary 1894-1994*, 18.

15. Donald Smith and Harold Klassen, in *Centennial City, Calgary 1894-1994*, 4.

16. Leishman McNeil, *Tales of the Old Town*, 27.

17. Donald Smith and Harold Klassen, in *Centennial City, Calgary 1894-1994*, 3.

18. *Ibid.*, 1.

19. Helen Godenberg and Elizabeth de Steur, *Once upon a Chinook*, 27.

20. Grant MacEwan, *Calgary Cavalcade*, 77.

21. *Ibid.*

22. *Ibid.*

23. Max Foran, *Calgary: An Illustrated History*, 64.

24. A. F. M. Brooke to Z. T. Wood, dated Calgary 14 June 1895. National Archives of Canada, RG 18, Royal Canadian Mounted Police Records, Vol. 370, file 179-1895, as quoted in *Centennial City*, 2.

25. *Eye Opener*, 2 July 1904.

26. Helen Goldenberg & Elizabeth de Steur, *Once upon a Chinook*, 57.

27. Grant MacEwan, *Calgary Cavalcade*, 84.

28. Max Foran, in *Centennial City, Calgary 1894-1994*, 18.

29. Max Foran, in *Centennial City, Calgary 1894-1994*, 16.

30. Grant MacEwan, *Calgary Cavalcade*, 86.

31. Max Foran, *Calgary: An Illustrated History*, 45.

32. *Ibid.*, 89.

33. Bob Edwards, *Eye Opener*, 23 February 1907.

34. Grant MacEwan, *Calgary Cavalcade*, 136.

35. Max Foran, *Calgary: An Illustrated History*, 100.

36. Grant MacEwan, *Calgary Cavalcade*, 137.

37. Helen Goldenberg and Elizabeth de Steur, *Once upon a Chinook*, Century Calgary, 1975.

38. Leishman McNeill, *Tales of the Old Town*, 28.

39. Max Foran, in *Centennial City*, 21.

40. Helen Goldenberg and Elizabeth de Steur, *Once upon a Chinook*, Century Calgary, 1975.

41. Grant MacEwan, *Calgary Cavalcade*, 198.

42. Max Foran, *Calgary: An Illustrated History*, 134.

43. *Ibid.*, 141.

44. Bob Edwards, *Summer Annual,* 1922, 24.

45. Alberta Department of Business Development and Tourism, Industries and Resources 1975, Table 41.

46. Harry Sanders, in *Centennial City*, 79.

47. A Plus-15 is an enclosed walkway 15 feet above grade which joins buildings across roadways.

48. Speech delivered in Calgary in 1912.

The Calgary Irrigation Company
Beyond the Banks
by John Gilpin

The federal government's passing of the North-West Irrigation Act in 1894 established the legal bases and priorities for the use of water in Alberta through to the present day. The catalyst for this measure was the need to regulate access to the Bow River during a drought. The Bow, more than any other river system in the drought-stricken region, was expected to fill the breach caused by the severe lack of rain. The federal government looked to the Bow River for its irrigation value. They needed to fulfill the terms of a contract with the Canadian Pacific Railway (CPR) and this could only be accomplished by offering irrigation as a solution.[1] Calgary area residents were equally enthusiastic about the irrigation potential of the Bow River system and by 1896, had created 70 of the 154 irrigation projects constructed or authorized.[2] Calgary politicians and businessmen also took the lead in promoting this type of agriculture by organizing the first irrigation conference in the West, creating the South-Western Irrigation League of the North West Territories, and lobbying for the establishment of an irrigation experimental farm.

Critical to establishing this link between Calgary, the Bow River system, and water management in Western Canada was William Pearce: bureaucrat, capitalist, and irrigation farmer.[3] As a senior official of the Department of the Interior, he helped formulate an irrigation policy, which emphasized Crown ownership of water and its development by private corporations. As a private citizen, he created the Calgary Irrigation Company (CICo.), which attempted to construct the largest irrigation project proposed prior to 1898. Owning a large plot of land along the Bow River gave Pearce the opportunity to conduct various experiments in irrigation agriculture. The company was also involved in the only serious challenge to the "first in time, first in right" principle which was the basis of the license system introduced in 1894. The CICo. illustrates the unique role Pearce played in the political, business, and agricultural history of the West and many of the problems confronting irrigation development through to the 1950s.

William Pearce began his career as a federal bureaucrat in 1874 when the Department of the Interior hired him as a surveyor. By 1881, his proven competence and enthusiasm for the work led to his appointment as Inspector of Land Agencies. This office was part of the newly established Lands Board which gave Pearce considerable influence in the administration of Dominion Lands policy. He moved to Calgary in 1881 to become Superintendent of Mines while continuing to handle various responsibilities for the Lands Board. The lack of mining activity, however, permitted Pearce to pursue his interest in the agricultural development of the semi-arid region of the West, which was dependent, in his view, on the efficient use of water. His introduction to water management through irrigation was the result of a trip to Utah and Colorado in 1881. A subsequent trip to Calgary in 1883 convinced him that irrigation was also required in Southern Alberta.[4]

In 1884, the need for water management was also recognized by the ranching community who requested the introduction of a program to maintain water reserves for livestock.[5] Pearce became its enthusiastic administrator since he believed that ranchers would maximize the economic benefits of the water supply. Settlers who fenced off springs and river courses minimized its economic potential. In addition to the aggressive administration of this program, he also suggested the introduction of a modified version of the American Desert Land Act to encourage large-scale irrigation development for hay production.[6] The 1889 annual meeting of the Dominion Land Surveyors Association provided him with a public forum to press the need for irrigation. The government's tolerance of Pearce's irrigation promotional activities came to an end and in 1891 when he was refused permission to give a second presentation on irrigation to the Surveyors Association and was advised to stop making public statements on the issue.[7] This action was in response to CPR and federal government fears that discussion of irrigation would discourage settlement.

Having been prevented from promoting irrigation as a government official, Pearce took his campaign to the private sector, convinced that it was a good investment opportunity. After a failed attempt in 1892 to interest A. M. Nanton, Manager of the Canada Mortgage Company, he created his own company, the CICo., in partnership with Calgary surveyor Peter Turner Bone, and Calgary lawyer John Pascoe Jeremy Jephson, who served as the other provisional directors. The major shareholders of were Turner Bone, William Pearce, and his wife. Between November 1892 and

August 1893, the system was planned and an Act passed by the Dominion Parliament to incorporate the CICo. plan. Construction began in 1893.

While waiting for authorization to build the system as originally planned, the CICo. made further surveys of the land south of the Elbow River and found that a much greater area could be irrigated by relocating the diversion point further upstream. Rather than obtaining an order in council approving their revised plans, as required by its own act of incorporation, the CICo. simply obtained the Minister of the Interior's permission, in August 1893, to begin construction immediately. Pearce justified his request to skip the formal approval process on two grounds. The first was that no other irrigation project using the Elbow River was underway. The second, was that any illegal actions taken could be made legal by subsequent amendments to the act of incorporation or by a general act regulating irrigation development.[8] By December 1893, $8 700 had been spent to build six miles (10 km) of main ditch along with headgate structures. The CICo. also started a land acquisition program, which included acquiring abandoned homesteads along with CPR and Hudson's Bay Company (HBC) land.

The haste with which Pearce, Jephson, and Turner Bone had initiated the development of the project created the first company crisis in January 1894, when they were advised that they had exceeded their authority as provisional directors because of their land purchase and construction program. From January to April 1894, the company obtained the necessary amendments to its charter to correct this mistake, while continuing its planning, construction, and land acquisition programs. Community support for its efforts was provided through the Calgary Branch of the South-Western Irrigation League of the North West Territories and the Calgary Town Council.[9] Its revised act received Royal assent on the same day as the North-West Irrigation Act that Pearce had simultaneously helped to draft while directing the affairs of his own company. The CICo. was thus poised in late July 1894 to make a formal request for authorization to complete the system and to launch an appeal in Britain for new investors to finance the work.

The Springbank challenge to the CICo., and indirectly to federal water resources policy in the West as outlined in the North-West Irrigation Act, began on July 26, 1894, at a meeting organized by leading members of the Calgary business community and a group of Springbank settlers. The main speaker was Senator Lougheed, who emphasized the value of irrigation, not only to every Alberta farmer, "but every resident in the towns and everyone who [had] a cent of money invested in the country."[10] He urged the community to organize and raise the funds to build a large irrigation system using water from the Elbow River. A petition was subsequently sent to the Territorial Government, which passed the Irrigation Ordinance on September 7, 1894. This legislation was necessary because the North-West Irrigation Act had deliberately failed to provide for the creation of community-based irrigation districts.

The most urgent task in the minds of the Springbank organizing committee was to stop the CICo., which announced in the *Canada Gazette* and the September 5 edition of the local press, that the company intended to create a 45 000 acre irrigation project. The Minister of the Interior, Mayne Daly, was asked to defer a decision on the CICo. request until an impartial investigation of their claims could be made.[11] Pearce was seen as using his position to gain special privileges over the rights of the settlers. The Springbank settlers and their supporters either did not understand or had chosen to ignore that the North-West Irrigation Act had extinguished riparian rights.[12] The Springbank Settlers filed their own plans to construct an irrigation system using the Elbow River in November 1894. When asked to respond to the Springbank protest, Pearce compared the two projects on legal grounds and more importantly on the principal of efficiency in the use of water and concluded that the CICo. was superior on both counts. He dismissed the Springbank protest as "malicious" and not a legitimate attempt to build an alternative system.[13] In private correspondence, he identified Senator Lougheed as the leader of the "clique" that was creating all the problems for the CICo.

The federal government's review of the Springbank protest and the CICo.'s application was made by J. S. Dennis in November of 1894. He concluded that the CICo.'s project was sound from an engineering point of view, having been "made on a accurate scientific basis."[14] He also noted that a satisfactory start had been made on its construction, with six miles (10 km) of main ditch and 10 miles (16 km) of lateral ditches having been completed along with suitable headgates at a total cost of $12 700. The legal position of the CICo. project was further strengthened by its prior rights to the Elbow River and the Company's right to the use of that water in an adjacent drainage basin. The legal issue was particularly important to Dennis, who pointed out the necessity of dealing with the first case of conflict arising from the *North-West Irrigation Act* upon principles that would apply in all similar cases in the future. The final point made by Dennis was that the Springbank settlers had an alternative supply of water, namely Jumping Pound Creek. Dennis suggested a plan which combined the use of this creek with storage reservoir development on its upper portion, and use of some water from the Elbow River during its flood stage. These recommendations were incorporated without revision into an order in council approved on February 23, 1895. The success of the CICo. in dealing with the Springbank protest came about, therefore, because the federal government was willing to adhere to the water licensing principal in the North-West Irrigation Act despite the fact that Pearce was in an obvious conflict of interest situation.

The end of the conflict between the CICo. and the Springbank settlers came with the May publication of the *Canada Gazette* reporting on the February 25, 1894, order in council and the submission of a final memorial by the CICo. to the Land Registrar in October 1895. The memorial described the land to be included in the project and estimated there would potentially be 300 water users.

Bringing the CICo. to the attention of the British investor was the immediate concern of the CICo. once the conflict with the Springbank settlers had been resolved. This task was primarily the responsibility of Turner Bone, while Pearce concentrated his more limited fundraising efforts in Canada. The Company based its appeal to potential investors by emphasizing the extensive and careful planning that went into the project and the absolute necessity of irrigation for growing crops in an area where drought was the "prevailing climate condition."[15] The results of this effort were, however, very disappointing because of a general decline in the price of Canadian stocks led by the CPR.

The British investors' lack of interest was shared by settlers who did not buy land and water to the extent the company anticipated, and showed little interest in learning about irrigation farming. As a result, by 1896, the number of water users peaked at 11 rather than 300, and the number of acres actually irrigated peaked at 400 rather than 45 000 acres.[16] No reference was made to the CICo. in the summary of results from irrigation included in the 1897 *Annual Report of the Department of the Interior*.[17] The end of the drought meant that irrigation was now perceived as unnecessary and expensive. Damage to irrigation works and the flooding of fields as a result of the heavy rains in June 1897, further reduced interest.

With the end of the drought, the CICo. developed a survival strategy based on the creation of two company farms combined with appeals for help to the territorial and federal governments. These farms were intended to demonstrate the value of irrigation to settlers, secure income for the company through the raising of crops, and provide work for company employees when they were not otherwise operating and maintaining the system. Bond guarantees were requested in October 1898, and a grant of $30 000 was requested in December of the same year. In return for this grant, the CICo. promised it would carry out studies to determine the appropriate value of the duty of water. However, the idea of company farms did not improve the company's appeal to private investors and both 1898 requests were rejected without explanation from the two levels of government.

Despite the lack of success in obtaining new funds and the lack of demand for irrigated land, the CICo. continued its construction program through to 1899. By that year the CICo. system consisted of two main canals with a total length of 60 miles (97 km). The first and largest of the two took water from a point on the Elbow River located at the north west corner of the Sarcee Reserve and transported it across the western end of the Reserve, and then north west towards Calgary but not actually into the town. The second canal took water from the Elbow River at the Stampede grounds and transported it to the Pearce and Walker Estates in Inglewood via a flume across the Elbow River just downstream from the Stampede grounds.[18]

By 1900, the failure to attract new investors, the lack of government support, minimal income from operations, and excessive amounts of rain finally forced the company to stop searching for ways to survive. The company went into liquidation in 1905, and its water licence was

Headgate on the Elbow River of the Calgary Irrigation Company. William Pearce and other company officials and investors can be seen standing on this structure. Glenbow Archives, NA-5673-6

cancelled in 1907. Pearce was no longer active in the company by the time these events took place largely because of the conflict with the Springbank settlers. In the Spring of 1905, Turner Bone took over the day-to-day management of the company upon his return from Britain while Peter Prince and A. E. Cross became the new directors. Pearce's family members remained the major shareholders, however, because there was no market for their stock. Pearce concentrated his effort on the development of his estate in Inglewood.

The CICo. had been created to prove that irrigation could be developed by the private sector but had demonstrated exactly the opposite. The principle cause of this result was its failure to adjust to the nature of the region's climate which was based on rainfall cycles and not on permanent drought. Its attempt to adjust to this change came too late to prevent its construction of a system, which was grossly under-utilized and a financial burden to operate. The end of the drought had the same effect on the interest in irrigation and the operation of irrigation systems in the Calgary area. The Calgary Hydraulic Company, established in 1893, with the same expectations, was in liquidation for want of new investment by 1898. Flood damage and redundancy caused by excessive rainfall in the late 1890s led to the abandonment of most of the remaining projects in the Calgary area by the turn of the century. The Calgary business community lost interest in the South-Western Irrigation League of the North West Territories and in establishing an irrigation experimental farm.

Calgary's declining interest in irrigation coincided with the success of the Lethbridge-based Alberta Irrigation Company (AIC [renamed the Canadian North West Irrigation Company]) which was controlled by Elliott Galt and associates. Its success after 1896 was, in part, the result of an agreement with the Church of Jesus Christ of Latter Day Saints, which ensured the establishment of a farming community that would remain during dry and wet years.[19] This agreement solved the problem that had defeated Pearce's effort on the Bow River and would later create similar problems for the CPR and the Southern Alberta Land Company on the Bow River after the turn of the century.

The fate of the CICo. did not change Pearce's view on the value of irrigation and how it should be implemented. Even in light of the CICo.'s steady decline, Pearce renewed his efforts to convince the CPR of irrigation's value, since he felt that the CPR had the resources to make the system a success. He emphasized the Mormon contribution to the success of the AIC and suggested that the CPR follow AIC's approach to land settlement.

Despite the lack of irrigation's initial success along the Bow River, use of the river for that purpose established the basis of Alberta water law and was a proving ground for federal and provincial water resource policy through to the Second World War. The water rights of all irrigation projects in Alberta today are based on the "first in time, first in right" principle of the North-West Irrigation Act. The partnership between the private sector and the federal government, which Pearce believed was the best way to implement large-scale irrigation development, was not changed until the 1950 federal-provincial agreement to expand the St. Mary Project originally begun by the Alberta Irrigation Company. The provincial government's emphasis on farmer-operated cooperatives, introduced in 1915, was based on the same ideas contained in the 1894 Irrigation Ordinance of the Territorial Government.

Notes

1. In the late 1880s the CPR rejected the land along the mainline between Medicine Hat and Crowfoot Crossing for inclusion in its land grant because it did not meet the criteria of "fairly fit for settlement." Rather than exchanging the land, the federal government tried to convince the CPR that irrigation would correct its deficiencies. See National Archives of Canada RG 15 Vol. 602 File 211000 Part 1 and 2 Reel T-13850 for the details on these negotiations. Legislation was passed in 1894 to provide for the creation of a CPR irrigation block between Medicine Hat and Calgary, but it was not created until the turn of the century.

2. "Schedule of Canals and Ditches constructed and in operation in Southern Alberta and Assiniboia, together with those which have been authorized to be constructed during 1896," *Annual Report of Department of the Interior*, 1896, Part III Irrigation, 3-7. The rapid increase in the number of applications to use water from the Bow River and its impact on federal government western land settlement policy is also documented in Order in Council 1447 approved May 15, 1895.

3. The only in-depth source of biographical information on William Pearce is "William Pearce and federal government activity in western Canada 1882-1904" by E. Alyn Mitchner. Edmonton: Dept. of History, University of Alberta, 1971. Additional biographical information is available in *The Canadian Prairie West and the Ranching Frontier* by David Breen.

4. William Pearce Papers, University of Alberta Archives, 9/2/7/4-6.

5. An overview of the role of Pearce in the development and administration of the stock water reserve program is available in *The Canadian Prairie West and the Ranching Frontier* by David Breen.

6. Report by William Pearce in 1885, *Annual Report of the Department of The Interior*.

7. William Pearce Papers, University of Alberta Archives, 9/2/6/4-1.

8. William Pearce Papers, University of Alberta Archives, 9/2/7/3-9.

9. Ibid.

10. *Calgary Herald*, 27 July 1894.

11. William Pearce Papers, University of Alberta Archives, 9/2/7/3-9.

12. Riparian rights means the rights to water possessed by owners of land adjacent to a body of water.

13. Defense of the CICo. written by William Pearce in October 1894, located in William Pearce Papers, University of Alberta Archives, 9/2/7/3-9.

14. Report by Dennis, 13 November 1894, attached to I. C. 447, 23 February 1895.

15. Company prospectus in Part 1 M3754, Glenbow Archives.

16. Annual Returns of the Calgary Irrigation Company, 1895 to 1905, Part 1 M3754, Glenbow Archives.

17. Irrigation Bulletin 3, *Annual Report of the Department of Public Works,* 1897.

18. The location of the upper canal is shown on maps produced in 1898 and 1901 by the Canadian Irrigation Survey, which are in the Glenbow Library map collection, call numbers G3502 S727J4 svar No. 3 1898 and G3502 S727J4 svar No. 3 1901. Both of these maps, however, show this canal extending into the Inglewood area of Calgary, which is incorrect. The location of both canals is also shown on registered plans IrrD, Irr3, Irr32, and Irr52 at the Land Titles Office and on plans G3502/C151J4/1894/J54 and G3504/C151: 3/151J4/1896/J54 at the Glenbow Library.

19. The contribution of the Church of Jesus Christ of Latter-day Saints to the success of the Alberta Irrigation Company is discussed in "The Mormons and the Beginnings of the Irrigation Industry in Alberta" by John F. Gilpin, which is part of *Regional Studies in Latter-day Saint Church History Western Canada,* editors Dennis A. Wright, Robert C. Freeman, Andrew Hedges, and Matthew O. Richardson. Department of Church History and Doctrine, Brigham Young University, Provo, Utah, 2000.

Alberta's Birthright
The Oil Industry in and Around Calgary
by David Finch

"Without oil," a commentator once quipped, "Alberta would be Saskatchewan." The petroleum industry has contributed enormously to the wealth and development of the most westerly prairie province. It has allowed Alberta to experience unprecedented periods of economic growth and has contributed hundreds of billions of dollars of income to the provincial treasury and to the economy. In 2004 alone, it provided the provincial government an income in excess of $10 billion – or about $3 300 for each of the three million men, women, and children in the province.

During the 90 years since the 1914 discovery of petroleum at Turner Valley – Alberta's first major oil and gas field – profits from this industry have funded a massive infrastructure, including roads, hospitals, schools, colleges, technical schools and universities, cultural institutions, museums, archives, libraries, agricultural programs, rural electrical systems and natural gas pipelines, dams, transit systems, provincial parks, and recreation areas, along with numerous other projects and programs.

But in addition to the frequently lauded benefits it has bestowed on the province, the oil and gas industry has also created and sustained a set of priorities that threaten the long-term viability of the resource-based economy and the quality of life of its residents. Though agriculture sustained the economy for many decades, without the discovery of petroleum the province would have remained a poor cousin of Confederation. Oil is Alberta's birthright, given by the vagaries of geologic deposition and political fiat. That unique birthright has allowed the people of Alberta to develop the provincial economy far beyond its agricultural potential.

Though the birthright is valuable, its price is also volatile. Oil and gas prices are dictated by the international marketplace and limited by regional transportation infrastructures. The strategic value of petroleum became evident after World War I as multinational oil companies expanded their empires around the world to acquired secure markets. Cheap gasoline quickly became the fuel of choice for transportation systems and the machinery of war. As a strategic resource, it was much more than a mere consumer commodity and its value fluctuated with international political, economic, and military realities.

The resulting cyclical pattern of demand for petroleum forced Alberta into a repetitive cycle of booms and busts. Each new discovery flooded the local markets, depressing the regional prices until pipelines to more distant markets once again elevated the price of oil to the world price, which in turn, again created an exploration frenzy that flooded the market with more product than the infrastructure could distribute. Repeating itself approximately every decade, the cycle binds the provincial economy to the international commodity markets in a manner that allows little provincial control over the pace and scale of development (Consequently, exploration companies that conduct geophysical and geological research seldom survive more than one or two boom and bust cycles and dedicated drilling companies suffer a similar fate).

By 1950, the wealth that poured into the provincial treasury from the petroleum industry exceeded any other source of taxation or income – including alcohol. The heavy reliance on oil and gas revenues accentuated Alberta's dependence on natural resource development and made it difficult for politicians or residents to create a long-term development plan for the provincial economy. The seduction by wealth – at the peak of the periodic boom – clouded the judgement process and prevented the formation of a wise, staged, and sustainable development strategy.

Fundamental to this short-sighted development process was the ideological fixation with free-enterprise and private ownership. In spite of the fact that most oil and gas is owned by the people of the province through their government, between the world wars entrepreneurs developed the resource in a wasteful, environmentally hazardous, and irresponsible manner that only reflected their short-sighted desire to maximize return on investment. Though the province attempted to control the development process by establishing a Conservation Board in the early 1930s, industry lawyers rendered it powerless until the late 1930s when the demands for oil during World War II (WWII) overrode the implementation of a sustainable development plan for the producing oilfields.

The Conservation Board attempted to control the development boom that followed the discovery of petroleum at Leduc in 1947 – though economic conservation was the only mandate for its first 50 years, the concept of environmental safety and conservation became more widely accepted by the public and the Board in the 1980s. The 1950s witnessed an unprecedented level of expansion and exploitation of the natural resources of the province by foreign or foreign-owned petroleum companies. The United States, whose interests and directives had controlled much of the Canadian West and the North during WWII, considered Alberta's oil as part of its own continental resource pool that could be exploited to counterbalance the less reliable offshore oilfields.

By contrast, until the 1940s, the U.S. had treated Mexican and Venezuelan petroleum in a similarly proprietary manner, but these countries, proud of their revolutionary heritage and their casting off the yoke of Spanish bondage, refused to allow the U.S. to plunder their oilfields indefinitely. Mexico nationalized its industry in the late 1930s. Venezuela flexed the power of its petroleum birthright by renegotiating its income from petroleum with the multinationals so as to reap 50% of the profits in 1943, and by becoming a founding member of the Organization of Petroleum Exporting Countries in 1959. Venezuela eventually nationalized its entire petroleum industry, protecting for itself the right to develop the petroleum reserves as it saw fit.

By contrast, Alberta allowed multinational oil companies to direct the development process as they saw fit. Though new provincial governments in 1935 and 1972 – Social Credit and the Progressive Conservatives – attempted to wrest some control over the development process away from the foreign-owned or foreign-controlled oil companies during their first years in power, they quickly lost their revolutionary zeal and accepted the economic wealth offered by the industry instead of holding out for fundamental change to the relationship between the elected officials and the companies whose allegiance was to foreign governments and investors.

At the national level, Prime Minister Joe Clark's short-lived Progressive Conservative government attempted to negotiate a national petroleum policy with the petroleum producing provinces in 1979 that would have expanded the role of the federal government in the development of the industry and encouraged Canadian ownership of the companies exploiting Canadian natural resources. However, Alberta's distrust for central Canadian politicians prevented Peter Lougheed from reaching agreement with the prime minister who hailed from High River, Alberta. As a result, Pierre Trudeau's Liberal government implemented its own version of an energy program in 1980, a considerably less onerous program than the one proposed by Clark, and the implementation of the much-maligned National Energy Program coincided with the drastic fall in the international price of oil that accompanied a worldwide economic recession. Though unwilling to take part in a Canadianization program with the federal government, Alberta was willing to allow the political and economic planners in the U.S. to dictate the development process in the province.

Over time, the weak control exerted by provincial and federal agencies over the petroleum industry was further compromised when governments throughout North America decided to decrease their regulatory control over all sectors of the economy. During the 1980s President Ronald Reagan and Prime Minister Brian Mulroney directed their regulatory agencies to pull back from enforcement and allow the petroleum industry to become "self-regulating" in order to further encourage industrial expansion and economic growth at the expense of environmental protection and a long-term and sustainable petroleum development program.

The ideologies and policies that have guided the Alberta petroleum development process contributed great wealth to the provincial economy but the cumulative effects of these decisions have created an uncomfortable social and political life in the province. The rate of discovery of the petroleum birthright peaked in the early 1950s and each year it has taken more and more oil and gas wells to bring an ever-decreasing quantity of product into production. According to the Conservation Board, in 1953 it took only 500 wells to add 2 billion barrels of oil to the storehouses – about 4 million barrels per well. In 1983 the 3 200 wells drilled found only 400 million barrels of oil – an average of less than 125 000 barrels per well – and in 2003, the industry drilled 16 411 wells in Alberta in a frantic quest to bring the dwindling resource into production.

This discovery rate is an important benchmark because Alberta's declining reserves encourage the petroleum industry to look elsewhere for oil and gas, thereby reducing its commitment to the development process in Alberta. Left behind are the cumulative effects of the development process, most of which industry is not called upon to mitigate. Though companies are responsible for cleaning up polluted industrial sites today, the costs of reclaiming numerous toxic historic sites have been borne by the provincial treasury – the people of Alberta.

Though the standard of living in Alberta is high, the quality of life for many Albertans is jeopardized by their exposure to toxic substances released by the nearly 400 000 oil and gas wells that have been drilled in the province – one for every seven residents – as well as processing plants and other facilities. Though overt violence against the industry is relatively rare, it has become more common in recent years and has even led to the murder of an oil company official by an irate landowner. Even the threat of potential pollution is enough to cause concern, as in the case of the development of sour gas wells on the southeastern boundary of the city of Calgary that could, in the event of a blowout, force the evacuation of hundreds of thousands of city residents as well as a major hospital.

The development of the oil sands in northeastern Alberta has provided an alternate and increasingly important source of petroleum production over the last three decades. It is not, however, without its own complications. The process that separates the hydrocarbons from the sand consumes massive amounts of water and natural gas. Also, recent construction projects to increase oil sands production have run far over budget, creating concerns in the investment community over these extremely expensive operations. Essentially a large mining operation, oil sands can be developed for decades if petroleum prices remain high and conflicts can be resolved. For example, companies with the rights to develop the natural gas that accompanies the oil sands are contesting the rights of oil sands operators to develop their properties in a manner that prevents production of natural gas. In addition, the Alberta government typically forgives taxes and royalties on oil sands operations until they become profitable, forgoing billions of dollars in lost revenue.

Finally, though Alberta has become wealthy, the economic costs to the people of Alberta have not been adequately calculated. Forgone economic rent from the decades of allowing the foreign-controlled industry to dictate the return to the people of Alberta amounts to many billions of dollars. Even the price the people of Alberta pay for oil and gas products is controlled by the Americans, through the Free Trade Agreement that forces us to sell our products to ourselves at the same price we sell to the Americans and prevents us from withholding supplies in the event of an inevitable energy crisis – a major concern given that the U.S. is currently importing a greater percentage (and total amount) of its petroleum than before the energy crisis of the early 1970s and that its own domestic supplies are dwindling as its consumption continues to set records. As a result, Alberta consumers pay an inflated price for gasoline at the pump and for natural gas to heat their homes. A product that was only worth 3 cents per thousand cubic feet a few decades ago is billed to Albertans during the winter at a rate in excess of $7.50 – 250 times as much. This rate does not reflect the price of the cost of production – of a natural resource that is mostly owned by the people of Alberta – but is instead inflated by the continental price for the commodity. (A commodity best used for heating homes that, in the most bizarre of contradictions, is shipped to California to generate electricity that in turn powers air conditioners.) Under an alternate resource development model that allowed us to pay the actual cost of production and allow our government to control the development process, the people of Alberta would not only pay much less for natural gas, we would also reap much more of the profits associated with the sale of this increasingly valuable natural resource. Acknowledging the need for conservation and energy efficiency, Alberta could become a world leader in wise use of the natural resources; encouraging conservation as well as investing its capital into research programs to expand the development of wind and solar energy systems for a global market.

In conclusion, the cyclical nature of the petroleum extraction industry in Alberta has taken the province on a rollercoaster ride of booms and busts with increasing regularity since the discovery of the first oil and gas field in Turner Valley in 1914. Attempts to diversify the provincial economy by public sector investment in an airline, high tech industries, and other speculative ventures have proved unsuccessful and cost the taxpayers billions of dollars. Similarly, the investment of the Alberta Heritage Trust Fund, which was to guard against tough times, has not alleviated the economic hardship of the periodic busts. Alberta's economy remains closely tied to the development of its natural resources, especially oil and gas.

Alberta's politicians, espousing free-enterprise and market-based theologies, have allowed foreign-owned and foreign-controlled companies to dictate the pace of the resource development process. Proclaiming fierce independence and an aversion to any policies emanating from the central Canadian government in Ottawa or from the majority of Canadians who live in Ontario and Quebec, Alberta has linked its future to priorities set in boardrooms in the United States and Europe rather than setting an independent course to benefit the provincial economy and the Canadian state as a whole. As a result, powerful foreign business leaders and politicians have set selfish development strategies that presumptuously include Alberta's petroleum as part of their global reserves.

Though Alberta's rate of discovery of oil and gas has been in decline since the 1950s – an anniversary that went unnoticed by the media – the cumulative negative effects on the people of the province have outlasted the benefits of the development process. As more and more wells are drilled and more pipelines are installed to move a shrinking quantity of petroleum products to markets, the social and environmental effects on the three million people who call Alberta their home are increasing in intensity.

There is no end in sight to the extraction of oil and gas in Alberta, but the birthright has been squandered. Short-sighted policies and ideological blinders have prevented the people of Alberta from diversifying the economy and creating a society that can outlast the boom and bust cycles and continue to expand. Instead of a stable economy, we celebrate our centennial in a province with the lowest minimum wage in the country, with education institutions starved of resources, and a health care system in crisis (and as one of the only two provinces that charges its citizens an annual premium for health care). The expensive infrastructure developed by an avowedly free-enterprise government in the 1970s and 1980s (in spite of the fact that it owned a bank, an airline, an oil company, and a major share in an oil sands project) needs a massive infusion of capital in order to survive. Alberta's cultural institutions are similarly strapped for cash and must beg for support from corporations that extract their pound of flesh by placing their names on the buildings where artists, playwrights, and musicians perform.

"Please God," the bumper sticker said during one of the downturns in the provincial economy, "give it to me just one more time and I promise not to piss it all away!"

Calgary Communities
From Development to Social Character
by Wayne K. D. Davies and Ivan J. Townshend

The term *community* is an imprecise one that can refer to a settle-ment as a whole, or to groups of people that owe their cohesion to their common associations, such as shared values or interests. But community, in the sense in which it is used here, is also used to refer to situations in which there are relationships and associations between peo-ple *within* a specific or common area, producing the functional as well as spatial linkages that define what creates community areas within cities. Most cities have examples of such territorial communities. However, in Calgary, the virtually complete coverage of community districts for the city as a whole, and the degree of activism of these associations within many of these areas, make them rather unique in the western world. Although Calgary communities may play a limited role in the structuring of the city compared to the more powerful forces of private developers and the decisions of municipal, provincial, or federal bureaucrats, these locally organized groups do play an important part in the life of the city, despite the general decline in the voluntary sector in western society in the last 30 years. This is partially due to increased levels of female labor force participation, which has meant there is less social capital avail-able to support voluntary and local residential activities, as well as the greater dependence on the car and other communication devices that have increased the spatial spread and flexibility of people's social and economic lives beyond their immediate neighborhood. Neverthe-less, communities in Calgary are far from dead, although they vary considerably in their degree of activity and influence, as well as in their morphology and social character, as will be shown in subsequent sections.

Figure 1 shows that there are 183 community districts in Calgary that are now recognized by the city. However, some of these areas, especial-ly the smaller ones in the inner city, have combined to form a single community association. The Federation of Calgary Communities (FCC), an umbrella advisory body established in 1961 by 47 different community associations, was created to represent the collective interest of the associations throughout the city.

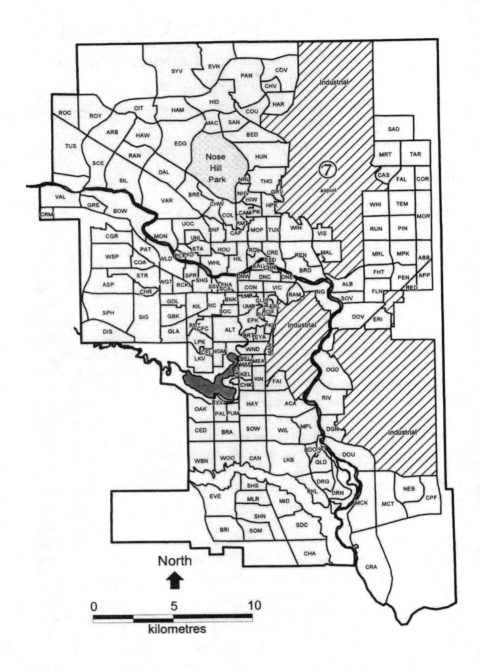

Figure 1. Calgary Community Districts, 2004.

Legend: Abbreviations of Community District Names.

ABB Abbeydale	DNC Downtown Core	MCK McKenzie Lake	SAN Sandstone Valley
ACA Acadia	DNE Downtown East Village	MCT McKenzie Towne	SCA Scarboro
ALB Albert Pk/ Radisson Hts	DNW Downtown Westend	MEA Meadowlark Park	SCE Scenic Acres
ALT Altadore	DOU Douglasdale Estates	MID Midnapore	SDC Sundance
APP Applewood Park	DOV Dover	MIS Mission	SHG Shaganappi
ARB Arbour Lake	DRG Deer Ridge	MLR Millrise	SHN Shawnessy
ASP Aspen Woods	DRN Deer Run	MON Montgomery	SHS Shawnee Slopes
BDO Bonavista Downs	EAG Eagle Ridge	MOP Mount Pleasant	SIG Signal Hill
BED Beddington Heights	EAU Eau Claire	MOR Monterey Park	SIL Silver Springs
BEL Bel-Aire	EDG Edgemont	MPK Marlborough Park	SNA Sunalta
BNF Banff Trail	EPK Elbow Park	MPL Maple Ridge	SOC South Calgary
BNK Bankview	ERI Erin Woods	MRL Marlborough	SOM Somerset
BOW Bowness	ERL Erlton	MRT Martindale	SOV Southview
BRA Braeside	EVE Evergreen	NGM North Glenmore Park	SOW Southwood
BRD Bridgeland /Riverside	EYA Elboya	NHU North Haven Upper	SPH Springbank Hill
BRE Brentwood	FAI Fairview	NHV North Haven	SPR Spruce Cliff
BRI Bridlewood	FAL Falconridge	OAK Oakridge	SSD Sunnyside
BRT Brittania	FHT Forest Heights	OGD Ogden	SSW Scarboro/ Sunalta West
BYV Bayview	FLN Forest Lawn	PAL Palliser	STA St. Andrews Heights
CAM Cambrian Heights	GBK Glenbrook	PAN Panorama Hills	STR Strathcona Park
CAN Canyon Meadows	GDL Glendale	PAT Patterson	TAR Taradale
CAP Capitol Hill	GLA Glamorgan	PEN Penbrooke Meadows	TEM Temple
CAS Castleridge	GRE Greenwood/ Greenbriar	PIN Pineridge	THO Thorncliffe
CED Cedarbrae	GRV Greenview	PKD Parkdale	TUS Tuscany
CFL CFB-Lincoln Park	HAM Hamptons	PKH Parkhill	TUX Tuxedo Park
CHA Chaparral	HAR Harvest Hills	PKL Parkland	UMR Upper Mount Royal
CHK Chinook Park	HAW Hawkwood	POI Point Mckay	UNI University Heights
CHN Chinatown	HAY Haysboro	PUM Pump Hill	UOC University of Calgary
CHR Christie Park	HID Hidden Valley	QLD Queensland	VAL Valley Ridge
CHW Charleswood	HIL Hillhurst	QPK Queens Park Village	VAR Varsity
CIT Citadel	HIW Highwood	RAM Ramsay	VIC Victoria Park
CLI Cliff Bungalow	HOU Hounsfield Hts/ Briar Hill	RAN Ranchlands	VIS Vista Heights
COA Coach Hill	HPK Highland Park	RCK Rosscarrock	WBN Woodbine
COL Collingwood	HUN Huntington Hills	RDL Rosedale	WGT Westgate
CON Connaught	ING Inglewood	RED Red Carpet	WHI Whitehorn
COR Coral Springs	KEL Kelvin Grove	REN Renfrew	WHL West Hillhurst
COU Country Hills	KIL Killarney/Glengarry	RIC Richmond	WIL Willow Park
COV Coventry Hills	KIN Kingsland	RID Rideau Park	WIN Winston Hts/ Mountview
CRE Crescent Heights	LKB Lake Bonavista	RIV Riverbend	WLD Wildwood
DAL Dalhousie	LKP Lincoln Park	RMT Rosemont	WND Windsor Park
DGN Douglas Glen	LKV Lakeview	ROC Rocky Ridge	WOO Woodlands
DIA Diamond Cove	LMR Lower Mount Royal	ROX Roxboro	WSP West Springs
DIS Discovery Ridge	MAC Macewan Glen	ROY Royal Oak	
	MAF Mayfair	RUN Rundle	
	MAL Mayland Heights	RUT Rutland Park	
		SAD Saddle Ridge	

In 2004 the FCC recognized 131 community association areas, each representing a formally organized territorial community district or set of districts. In origin, these community areas were based on the growth of local informal ratepayer associations and community clubs. Although both were place-based associations, the former were concerned primarily about the provision of facilities and services, such as paved streets, lighting, and sanitation, as well as local tax rates; while the latter dealt mainly with the development of recreational associations and social facilities for the residents. Two of the earliest community associations were those in Bridgeland in 1908, and Scarborough in the 1920s, in which the former organized local recreational activities and raised money for a local community hall, whilst the latter was to be the first to be called a "community association." Neilson (1975, 31), writing about the ratepayers' association in Bowness in the early 1930s, noted that "the ratepayers association was the backbone of the social life of the community and provided most of the fun and games of local residents," such as dances, box socials, charity benefits, and later, children's sports.

By the 1930s some of these community associations began to register themselves under the Alberta Societies Act, adopting specific by-laws and constitutions. Like all non-profit registered organizations, they were bound by law to file annual financial reports with the Alberta Corporate Registry. The official registration of these locality-based associations – variously described as clubs, associations, ratepayers associations, and community associations – all within specific areas, makes it possible to accurately measure the growth of these associations. By 1950 there were 10 registered associations. These grew to 41 by 1960; 67 by 1970; 100 by 1980; and 123 by 1990. New community associations are formed in virtually all newly established subdivisions and community districts. By 2004, the 183 designated community districts in the city were represented by 131 separate community associations. Almost all of these (94%) are members of the umbrella Federation of Calgary Communities.

There is no comprehensive, regular, city-wide enumeration or monitoring of the array of different community association activities in the city of Calgary. The only complete survey to date was produced by Townshend (1992). Although the precise numbers have probably changed, this survey is still useful in showing the way that the various indicators of community association activity vary.

Townshend's results showed that 80% of the community associations in Calgary had some kind of community hall or community centre. These were mainly developed as a result of local citizen fundraising efforts, supplemented by provincial matching grants and low cost land leases from the city. However, in recent years a few developers, such as Carma in Tuscany, or Qualico in Crestmont, have built halls or "resident clubs" in their new communities to encourage the growth of the local community association and to help sales of houses in these developing areas. In 1992 the community centres or halls in Calgary had a median value of $472 000, but ranged from $29 000 (Elboya) to $4 450 000 (Acadia). These facilities also varied considerably in size, with an occupant capacity ranging from 50 (Elboya) to 1 200 persons (Thorncliffe), but with a median of 225 persons for the community halls as a whole. These larger community buildings are not simply a hall, meeting rooms, and kitchen facilities, but may include tennis courts, gyms, local pubs, and swimming pools or hockey rinks. The buildings constructed in the late 1960s and 1970s tend to be the largest in the city, reflecting the prosperity of the time and the availability of matching grants from the province.

The communities also vary considerably in the number of different functions or activities that are carried out by local members. Townshend's review of all such activities in one year revealed that there are generally seven major types of activities: Sports and Sports-Related Instruction Programs; Educational/Instructional Programs (non-sport related); Fitness and Lifestyle Programs; Community Environment and Aesthetic Programs; Community Socials and Special Events; Community Safety, Security, and Information Programs; and Charity, Goodwill, and Social Service-Related Programs. Yet the associations vary considerably in the number and mix of activities offered throughout the year. Some communities, such as Dalhousie and Varsity, offered more than 30 different functions in one year, while others, such as the Downtown community association, offered no activities during the year. The mean value of 8.5 programs per year for the communities as a whole shows that these organizations are generally active. But it is also worth noting that not all of the activities are run by, and for, the community members. Many community associations have a significant number of activities carried out through co-sponsorship arrangements with the city's Parks and Recreation department, with a mean of 4.5 such co-sponsored functions for the communities as a whole.

	5 Lowest Community Associations		Value	5 Highest Community Associations		Value
Facility Value median **$472 5000**	MCK	McKenzie	$8 000	ACA	Acadia	$4 450 000
	EYA	Elboya	$29 000	THO	Thorncliffe/ Greenview	$4 000 000
	UMR	Upper Mount Royal	$60 000	WHL	West Hill- hurst	$3 412 500
	SHG	Shaganappi	$85 000	BOW	Bowness	$3 100 000
	BNF	Banff Trail	$100 000	HUN	Huntington Hills	$2 913 750
Facility Capacity median 225	EYA	Elboya	50	THO	Thorncliffe	1200
	SHG	Shaganappi	60	WHL	West Hill hurst	840
	STA	St. Andrews Heights	70	BRD	Bridgeland	800
	SPR	Spruce Cliff	80	BOW	Bowness	675
	BNF	Banff Trail	85	DRN	Deer Run	610
Annual Income median **$64 459**	DNE	Downtown East	$0	HUN	Huntington Hills	$1 210 088
	APP	Applewood	$579	THO	Thorncliffe/ Greenview	$1 090 978
	MRT	Martindale	$2 104	LKB	Lake Bonavista	$863 942
	MAC	MacEwan	$2 872	BOW	Bowness	$794 994
	UNI	University Heights	$2 878	ACA	Acadia	$771 344
Household Membership % median 15.5%	DNW/DNC	Downtown	0	SCA	Scarboro	78.74
	APP	Applewood	1.65	PKD	Parkdale	78.20
	BRD	Bridgeland	1.91	MEA	Meadowlake Park	59.68
	RIC	Richmond	2.03	PKL	Parkland	50.48
	EYA	Elboya	3.41	WLD	Wildwood	50.07
Number of Locally Sponsored Programs in one year median 6.5	APP	Applewood	0	DAL	Dalhousie	37
	ERL	Erlton	0	VAR	Varsity	30
	BRT	Brittania	0	THO	Thorncliffe/ Greenview	27
	RID/ROX	Rideau/ Roxbury	0	SIL	Silver Springs	25
	CFC/CFH/CFL	Canadian Forces	0	HIL/SSD	Hillhurst/ Sunnyside	24
Number of Shared Programs in one year median 2.5	APP	Applewood	0	TEM	Temple	24
	BRE	Brentwood	0	DRN	Deer Run	22
	REN	Renfrew	0	MPK	Marlborough Park	22
	EDG	Edgemont	0	SIL	Silver Springs	19
	HIW	Highwood	0	DOV	Dover	16

Table 1. Selected Indicators of Community Associations, 1992.

Despite the variations in the level of activity and the size of buildings, it cannot be claimed that all residents of a community district are active members of these associations. Oroposa (1989) and others have shown that in North America, most community associations do not have membership levels above a fifth of the local households. This is reflected in Calgary where the survey showed that on average only 18.9% of households were enrolled as members in their local association, even though the typical annual fee of $20 was a modest amount. Again, however, Table 1 shows the wide range in memberships levels between the community associations, with five communities having over 50%, and five communities with under 4% of households enrolled as members in the local association. The annual operating budgets and incomes of these associations also shows major variations, with a median income of 152 000 dollars, yet with extremes of under 600 dollars in Applewood and 1.2 million dollars in Huntington Hills in 1992. Most communities finance their activities by a number of actions. For some of the smaller and older communities, a significant share of annual revenue is derived from activity fees and renting out their hall and facilities to various groups, such as dance groups, bingos, and day cares, although on average, rentals only account for 23% of community association incomes for the city as a whole. The larger entities also raise a significant amount of their income from a series of other activities, with the larger associations persuading members to volunteer to spend two or three nights helping in the provincial casinos, which may bring in over 50 000 dollars for the association.

Attempts to quantitatively explain these variations by the socio-economic status, family, or ethnic status of various areas did not produce adequate explanations for the level of community activity variations (Davies and Townshend, 1994). Therefore, the more plausible explanation at work seems to be the enthusiasm of local residents to generate and participate in community activities. However, there is a tendency for the poorest and the wealthiest areas of the city to have lower levels of community activity, a product of private clubs providing social facilities in the richer areas, and perhaps a lack of organization and participation of the residents in the lower income areas. By contrast, some of the biggest community facilities are found in the middle income suburban areas built in the late 1960s and 1970s, but again not all these areas have extensive community facilities.

But community associations are much more than a vehicle for socialization among residents or the delivery of various services to their local area. The community associations are voluntary organizations of local residents that fulfill four other main functions. One is the *modification or improvement of existing conditions*, such as helping in the creation of small parks on previously identified wasteland sites, such as Tom Campbell's Bluff overlooking the Calgary Zoo. Another typical example is the modification of traffic flows through a residential area, such as the closure of roads to through-traffic, or the addition of stop signs, although these are usually recommendations that have to be approved by the city's traffic department. Some of the communities, such as Marlborough Park in the east, have, with the co-operation of the police and judicial services, established community courts for young offenders in recent years. This system of community justice usually involves some measure of community service as punishment for the lower grade crimes, rather than pushing first time offenders into the criminal system where they run the risk of being labelled as criminals and beginning a life of crime.

Another important function is the *identification of missing needs or resources*. One important example is seen in the way that communities have often banded together to lobby city hall, such as for more parks in particular areas of the city. Perhaps the best recent example of this is the fact that there are over 25 new communities on the edge of the city in 2004 that do not have a school, due to the limited financial resources of the school boards, even though land is zoned for such functions in these community districts. This means that children are bussed out of their local area, to the detriment of establishing local ties. These communities are constantly lobbying the government to provide schools in their area. In the 1970s, the activist inner city community of Hillhurst-Sunnyside, recognizing the need for social housing, raised funds to create a number of social houses for seniors and low income people in their area, although this activity was spun off to a separate organization in the 1990s. Other examples of the provision of additional services can be identified. For example, communities such as Strathcona Park have persuaded residents to pay more city taxes to cover the costs of more frequent grass cutting and maintenance in order to improve the look of the area.

Still another important function is the activity often called *turf defence*, in which residents unite in opposition to the widening of roads through a community area, or the addition of halfway houses, shopping areas, or other facilities that residents may not want. However, not all such actions have been successful. For example, in the mid-1990s, Dalhousie and nearby associations tried to prevent the building of a new shopping centre on the site of a former mobile home park bordering

Crowchild Trail. They were unsuccessful in their efforts and the Dalhousie Station shopping centre was subsequently built. One of the most dramatic and successful examples of this kind of turf-defence can be seen in the case of Hillhurst-Sunnyside, one of the most active of all community associations (Stanley 1985). Like many inner city areas in North American cities experiencing transformation during the 1960s and 1970s (Ley 2000), there was massive development pressure in the late 1960s to transform the Hillhurst-Sunnyside area into offices and apartment blocks. Through the community association, its citizens mobilized to prevent wholesale redevelopment and to maintain the single home character of the area, although many parts of the community have been gentrified in last 30 years. But the most comprehensive alteration of a community area through the influence of community activity can be seen in the case of Chinatown. Although this area has only 1 210 permanent residents today, mainly seniors in several high-rise apartment blocks, it contains over 170 commercial and professional activities, an increase from the 30 in 1961. Hence the area has become an important economic core for the expanding Chinese community. However, in the late 1960s, it was threatened with extinction due to inner city renewal and new highway projects. At that time, a group of concerned people of Chinese heritage in the Sien Lok society began the process of persuading the city to adopt an area redevelopment policy to rescue the area and to make it distinctive by the use of Chinese symbols in road signs and light standards, and to encourage all new development to adopt architectural styles to reflect the Chinese heritage. This was confirmed by the city's Area Design Brief in 1976. The centerpiece of these changes was the construction of a new cultural centre, library, restaurant, and community hall in 1992. This was a replica of the Temple of Heaven in Beijing, and was built by craftsmen from China with money raised by the Chinese community throughout the city rather than only from within the local area. In this case the threat of development began the process of transformation that added important new resources and a new architectural style to Chinatown, so the area has become a cultural and economic core rather than a residential area.

In several of the above examples the community association can also be seen to have acted as a *vehicle of opinion* to city hall. But in Calgary this is not simply a case-by-case response to perceived needs or problems. All proposed major planning and development changes by the city are now routinely passed on to community associations for their opinion. This means that the grass roots are given a voice in the discussion of these changes, although the final decision is always made by the city council. This is justified by the judicial fact that the municipality is the responsible level of government for its administrative area, so community activity has no formal role. This, of course, is the major weakness of the community associations; they have no legitimate and separate role in the governance of cities, or rather in their own area. In addition, having no mandatory taxing powers and no legislated claim to a share of city tax revenues, except by sharing programs with the city, means that their activities are always circumscribed by their ability to raise money for local activities. This is in contrast to communities in many western countries where local communities are allocated a proportion – usually under 2% – of city taxes for their discretionary use within the local area. One emerging problem for community associations is the aging of many community halls and the need for renewal and repair. It is unlikely that many community associations can raise the money to finance these renovations from their own resources and it is still problematic whether the city is prepared to help with the substantial costs that will be involved.

Calgary communities also vary considerably in their morphology or design. The initial residential areas were based on a grid-iron form, a subdivision of the township and range system that allocated land in the Prairie provinces. This grid had the advantage of precisely locating each plot to be sold and settled and provided an exact city address based on the system of streets running east and west of a centrally located Centre Street, and avenues running north and south of the Bow river, although local topographic variations have caused some modifications of the simple system. However, distinctive community areas did emerge within the grid – areas usually defined by major traffic arteries or natural barriers that provided boundaries to the various areas that were given distinctive names by the early developers. Exceptions to this typical grid development can be seen by upper- and middle-income areas, such as Mt. Royal and Scarborough. In the early twentieth century the Canadian Pacific Railway land development unit adopted the planning principles of high income suburban areas in the U.S.A. and garden cities in the United Kingdom (Davies and Herbert, 1993). This meant that both community districts were built according to a defined master plan for these areas, with curvilinear streets, larger lots, and the addition of open spaces and trees to create a more rural setting.

In the late 1950s the city adopted the principles of neighborhood unit planning for all new residential areas, linked to the modifications in design originating in post-war British and eastern Canadian new towns. This type of planned urban development meant that new houses could not be built independently by adding houses on to the pre-existing grid; instead, developers had to create a master plan for each of these new residential areas, or community districts, that had to be approved by the city, before individual builders were able to build on the various plots. Although these community plans varied in detail, they were alike in several important ways in that they tried to encourage community co-operation and provide services. Most tried to reduce through-traffic by banishing main roads, or at least most of them, on the outer boundaries of the area; a central area was created to provide a park, elementary school, and small local shopping area, which sometimes was placed on the edge of areas; typically, 10% of the area was left for recreational purposes, and the internal road system began to adopt the curvilinear patterns previously only found in upper income areas. In some cases, such as Varsity Village, the addition of walkways at the back of houses enabled access to the recreational facilities and local school without, as far as possible, crossing roads. A crucial part of the planning was that these were almost exclusively residential areas, apart from the small shopping area, since industrial activity was now banned in these zones.

Through time there has been a modification of the initial neighborhood principles, in what is now called planned urban development, by the addition of many new features. One was the addition of cul-de-sacs, which were intended to reduce traffic flow and to encourage household co-operation, although examples can be found in the earlier phase. A further development of this was the deliberate subdivision of some areas into groups of houses or cells, with an internal connecting road and with a distinctive name. Another was a stricter adherence to the practice of putting main roads on the outside of the area, with smaller local traffic roads and a limited number of entrance roads, although some communities still have major roads cutting through the area. Noise barriers were also added on the outside of the community to reduce traffic noise, either retro-fitted by concrete walls, or low earth mounds, or even fences on the outer boundaries. By the late 1980s more imposing entrance features were developed, such as a larger wall, with a distinctive community logo at the main entrances to the area. In addition, increasing amounts of recreational land were developed within the area.

However, a unique feature of Calgary's new community areas, from the planning of Willow Park and Lake Bonavista by Keith Developments in the late 1960s, has been the creation of new residential communities around a major recreational feature, such as a golf course in the case of the former and a lake in the latter. By 2004 there were nine communities within the city designed around a golf course and seven around a lake and a surrounding recreational area. These lake areas are only accessible to residents of the area who maintain the facilities by means of a mandatory annual fee that all homeowners in the community have to pay. Most of the initial golf course-centred communities also operated on this principle, with community residents able to join on favorable terms, but many are now private facilities.

Architectural controls, such as house color and roofing materials, is typical of the new areas, and is enforced through restrictive covenants. Finally, the adoption of a distinctive name by developers can be seen in the communities. The trend has been to use names of high income areas from other parts of the world, or names that reflect water, trees, extensive acres, and heights – all designed to create a positive image of the area to attract would-be buyers. Within these areas the city initially adopted a principle that all internal roads in the community should begin with the first letter of the community name, although subsequently the community name has been used. An example of the latter is Silver Springs Boulevard in the community of Silver Springs.

During the past 20 years two other new trends can be recognized. One is a greater concern for environmental issues, which has led to the decision to maintain any distinctive initial ecological areas in the zones to be developed, so that pre-existing landscape features such as small copses of trees, rocky areas, streams, gullies, and especially sloughs, are preserved as recreational features. For instance, in the new area of Bridlewood the local slough has pathways around and across it, with indicator boards to draw attention to the distinctive fauna and flora. Another trend has been the addition of more and more open space in the plan beyond the provincial land-use legislation standards.

A more recent trend stems from the adoption of *new urbanism or neo-traditional* urban planning principles in a few areas, most noticeably MacKenzie Towne. By planning for higher residential densities and more integrated land-use functions, these community designs aim to address growing concerns about the growth of low-density suburban sprawl. This has led to the adoption of higher densities through smaller lots and townhouse development, and the plan for the incorporation of employment zones other than shopping areas in the community area. Residential streets are made narrower to slow vehicular traffic, garages have been removed to the back of houses, and homes are typically constructed with a front porch to encourage street life and community interaction. In addition, the whole area is being built in distinctive clusters of development, labelled as various "villages." Finally, the new communications revolution has led some developers in the late 1990s to create "wired" or "e-communities" in which all homes are connected to the internet and to one another through a neighborhood intra-net, which is another attempt to foster community cohesion, just like the 1920s neighborhood unit design principles. Lake Chapparal was one of the first of these areas, although the presence of a lake shows that many communities have several of these design and content features. The missing trend in North American contemporary community design in Calgary is that of real gated communities, except in a few senior citizen complexes within the community as a whole, for such developments have been prevented by City Council. However, the separation of so many of Calgary's community districts, through their limited access points and their traffic noise fences and earthen boundaries, would make it easy to transform such distinctive entities into gated areas if the need arose.

The community areas of Calgary also vary in their social character. Figures 2 and 3 are graphs that show the variations between these areas in some of the key features that have been shown to differentiate social areas in cities through multivariate analysis (Davies and Murdie, 1991), but using key indicators from the 2001 census in this case. Each community district is identified by a single dot on each graph, according to its values on the two chosen variables. Figure 2 shows a clear separation of the communities by the variables that provide a measure of economic status and family size. Most of the high status communities are located in a sector running south-west from the Mt. Royal district, whereas the lower income areas are found in the north-east. However, the family size variable separates upper-income areas, such as Rideau, that have low family size, as well as differentiating the downtown and inner city areas such as Victoria Park and Bankview which have low-income and small households, from the larger family, low-income areas of the north-east. In Figure 3 the difference between communities with mature and old people and those with high numbers of visible minorities born overseas is also clear. The most distinctive community is Chinatown, with over 97% visible minority and 57% elderly. As for the others, the graph shows a difference between the relatively new north-east suburban communities, such as Coral Springs, Monterey Park, and Applewood, that have high levels of visible minorities yet few elderly. However, the Eagle Ridge and Palliser areas, that are part of the south-west high status sector, have more older people and few minorities. Many of the inner suburban areas that were built in the 1960s, such as Glamorgan and Killarney, now contain an aging population, which often means there are low levels of participation in the local community associations, leading to fears of their survival. These two graphs represent some of the most important features of the variations in the social character of the community areas. However these are only the most basic variations; other census-based variables, and especially cognitive and attitudinal dimensions (Townshend and Davies, 1999; Davies, Chan, and Townshend, 1999; Townshend, 2001), could be used to show the nuances between the various areas, providing a more detailed description of the social mosaic of the city.

Most of Calgary has been built during various phases of suburban expansion during the last century. However, this does not mean that the city is without differentiation in these areas. It has been shown that residential communities within Calgary still play an important role in the life of the city, but vary considerably in the functions or levels of activity carried out within the areas, as well as in their designs and social character. Within the wider context of Canadian cities, it can be argued that Calgary communities may be the most distinctive sets of areas in the country, given the way that many have pioneered so many different activities and show such distinctive designs. Obviously this essay has focused only upon the locality-based associations and districts within the city. For many people, other types of community, without a necessary inclusive locational basis of community associations, such as ethnic or church groups, also play important roles for their members. This means that in the context of an increasingly connected world, it is important not to forget the importance of local communities, of whatever type in the life of a city such as Calgary, even though so many of our linkages may be to workplace, interest groups, and family that may not be spatially contiguous.

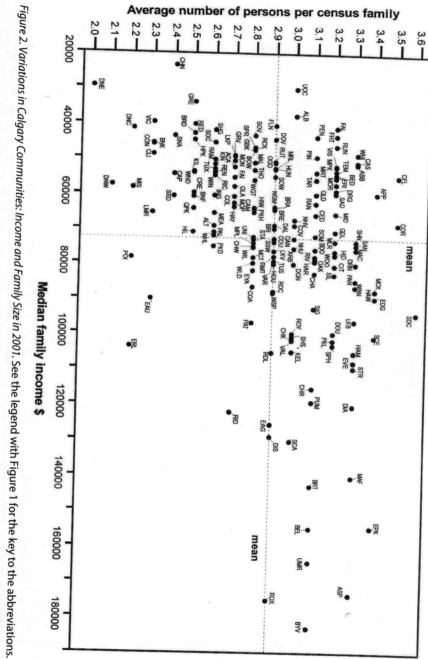

Figure 2. *Variations in Calgary Communities: Income and Family Size in 2001. See the legend with Figure 1 for the key to the abbreviations.*

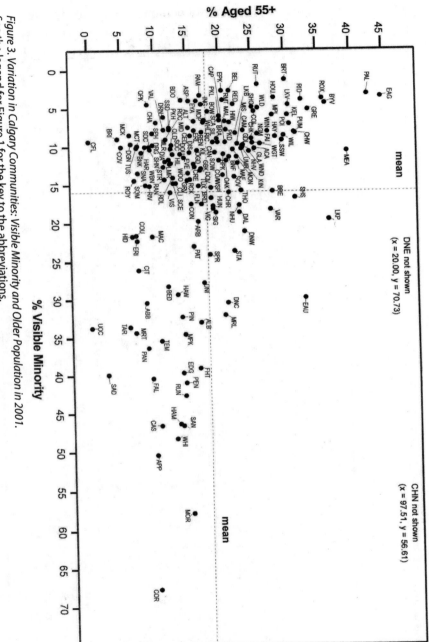

Figure 3. *Variation in Calgary Communities: Visible Minority and Older Population in 2001.*
See the legend for Figure 1 for the key to the abbreviations.

References

Davies, W. K. D., Chan, J., and Townshend, I. J., 1999, "How Do Communities Differ? Empirical Evidence for Behavioural and Cognitive-Affective Dimensions of Community" in Aguilar, A. and Escamilla, I. (eds.), *Problems of Megacities: Social Inequalities, Environmental Risk and Urban Governance*, Universidad Nacional Autonoma de Mexico, Institute of Geography, 529-542.

Davies, W. K. D. and Herbert, D. T., 1993, *Communities Within Cities*, London and New York: Belhaven and Halstead-John Wiley.

Davies, W. K. D. and Murdie, R. A., 1991, "Measuring the Social Ecology of Canadian Cities" in D. Ley and L. Bourne (eds.) *Social Geography of the Canadian Cities*, Kingston: McGill-Queen's University Press, 52-75.

Davies W. K. D. and Townshend, I. J., 1994, "How Do Community Associations Vary," *Urban Studies*, 31 (10), 1739-1761.

Ley, D., 2000. "The Inner City" in T. Bunting and P. Filion (eds.) *Canadian Cities in Transition*, Second Ed., Don Mills, Ontario: Oxford University Press, 274-302.

Neilson, D., 1975, "Bowness," in H. Surplis (ed.), *Communities of Calgary: From Scattered Towns to a Major City*, Calgary: Century Calgary Publications, p1-64

Oroposa, R. S., 1989, "Neighbourhood Associations, Political Repertoires and Neighbourhood Exits," *Sociological Perspectives* 32(4), 434-452.

Stanley, Harold L., 1985, "Evaluation of Citizen Participation in the Planning Process in Hillhurst-Sunnyside." Unpublished MDP Project, Faculty of Environmental Design, University of Calgary.

Townshend, I. J., 1992, Calgary Community Associations. Unpublished MA Thesis, University of Calgary, 1992.

Townshend, I. J., 2001, "The Contribution of Social and Experiential Community Structures to the Intra-Urban Ecology of Well-Being," *Canadian Journal of Urban Research*, 10(2), 175-215. Special issue on urban quality of life.

Townshend, I. J. and Davies, W. K. D., 1999, "Identifying the Elements of Community Character: A Case Study of Community Dimensionality in Old Age Residential Areas," *Research in Community Sociology*, Volume 9: 219-251.

Contributing Authors

DAVID BIRRELL – *"FM159"*
A geophysicist and teacher, Dave is currently involved in the development of interpretive information regarding the Canadian Rockies. He is the author of several books including *Calgary's Mountain Panorama* and *50 Roadside Panoramas of the Canadian Rockies*. He lives in Nanton, Alberta, where he is director with the Nanton Lancaster Air Museum, focusing on display and website development.

JIM BOWMAN – *"A Francophone Community Leader"*
Jim was born in Edmonton and educated at the Simon Fraser University and the University of British Columbia. He has worked as a professional librarian and archivist in British Columbia and Alberta, and is presently at the Glenbow Archives. He lives in the Calgary community of Mission, where he is active in community politics and serves as chair of the Friends of Rouleau House/Les amis de la maison Rouleau.

JENNIFER COOK BOBROVITZ – *"Reasoned Speculation"*
Jennifer is the archivist-curator for Calgary's historic Lougheed House. She has worked as a teacher, chief librarian for the *Calgary Sun*, archivist for the Glenbow Museum, and as Calgary Public Library's local history librarian. Jennifer has written extensively about heritage for the *Calgary Herald*, *Calgary Real Estate News*, *Alberta History*, *Legacy*, and *Glenbow* magazines. In 2003 she won the Heritage Canada Foundation's Award for Journalism and the City of Calgary's Heritage Award.

BRIAN BRENNAN – *"A Warrior Among Businessmen"*
Brian is an award-winning Alberta journalist and author who specializes in books about the colorful personalities and social history of Western Canada. Titles include *Romancing the Rockies*, and *Scoundrels and Scallywags*. Born and educated in Ireland, he is also the author of *Máire Bhuí Ní Laoire: A Poet of Her People*. He was the first winner of the Dave Greber Freelance Writers Award 2004, won two Western Magazine Gold Awards, and the national Hollobon Award.

352 Remembering Chinook Country

TRUDY COWAN – *"Reasoned Speculation"*
Trudy Cowan has long worked with museums and historic sites at the Glenbow, Fort Calgary, Alberta Historical Resources Foundation and as a private consultant. For the past 17 years, she has co-ordinated efforts to restore and reuse Lougheed House. Dr. Cowan has also served Canada's heritage at the local, provincial, and national levels, including the CCHS, Historic Sites and Monuments Board of Canada and Heritage Canada Foundation.

LOUISE CRANE – *"Role Models for Today"*
Louise is a Métis of Cree descent. She is a graduate of the Heritage Resource Management Program at the University of Calgary. Her career brought her from Fort George Buckingham House, interpreting the history of the Aboriginal women in the fur trade, to Lac La Biche Mission and residential schools, to St. Albert and the role of the Métis in establishing community to Fort Calgary and the importance of Métis in Calgary's history.

WAYNE K. D. DAVIES – *"Calgary Communities"*
Dr. Davies was educated in the University of Wales and taught in the Universities of Southampton and Swansea before coming to the University of Calgary where he is Professor of Geography. He has written over 120 papers and chapters in various areas of human geography and has authored or edited 10 books, the last two of which are *Writing Geographical Exploration* (University of Calgary Press, 2003) and *Monitoring Cities* (with I. Townshend, International Geographical Union, 2002).

CHERYL FOGGO – *"My Home is Over Jordan"*
Cheryl is a successful journalist, poet, screenwriter, playwright, fiction and non-fiction author, and young adult novelist. Several of her works have been nominated for provincial and national awards, while the documentary she wrote and directed, "The Journey of Lesra Martin," won the bronze award at the Columbus International Film and Video Festival. She is currently working on a new novel and another documentary film.

DAVID FINCH – *"Alberta's Birthright"*
David holds the M. A. in Canadian History from the University of Calgary and is the author of more than a dozen books on the history of the Canadian West.

MAXWELL FORAN – *"Apostle of the Arts"*
Max Foran is the biographer of Stanford Perrott and has written widely on Calgary and other Western Canadian subjects. He is presently Assistant Professor in the Faculty of Communication and Culture at the University of Calgary.

JOHN GILPIN – *"The Calgary Irrigation Company"*
John is a Calgary-based historian who has written on the urban and business history of the West as well as the development of irrigation. His publications include *Edmonton, Gateway to the North: An Illustrated History; Prairie Promises: History of the Bow River Irrigation District;* and *Quenching the Prairie Thirst: A History of the Magrath, Raymond, Taber and St. Mary River Irrigation Districts.*

JENNIFER HAMBLIN – *"Everybody's Favorite"*
Jennifer is a contract archivist and reference librarian at the Glenbow Museum. With Masters Degrees in History and Library Science, she enjoys researching and writing about Alberta history. She is currently co-authoring the biography of George and Norma Piper Pocaterra.

FAYE REINEBERG HOLT – *"From the Heart and Pocketbook"*
Faye is a writer, editor, speaker, and workshop instructor. She has published 10 books on topics related to Western Canada's social history. Her most recent book, titled *Prairie Twins: Alberta and Saskatchewan Photographic Memories 1905-2005,* celebrates the 100th birthday of the two provinces.

SALLY JENNINGS – *"Urban Planning in Calgary"*
Sally is a writer, editor, teacher, and urban planner. She has compiled the Chronicle of Significant Alberta Architecture and was co-chair of Doors Open and Calgary Architecture Week 2004. Sally is also co-founder of the Calgary Civic Trust and edited their conference proceedings, *Heritage Covenants & Preservation* (UofC Press, 2004). Aside from academic editing, she is currently writing books on travel and urban planning.

KARIM-ALY KASSAM – *"Muslim Presence in Alberta"*
In 2003, *Alberta Venture Magazine* named Professor Kassam among the 50 most influential people of Alberta, and in 2004 *Maclean's Guide to Canadian University* named him one of the most popular professors at the University of Calgary. Whether teaching Economic Development in the classroom, or serving communities worldwide, Karim-Aly derives deep personal satisfaction from helping others grow to their full potential.

BRENDA MCCAFFERTY – *"Polo Anyone?"*
Brenda is a fourth generation Calgarian and archivist of the Legal Archives Society of Alberta (LASA). After graduating with a degree in History from the University of Western Ontario, Brenda began her career in 1990 with the Glenbow Archives and worked for several years at the City of Calgary Archives. She has been employed with LASA since 1999 and resides in Calgary with her beloved husband Sean and children Erin and Conor. They enjoy travelling and exploring the historical sites of Southern Alberta.

VERNA MACKENZIE – *"Our Prairie Origin"*
Verna Tate MacKenzie is a native Calgarian, born in 1916. She worked the fields of teaching, merchandising, and banking. Verna has always been interested in the early history of Calgary and Alberta, as well as the arts and writing. As a member of the CCHS, Verna has the opportunity to explore her interests and share her wealth of information.

DAVID MITTELSTADT – *"Calgary's Early Courts"*
David attended the University of Calgary and the University of Western Ontario, and holds a Master of Arts in History. He presently works in Calgary as a historian and heritage consultant. He has written a book about Alberta's historic courthouses, *Foundations of Justice*, which will be published by the University of Calgary Press in 2005. He has recently completed another book, on the history of skiing in Calgary, to be published by Rocky Mountain Books. His work has also appeared in *Legacy* magazine.

FRITS PANNEKOEK – *"A Strong-Minded Woman"*
Frits Pannekoek is Director of Information Resources and Associate Professor at the University of Calgary, as well as the author of several books and numerous articles on Western Canadian history.

BOB PEARSON – *"Live, On the Air"*
Bob holds a Master of Arts Degree in History from the University of Calgary. He has a keen interest in the history of old time radio. Bob has worked as an interpreter at museums and historic sites for many years. Currently, he is employed at Fort Calgary.

J. KENNETH PENLEY – *"Shall We Dance?"*
Ken is a native Calgarian and retired pharmacist. He has been a volunteer for the Historical Society of Alberta and the CCHS with an interest in local history. Ken produced and was the co-author of the book, *The History of Pharmacy in Alberta*.

KATE REEVES – *"Some Things Remembered"*
Kate is a past president of the CCHS as well as the United Church of Canada ANWC Historical Society. While the archivist at Knox United Church in Calgary, she researched and led tours of the three downtown sandstone churches for her Museum and Heritage Studies. This was followed by three summers at the 1875 McDougall Stoney Mission historic site near Morley. Kate loves old churches and is presently with Wild Rose United Church in Calgary.

HARRY SANDERS – *"All Things Remembered"*
Harry is a Calgary-based freelance writer, historical consultant and reference archivist. He studied history at the University of Calgary and has worked for the Calgary Public Library, the City of Calgary Archives, the Glenbow Library and Archives, and the Jewish Historical Society of Southern Alberta. He is a past president of the CCHS. He is author of several books including *Historic Walks of Calgary*.

DAVID SCOLLARD – *"McClelland & Stewart West"*
David has played various roles in Canadian book publishing, including Sales Manager at Ryerson Press, Managing Editor at McClelland & Stewart, and Editorial Director at McClelland & Stewart West. In 1999, he co-founded a Calgary-based literary publishing company, Frontenac House.

DON SMITH – *"Color Conscious"*
Author Donald B. Smith has taught Canadian History at the University of Calgary since 1974. Born in Toronto in 1946, Dr. Smith was educated at the Université Laval, and at the University of Toronto where he earned his Ph.D. Besides three biographies in the field of Native History, he has co-edited such books as *The New Provinces, Alberta and Saskatchewan, 1905-1980* (with the late Howard Palmer), and *Centennial City: Calgary 1894-1994*. His history of Calgary, *Calgary's Grand Story*, will be released in the summer of 2005.

CAROL STOKES – *"To Market, To Market"*
Carol Stokes, BPE, BA, BFA, has worked in Corporate Records, Archives at the City of Calgary since 1998. Through her work she has discovered that the municipal government of Calgary has a rich and interesting history, and that issues facing citizens and government do not really change over time.

JACK SWITZER – *"Calgary's Jewish Community"*
Jack is the editor of *Discovery: The Journal of Jewish Historical Society in Southern Alberta*. Since retiring from the Business faculty of Southern Alberta Institute of Technology, he has devoted his time to research and writing about Alberta Jewish History.

LYNNE THORNTON – *"McClelland & Stewart West"*
In addition to her role as Business Manager of McClelland & Stewart West, Lynne has been a publishing consultant, writer, events manager, actress, theatre producer, and public relations manager for organizations as diverse as the Alzheimers Society and the Royal Tyrrell Museum.

IVAN J. TOWNSHEND – *"Calgary Communities"*
Dr. Townshend is associate professor at the University of Lethbridge. He has wide-ranging research interests and publications in human geography, specializing in the social ecology of cities, the geography of neighborhood experience, and its links to community differences in well-being. He has co-edited, with W. Ramp, J. Kulig, and V. McGowan, *Health in Rural Settings: Contexts for Action* (University of Lethbridge Press, 1999), and with W. K. D. Davies, *Monitoring Cities: International Perspectives* (International Geographical Union, 2002).

PATRICIA WOOD – *"Calgary and the Tsuu T'ina Nation"*
Patricia K. Wood is associate professor of Geography at York University. Her research interests concern citizenship and the politics of diversity, particularly with reference to Aboriginal people and immigrants. She is the author of *Nationalism from the Margins* (McGill-Queen's, 2002) and with Engin F. Isin, *Citizenship and Identity* (Sage, 1999).

BILL YEO – *"Gateway to the Rocky Mountains"*
Bill grew up in Southern Alberta, attending schools in Nanton and Calgary. He has worked as a landman, school teacher, and public servant. After 20 years with Parks Canada, he left to become a freelance researcher and writer, and was awarded the commemorative medal for the 125th Anniversary of Confederation.

SPECIAL THANKS TO
FREDERICK HUNTER
"The Legend of Jimmy Smith"

Frederick "History" Hunter has long been a familiar and respected figure in Calgary's historical/heritage, arts/culture, and social activism communities. He is an accomplished member of, or affiliated with, numerous academic, scholarly, and learned societies, as well as many Royalist, Loyalist, and British Empire, and Canadian patriotic organisations and other special interest groups, and intellectual pursuits. He has served as a General Faculties Councillor and Senator of the University of Calgary, and as a Director of its Alumni Association, of which he was the first official Historian and Archivist. As a University official, Hunter has sat on more than 40 different Boards, Commissions, Committees, and Services, initiating a considerable number of reforms and instituting various projects and programmes whose effects still continue to be felt on Campus to this day. Awards received for these and other contributions have been legion.

A staunch traditionalist, Hunter was an original founding member of The Monarchist League of Canada, was elected to the prestigious Royal Stuart Society by its International Grand Council, and Council of Honour, and holds the Medal of The Society of King Charles the Martyr, amongst other similar distinctions. He is regarded as a leading authority on the topics of heraldry, vexillology, tartanry, protocol, proper usage of titles and forms of address, as well as an expert in the field of pedigrees of the Reigning Dynasties and Noble Houses, and Families of Europe. Likewise, he has lectured widely on the related subject of British-Israel philosophy, the symbolism and descent of the Imperial Crown, ancient bloodlines and their modern status, etc.

Locally, Frederick's lengthy career of community and public service has taken many turns and permutations. For example, he personally selected the names for the streets and other features of Huntington Hills and is currently the official Historian of two other City Subdivisions (Bankview and South Calgary). In fact, both sides of his family have been honoured by the naming of collections of Calgary roadways. He was a member of the Mayor's Committee on Open Government Studies, (COGS), and his compilations concerning the Histories of Calgary's Town and City Councils have on two occasions been the theme of exhibitions mounted in the Municipal Atrium of the City Hall Complex. A guiding light behind the Calgary Cemeteries and Historical Commemorations Committee, which arranges, co-ordinates, and oversees erection of historical markers and monuments, he has often, in this capacity, accompanied, escorted, or conducted tours for children and adults alike through local cemeteries and other sites of interest. For several years, he was the Festival Co-ordinator in charge of the annual Historic Calgary Week Festival, which he twice brought to its zenith of nearly 100 events, covering a full two-week period, an achievement never equalled before or since. At present, to mention but a few of the activities with which he is associated or involved, he serves, amongst other things, as a Judge for both the annual Calgary and District Heritage Fair and the Great Canadian Geography Challenge, and as a Research Consultant in Genealogy for the Calgary Family History Centre.

As an historian of note, both in Southern Alberta and abroad, Hunter is best renowned for his scrupulous attention to detail and accuracy, and for researching, debunking, or exploding countless long-standing urban myths. As such, much of his time now is spent correcting factual errors perpetrated and perpetuated by his colleagues past and present.

As an activist and ardent supporter of a plethora of left-wing causes, Frederick Hunter gained widespread attention as one of some 40 or so valiant Defenders of Freedom who occupied Olympic Plaza and courageously maintained a continuous round-the-clock vigil for 30 days and nights through all weather conditions, standing firmly, resolutely, and defiantly against all threats and opposition, in protest of the arbitrary Bush attack on Iraq during the spring of 2003. As a Freedom Fighter, some of the concerns which he vehemently addresses and fights include "Yankeeism," militarism, police and the "Police State," prosecutors, the judiciary, authoritarianism or control of any kind, right-wing thought in general, and the concepts of money, and of monetary or economic systems of any sort, to abolition and dissolution of all of which, as well as the ultimate destruction of the "Benighted States" (which he sees as the root of all the world's ills), his life remains principally and primarily dedicated and devoted.

The Chinook Country
Historical Society Directors

First executive of the Calgary Branch, 1959-1960

Jack D. Herbert, President
Benton Mackid, First vice-president
J. Burnham Toft, Second vice-president
Sheilagh Jameson, Secretary
Sheila Johnston, Treasurer

Directors:

Hugh A. Dempsey, C. Reg Gladden, T. R. H. (Tom) Hicks
Una MacLean, T. R. (Pat) McCloy, Georgina Thomson

Presidents of the Historical Society of Alberta, Calgary Br.
(some dates are approximate)

Jack D. Herbert, 1959
Benton S. Mackid, 1959-1962
Rev. J. Ernest Nix, 1962-1963
J. Douglas Middlemass, 1963-1965
Capt. J. R. Schmitz, 1965-1967

Presidents of the Chinook Country Chapter Historical Society of Alberta
(some dates are approximate)

Ken Taylor, 1969-1970
William R. Sampson
G. L. (Grant) Weber
D. B. (Dave) Coutts, 1974-1975
Henry Klassen, 1978-1980
Stephen Bateman, 1980-1982
Elise Corbet, 1982-1984
Neil Watson, 1984-1986
Marianne Fedori, 1986-1988
Trudy Cowan, 1988-1990
W. B. Yeo, 1990-1992
Al Mogridge, 1992-1993

Presidents of the Chinook Country Historical Society

Al Mogridge, 1993-1994
Harry Sanders, 1994-1996
Diana Mansell, 1996-1998
Kate Reeves, 1998-2000
Mike Kampel, 2000-2001
Vivian Sampson, 2001-2003
Rotating presidency, 2003-2004
Diana Ringstrom, 2004-